The Tate
A HISTORY

Frances Spalding

The Tate
A HISTORY

Tate Gallery Publishing

ISBN 1 85437 231 9
A catalogue record for this book is available
from the British Library

Published by order of the Trustees of the Tate Gallery
by Tate Gallery Publishing Limited
Millbank, London SW1P 4RG

Designed by Caroline Johnston
Printed in Great Britain by BAS
Over Wallop, Hampshire

Contents

Acknowledgements

My thanks go first of all to Nicholas Serota and the Trustees of the Tate Gallery for inviting me to write this book, and for the access to information this gave me. When talk of the approaching Centenary first began, Corinne Bellow, then Head of Information Services, volunteered to make tape-recorded conversations with various people who had been or who still are associated with the Tate. These have been an invaluable source of help. In addition, I am indebted to the following for insights and information: Ronald Alley; Fay Ballard; Anne Beckwith-Smith; Lewis Biggs; Sir Alan Bowness; Natalie Brooke; Martin Butlin; Michael Compton; Frank Constantine; Alexander Dunluce; Lucy Dynover; Dennis Farr; Sarah Fox-Pitt; Robin Hamlyn; Patrick Heron; Sir Howard Hodgkin; Richard Humphreys; Lord Hutchinson; Stephen Keynes; Jeremy Lewison; Jenni Lomax; Judith Jeffreys; Richard Morphet; Edward Morris; Lord Palumbo; Leslie Parris; Roy Perry; Sir Norman Reid; John Richardson; Lord Rogers; Nicholas Serota; Sir Dennis Stevenson; David Sylvester; Sean Rainbird; Denise Riley; Jane Ruddell; Michael Tooby; Pauline Vogelpoel; Catriona Williams; Peter Wilson; Simon Wilson; Andrew Wilton. I am especially grateful to my editor, Judith Severne, and to the staff of the Tate Gallery Archive and Gallery Records who were unstintingly helpful. But three people in particular have been crucial in the making of this book: Corinne Bellow, owing to the usefulness of her tape-recordings, her encouragement and long-standing commitment to the Tate; Krzysztof Cieszkowski, Assistant Librarian, who has the historian's love of minutiae and also prepared the list of exhibitions; and Jennifer Booth, the Archivist, whose grasp of the vast collection of material in her care is both encyclopedic and humane.

I

The Potent Tate

In a memorable passage in *A Room of One's Own*, Virginia Woolf observed that great works of art 'are not the product of single and solitary births; they are the product of many years of thinking in common, of thinking by the body of the people, so that the experience of the mass is behind the single voice.' The same may be said of great institutions. Though the name of the Tate Gallery associates it with its original donor (not at his own request but owing to the pressure of popular opinion), its origin owed much to a ground swell of interest in British art which during the nineteenth century regularly disturbed the nation's cultural life. Ever since the moment of its inception the Tate has drawn on a kaleidoscope of human energies – on the skills, passion, knowledge, vision, resourcefulness and generosity of many. It has also been shaped by particular historical conditions; by the changing agenda set by the cultural and political issues of the day; and by subtle shifts in power between government and Trustees, Director and Chairman. Like most institutions, the Tate is a complex, constantly changing entity, which in the course of its first hundred years has frequently been the subject of heated debate. Both its critics and its admirers attest to the fierce, possessive affection it arouses, while it continues to occupy a central role within our cultural life.

One factor in the Tate's history, as in that of other national collections, has been the British government's ambivalence towards the arts: time and again a strong desire for prestigious public art collections has been balanced by an equally strong reluctance to spend public money on acquisitions and upkeep. When the British Museum was founded in 1753, the £300,000 needed to fund and house the purchases did not come from state funds but was raised by public lottery. In 1762, and again in 1764, Parliament gave the Museum a grant of £2,000, followed by further subventions of the same amount, which increased eventually to £3,000. Even by the standards of the day these grants were grossly inadequate for a national collection. The Museum's expenses regularly exceeded its annual income from the original endowment and the difference had to be made good from money grudgingly voted by Parliament. Not until 1835, by which time the National Gallery was eleven years old, did Parliament show signs of a more responsible attitude towards our national art collections. That year a Select Committee of the House of Commons was appointed to enquire into 'the best means of extending a knowledge of the Arts and of the principles of design among the people (especially the manufacturing population) of the country, and also to enquire into the constitution, management, and effects of institutions connected with the Arts'. Among its conclusions was a clear directive:

It appears to your Committee, that some portion of the [National] Gallery should be dedicated to the perpetuation and extension of the British School of Art. Pictures by living British artists of acknowledged merit might, after they have stood the test of time and criticism, be purchased for the national collection; especially such paintings as are more adapted, by their style and subject, to a gallery than a cabinet.

At the time of this report the National Gallery was confined to six rooms. British painting had been included in its collection from the start, but it remained the poor relation of the foreign schools, even in the 1890s, by which time the National Gallery had expanded into fifteen rooms. Although the British government was aware of the state collections being amassed in France, its doctrine of laissez-faire discouraged state intervention in the arts and it was left to private collectors to take up the 1835 recommendation.

Certain individuals had already begun to open their collections to the public. A select audience visited Earl Grosvenor's collection of Old Master and British paintings between 1808 and 1819, after which it was more publicly displayed in a purpose-built gallery. Sir John Leicester (later Lord de Tabley) also built a gallery which opened in 1806 for the public display of his pioneering collection of British paintings. Both these collections would have inspired Robert Vernon, the prosperous London horse dealer, who in 1847 presented to the nation a selection of 157 pictures from his collection.[1] Ten years later another collector of British art, John Sheepshanks, donated 236 British paintings to the South Kensington Museum. This practice of collecting, exhibiting and later donating British painting to the nation was accompanied by wider debates about the significance of the national school and its status in relation to the achievements of foreign schools.

When he moved into 50 Pall Mall in 1832, Robert Vernon found himself in close proximity to the National Gallery, then housed in the home of the collector, John Julius Angerstein, at 100 Pall Mall. A few years later it moved to its present site in Trafalgar Square, sharing the building until 1868 with the Royal Academy. Within a short period the large numbers of paintings being acquired began to create congestion in the already crowded rooms. As a result, certain pictures had to be shown elsewhere; some seventy modern British pictures which Vernon had donated to the nation remained in his Pall Mall home until they were moved for exhibition to Marlborough House, where they remained for many years. In 1856 they were joined by thirty-four works by Turner, which had just been released to the National Gallery by the Court of Chancery following the settlement of Turner's complicated will. In 1859 both the Vernon paintings and the Turners were moved into a building next door to the South Kensington Museum. After the National Gallery had been enlarged in 1876, they were moved again, to Trafalgar Square. By then, however, a precedent had been set for exhibiting British painting in separate premises and this had heightened awareness of the need for a national gallery of British art.

The man who had first conceived of a public national collection of British art

1 Sir Henry Tate, Bt. Contemporary engraving
from photograph, 1897

was the sculptor Sir Francis Chantrey. In his will of 1840, which did not come into effect until after the death of his widow in 1876, he created a bequest specifically for the purchase of painting and sculpture produced within the shores of Britain. Chantrey made no provision for a permanent home for this collection because he was confident that in time the government would provide it. But thirteen years after the Chantrey Bequest began, nothing had been done, despite the weight of public opinion: it was not government authority, but the determination of a self-made man from Liverpool that was to instigate a new national gallery.

Born in 1819, the seventh son of a Unitarian minister, Henry Tate entered the grocery trade in Liverpool at the age of thirteen and seven years later became a master grocer, having bought his own business. After a further six years he owned a chain of shops and had begun to expand into the wholesale trade, buying whole cargoes and disposing of what he could not retail himself to his fellow tradesmen. In 1862 he began refining his own sugar. This demanded more than good business sense, for the process of sugar extraction required an understanding of science and technology as well as heavy capital investment. Tate took advantage of a patent which others had turned down, for the production of dry, granulated sugar. The success of this enabled him to expand his business and to open another refinery in London, at Silvertown in the East End. It was there that he experimented with another patent, the Langen cube process, patented by Eugen Langen of Cologne.[2] It caused the demise of the tall cones of loaf sugar which had been such a feature in grocer's windows at Christmas time. Instead of the cone, which needed to be cut up, Tate substituted the neat, white cube which quickly became a familiar aspect of the tea-table. Such was the demand for this new commodity that the Silvertown refinery thrived, queues of casual labour forming each day outside the gate, for Tate also had the reputation of being a good employer. Meanwhile, he had moved himself and his family into a large mansion called Park Hill at Streatham Common. It was here he began to indulge his interest in art.

In order to do this, Tate added a picture gallery to this stately house with its sweeping carriage drive. Though he bought single works by John Constable, John Crome and William Etty, his taste had been largely shaped by Royal Academy summer exhibitions. He acquired examples of late Pre-Raphaelitism, narrative, animal, and landscape paintings; decent, affecting, uncontentious pictures which also brought him an incidental pleasure – the friendship of artists. He began holding an annual 'painters' dinner, usually on the evening before the Academy's private view of the summer exhibition. A feature of these dinners were the strawberries, which in Tate's well-tended greenhouses invariably ripened before Easter.

Though it is said that these occasions ranked second in importance only to the Academy banquet itself, Tate himself was a rather shy, undemonstrative man who preferred to remain in the background. He never forgot the deficiencies of the social system in which he had been brought up and as a philanthropist he gave large sums of money towards improvements in education, both secular and religious, and concerned himself also with mental and physical welfare, with libraries and hospitals, his giving always reflecting a desire to achieve the greatest good for the greatest number of people. During his time in Liverpool he had made considerable benefactions to University College in Victoria Street, paying for a wing to be built which housed the library, and endowing the Hahnemann Hospital with £20,000. His interest in the Unitarian Church led him to donate £10,000 for the library of Manchester College, Oxford, together with £5,000 to promote and encourage the theory and art of preaching.[3] He also founded the Tate Institute at Silvertown 'for the benefit of the industrial classes of Silvertown and its neighbourhood'. Although in Liverpool he had been for a short period a Liberal member of the City Council, he preferred to take no part in public life. Speech-making was anathema to him, and at events where as donor he was expected to speak, he often developed a diplomatic illness and arranged for someone else to read the words he had prepared. At the heart of this man, who invested in people, was a humility which seemed unaffected by his material success.

What may have helped this quietly generous philanthropist to become a more visible national benefactor was the arrival of his second wife.[4] His first wife died in 1883 and two years later, at the age of sixty-six, he married the thirty-five year old Amy Hislop, their introduction having been effected by the Brixton Independent Church which was run by a man with strong Liverpool connections. Amy Hislop appears to have had a taste for fancy-dress balls and for sitting on platforms with the Prince of Wales. With this young, extrovert woman at his side, Tate now made generous benefactions towards the establishment of public libraries in south London. He made an anonymous offer of £15,000 for a large central library to be built in Brixton, on the condition that the cost of its maintenance would be borne by the Library Commissioners. When it opened in 1893 he did not absent himself, but, somewhat hot and ruffled, sat on the platform to the right of the Prince of Wales. Between them sat Mrs Tate, looking cool, but supremely happy.

The history of the Tate Gallery begins with the letter Henry Tate wrote to the National Gallery on 23 October 1889. In this he offered to donate a collection of modern British art, valued at around £75,000, on three conditions: that a room or rooms be provided or built for its reception; that this should be effected within two or, at the most, three years of the acceptance of the gift; and that, when hung, the pictures should be called 'the Tate Collection'. His letter went before the National Gallery Board of Trustees on 7 January 1890 and appeared on the agenda immediately before an item dealing with the National Gallery's urgent need for an extension. Initially, in the absence of the Director, the Gallery's Keeper, Mr Charles Lock Eastlake, told the Treasury that the Gallery wished to accept Tate's offer, provided that the 'absolutely necessary structural extension' was built. However, the Director, Sir Frederic Burton, eventually had to turn down Tate's offer on the grounds of want of space. In addition, it was pointed out that Tate's request for a room or rooms devoted solely to his collection ran counter to the historical and educational system on which the National Gallery was based. Tate therefore renewed his offer to the Chancellor of the Exchequer, George Goschen, making the additional demand that the Lords of the Treasury sanction the establishment of a separate institution and agree to render annual grants, to make it a worthy repository of national talent and to make possible loans to the provinces. Not a single painting was to be collected until a suitable gallery had either been erected or found.

Tate's offer was made known to the public in the spring of 1890, at the same time that the landscape painter James Orrock read a challenging paper at the Society of Arts on the need for a fuller, less haphazard representation of British art in the National Gallery. Orrock's speech and Tate's offer were linked in a leading article in *The Times* (13 March 1890) which concluded:

> A wealthy country like ours, which possesses so fine a national school as we do – a school of landscape and a school of portraiture containing so many elements of greatness – ought to be able to stop the mouths of foreign critics by showing them a really representative and choice collection … Why cannot we have in London, started partly by voluntary effort and afterwards subsidised and directed by the Government, a gallery that shall do for English art what the Luxembourg does for the French? … the time has come for the creation of a great British gallery.

So vigorous was the debate aroused by Tate's offer that *Punch* (22 March 1890) announced that 'the King of the National Picture Donors is henceforth "the Potent Tate"'. But he was also the subject of some unkind cuts, for aspersions were cast on the taste of this 'sugar boiler' and the suggestion was made that the National Gallery should be allowed to select the best in his collection and reject the rest. Tate held out against this idea and kept to his purpose, ignoring the slurs and ungrateful remarks. But he did, at this time, attempt to commission a painting from Sir Frederic Leighton, hoping perhaps to add an element of classical grandeur to his collection. Many of the pictures in his collection suggest that he was less interested in the technical or aesthetic merits of a painting than in its sentimental value. A more modish collector might have been aware of the Glasgow School and of the new interest in effects of light that were steadily eroding the importance formerly given to subject matter. Instead, Tate liked tear-jerkers – Frank Holl's *Hush!* and *Hushed*, for example – and he bought some of the great icons of Victorian story-telling: Millais's *The Vale of Rest*, *The North-West Passage*, as well as *Ophelia*, Luke Fildes's *The Doctor*, Stanhope Forbes's *The Health of the Bride* and Quiller Orchardson's psychological dramas (*The First Cloud*, *Her First Dance* and *Her Mother's Voice*).

The gallery of modern British art which Tate now had in mind seized the imagination of the public, and in the course of the spring and summer of 1890 various sites were proposed. Attention was focused on a suite of rooms in Kensington Palace which dated back to William III, had painted ceilings and elaborate mouldings and had been left for half a century uninhabited, shut up and inaccessible to the public. Another suggestion, which came from Sir Charles Robinson, Surveyor of the Queen's Pictures, was that a gallery should be built in the grounds of Kensington Palace. Sir James Linton, President of the Royal Institution, declared it 'an ideal site', despite the difficulties presented with regard to public access. An East End parish urged the claims of Whitechapel, whilst others suggested that St George's Barracks at the back of the National Gallery should be moved to make space for a new extension. Initially George Goschen and his advisers favoured the Eastern and Western Galleries in the South Kensington Museum, which had housed various kinds of scientific exhibits but were about to be vacated. A committee of experts, including Sir Frederic Leighton and Sir Frederic Burton, examined them and reported favourably on their adaptability, though these galleries were in fact a jumble of rooms intended for art collections of a very different character, in a building that was still in an unfinished state. Some fifty steps had to be climbed in order to reach these galleries and they were separated from each other by a long corridor. The art dealer William Agnew, writing to *The Times* (22 July 1890), regarded it a makeshift plan, 'a paltry and unwitting issue of a large matter'. His letter drew from *The Times* leader in the same issue one positive conclusion: 'When a man in Mr Agnew's position takes up a proposal of this kind, it may be assumed that the thing is wanted.'

It was now understood that the search was on for a gallery which would receive not only Tate's collection but also other works scattered among various institutions. The debate was galvanised by the sudden announcement, made through *The Times* journalist Mr T. Humphry Ward, that an anonymous donor had offered £80,000 to cover the cost of a new building. It soon became known that Henry

2 Sir John Everett Millais, Bt, *Ophelia*, 1851–2

Tate was the donor and that the condition attached to this new benefaction was that he should have the right to approve the site. The Prince of Wales was anxious that Tate should be given a site for his gallery on the Kensington Gore estate, and so Tate had been shown a plot of land on the corner of Exhibition Road and Imperial Institute Road which had been set aside by the government for the proposed Science Museum. Tate now made this site conditional upon the acceptance of his offer. However, the suggestion that art should push out science caused the entire scientific body to protest; questions were asked in Parliament and a protest, published in *The Times* (28 April 1891), was presented to the Prime Minister signed by leading scientists of the day. By way of reply Lord Cranbrook and Goschen received a deputation at the Privy Council Office on 12 May 1891 at which an assurance was given that the interests of science would be carefully guarded: the future Science Museum was not to be moved.

When Tate sent Millais's *The Vale of Rest* to the Guildhall Art Gallery in March 1892, for an exhibition of works lent from private collections and shown free of entrance charges, he must have despaired of ever seeing his collection in the public domain. The *Daily Telegraph* (8 March 1892) opined: 'it is a little unwise, as well as rather churlish, to subject a princely donor to all the annoying delays and vexatious snubs which are usually reserved for those who penetrate in to the mysterious Kingdom of Red Tape.' One recent snub had concerned a vacant plot of land between Temple Avenue and Sion College in the City which the Corporation of London preferred to hold back, hoping for a more handsome offer from the Salvation Army. But the final straw, in Tate's opinion, had been Goschen's offer of another plot along the Exhibition Road occupied by the Art Needlework Society. In a letter to *The Times* (5 March 1892) Tate dismissed it as 'totally inadequate'. He had offered to erect a new building, he said, 'to save British art from the humiliation of being housed in those tunnel-like edifices [the Eastern and Western Galleries]', but difficulties, delays and uncalled for opposition had left him with no recourse but to withdraw his offer.

A change of government saved this dire situation. At the August 1892 election the Conservatives, in disarray and defeated by Irish Home Rule, gave way to the Liberals. Goschen's successor as Chancellor of the Exchequer was the elderly Sir William Harcourt. He later boasted that, in the course of a half-hour conversation with Henry Tate, he had reopened negotiations, dissolved deadlock and resolved matters conclusively: a new palace of art was to rise on the site of the old Millbank Penitentiary.[5]

The suggestion that the land occupied by the Penitentiary should be put to other use had first been made by John Ruskin in a lecture in 1867, and had been echoed by Sir Edmund Du Cane in a letter to *The Times* (17 March 1892), at a time when the land was being transferred to the Commissioners of Works under the Millbank Prison Bill, then before Parliament. What recommended this plot for the purposes of a gallery, as Du Cane pointed out, was that it 'furnished conditions of air, light, and space which very few others could equal'.

In the minds of many, however, both the prison and the area had a malodorous air. By the end of its malfunctioning and disease-ridden existence the Penitentiary had been known as a centre of chronic rheumatism, ague and neuralgia. Existing close to the river, it was surrounded by decaying buildings, obsolete machinery, coarse grass and rank weeds, whilst at its back, behind a burial ground, sat two gasometers. Begun in 1812, Millbank Penitentiary had been the largest prison in Europe at the time of its opening.[6] It remained England's principal prison for both male and female convicts for several decades, having originally been the great depot from which convicts were shipped to Australia. In layout it reflected ideas laid down by Jeremy Bentham, who had first suggested that all the parts of a prison building should radiate from an 'inspection-station' at its core. Millbank's massive structure was composed of six polygons which grew out of a central hexagon, inside which sat the governor's house. The corridors totalled some three miles in length and there were 1,550 cells. The prison acquired particular notoriety for its use not only of the 'solitary system', which for a period was applied to prisoners during the first three months of their sentence, but also for its use of underground cells known as 'the dark', as a punishment for indiscipline. It occupied twenty-four acres, two-and-a half of which were to be set aside for the new gallery. In the early stages of planning it was suggested that the gallery should be surrounded by a park, but in the eventual division of the site the building of a military hospital and a housing scheme for 'artisans' made this impossible.

In addition to its association with crime, Millbank seemed inaccessible. Journalists complained that it could only be reached through some of Westminster's shabbier streets or via the rookeries of Pimlico. Though these claims exaggerated

3
'TATE À TATE.
[Mr. Tate has withdrawn his munificent offer.–*Daily Paper*]
Goschen.– "Much Obliged, but we are a Nation of Shopkeepers
and We don't want any Art To-day, Thank You.'"
Cartoon from *Fun*, 16 March 1892

4 Millbank Penitentiary, 1829. Engraving by James Tingle after a
drawing by Thomas Hosmer Shepherd

the difficulties, the Millbank site continued to be inadequately served by public transport for many decades and therefore somewhat cut off from central London. This problem did not, however, delay the decision to transform a melancholy site into a place of national significance. The penitentiary was pulled down and by December 1893 the foundations of the new gallery were being excavated by seventy or eighty men. The prison had in places been built on loose shingle and had subsided so seriously that one morning all the cell doors in one of the wings were found jammed fast and impossible to open. It was therefore decided to carry the foundations for the Gallery down through the alluvial mud of the primeval marshes to the solid gravel overlaying the clay. Concrete was poured in underneath what was to be the central part of the gallery, to a depth of five feet. Rumours went round that human remains had been removed from the Millbank prison site, but these were scotched by Tate's architect, Sidney Smith.

Sidney R.J. Smith (1858–1913), who had opened an independent practice in 1879, worked in an eclectic style and had specialised in public architecture in south London. He had designed the concert hall at the Royal College of Music, the library for Bedford College in Regent's Park, and four public libraries, all of which benefited from Tate's benefactions. He had also designed a carriage entrance, picture gallery and large garden folly for Tate's house at Streatham Common. But a national gallery of British art, as Tate envisaged it, would be Smith's *magnum opus*, and he proudly appended the name of this project to his headed notepaper. Tate instructed him to spare no effort in obtaining information concerning the best-lit galleries, and Smith therefore went on an inspection tour of art galleries on the Continent and in the provinces. He would also have been keenly aware of Wilkins's National Gallery in Trafalgar Square and, more generally, of the way in which classical rhetoric and structural resemblances to palaces and ancient temples could be used to signify tradition, learning, authority and other attributes.[7]

Smith's first design, submitted for the South Kensington site on the corner of Imperial Institute Road, had been rejected by Goschen, who thought it too light

5 One of several proposed designs for the Tate Gallery
made by Sidney R.J. Smith

in scale for a civic building. Rethinking his ideas for the Millbank site, where the outlook over the river encouraged a temple-like central façade, Smith drew on every architectural device in his repertoire. He now conceived a building which, raised on a rusticated basement, rippled with columns and pediments and semi-circular bays. A domed tower surmounted the palatial central block, at each corner of which sat a domed minaret. Two further domes appeared on the porches at the end of each wing. On the top of these and on the main dome, Smith envisaged gesticulating winged sculptures, a final exuberant touch linking earth and heaven.

If Smith thought he had succeeded in designing a truly imperial building, he must have been disappointed to learn of Harcourt's reactions. Henry Tate showed the Chancellor of the Exchequer Smith's new elevation on 22 February 1893. 'I don't consider it belongs to my province to interpose much in the question of design,' Harcourt admitted in a memorandum, 'but I confess I thought that the addition of the pretentious dome and cupolas of a gimcrack order of decoration anything but an improvement. They are a good deal in the pretentious style so much in favour in the modern debased municipal architecture which predominates in provincial public buildings.' The advice he sent Smith was that he should visit the Fitzwilliam Museum in Cambridge, 'which is the nearest analogue to his own building, and which is one of the few successful edifices of the last half century. The severe exclusion of meretricious decoration is its signal merit.'[8] Harcourt was not alone in thinking Smith's design erred in its excess; certain Royal Academicians, whose work was represented in Tate's collection, expressed concern over the height of the central dome for they feared it would dwarf their art.

Smith went back to the drawing-board, submitted alternative designs and towards the end of 1894 the final scheme emerged. The central dome was reduced in height and partly obscured by a substantial vestibule behind the front portico, which now extended out towards the river. All the smaller domes had vanished along with the niched statuary which had earlier punctuated the main facade. But though the pediment of the portico was to be left empty, a figure of Britannia was to sit on top with a lion and unicorn on either side. In addition, the plan of the new Gallery had been designed with a future extension in mind, the initial construction forming only part of what would become a symmetrical and harmonious whole.

By October 1896 enough scaffolding had been removed for the public to gain an impression of this great new building. Opinion was immediately divided. What seemed satisfactorily monumental to some appeared coarsely classical to others, its mouldings exaggerated and its dome unimposing. 'There is something heathenish about its heavy pillars and frowning portico,' announced the *Spectator*. The heavily rusticated basement frontage and returns gave an effect of great massiveness; but it was precisely this kind of heavy, graceless detail that later drew from the architectural historian Nikolaus Pevsner the observation that Smith had used the late Victorian grand manner 'with neither discretion nor with originality'.[9]

Though it has never pleased the cognoscenti, Smith's building was to become a landmark: a very serviceable, dignified monument which inspired such affectionate respect among the public that in the 1960s an attempt to clad its façade with a modern extension was resisted. Its huge walls of solid brickwork and concrete go down twenty feet below the ground, the arched basement rooms evoking the subterranean levels of an old feudal castle. These basement rooms in the initial building were never intended to be used as galleries but were to house a picture-cleaning and framing room, a dining hall for staff, offices, attendants' rooms, boiler house, heating apparatus and dynamo.

By February 1897 about half of the interior had been completed and the heating had been set going to help dry the walls. Floors of polished oak had been laid, and the Corinthian order of the portico had been followed by Ionic pillars of Portland stone in the vestibule and Doric columns in the central hall under the dome. Here a carved inscription was already in position: 'This gallery and sixty five pictures were presented to the nation by Henry Tate for the encouragement and development of British art and as a thank-offering for a prosperous business career of sixty years.' Another inscription, still in the process of being made, read: 'The building was opened by the Prince of Wales on the 21st July 1897.'

Nine days before this event, as the *St James's Gazette* reported, the outside of the Gallery still bore the chaotic appearance of a builder's yard. Inside, the recently ennobled Sir William Agnew had hung Henry Tate's collection in the large gallery to the west of the central hall. In the place of honour was the late Lord Leighton's *And the Sea Gave Up the Dead which Were in It*, a rather ghoulish picture which had originally been intended for a cathedral. The works by Millais were, however, the chief feature of the collection, whilst Luke Fildes's *The Doctor*, which had been painted for Tate's collection, drew much attention, as did Lady Butler's *The Remnants of an Army* with its wounded rider and desperate-looking horse struggling to reach distant ramparts from which help is arriving, a picture that is said to have stirred the pulse of the nation when it was first exhibited. In the gallery on the opposite side of the central hall, the Director of the National Gallery Sir Edward Poynter had been responsible for hanging a selection of pictures from the National Gallery, including William Powell Frith's *The Derby Day*. He also took charge of two other galleries filled with works that had been bought under the terms of the Chantrey Bequest. Each of these rooms led into small octagon galleries in which hung pictures by George Frederic Watts, given by the artist to the nation. At Watts's request these two galleries had been repainted a rich red instead of the sober green or dull purple-brown that prevailed elsewhere.

The total cost of the building to Tate had risen to £105,000. It saddened him that his friend Millais, whose statue to this day stands guard outside the gallery, never saw it. Tate told the *Daily Mail* (8 May 1897): 'Photographs of the building in a forest of scaffolding were submitted to the late Sir John Millais, my deeply regretted friend, shortly before his death, and he endorsed in pencil the two words "Quite satisfied" beneath them.'

Tate had earlier been anxious that the press should be correctly informed about the naming of the new gallery. He had hastily written to the *Daily News* (4 December 1893) to correct the misapprehension that the gallery would be named after him. 'I do not wish it to bear my name, and I most certainly do object to its being called "the New Tate Gallery". I have recommended the Government to call it "the National Gallery of British Art", and I hope it will be known by that name for all time.' The final gallery fell short of Tate's expectations: it was neither independent, being an annexe of the National Gallery, nor was it a gallery of British art but of modern British art. Only in time were Tate's ambitions for the gallery to be fulfilled. Its official title, on opening, was the National Gallery of British Art at Millbank, but it was popularly referred to, even in the pages of *The Times*, as the Tate Gallery.

At four in the afternoon on 21 July 1897 the Prince of Wales arrived at the steps of the Gallery accompanied by various members of the royal family. A guard of honour had been mounted up the steps by the Artists' Volunteer Corps. A host of notables were present, including Arthur Balfour, Sir William Harcourt and Sir Edward Poynter. At the entrance Henry Tate presented the Prince of Wales with a handsome gold key and requested him to unlock the Gallery, while Mrs Tate offered the Princess of Wales a bouquet of orchids in the shape of the Prince of Wales's feathers. Once inside, the royal family passed through one gallery devoted to the Chantrey Bequest into one of the octagon galleries, and finally into the room housing the Tate collection where a large number of Tate's relatives were gathered. As so often happens at major public events, fashion vied with art in newsworthy importance. 'The Princess of Wales', noted *The Times* (22 July 1897), 'wore a dress of pearl gray figured silk trimmed with petunia velvet and gray chiffon, and a toque of deep mauve poppies with a black plume.' When the official party was seated on the platform, Leighton's *And the Sea Gave Up the Dead which Were in It* provided an incongruous background 'against which', the *Daily Graphic* (22 July 1897) noted, 'the bonnets of the ladies stood out with gay irrelevance'.

Over three weeks later, on 16 August 1897, the Gallery opened for the first time to the public. From ten o'clock in the morning a stream of people poured in. Newspaper reports noticed that though 'carriage folk' came in considerable numbers, the majority of the visitors were working men and women from the immediate neighbourhood. There were also crowds of board-school children whose attention was divided between the pictures and the fountain that played in the central hall. Entrance was free, except on Thursdays and Fridays which were deemed students' days, when admission cost sixpence. It was also intended to keep the Gallery open on Sunday afternoons between April and September.

Tate himself was often seen in the last years of his life making a tour of the galleries on Saturday afternoons. He had been made a baronet in 1898 and his continued benefaction to the Gallery made possible the building of the first extension, plans for which had been exhibited at the 1897 opening. This rear extension added nine further rooms and a sculpture hall to the Gallery. Though his wife was present at the opening ceremony, Tate himself was unable to attend; he died a few days later. At the request of Lady Tate, the Gallery did not close on 9

December 1898, the day of his funeral, but remained as he would have wished it – open to the public. However, in the room where his collection hung, a wreath of bay leaves ornamented his bust portrait.

It may have disappointed his wife, if not Henry Tate himself, that Queen Victoria had declined an invitation to open the Gallery in 1897. Age and ill health meant that she now mostly took her exercise in the grounds of Buckingham Palace in her garden chaise. But on 11 May 1900 she went for a public drive in an open landau drawn by four horses, with postilion and outriders. With her in the carriage were her eldest daughter Princess Victoria of Schleswig-Holstein and a lady-in-waiting. On these now rare outings the Queen's entourage normally followed an accustomed route, but on this occasion it was altered so that Her Majesty, as *The Times* reported (12 May 1900), could be shown 'the Tate Gallery'. Crowds bordered the main thoroughfares and cheered loudly as the Sovereign approached. When the carriage reached the Embankment, it slowed down in order that the Queen might, with the aid of her spectacles, cast a regal if waning eye over a site previously associated with suffering and crime. 'None who can remember the old Millbank prison', Balfour had remarked in his speech at the opening ceremony, 'could, in their wildest imagination, have conjectured that in so short a period, by the generosity of one man, so vast a transformation could have been effected.'[10]

Entrance Hall, Tate Gallery, London

6 A postcard of the entrance hall, 1897

2

The Search for Identity

The National Gallery of British Art, despite the pomp and ceremony that had surrounded its opening, very soon became the subject of adverse criticism. One reason for this was that its identity, still inchoate, was to a large extent shaped by its relationships with others. These included its original donor, Henry Tate, who had contributed sixty-five of the 245 pictures on view; the Royal Academy, which was responsible for the administration of the Chantrey Bequest; and, inevitably, the National Gallery. Decisions had been taken at Trafalgar Square early in 1897 as to what British paintings in the national collection should be sent to Millbank. The parent institution had decided that only 'modern' pictures should be transferred, by which the Trustees meant paintings by artists born after 1790. This cut-off date conveniently kept Constable and Turner for Trafalgar Square. However, in order to give Millbank a good start, the Trustees did, at Lord Carlisle's urging, permit the transfer of a few Constables, on the understanding that any loan to Millbank could immediately be returned to Trafalgar Square if the Trustees requested it. But even the 1790 resolution was not strictly adhered to; several Landseers remained at Trafalgar Square where a reduction in numbers meant that British painting, rehung in the western wing, could now be seen in a less crowded and more telling display. Far from ceding British art to Millbank, the National Gallery was now able to display it with better focus.

As an annexe to the National Gallery, the Gallery at Millbank was inevitably cast in an inferior position. Not only was its collection vested in the Trustees of the National Gallery, but its management was accountable to the Vote Officer at the senior institution. In February 1897, the annual cost of maintaining the new establishment had been reckoned to be £2,444 per annum. This sum included a salary of £500 for its Keeper, £200 for the Clerk, five attendants at £80 each, four porters at £47 each, one messenger at £50, six housemaids at £22, six police constables at £124 each and one police serjeant at £160. Further estimates were given for the cost of uniforms for the attendants, for picture-framing, carriage and postage. But no purchase grant was allocated the Gallery until 1946. Thus the Chantrey Bequest, which produced annually a sum of around two thousand pounds, was of primary importance to the development of the collection. Yet though work bought through the Chantrey Bequest became the property of the National Gallery of British Art, no one at Millbank had any say over the purchases, responsibility for which rested with certain members of the Royal Academy Council. This anomaly was to become the cause of fairly continuous dissatisfaction.

7 Portrait of Charles Holroyd by Alphonse Legros, 1907

Staff for the new Gallery had been appointed between February and July 1897. The first Keeper was a member of the Royal Society of Painter-Etchers, the artist and scholar Charles Holroyd. At the Slade he had been a star pupil of Alphonse Legros, with whom he had travelled round Italy in 1896. Holroyd's chief contribution to the Gallery was the formation of a collection of work by Alfred Stevens. If nowadays this artist–craftsman arouses limited interest, in the late Victorian period he was regarded as a latter-day Michelangelo. Painter, designer and sculptor, he was best known for his Wellington Monument in St Paul's Cathedral, a complex ensemble of architecture and sculpture which was left unfinished at the time of his death in 1875. His admiration for Italian art coloured everything he did, whether it was designs for Dorchester House in Park Lane, for the cupola in the British Museum Reading Room, vases for Minton or the house he built for himself, 9 Eton Villas, on Haverstock Hill. There he died at the age of fifty-seven, worn out, it is said, by the strain caused by the Wellington Monument and by his lack of official recognition. His influence, however, lingered on through the work of his pupils, among them Godfrey Sykes, Reuben Townroe and James Gamble, who left their stamp on the Victoria & Albert Museum and the Albert Hall.

Holroyd's espousal of Stevens was the first sign of the Gallery's willingness to stand apart from establishment taste. Nevertheless this able administrator, who ensured that the building was kept in very good order and the parquet floors well polished, failed to find a way of opposing the preponderance of weakly anecdotal painting which in the minds of serious artists established the Tate as a dumping ground for Victorian mediocrities. It had also received from the National Gallery, somewhat anomalously given its remit, certain modern foreign paintings, among them Rosa Bonheur's *Horse Fair*; but as these were mostly Barbizon school, they merely reinforced the Tate's conservative look. Neither at the National nor at the Tate was there any display of more recent French art, for the Trustees of the National Gallery shared the English suspicion of all things French: '"French" in painting, to the old-fashioned Briton,' recalled the painter Alfred Thornton, 'still connoted lubricity, bloodshed and a pursuit of the ugly.'[1]

The Tate's 'splendid isolation' was further enhanced when the temporary bridge, which had terminated in front of the Gallery, was removed after the completion of the new Vauxhall Bridge; and by the fact that no omnibus passed its door. Nevertheless, by 9 June 1898, having been open some ten months, the Gallery had received 104,275 visitors on public days and 15,795 on student days. One of the first publishers to take advantage of this new audience for art was Macmillan, which in 1898 brought out Edward T. Cook's *A Popular Handbook of the Tate Gallery*, its title employing the name by which the Gallery was familiarly known.[2] The first official publication was the Gallery's own *Descriptive and Historical Catalogue* in 1897. This focused the reader's attention on what could be seen in each painting, on the subject rather than the execution, and made no attempt to evaluate or discuss aesthetic merit. As a result, these descriptive catalogues served only to reinforce the public's expectation that every picture should tell a story and depend on mimetic veracity. There was also an inclination at this time towards nationalistic interpretations. When in 1897 the *Sunday Times* published its *Short Guide to the Tate Gallery of Contemporary Art* (another instance of the decision to ignore the Gallery's official title), it noted that in Briton Rivière's painting of a polar bear, *Beyond Man's Footsteps*, the white bear, red sunset and the blue ice were 'painted in the colours of the Union Jack'. Meanwhile, the Gallery's isolated location meant that the need for catering services soon became apparent. In January 1898 a Mr F.E. Henley offered to contract for the supply of light refreshments. His offer was turned down owing to shortage of space; but six months later, by which time the extension was well under way, the Trustees responded differently to a similar request from a Mrs Heimpel and Miss E. de G. Bedford of 52 Lower Sloane Street. The Trustees now thought it 'desirable that a refreshment stall should be established … and that it should be provided under the management of some lady or ladies'.[3] Approval was given by H.M. Office of Works and Mrs Heimpel remained in charge of the Refreshment Department for the next thirteen years.

The opening of the extension in 1899 doubled the capacity of the original building and incorporated a sculpture gallery. The collection, meanwhile, grew more slowly, owing to the lack of purchasing funds and the disinclination on the part of the National Gallery Trustees, more used to dealing with Old Masters, to accept gifts if the paintings in question challenged their preconceptions about art. Among the works they accepted were Millais's *The Order of Release 1746*, bought by

Sir Henry Tate for the Gallery a year before he died, and *The Boyhood of Raleigh*, also by Millais, which Lady Tate purchased for £5,250 in 1900 and immediately gave to the Gallery. Much of the appeal of this sentimental late work, for those who had known Millais, lay in the fact that his sons, Everett and George, had posed for the young boys in whom the old sailor is imparting his love of adventure. This same year, subscribers to the Burne-Jones Memorial Fund presented the Gallery with *King Cophetua and the Beggar Maid* with the expressed hope that for six months it would first hang at the National Gallery in Trafalgar Square. Such slights were continually to aggravate the Tate's relationship with its parent institution. Tradition has it that the huge basement studio built into the northeast corner of the 1899 extension had been purposely designed for Sir Edward Poynter, the National Gallery's Director who, since 1896, had also been the President of the Royal Academy. Whether or not he ever used this studio, his association with it underlines how invasive was the authority stemming from Trafalgar Square.

Neither Burne-Jones nor Millais could save the Gallery's reputation, which was gradually becoming the laughing stock of intelligent people. The art critic M.H. Spielman wrote in the *Graphic* on 5 September 1903: 'The Tate Gallery is slowly changing its character, in certain respects not for the better. This is not the fault of the keeper, Mr Holroyd, who is efficient as an administrator as he is talented as an artist and scholarly as a writer: It is the policy of the governing body.' Spielman instanced the National Gallery's habit of dispatching to Millbank less good modern paintings by non-British artists such as Horace Vernon and Ary Schaffer; he regretted the introduction of painting into the sculpture gallery; and he saw that the Chantrey Bequest, far from strengthening the Tate's collection, had so far added little more than a weakly humorous and sentimental vein of anecdotalism. It was this that gave the future author of *Le Grand Meaulnes*, Henri Alain-Fournier, during his 1905 visit to the Gallery, the impression of art 'so very Dickensian with its little old-world values, attracting by its humour, the delicacy of faded colours, scrupulous attention to detail'. He felt intimidated to find himself alone in a gallery full of Watts's philosophical allegories, thought the palm trees got in the way of the art in the sculpture gallery and observed that the Gallery was, 'like all English museums, spotlessly clean, disconcertingly polished'.[4]

No amount of hygiene could improve the quality of the pictures. The spick-and-span galleries only made it more glaringly obvious that the terms of Sir Francis Chantrey's will had not been fulfilled. This sculptor, who personified just the kind of professional success that the Royal Academy hoped to promote, had risen, with a little help from his wife's dowry, from poor craftsman to wealthy, fashionable artist, much in demand for bust portraiture and funerary monuments. He had been elected a Royal Academician and had bequeathed his personal estate so that, after the death of his wife, it would be directed towards the encouragement of British painting and sculpture. His residuary estate amounted to £105,000 and the income from this was to be spent on 'works of Fine Art of the highest merit in painting and sculpture that can be obtained either already executed or which may hereafter be executed by Artists of any nation Provided such Artists shall have actually resided in Great Britain during the executing and completion of such works.'

The broad terms of the will meant that Chantrey purchases could have encompassed paintings by Monet, Sisley or Pissarro, all of whom had painted in England. But ever since the first purchase, in 1877, the Academicians in charge of the Trust had rarely looked beyond the walls of Burlington House: by 1903 only five of the 110 works in the collection had been purchased outside the Royal Academy and some £60,000 had been spent. As early as 1884 Sir Robert Peel had drawn the attention of the House of Commons to the unsatisfactory nature of Chantrey Bequest purchases. In the early 1890s the critic George Moore stated the problem bluntly in the *Fortnightly Review*: 'The Academy has the handling of the Chantrey Bequest Funds, which it does not fail to turn to its advantages by buying pictures of Academicians which do not sell in the open market, at extraordinary prices, and imposing on the public the standard of Art which obtains in Academic circles.'[5]

The person who became the real scourge of the Chantrey Bequest was D.S. MacColl, art critic of the *Saturday Review*. In April and May 1903 he published two articles attacking the administration of the Bequest, and afterwards reprinted these, together with other matter, in a small book entitled *The Administration of the Chantrey Bequest*. He made the public aware of the sums of money that had been spent on scores of saccharine subjects, such as Joseph Clark's *Mother's Darling*, whilst the work of Dante Gabriel Rossetti, Ford Madox Brown, William Holman Hunt, Legros and J.A.M. Whistler was ignored. The fact that Whistler was as yet unrepresented in an English national collection while his famous portrait of his mother hung in the Luxembourg seemed to MacColl a terrible indictment. MacColl lambasted those who had 'administered the Trust with a laxity and view to their own interests implying either culpable ignorance of its terms, or a policy that amounts to a breach of trust' and he poured condemnation on the Royal Academy: 'The Academy can no longer pretend to speak for the general body of artists in this country or to command their confidence and that of the cultivated public ... the Academy has sunk to the level of a sectional institution.'[6]

As a result of widespread newspaper agitation, largely stimulated by MacColl, Lord Lytton moved in the House of Lords 'That a Select Committee be appointed to enquire into the administration of the Chantrey Trust and if necessary make recommendations'. It convened in November 1904 and was chaired by Lord Crewe. Ten meetings were held at which witnesses were examined. The Committee concluded that the Chantrey collection contained 'too many pictures of a purely popular character, and too few which reach the degree of artistic distinction aimed at by Sir Francis Chantrey'.[7] Although it found no grounds for any imputation of corrupt or interested behaviour, it urged a wider interpretation of Chantrey's will and recommended that more attention should be paid to exhibitions outside the Royal Academy. But no alteration in its administration was sought. As a result, there was little significant improvement in the purchases, and when in 1911 Lord Curzon began his inquiry into the National Gallery of British Art the issue of the Chantrey Bequest had to be reopened. One instance of a missed opportunity was the Wilson Steer retrospective mounted by the Goupil Galleries, London, in 1909. The discerning collector Sir Hugh Lane bought three pictures from this show, and another was sold to Johannesburg Art Gallery, but the Chantrey Bequest bought none.

As Gordon Fyfe has observed,[8] disputes over the Chantrey Bequest took place in an era when the balance of cultural power was shifting towards the professional classes. The Royal Academy, with its calendar of dinners and private views, was very much a part of a social season which helped sustain aristocratic identity. At the same time, the creation of such institutions as the National Gallery and the Tate meant that aristocratic habits of collecting had shifted away from courtly society into the more bourgeois, nationalistic environment of a professional museum. To ease this transition, aristocrats were invited to become stewards of national treasures by sitting on museum boards as trustees. At the same time an enlarged state enhanced the power of the professions and the civil service. In time the Tate, with the Treasury behind it, was to challenge confidently the prerogatives of the Royal Academy, as reflected in the Chantrey Bequest purchases. And the outcome of this struggle was that the Royal Academy gradually lost its shaping power over the making of a national collection.

★   ★   ★

Disappointment over the Chantrey Bequest was to some extent mitigated by the work of the National Art Collections Fund, founded in 1903 by D.S. MacColl, Roger Fry and others. The aim of the NACF was, like the Société des Amis du Louvre, to raise money in order to assist public museums and art galleries in the acquisition of works of art which might otherwise disappear abroad. The foreign exodus of works from great private collections had begun when the Harcourt Death Duties came into effect in 1894 and for the first time all forms of property, landed or other, were brought into a pooled value for the total estate at a person's death. The exodus was further stimulated around the turn of the century by an agricultural depression, combined with higher taxes, which left some owners of private collections in need of ready cash. It was through the NACF that the Tate acquired in 1905 its first Whistler – *Nocturne in Blue and Gold: Old Battersea Bridge*.

Ironically, the avant-garde Whistler was partly to blame for the lack of English interest in French Impressionism. He had done much to enhance awareness of tone, and the low-key harmonies found in his paintings made the chromatic divisionism of the French Impressionists seem garish. As a result, when the Parisian dealer Paul Durand-Ruel exhibited 315 French Impressionist paintings in London in 1905, fewer than ten paintings sold. Inside the Gallery at Millbank the English retreat from colour was further pronounced on dull days by the absence of lighting. Electricity had been installed at basement level, but the galleries had been left deliberately unlit, in keeping with the policy that prevailed at the National Gallery

8 James Abbott McNeill Whistler, *Nocturne in Blue and Gold:
Old Battersea Bridge c.*1872–5

and elsewhere. When the Wallace Collection daringly sanctioned the use of artificial lighting in its galleries in 1905, questions were asked in Parliament whether
the National Gallery and the Tate would follow suit. The answer was negative:
the Trustees objected to the exhibition of pictures under artificial light, and
because fog had closed the Galleries on very few occasions over the past three

years, it was argued that the figures available did not justify the expense of installing electric light.

Change was slow in coming. When Sir Edward Poynter resigned from the Directorship of the National Gallery in 1905, his post was left vacant for a year. Various names were considered and the job was finally offered to the painter, critic and authority on Italian art, Roger Fry, who for some months had been courted by the Metropolitan Museum of Art in New York. He was in fact en route to America when a telegram, offering him the National Gallery, reached him at Queenstown. Tempted though he was to turn round and return home, he felt morally committed to the Metropolitan, and instead Charles Holroyd, who had been knighted in 1903, became Director of the National Gallery. During his ten years at Trafalgar Square he was to make some notable additions to the collection, accepting the George Salting bequest of 192 pictures and acquiring Velázquez's *Rokeby Venus* and Hans Holbein's *Christina of Denmark, Duchess of Milan*, among other works.

Holroyd left Millbank on a note of triumph. He accepted the dealer J.J. Duveen's offer of John Singer Sargent's *Miss Ellen Terry as Lady Macbeth*, bought Charles Furse's large, breeze-filled picture *Diana of the Uplands* with money from the Clarke Fund which had to be spent on British art, and arranged for fourteen Turners, formerly hung in offices at the National Gallery and only shown to the public on request, to be transferred to the Tate along with twenty-one other works by Turner which had been repaired, cleaned and framed. These paintings, the majority of which had been left unfinished at the time of the artist's death, had never been exhibited. When they went on show at Millbank early in 1906 Londoners flocked to see them.

The appointment of D.S. MacColl as Holroyd's successor seemed to imply official approval of the anti-Academy lobby and the need for the gallery to evolve an independent policy. It is not known whether MacColl submitted an application or was invited to apply,[9] but ironically the man who had so severely castigated Chantrey Bequest purchases now found himself responsible for seven rooms full of these pictures which he regarded as an affront to all true lovers of art.

MacColl had originally intended to build on his Presbyterian upbringing and follow his father into the Church. While studying for ordination at University College London he had lived at home in Kensington, an area of London that brought him into contact with artists and writers. He took drawing lessons in his spare time and increasingly longed for a career in art. Eventually he abandoned the Church and became an Oxford Extension lecturer. He toured most of the major European galleries and began writing art criticism for the *Spectator*. At the same time he enrolled as a part-time student at the Westminster School of Art and became an advocate of the New English Art Club, which had been set up as an alternative exhibiting forum to the Royal Academy. His independent mind enabled him to defend Degas's *L'Absinthe* during the controversy aroused by its subject matter when the painting was shown in London in 1893. Three years later he became art critic of the influential *Saturday Review*.

9 Portrait of D.S. McColl by Donald Maclaren, *c.*1906

It was in this position that he had first cast an eye over the Tate and not liked what he saw. He watched as the building at Millbank was erected and wrote: 'The building cannot be pronounced an addition to the architectural beauties of London. A centre block humped over wings of mean proportions is the effect of the masses; the smaller features are heavy or thin, and the details vulgar. The old prison was a building of much greater character and taste.'[10] Nor was he an admirer of Henry Tate's collection ('the Agnew type – that is to say, pictures of the year by popular Academicians') or of the Chantrey pictures ('a terrible indiscriminate collection').[11] He also made known his opinion that the Gallery should have its own constitution, management and independent Trustees and he went on campaigning for these until they were achieved in 1917.

He had become renowned for fierce and unrepentant attacks on the degeneracy of the Royal Academy, on the 'trashy mosaics' with which William Blake Richmond had covered the arches, clerestory and ceilings in St Paul's Cathedral, and on conventional prejudices about art. He defended Manet and Degas but was less certain about the French Impressionists and made no attempt to buy their work for the Tate during his time as Keeper. When he took up his appointment in June 1906 his salary was £350 per annum, rising by £20 increments annually to £500. Though he brought to the job an incisive intellect and learned mind, he did not initially have the habits of a bureaucrat, as his memoirs recall:

Imagine me, up to a mature age, rising not always or even often with the lark, but at any convenient hour; putting off the writing task till the last moment, and simmering up to it in an armchair by the fire; never keeping accounts more elaborate than the most meagre of bank pass-books, and dreading of all things in life the giving of orders to subordinates and keeping discipline. Could there be a worse training?[12]

It astonished MacColl how difficult it was to obtain a desk. When the need for one was communicated to the Treasury, it brought into action a complicated system of checks against expenditure which involved visits from various officials and the sending of polite reminders until, after a very long time, a desk arrived, which, as MacColl writes, 'had an exotic and theoretical air, as of a form sought in the heaven of ideas by one who had never met the object in the phenomenal world'.[13] Still more aggravating was the realisation that as Keeper he had no official power to acquire works of art for the collection: there was no purchase grant, and because he attended Board meetings at Trafalgar Square in an ex-officio role he had no vote on acquisitions under discussion. 'It was', he concluded, 'harder to get a picture in than it would have been to steal one of those already there.'[14] Moreover, he resented the lordly types on the Board of Trustees who paid scant attention to anything in print but attached excessive importance to things said to them by their neighbour at the dinner table or in their club. Yet he soon cracked their method, which was based on the principle of obstruction.

I, who had avoided committees like the pest, had to learn the lesson that nothing makes a committee of this complexion so suspicious as does an air of conviction. An acquisition recommended on its merits had a very bad chance, and the late Lord Carlisle, a very uncharacteristic specimen of his order, taught me that the way to appeal to his colleagues was to disparage the work of art on its merits and advocate it as a matter of 'policy'. When this was done for me and I could remember a few emollient phrases like 'with all deference' I had a relative success, and things did slip through.[15]

Towards the end of 1906 Charles Aitken, Director of the Whitechapel Art Gallery, mounted an exhibition of Jewish art and antiquities. MacColl let it be known that he would like to have William Rothenstein's *Jews Mourning in a Synagogue* for the Tate, and as a result in February 1907 the Revd Canon Barnett, who sat on the Whitechapel Art Gallery Committee, wrote on behalf of various donors, offering to give to the Gallery Rothenstein's painting or a similar picture in commemoration of this exhibition. MacColl helped obtain its acceptance. He also worked obliquely for the Gallery by sitting on the Executive and Purchasing committees of the National Art Collections Fund and in the course of time was able to ensure that several works by Philip Wilson Steer entered the Gallery's collection through the NACF.

His friends regretted that his official position had silenced a very fine critic. But MacColl was active on many fronts, achieving changes from within. He pushed through a new rule concerning copyright: permission to photograph or copy a work by a living artist could not from now on be given without the artist's permission and, if requested, a fee. He drew up a 'Desiderata' list in which he signalled his commitment to Steer: 'Steer is likely to rank in the future as the greatest English painter of his generation. He is represented at Dublin, Melbourne, New York and by his portrait in the Uffizi, but by nothing in Great Britain, where the neglect of the Chantrey fund has been imitated in Provincial Galleries.'[16] He recommended also the names of Augustus John, Walter Sickert and William Rothenstein. He also merged the Tate Gift in with the general collection, weeded and rehung the main galleries, devoted one to the Alfred Stevens collection and strengthened the Pre-Raphaelite section. Furthermore, he also took part in discussions in March 1909 that led to the founding of the Contemporary Art Society, which, like the NACF, helped place works of art in public institutions. In the course of all this work he moved to Hampstead (an area that was to house four Tate directors) when his son began attending University College School, and he occasionally lectured at the Slade and elsewhere.

The climax of MacColl's career was the opening of a Turner wing on 29 July 1910. As a result of the interest caused by the Turners which Holroyd had brought to light in 1906, Lionel Cust, the Keeper of the National Portrait Gallery, had drawn attention in a letter to *The Times* in August 1906 to the existence of a vacant plot behind the Tate that was earmarked for another use, and to the fact that no suitable place had yet been found for displaying the Turner Bequest. In his will Turner had left 180 oils and an estimated nineteen thousand drawings and watercolours to the nation, with the stipulation that the National Gallery should, within a period of five years, build a gallery to house this collection of work. A further codicil modified this condition on the understanding that a gallery would be built within ten years of his death. However, Turner's relatives, who had been all but disinherited, sued the executors for a share of Turner's £140,000 estate, and a lengthy case dragged on for some five years until a compromise settlement was reached in 1856. At that time the British government was totally absorbed by the Crimean War. Faced with a shortage of funds, the lack of a suitable building and tiresome legal complications, it side-stepped Turner's stipulation by simply sending the oils to the National Gallery and the rest of the collection to the British Museum. Though retained by these institutions for 'the Benefit of the Public', the public had since seen little of the Turner Bequest as much of it had never come out of store.

The government had proposed building a stationery office on the vacant site to the rear of the National Gallery of British Art. Protests were made and MacColl and others helped secure this site for future gallery expansion. Next, a private individual came forward with an offer of £20,000 for the erection of a new building on the condition that Turner's pictures should be housed within it. On 6 May 1908 the first Commissioner of Works, Lewis Harcourt (son of Sir William) announced that, owing to the generosity of J.J. (afterwards Sir Joseph) Duveen, an additional five rooms on the main floor, with others below, would be built in

10 Sir William Rothenstein, *Jews Mourning in a Synagogue*, 1906

order to house the bulk of Turner pictures currently stored at Trafalgar Square. Work on the building began in August 1908, under the control of Duveen's architect, W.H. Romaine-Walker. Duveen himself died before its completion and his son, Joseph Duveen, paid for the staircase that linked the upper floor with the two lower galleries. Both floors were wired for electric lighting, creating an anomaly as the galleries in the older part of the building were still without it. When finally this new Turner wing opened in July 1910, there was no official ceremony owing to the recent death of King Edward VII. But King George V paid a private visit on 9 July and the public was admitted on 18 July.

Overseeing the creation of these new galleries had added greatly to MacColl's workload. Like many others, he had been taught to admire Turner by Ruskin. Together with Holroyd and Turner's biographer, A.J. Finberg, he had hung the pictures and produced what *The Times* (19 July 1910) called 'the best catalogue of the vast Turner bequest that has ever been made'. In the first gallery, which was over a hundred feet long, the paintings hung on a rich Venetian damask which gave way, elsewhere, to dull-gold wall coverings framed in white. The completion of this project left MacColl physically exhausted. In December 1910 he managed to stagger round Roger Fry's *Manet and the Post-Impressionists* exhibition at the Grafton Galleries, but he was suffering from heart strain and too ill to take a leading role in the controversy it engendered. The authorities must have been informed of his need for a less arduous post because, while recuperating in Italy with his wife, he heard that Asquith had recommended his appointment as Keeper of the Wallace Collection, from which Sir Claude Phillips was retiring in January 1911. As a result, MacColl informed his Trustees that he was leaving the Tate out of necessity and with great reluctance. It must have been some consolation that his successor Charles Aitken, though a very different character to himself, was a person of whom he approved.

11 The new Turner wing in 1910

3

The Curzon Report

When Charles Aitken began work as Keeper at the Tate on 7 March 1911 he did not arrive, as MacColl had done, with the reputation of a fighter. On the contrary, as John Rothenstein later wrote, he seemed ordinary in comparison with Mac-Coll: 'his intelligence was relatively pedestrian; his powers of expression were limited; he was a dry, retiring, quite unimpressive person who, had he not been Director of the Tate, might have lived out his life without leaving any particular mark.'[1] Yet, saddled with the responsibilities of the job, as well as the opportunities it offered, he proved adept in moments of crisis, knew when to exert pressure on others and was an able administrator. His many small acts of generosity grew out of his caring attitude towards his staff, and in his will he left £1,000 for the establishment of a staff welfare fund, today known as the Aitken Fund. But above all what emerged in Aitken during his time at the Tate was, as Rothenstein records, 'clarity and liberality of mind, firmness of purpose and a burning devotion'.[2]

Aitken had spent many years of his life teaching at Colet Court (the preparatory school to St Paul's) and elsewhere, before becoming Director of the Whitechapel Art Gallery in 1900. There he organised, in the opinion of William Rothenstein, 'some of the best picture exhibitions to be seen at that time in London'.[3] He was motivated by the belief that the value of art lay in its capacity to contribute to the moral and social welfare of humanity. But his evangelical outlook was hidden behind an austere exterior: a shy bachelor, slightly prim in manner, he lived at 28 Church Row, Hampstead, and swam every morning in one of the ponds on the Heath before arriving for work at the Tate. Like MacColl, he had scant enthusiasm for the Chantrey pictures but admired the Pre-Raphaelites, whose paintings were always well hung at Millbank during his era. He was also to some extent responsive to new talent and alerted William Rothenstein to the work of Gilbert Spencer while this artist was still at the Slade. But Aitken's frosty shyness unfortunately lost the Tate the early twentieth-century paintings which William Rothenstein's brother Charles (who changed his name to Rutherston during the First World War) gave to the City of Manchester. Having initially approached Aitken with the idea of offering these works to the Tate, Rutherston had been put off by what he felt was slighting encouragement.

Before a year was out, Aitken had submitted a paper to the Trustees outlining his suggestions for the Gallery. The lack of any regular purchase grant with which to increase the collection, he argued, made necessary loan exhibitions which would create change and bring fresh interest to the Gallery. Two such exhibitions

12 Portrait of Charles Aitken by Stephen Bone, exh.1932

were held during the first year of his Keepership: one of Alfred Stevens's work and another of Pre-Raphaelite paintings from Birmingham, lent while its City Art Gallery was being rebuilt and extended. The success of these two events convinced the Trustees that loan exhibitions were advantageous to the Gallery, and it was agreed to ask the Treasury for the provision of £120 a year to cover the expenses involved. This request was initially declined, but Aitken would not admit defeat on this issue and loan exhibitions of work by Alphonse Legros and Whistler in 1912 were followed by Pre-Raphaelite paintings from Lancashire collections and a major William Blake exhibition in 1913.

It worried Aitken, coming from the Whitechapel Art Gallery where electric light had been installed, that, owing to the absence of electric light in most galleries, the attendants turned visitors out of the Tate on dark or foggy days or as soon as daylight failed, owing to the difficulty of providing adequate surveillance. As a result, the Gallery was scarcely ever open when the majority of the public was free to visit it. Aitken informed his Trustees that he had seen 'large numbers of poorer visitors on Saturday afternoons forced to limit their brief visit to the Gallery',[4] and argued that, because this class of people found the Tate more intelligible than the National Gallery, electric light should be inaugurated first at Millbank.

Aitken was the first to suggest that money earned through entrance fees, as well as the net profit from the sale of prints, photographs and catalogues, should be appropriated for purchases. There were now some nine hundred works in the

Gallery's collection, but only thirty of these (with the exception of a hundred drawings by Alfred Stevens which had been bought for £1 each) had been purchased, and only nine with government help. Aitken was in addition the first to talk of 'gaps' in the collection which, he said, made it impossible to hang any clear representation of contemporary art. He saw clearly that the Chantrey purchases set up an unfortunate double standard, as would-be donors found pictures in the Gallery 'inferior to those offered by them and with justice rejected by the Trustees'.[5] Aitken also made the entrance to the Gallery more dramatic by placing either side of the main door on Portland stone pedestals Sir Charles Lawes-Wittewronge's *The Death of Dirce* and Henry C. Fehr's *The Rescue of Andromeda*. And, like MacColl, he expressed dissatisfaction with the fact that salaries at the Tate were far below those of corresponding officials in other galleries of similar rank.

In April 1910 the Director of the National Gallery had requested the return of the modern continental paintings on loan to the Tate. Their presence had been an anomaly in the National Gallery of British Art ('better known perhaps as the Tate Gallery', as Sir Edward Poynter admitted in his preface to the illustrated catalogue published by Cassell & Co. in 1913), and at some point Lady Tate had reminded Holroyd of the nationalistic purpose behind her late husband's gift. As a result, if a private donor gave a modern foreign picture to the nation, the nation did not quite know what to do with it. This became evident in May 1912 when the National Gallery accepted the gift of Giovanni Boldini's portrait of the famous beauty and art critic, Lady Colin Campbell. Hung among the Old Masters at Trafalgar Square, it seemed foreign, flashy and horribly new. 'The fashionable portrait painter is interested in the *monde* to which his subject belongs', announced *The Times* (8 May 1912) apropos this picture. 'He uses all his art to emphasize, not the essence of character, but a trivial relation; and whatever his skill in doing so, his art is condemned to triviality.' In the ensuing discussion both *The Times* and Sir Charles Holroyd recognised the need for a gallery in London which would house modern foreign art. The person who made this need pronounced was the Irish dealer and collector, Sir Hugh Lane.

The troubled history of the Lane Bequest began in 1913. By this date Lane had already donated a large part of his collection to the Dublin Corporation but had kept in reserve a choice collection of French pictures, among them Renoir's *The Umbrellas* and Manet's *Music in the Tuileries Gardens*, which he used as a lever to persuade the Dublin authorities to build a permanent gallery for modern foreign art. These negotiations broke down in 1913 and in September his continental paintings were sent to London, on the understanding that the National Gallery would exhibit them and this might lead to the creation of galleries for modern foreign art. Lane also made a will leaving these pictures to the National Gallery in London. But in December 1913 Lane was appointed Director of the National Gallery in Dublin, and though his relations with the Dublin Corporation did not improve, he at some point decided to revoke his earlier decision and wrote a codicil leaving his paintings to Dublin on the condition that a gallery should be provided for them within five years of his death. He may have been influenced by London's qualified reaction to his collection, for the National Gallery proved unwilling to exhibit his thirty-nine paintings *en bloc*, as Lane requested. And though MacColl and others urged Lane to show his collection at the Tate, Holroyd objected to this: he was mindful that Lady Tate, already alienated over the addition of the Turner galleries, about which she had not been consulted, resented the appearance of foreign art at Millbank.[6]

As a result, Lane's pictures were not exhibited in London in his lifetime. He died aboard the *Lusitania* when it was sunk by a German U-boat in 1915, after which it was discovered that the codicil to his will, though signed, was not witnessed and therefore not legally binding. A fortnight before he sailed for America, Lane had called at the Tate and learnt from Aitken that a donor had offered to pay for the building of modern foreign galleries in which Lane's pictures could be exhibited. Lane's positive reaction to this news confirmed English authorities that they should press for what was legally theirs, in opposition to Lane's relatives and friends, including Lady Gregory, who argued that Lane's final wish should be respected and his paintings be returned to Dublin. The Chief Secretary for Ireland interceded on behalf of Dublin's National Gallery, and MacColl published a riposte in the journal *Nineteenth Century*, arguing fiercely that the Trustees in London should not relinquish their claim to these paintings. After this the National Gallery Trustees passed a resolution that without delay Lane's pictures should be exhibited at Trafalgar Square.[7] They went on display in 1917.

By then the whole scope and constitution of the Tate had been reviewed by a committee of National Gallery Trustees, chaired by Lord Curzon, a former Viceroy of India. His committee had begun work in 1912 and one of the issues it addressed had been the need for a modern foreign gallery. It was MacColl who had argued not only that such a gallery would help secure Lane's pictures but that a further benefaction could be obtained from Joseph Duveen.[8] When Curzon intimated that such an offer would be acceptable to the Trustees, MacColl spoke with Duveen who agreed to finance a new wing. But before anything could come of this development, the First World War intervened.

As it turned out, the first destructive act against the nation's art was perpetrated not by enemy forces but by a small woman in a tight-fitting grey coat and skirt who entered the National Gallery at Trafalgar Square on 10 March 1914 and, with the aid of a small axe, broke the glass protecting Velázquez's *The Toilet of Venus* (*'The Rokeby Venus'*) and gashed the canvas in seven places. Miss Richardson (nicknamed 'Slasher Mary' by the newspapers) gave two reasons for her attack: the first was that it was directed at men who 'gaped all day' at the recumbent figure; the second, that she was attempting to destroy this most beautiful figure because the government was destroying Mrs Pankhurst, the most beautiful character in modern history. Both the National Gallery and the Tate closed for a fortnight to consider precautionary measures. Then on 22 May 1914 a Suffragette made a still more savage onslaught on five Bellinis at Trafalgar Square and both Galleries closed permanently until August, when, owing to the onset of war, the

Suffragettes declared an end to the use of violent acts to draw attention to their political campaign. During the period of closure students had still been admitted on student days, but access was restricted to certain rooms in which attendants and constables were heavily concentrated.

Though a few Tate pictures were sent to provincial galleries when war began, the majority stayed at Millbank and the Gallery remained open until 1916. Not until the onset of Zeppelin attacks were further precautions taken; and in July 1917 some paintings from both the National Gallery and the Tate were deposited on the platform of Aldwych tube station. In March 1918 a further exodus took place when the Ministry of Pensions, which had moved into the Gallery at Millbank, requested more space for their staff and records; as a result, a large part of the Tate's collection was moved to the Post Office vault, leaving behind only works of secondary importance and those which, owing to their size, weight or condition, would have been dangerous to move.

But in 1915 the Gallery turned its back on the war and mounted a small loan exhibition of the work of Alfred Stevens to celebrate Sir William Blake Richmond's gift of a bust of Stevens by Edouard Lanteri. In addition, the Alfred Stevens Memorial Committee, of which Legros was President, donated a cast of Stevens's Dorchester House fireplace. Stevens's draughtsmanship was highly admired at this time and it was decided that the gallery in which this exhibition was shown should henceforth be called the 'Stevens Room'.

Shortly before this exhibition opened, MacColl had brought to light a large number of cartoons, drawings and paintings made by Stevens for the projected decoration of Dorchester House. Among these was a gigantic spandrel cartoon of the prophet Isaiah, which, long after the vogue for Stevens had passed and much of his work had been transferred to the Victoria & Albert Museum, remained in this gallery, hidden behind boards, to be rediscovered in 1989 when a false wall was removed. To assist the visitor to the 1915 exhibition, the Clerk at the Tate had made a set of sketches reconstructing, as far as was possible, the groups of figures with which Stevens had intended to ornament the dining-room at Dorchester House.

J.B. Manson, a former bank employee and painter, had taken up the post of Clerk at the Tate on 9 December 1912. His wife Lillian had formed a warm friendship with Aitken, and the previous summer the Mansons had stayed with him at Alfriston in Sussex, where he had the use of a house for visits and holidays. Aitken had asked Manson to help with the hanging of a show at the Tate and had been so pleased with the result that he had suggested to Holroyd that Manson be taken on to the staff. A post had fallen vacant in July when it had been discovered that the former Clerk had been converting to his own use some of the Gallery's petty cash. With three others, Manson sat the normal civil service exam procedure and easily came out the best. But he did not really want the job. His wife, however, mindful of their two daughters, regarded it differently and as a result Manson, at the age of thirty-three, entered the Tate on a salary of £150 a year, while continuing to paint furiously at weekends.

Manson is said to have influenced Aitken's taste, weaning him away from old allegiances and converting him to French Impressionism.[9] He also drew attention to the Camden Town Group at a time when its leader, Walter Sickert, still lacked official acceptance. A Sickert was offered to the Trustees in 1915 at a time when Sir Charles Holroyd was recovering from a heart attack. He wrote to his Keeper, C.H. Collins Baker: 'tell the Trustees that I think it is a very good Sickert – but the question is whether he is important enough for the Tate. I think not; but as an old friend of the artist perhaps I am a prejudiced judge.'[10]

Holroyd blamed his poor health on the lack of staff at the National Gallery which obliged him to curtail his holidays and shoulder much anxiety. He resigned in 1916 and died the following year. The situation was no better at the Tate where the Keeper and the Clerk were jointly responsible for the care of the collection, the office work and the supervision of the staff. Manson's services were regarded as indispensable to the Tate. He was therefore exempted from military service, and in 1917 promoted to Assistant Keeper.

By then the Gallery had closed, the Ministry of Pensions had moved in, and, at the request of the nearby Queen Alexandra Military Hospital, space had been set aside as a Recreation Room for convalescent patients. Owing to the necessity of concentrating the national resources on war, the National Gallery's purchase grant had been suspended and both the National and the Tate were now entirely dependent on gifts and bequests. In this way the Tate gained Whistler's *Miss Cecily Alexander: Harmony in Grey and Green*, bequeathed by W.C. Alexander (subject to the life interest of his two daughters), and John Singer Sargent's rakish portrait of *Lord Ribblesdale*, bequeathed by him in memory of his wife and two sons, both killed in action. In addition, Asher Wertheimer let it be known that he wanted to leave to the nation a series of family portraits by Sargent which went on show at Trafalgar Square in autumn 1916 but were eventually to come to the Tate. In August 1916 Aitken proudly told the Trustees that the growing importance of the Tate as the national gallery for British art had attracted an estimated £100,000 worth of bequests and gifts over the last year.

Aitken's greatest achievement during the war was undoubtedly his acquisition of some of William Blake's illustrations to Dante's *Divine Comedy*. These had been commissioned by John Linnell and remained in the possession of the Linnell family until they were offered for sale at Christie's on 15 March 1918. Aitken had approached Herbert Linnell about these drawings at the time of the Blake exhibition at the Gallery in 1913, by which time the Tate already possessed several important tempera paintings by Blake. It had acquired *Nelson* and *Bathsheba* after the 1913 exhibition but none of the Dante illustrations, few of which were completely finished, since Blake died while working on the project, and only seven of which had been engraved. Now they were to be sold as one lot. Aitken drew up a list of benefactors and must have approached some with limited success as certain names on his list are annotated 'tried too often'. He also obtained money from the Clarke Fund through the National Gallery and from the National Art Collections Fund. And by forming a consortium with other interested public art galleries and private individuals, he succeeded in acquiring the collection for 7,500 guineas. Though the subsequent division of these drawings among the various parties within the consortium may seem regrettable, the Tate managed to acquire twenty Dante drawings, among them some of the finest in the series.[11]

Despite wartime circumstances, this was a crucial period in the Tate's history, for the Curzon Report, submitted by his committee in 1915, had been issued by H.M. Stationery Office (and therefore presumed incorrectly to be a government report) and had laid down recommendations which eventually formed the basis of the main charter of the Tate. The committee's brief had been to look at 'the Retention of Important Pictures in This Country and other matters connected with National Collections', and it had conducted a wide-ranging enquiry into, for instance, government fiscal policy, purchase grants and the sale of works of art to foreign buyers. It proposed the rationalisation of collecting policies pursued by the Tate, the National Gallery, the Victoria & Albert Museum and the British Museum with regard to British art, and particularly watercolours. Both Aitken and MacColl were interviewed by the committee and their recommendations influenced the conclusion that the Tate should become the home of two national collections: historic British art and modern foreign painting. But the National Gallery Trustees who had sat on Curzon's committee and written this Report were none too enthusiastic about the latter. 'We have not in our mind', they declared, 'any ideas of experimentalising by rash purchases in the occasionally ill-disciplined productions of some contemporaneous continental schools, whose work might exercise a disturbing and even deleterious influence upon our younger painters.'[12]

When Holroyd resigned as Director of the National Gallery the following year, Aitken seized the opportunity to implement the recommendations of the Curzon Report. He wrote to Holroyd's successor, C.J. Holmes, soon after he took over in August 1916, informing him that the Treasury was ready to act if required to do so by the Trustees. As a result, the Tate was given its own Board of Trustees and its Keeper advanced to the position of Director. The new Board, which met for the first time on 3 April 1917 under the chairmanship of Lord Plymouth, was responsible for management, administration and staff discipline but not for the Tate Gallery's financial matters, which remained subject to the Accounting Officer at Trafalgar Square. Its collection also remained vested in the Trustees of the parent institution.

Nevertheless, a separate Board meant more attention could be given to the affairs of the Tate. Three of the National Gallery Trustees sat on the Tate Board, as did the older institution's Director and Keeper as ex-officio members. A Treasury minute advised that additional Trustees should be 'a selection of gentlemen with a knowledge of or interest in modern and contemporary art'. Among the first who fell into this category were MacColl (the Tate's previous Director); Lord Henry Cavendish Bentinck, collector and chairman of the Contemporary Art Society; and J.R. Holliday, who had advised on the collections at Birmingham. But because the new Board was still rather heavily weighted with aristocrats, it did not

13 William Blake, *Dante and Virgil Approaching the Angel
who Guards the Entrance of Purgatory*, 1824–7

satisfy the Royal Academy and other art societies who requested that professional artists should be included. A Treasury minute of 6 July 1920 thus provided for
the inclusion of practising artist-Trustees on the Board. Architects were eligible
under this category and among the first three artist-Trustees to be appointed was
Sir Aston Webb, who had designed the extension that had transformed the South
Kensington Museum into the Victoria & Albert Museum. His fellow artist-
Trustees were the painter Charles Sims and the printmaker Muirhead Bone. All
three were Royal Academicians, which brought a tactical advantage, for the Royal
Academy now became more flexible over the management of the Chantrey
Bequest, which the Curzon Report had severely criticised. It was agreed to set up
two Recommendation Committees, one for painting and the other for sculpture,
each composed of three Academicians and two Tate Trustees. However, though
these advised on purchases, the Royal Academy Council retained its right of veto
– a fact that was to produce aggravation in years to come.

One practical effect of the Curzon Report was the transfer in 1919 of over two
hundred British pictures, including Hogarth's *Marriage à la Mode*, from Trafalgar
Square to Millbank. Now that it had become not only the collection of British art

of all periods but also modern foreign painting, some change in its official title became necessary; and in 1920, the same year that telephones were installed, the Tate was designated the National Gallery, Millbank. It was still, however, closed. Though all the works of art which had been deposited in Aldwych Underground station and in the Post Office vault had been returned by March 1919, the Ministry of Pensions was slow to move out and the entire building was in need of a thorough redecoration. When in 1921 the Gallery finally did open again to the public, its walls reflected a shift in taste: instead of heavy brocades, modern fabrics, with broken texture but without pattern, provided the background for the paintings. Impressionist paintings hung on pale neutral tones, darker shades of fawn appeared in the eighteenth-century and early nineteenth-century rooms, and the Pre-Raphaelites looked resplendent against a reddish-purple ground.

The Gallery had first appointed an official lecturer in 1914. But H.S. Teed, who took up the post, enlisted in the army the following year, and Edwin Fagg was appointed in his place. Fagg remained in position after the war and took a special interest in modern foreign art, publishing *Modern French Masters: An Introduction and Complete Handbook to the Modern Foreign Work in the National Collection* in 1930. As the title of his book indicates, the notion of two separate collections of modern foreign art, one at the Tate and the other at the National Gallery, did not then exist and the various transfers between the two institutions make it difficult in some instances to ascertain the whereabouts of pictures at a particular moment in time. The representation of modern French painting had been improved by items from Degas's collection, purchased at his studio sale in March 1918 by means of a special government grant. But the choice of acquisitions had rested solely with C.J. Holmes and had been made with the National Gallery in mind, though some of the purchases eventually came to the Tate. On the other hand the National Gallery did agree to transfer to the Tate the thirty-nine paintings in the Lane Bequest, which ranged through Corot and the Barbizon painters to some very fine examples of French Impressionism.

Meanwhile, the Clarke Fund for British art, amounting to some £576 per annum, had been placed at the Gallery's disposal; and Joseph Duveen's architect, W.H. Romaine-Walker, had submitted plans for new galleries which would house modern foreign art. But the development of the Tate during the 1920s was to be persistently undermined by the conservatism of the Trustees. When a painting formerly owned by Delius, Gauguin's *Nevermore*, was offered to the Tate by the Goupil Gallery in 1921 for £1,800, it was declined.[13] The reasons are not recorded, but the cumulative impression gained from this and other instances of works declined, is that a shortage of money was combined with a dilettante, half-hearted interest.

★   ★   ★

Joseph Duveen had first shown his willingness to benefit the Tate by paying for a staircase to link the two floors in the Turner wing, which had been built with his father's money. In November 1915 he offered to redecorate the lower ground-floor galleries in this wing and to provide stands for the proper display of Turner's *Liber Studiorum* at a cost of £550. His architect Romaine-Walker and his younger assistant Gilbert Jenkins undertook the work and they pleased Aitken by using a silk wall-covering that was more subdued than the glossy satin in the big upstairs top-lit gallery. But it was Duveen's offer, first made in 1915 and ratified the following year, to pay for a set of modern foreign galleries which marked him out as a major donor.

Duveen's father, Joseph Joel, and his uncle, Henry, had set up the firm Duveen Brothers, which dealt in porcelain, tapestries, furniture and silver. This highly successful business, which operated in America and in England, had begun when Joseph Joel's mother, the wife of a Dutch blacksmith, had sent him to England to sell the Delft pottery she had collected. He had set up a Delft and furniture shop in Hull, where his son Joseph was born, but soon moved shop and family to Oxford Street in London. Like his seven brothers, Joseph worked in this shop, learning the skills of the trade. By courting experts, he then managed to persuade his father to extend the business into painting and sculpture and made his debut in this field in 1901 when he paid £14,050 for John Hoppner's *Lady Louisa Manners*, which was then the highest price ever paid for a painting at a British auction. As S.N. Behrman has observed, Duveen 'noticed that Europe had plenty of art and America had plenty of money, and his entire astonishing career was the product of that simple observation'.[14] He paid and got higher prices than other dealers, forged a unique link with Bernard Berenson by asking him to act as his paid adviser on Italian pictures, and became a virtuoso salesman, cannily playing on his clients' tastes, strengths and weaknesses. There was nothing Duveen could not get for them, from berths on fully booked ships to houses or even wives. He was crucial to certain American collectors, among them Andrew Mellon, founder of the National Gallery of Art in Washington, Samuel H. Kress and Henry Frick. When shown pictures bought from other dealers, he made outrageous remarks such as 'I sniff fresh paint', which sometimes resulted in lawsuits. Though based in New York, he continued to regard London as his home and operated from Claridges, where he always stayed when in town, transforming his suite into a small art gallery. His huge success enabled him to make generous benefactions, both public and private. Over the years he gave £200,000 to the British Red Cross, paid for the rehanging and redecoration of the Wallace Collection as well as additions to the Tate, the National Gallery, the National Portrait Gallery and the British Museum, and made a generous donation towards the endowment fund for London University's Courtauld Institute of Art. When he acquired Hogarth's *The Graham Children*, he had a ready customer in Mellon but instead presented it to the National Gallery. Nevertheless, the irony remains that, while making these munificent gifts to the nation, he was simultaneously denuding England by selling its art treasures abroad.

In 1919, the year that he was knighted, Sir Joseph Duveen presented Gauguin's *Faa Iheihe* to the Tate. In 1922 he began giving £200 a year to the Gallery for the

14 Paul Gauguin, *Faa Iheihe*, 1898

purchase of watercolours and drawings. And the following year he was one of several individuals who helped pay for Boris Anrep's complex but suitably subdued mosaic pavement, based on subjects taken from Blake's *Marriage of Heaven and Hell,* which was placed in the octagon gallery in the south-west corner of the Tate. The original pink terrazzo pavement had been damaged in a Zeppelin raid, and Mr and Mrs J.L. Behrend, the patrons of Stanley Spencer's Burghclere Chapel decorations, had instigated its replacement by offering £250 towards an Anrep mosaic in 1921.[15] Their offer was accepted in 1922 and the work completed in 1923. By this date Duveen had pledged £25,000 towards the building of the modern foreign galleries, an offer that increased to £30,000 when he decided that a gallery in honour of the American artist John Singer Sargent should be part of the new scheme to house, among other things, the Wertheimer portraits, currently on show at the National Gallery. It was also to house Sargent's oil study for *Madame Gautreau,* which Duveen donated to the Tate in 1925 together with two other works, Augustus John's *Madame Suggia* and Sargent's *Claude Monet Painting at the Edge of a Wood.*

If Aitken and his Trustees welcomed the prospect of new galleries, they felt less confident about what to put in them. At the sale of Degas's collection in Paris in 1918 the Director of the National Gallery, C.J. Holmes, had refused to purchase a Cézanne and returned home with some of the special govenment grant unspent. In the spring of 1921 Aitken rejected two Cézannes which the collector Gwendoline Davies, daughter of a Welsh industrialist, had offered to lend to the Tate. Hugh Blaker, Miss Davies's adviser, wrote an indignant letter to the *Observer* on his behalf, to which Aitken replied in conciliatory manner, arguing there was little room for foreign art until the new galleries had been built. The *Burlington Magazine* then entered the debate and in an editorial excoriated Aitken for failing to see 'that the surest way of encouraging gifts is to welcome suitable loans'. It continued: 'Although ... opinion ... varies greatly regarding the relative merit of the painters of modern France, all have come to an agreement about Cézanne ... universally recognised as the father of the whole movement, and ... now given a place in great public collections throughout the world. A Gallery of Modern Foreign Art without Cézanne is like a gallery of Florentine art without Giotto.'[16]

Despite the criticism it had incurred, the Tate continued to do nothing about Cézanne. It declined a *Portrait of Madame Cézanne* in January 1922, on offer at

15 John Singer Sargent, *Ena and Betty, Daughters of
Asher and Mrs Wertheimer*, 1901

£8,000, despite the fact that minutes for the Board meeting held on 16 November 1921 record that Sir Joseph Duveen was willing to provide money for the purchase of a Cézanne. In May 1922 the Board looked at four photographs of Cézannes offered by M. Figuet and decided 'none of the pictures were suitable at the large prices'. The following month the dealer Percy Moore Turner who ran the Independent Gallery offered the *Portrait of Madame Cézanne* at the reduced price of £7,000. It was again declined. Though Duveen donated a Cézanne print in 1927, a Cézanne oil did not hang in the Tate until 1929 when one was lent by Samuel Courtauld. In 1933, owing to a bequest from C. Frank Stoop (a Dutchman who had lived in London), two canvases by Cézanne marked the long-overdue entry into the Tate collection of Cézanne as a painter.

The Tate's acquisition of French art during the 1920s would have been dismal had it not been for the rayon manufacturer, Samuel Courtauld. He had been impressed by Hugh Lane's French pictures at the National Gallery in 1917, took advice from Percy Moore Turner among others, and in 1923 transferred £50,000 into a trust for the purchasing of modern foreign art on certain conditions: the trust was to be named the Courtauld Fund, it was to be administered by a committee, and purchases were to be confined to a specific list of French artists.[17] The Courtauld Fund transformed the Tate's foreign collection. By February 1924 six pictures had been bought, among them Vincent van Gogh's *Sunflowers* and his *Chair and Pipe*. To these were added, over the next three years, superb paintings by Manet, Monet, Cézanne, Bonnard, Sisley, Renoir, Pissarro, Toulouse-Lautrec, Degas and Utrillo, as well as one of the key paintings in the history of Post-Impressionism – Georges Seurat's *Bathers, Asnières*. The Courtauld Fund Collection went on show as a unit in the winter of 1925–6 and, before it was merged with the rest of the collection, received very full and favourable notices in the press. By January 1926 the entire £50,000 had been spent, but Courtauld added a Cézanne, *Aix: Paysage Rocheaux*, at a cost of £4,500.[18] Simultaneously he was building his own collection of French art which he bequeathed to the Courtauld Institute of Art after it became established in the collector's own home, Home House, in Portman Square.

After the war, non-essential building had been delayed owing to the urgent need for labour and materials for domestic housing. In the long lead-up to the opening of the modern foreign galleries Aitken, having been chastised by the *Burlington Magazine*, began to accept and request loans of foreign works. William Burrell's outstanding collection of mostly French art went on view at the Tate in March 1924, as did paintings by Renoir, Degas, Monet and Corot, which the printer Jacques-Emile Blanche had been persuaded to lend. Meanwhile, Irish protest over Hugh Lane's bequest was still voluble and actively supported by Lane's aunt, Lady Gregory; and the Tate, aware of the need to satisfy Lane's demand that permanent accommodation should be found for modern foreign art, at one point asked Duveen not to wait for the completion of the Sargent Gallery before opening the other three new galleries. However, the architects worked overtime in order to have all four galleries ready for the spring of 1926. A crisis arose when

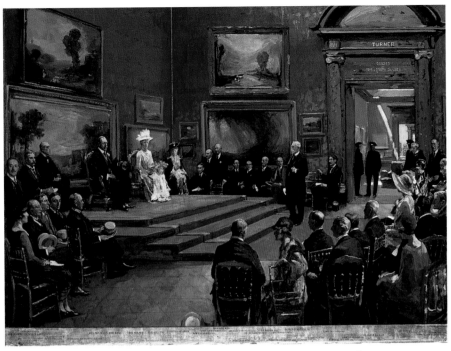

16 Sir John Lavery, *The Opening of the Modern Foreign and Sargent Galleries
at the Tate Gallery* exh. 1929

George V, having initially agreed to perform the opening ceremony, cancelled the arrangement, mindful of the political embarrassment which the association of Duveen's galleries with the Lane Bequest would afford. The Trustees asked Lord Crawford to intercede on their behalf, as it was felt that Duveen would interpret His Majesty's refusal as a rebuff, and it would seem to imply a decision in favour of the Irish claims. The opening date was postponed until the Lane pictures were no longer 'sub judice', and the King and Queen attended the ceremony which took place at 3 pm on 8 June 1926. Though Lane's thirty-nine Impressionist paintings formed the nucleus of the collection, all references to his pictures were removed from the address which was written by MacColl.[19]

Duveen had insisted that the modern foreign galleries should correspond fairly closely with the galleries built by his father. He had used the same architect as his father – Romaine-Walker – but had asked a younger man, Charles Holden, who had built the British Medical Association Building on the corner of Agar Street and the Strand and was later to work for Frank Pick on certain London Underground stations, to work with him. In addition, an experimental anti-reflection gallery, a long corridor-like space with walnut columns, was designed by Gilbert Jenkins. When opened, the new extension offered a magnificent vista from the big Turner room into two further galleries devoted to French Impressionists and Post-Impressionists, with Puvis de Chavannes's *Beheading of St John the Baptist* visible on the end wall. Duveen, with a dealer's love of showmanship, had

17 The Sargent Gallery in 1926

spared no expense in the decoration of these galleries. Various ingredients – green marble doorways, brown silk wall-hangings, painted and gilt ceilings, walnut seats and marble-bordered parquet floors – created an atmosphere reminiscent of old Italian palaces. In addition, a new system of ventilation had been installed which purified the air, and the artificial lighting had been subdued by concealing its source.

Since the cost of these four rooms, as well as five other lesser rooms on the lower floor, had far exceeded the original estimates, it was decided in the final stages that the Tate could not ask Duveen to pay for an additional staircase and lavatories. (In 1923 the Tate had only two water-closets for men and two for women, as against the eleven for women and eight for men at the Victoria & Albert Museum.) As a result, only the staircase was added. The Trustees held out against Duveen's wish that a portrait of his father and a bust of himself be exhibited in these galleries in perpetuity. But lettered inscriptions by Eric Gill, 'Erected by Sir Joseph Duveen MDCCCCXXVI', over the doorways to the new galleries were permitted. Also at Duveen's request Sir John Lavery was given facilities to paint the opening ceremony.

The press was enthusiastic and the addition of these new galleries was seen to raise the stature of the Tate in relation to other galleries in Europe. With the Courtauld Fund and Lane pictures integrated among loans of other foreign paintings, the Gallery now offered a broader view of art and an antidote to the artificiality and convention that had marred its reputation in earlier years. When Alfred H. Barr, Jr composed a brochure to aid the establishment in New York of a permanent museum of modern art, he instanced, as part of the rising tide of interest in modern movements in art, the 'most remarkable activity' in London that had given the Tate 'magnificent rooms of modern French paintings'. Barr went on to express his hope that in time New York would have a collection 'which would place her at last on a par with Paris, Berlin and London'.[20]

4

The Flood and After

A visitor to the National Gallery, Millbank, in 1925 would have been offered a largely chronological route through British art, beginning with Hogarth and taking in rooms devoted solely to G.F. Watts and Alfred Stevens as well as the Turner wing before ending with present-day art. This journey is recorded in the Gallery's first illustrated guide, published that year. A more significant landmark, however, was the report published in 1927, *National Gallery, Millbank: A Record of Ten Years, 1917–1927*.

This report, like others that followed, drew the attention of the public to matters on which the Trustees hoped to influence government policy. In 1924 the Tate's Trustees had voted to abolish entrance charges on student days, only to find that the Treasury opposed their decision. Aitken had afterwards written to C.J. Holmes: 'I am sorry about the fees, as I am sure they are a mistake here, particularly in view of the small amount they provide … In view of all that has been given to the gallery, fees and grants are merely useful fleabites. "Atmosphere" is everything and free entrance and good attendance help atmosphere.'[1] When, in April 1924, the entrance fees on paying days had been reduced from 1s to 6d the average attendance on these days had risen from 127 to 344. The 1927 report strongly argued that it was 'a false economy' to charge for entrance as it sacrificed attendance and tended to discourage the public from coming on other days, 'as few can keep in mind which days are free'.

Another point of contention raised by this report was lighting. On several occasions the Tate's request for artificial lighting had been turned down on grounds of economy. Recently a minimum system of 'Pilot-lighting' had been installed which made it possible to supervise visitors and therefore keep the Gallery open on foggy days, but which did not really enable the visitors to see the pictures. An additional problem for Aitken was that the ex-servicemen employed as attendants were often low in health and morale, and frequently had to be dismissed for failing in attendance, for lack of punctuality, for drunkenness or for sleeping on the job. One police pensioner was dismissed for his habit of chewing tobacco and spitting it out in the front hall.

In the aftermath of the Curzon Report, the Tate had been allowed to withdraw from permanent exhibition works regarded as unworthy of display. This had in effect liberated seven galleries hitherto allocated to the Chantrey Bequest. There had been some improvement in Chantrey purchases since the advent of the Recommendation Committees, in that the Royal Academy refrained from buying anything definitely unacceptable to the Tate. But on the other hand, the Trustees

18 Sir Stanley Spencer, *The Resurrection, Cookham*, 1924–7

often had to accept a painting or sculpture which suited the needs of the collection much less than other things they would have liked to acquire. Then, in 1926, and again in 1927, the Academy rejected all the Recommendation Committee's proposals marking the onset of an uneasy period in the history of the Chantrey Bequest, with the Tate at one point withdrawing from the Recommendation Committees in protest.

Since the death of Lord Plymouth in 1923, Viscount D'Abernon had been Chairman of the Tate Trustees. Formerly the head of an Anglo-Turkish bank, he was often absent from Board meetings owing to his appointment as British Ambassador in Berlin. However, he did not lack experience, having formerly been a National Gallery Trustee under the chairmanship of Lord Curzon, and he was the vital link between the Tate and Duveen. D'Abernon found Duveen an exhilarating companion and, in turn, Duveen looked on D'Abernon as one of his closest London friends – not without justification, for in 1926 and again in 1932 D'Abernon sent the Prime Minister a report on all Duveen's benefactions, as part of a move to obtain for him the honours he craved.

Under D'Abernon's chairmanship the Board underwent extensive change in 1927: MacColl, Bentinck and Holliday left, to be replaced by the Hon. Evan Charteris, Samuel Courtauld and Sir William Burrell. Three new Royal Academy artists arrived – Glyn Philpot, Walter Westley Russell and Henry Poole – and were joined by the former Royal College of Art professor, the painter William Rothenstein. Meanwhile, at the National Gallery in Trafalgar Square A.M. Daniel became Director in 1929 and W.G. Constable his Assistant Director. During this period J.D. Innes, J.S. Cotman and Richard Wilson were the subject of Tate exhibitions, sixteen of which took place in the 1920s. One of these, in 1927, acknowledged the vogue for the 1890s artist Charles Conder, MacColl writing the catalogue introduction. Other loan exhibitions featured the Swedish sculptor Carl Milles, Thomas Rowlandson, Philip Wilson Steer, Jugoslav art and the East London Art

19 J.M.W. Turner, *The Ponte Delle Torri, Spoleto, c.*1840–5

Club. For the last of these, work from an exhibition at the Whitechapel Art Gallery had been selected by Sir Joseph Duveen, who underwrote a national scheme to help young artists hold exhibitions at home and abroad.

Duveen's benefactions to the Tate had not ended with the opening of the new galleries. In 1927 he donated Stanley Spencer's *The Resurrection, Cookham*, which, owing to its use of distortion and its interpretation of the subject in local terms, became the focus of a widespread controversy and, as a result, one of the pictures most readily associated with the Tate. Duveen himself was a constant visitor to the Gallery, especially to his father's Turner wing where he would stand for ages in front of Turner's *Bridge and Tower* (now called *The Ponte Delle Torri, Spoleto*). 'If I owned that picture,' he is on record as saying, 'I should want nothing else in the world.' But as he did not own this painting, his ambitions were more complex: when he began piloting Ramsay MacDonald around London galleries, it seemed a disinterested act, but after MacDonald became Prime Minister for the last time, Duveen was made a baronet and also a Trustee of the National Gallery in Trafalgar Square – a distinction which had never before been conferred on an art dealer.

Duveen, keen to stimulate young artists' interest in mural painting, had supplied money for the decoration of the Boys' Highways Club in Shadwell by two Slade students, Mary Adshead and Rex Whistler, under the supervision of Professor Tonks. In 1925 he offered to pay £500 for a wall decoration in the Tate Gallery's

Refreshment Room. This rather grim and gloomy room, which had a row of hideous iron pillars punctuating its space, helped create the impression that what was on offer was an impromptu picnic in a boiler room. Once Duveen's scheme had been approved by H.M. Office of Works, a small committee was formed (Professor Tonks, Archibald Balfour and Charles Aitken) to select an artist and to arrange all details, such as the hiding of unsightly waterpipes behind a false wall. The commission was given to twenty-one year old Rex Whistler who was paid five pounds a week (earning £400 in all), on top of which, at Duveen's suggestion, he was given a £100 bonus. Having demonstrated his gift for imaginative decoration at Shadwell, Whistler devised, with the help of Edith Olivier, a story entitled 'In Pursuit of Rare Meats'. With grace, wit and fantasy, in a manner not dissimilar to William Walton's music for Edith Sitwell's *Façade*, Whistler traced the imaginary journey of a hunting party, which is seen leaving a palace in one corner of the room and rides through various countries, hunting for truffles in the oak woods of France, spearing sturgeon, and meeting strange beasts, including a unicorn and a ghost. On the wall pierced with windows it passes through China with its Great Wall, through Peru, and finally ends in a Claude-like landscape. As David Cecil observed of this mural, its ironic Romanticism mischievously mocks its own sentimental response to the picturesque.[2] The murals successfully transformed the Refreshment Room into one of the most talked-about venues in London after it reopened on 30 November 1927. At the time the only other comparable restaurant was Boulestin's, decorated by Allan Walton.

Painted in a mixture of wax and oil, Whistler's murals survived the great flood of 1928 which covered them to a depth of eight feet. Over Christmas 1927 there had been heavy falls of snow outside London in the Cotswolds. Early in the new year a sudden thaw doubled the daily flow of water down the Thames. On the evening of 6 January 1928 a south-westerly wind stiffened and blew with gale-like ferocity. When the tide turned on the ebb, it surged back upstream with turbulent violence and met the wind. The force and turmoil of the water was such that barges and boats were tossed about as if in a storm at sea. In the early hours of 7 January the Thames embankment wall collapsed near Lambeth Bridge. Soon after, the wall in front of the Tate Gallery was breached. The flood tore away 165 feet of wall, the water sweeping across the road and roaring into the lower galleries. Nothing could stop it; doors were unhinged and masonry pushed aside. Many people in nearby houses had to swim for their lives and some were drowned. It was estimated afterwards that flood damage had rendered some four thousand families homeless.

Aitken was summoned to the Tate at 5 am. He contacted Manson and took a cab to Millbank, wading through water on foot for the last part of his journey. Messages were sent to his staff and he arranged for pumps to be at hand. When his assistants arrived he led a party of them through deep and icy water. At one point he stumbled and fell into an open manhole and was completely submerged. Only prompt action saved him from drowning. Pumps worked throughout the day and the level of water began to fall. Officials from other galleries, as well as many private individuals, among them Sir Robert Witt and Sir William Burrell, gave a hand in the work of salvage.

Though the bulk of the Tate's collection was situated in the galleries on the main floor, nine of the lower-floor galleries were hung with pictures, including a loan collection of Rowlandson's drawings, a number of modern foreign pictures lent by Burrell and others, and a display of Landseers. All these pictures had to be rescued from a confusion of floating cases and objects. On this floor, too, were the Turner portfolios, housed in Solander boxes in four wooden presses which were completely submerged. Though they had been covered with mud for some hours the Turner watercolours, to Aitken's surprise, had not run. They were spread out over the floors of the upper galleries and dried with blotting paper, as were the sketchbooks, sheet by sheet, under the supervision of Edwin Fagg, the Gallery's official lecturer. He was assisted by the Turner authorities A.M. Hind and A.J. Finberg, MacColl and members of staff from the Victoria & Albert and British Museums. But in the early stages of this salvage operation, some helpers had been seen wringing Turner drawings out like old rags.

All telephones, lighting and heating services were out of use. There was practically no glass left in the windows at basement level and, in the opinion of the chief surveyor, a large amount of water had found its way into the building from under the floor, because the old vaults of the Millbank Prison had not been completely filled in. But there was no damage to the outer and main walls of the Gallery which rested on deep foundations.[3] The Gallery's store of catalogues, postcards and paper was ruined and its library of art books seriously damaged. In all, 226 oils had been submerged. Of these, sixty-seven were slightly damaged, twenty-six seriously damaged but capable of repair, eighteen were damaged beyond repair and 115 had been submerged but were not damaged. In time the Treasury was to provide £8,700 for restoration and repairs to paintings and frames, and to assist with replacement books for the library.

In order to reassure the public that the main bulk of the collection was undamaged, the Trustees agreed to reopen the Gallery as soon as possible. It partly opened on 23 January 1928, more galleries going on view in February and March. But the aftermath of the flood seriously impeded development, for until a new embankment wall had been completed the storage space and exhibition galleries on the lower floor could not be considered safe. One large main-floor gallery had to be turned into a store, as did one of the corridors leading to the sculpture hall. The Boardroom and library were relocated upstairs, as were the curators' offices, a gallery over the front portico being converted for this purpose. Finally, the Tate lost a large part of the Turner Bequest when the Board sanctioned the removal of the drawings and watercolours to the British Museum and the Victoria & Albert Museum.

At the request of the Board, Duveen agreed to pay for the cost involved in creating storage space on the main floor. But when plans were submitted to him, he objected to the change of level which the plan entailed and he suggested another. This was in turn found unsatisfactory, and in the autumn of 1928 Duveen returned to the Board with an offer to rebuild three-fifths of the basement area, together with a grand new gallery for foreign sculpture which he had originally offered to build in 1927. He initially wanted to extend back on the east side of the building, in order to create a side-wing that would balance the modern foreign galleries. But the Board wanted to extend back from the existing sculpture gallery and eventually Duveen agreed to this, for he realised that if a central doorway was opened up in the existing British sculpture gallery, and the old Tea Room was removed, another magnificent long vista could be created on the same axis as the main entrance. At Duveen's request, Romaine-Walker & Jenkins began to draw up plans for a series of sculpture galleries, including a central octagonal gallery, as well as another staircase which would lead down to the Refreshment Room. The choice of architects depressed Aitken who did not think highly of either the Turner wing or the modern foreign galleries. 'I have done all I could since 1916 to try to get Sir Joseph to employ architects with really fine taste', he told Lord D'Abernon, 'but without success'.[4]

While plans for the new sculpture galleries went ahead, Aitken had his attention caught by the proposal to erect at Battersea a vast new power station. Both the Tate and the National Gallery sent a deputation to the Prime Minister to protest against it. Aitken wrote:

> The proposed concentration of coal combustion on a scale unprecedented in this century must entail the emission of large quantities of sulphuric acid and the discharge of large quantities of dust and grit. As the prevailing winds in London are from the south-west, the normal flow of fumes from the proposed power station at Battersea would pass directly over the chief national galleries and museums with their priceless collections.[5]

This objection, which presaged the huge protest later aroused by Bankside power station, did not prevent the building of the Battersea power station, but it caused the government chemist to look into the elimination of sulphur fumes. Further experiments were carried out four years later when a 100,000 kilowatt turbo-alternator generating set was installed at Battersea.

Aitken's readiness to act over environmental issues exceeded his interest in modern sculpture. At the time of the Gaudier-Brzeska memorial exhibition in 1918, there had been a slight altercation between him and the sculptor's executor, Sophie Brzeska, who had asked for some of Gaudier's sculptures to be taken into safe-keeping. In return, she had offered to give to the Tate some of his drawings but then became angered because, through a misunderstanding, Aitken had taken four on approval, whereas she only intended giving two. The matter had been quickly rectified, but, as Roger Cole has observed,[6] it may have coloured Aitken's subsequent response to Gaudier's work when, in April 1926, twenty-five pieces of sculpture, thirteen oils and pastels and 1,630 drawings by Gaudier-Brzeska suddenly cluttered the Tate's Boardroom. Sophie Brzeska had died in a mental asylum, intestate. Advertisements to alert any possible beneficiaries had been placed in four newspapers, but none had been sent to any Polish or French newspapers

20 Detail from *The Expedition in Pursuit of Rare Meats,* murals designed
by Rex Whistler for the Refreshment Room, 1926–7

21 London Underground poster designed
by Rex Whistler, 1927. *London Transport Museum*

22 The Thames in flood in 1928, with workman building a wall of sandbags

23 Men carrying pictures to safety during the flood of 1928

where they might have been seen either by her or Gaudier's relatives. After a grant of admission had been made, the nation became the beneficiary of all Sophie Brzeska's possessions and papers which now had to be offered to a national collection. Aitken, occupied with the forthcoming opening of the modern foreign galleries, did nothing about the contents of the Boardroom for five months. He then told the Treasury Solicitor that much of the work seemed slight and rather mannered, and that he thought the Trustees would have little interest in it. He agreed to invite discussion on it at the Board meeting in October, but was chiefly concerned that the whole collection should be removed from the Tate's premises as soon as possible.

Owing to the shortage of office space, the Tate Boardroom doubled as an office for one of the assistants to the Director, H.S. Ede. Better known as 'Jim' Ede, he had fought and been wounded in the First World War, after which he had spent a year at the Slade before taking up the post of Lecturer at the National Gallery. A year later, in 1921, he had moved to the Tate as an assistant, with Manson, to the Director. 'What shall we give Ede to do?' he remembered his superiors saying,[7] and at first all that could be found were minor jobs such as the unpacking of dusty packets of postcards. It fell to him to collect the weekly wages from Trafalgar Square. He would return to Millbank by bus, and once got off leaving his bag with all the wages in it on board. Realising what he had done, he sprinted fast over the bridge, caught up with the bus and retrieved the bag.

Ede's taste in art was more advanced that that of Aitken or Manson and he took more interest in Picasso than in the Pre-Raphaelites. At the time of the 1928 flood he had been commended for his salvage work, but while wading through muddy water and feeling something knock against his shins, he had reached down and pulled up Watts's *Hope*, the one painting he had hoped never to see again, and had been sorely tempted to put his boot through it.

Association with the Tate brought Ede certain advantages: when sent to Paris on estate duty office business, he found that Picasso and others were willing to see him and he gained access to studios that would otherwise have been closed to him. 'It is amazing the interest which is taken here in painting', he wrote to Aitken from Paris in 1927. 'I am seeing pictures from 8 am till sometimes midnight.'[8] It was, however, disappointing to find on his return that his colleague, Manson, showed no interest in the artists he had seen or the lists of paintings he brought back. After a three-day visit to Holland, during which he had tea with van Gogh's sister-in-law, Madame Gosshalk-Bonger, Ede informed the Tate that it could buy six paintings by van Gogh for £5,000. Though steps were taken to view the paintings, the offer, in Ede's opinion, was grossly mishandled and eventually nothing was bought.[9]

Ede found a more positive outlet for his interests through the Contemporary Art Society (CAS), for which he acted as secretary, under the chairmanship of Sir Edward Marsh. However, it soon became obvious to the administration at the National Gallery that his involvement with the CAS was having a detrimental effect on his work for the Tate. In April 1927 Ede had to justify himself to C.H. Collins Baker:

> I have very great hopes of making the CAS a source of permanent and considerable revenue to the Tate Gallery ... When I took over my duties in the CAS its yearly turnover was £800. Last year it was £4,600. This large increase is perhaps slightly due to me in that I revived the interest in the society and by constantly writing to the members and talking to them have spread its activities ... For my share in this I get £30 p.a. which doesn't at all represent the financial value of what I do. I find it useful of course but could raise considerably more if my time was free ... The question of outside work sapping your energy from your official job is a thorny one ... Were I to be just a clerk and keep my office hours and those only I would as you know get nowhere and the Tate would get nothing adequate for I should soon become even duller than I am.[10]

Collins Baker, irritated by the constant minor errors that appeared in Ede's paperwork, was not mollified by this letter. He replied: 'I am quite ready to believe that you think those other things, [the CAS] are of great importance to the gallery, and I daresay you are right. But unless you get into the way of never touching that outside work until every detail of your official work has been cleared thoroughly, you are sure to find that you confuse and fluster yourself.'[11] When the following January Ede requested the appointment of another assistant, he was told that, in the Treasury's opinion, the fact that he had managed to do CAS work in official time was a major snag.

Yet Ede had a better idea of what was needed in a Tate curator than Manson or Aitken. He had an active interest in contemporary art, was friendly with certain artists and collectors, including Frank Stoop, visited exhibitions, read the critics, and kept an eye on saleroom prices. And when Gaudier-Brzeska's work suddenly appeared in his office in 1926, he knew better than Aitken its value and significance.

The critic R.H. Wilenski had been asked by the Treasury to value the collection. Taking into account the selling price of a work of art, as opposed to what it might fetch in a dealer's gallery, and also the fact that when works of art appear on the market in large quantities their value is diminished, Wilenski's objective and considered opinion was that the Gaudier-Brzeska collection should be valued at £250.

To Aitken's surprise, the Trustees were more favourably impressed by Gaudier-Brzeska's work than he had expected. They viewed it in October and again at the Board meeting in November, at which they selected three sculptures and seventeen drawings, on the understanding that the Treasury was prepared to offer these as a permanent loan.[12] A further three sculptures and eighteen drawings were accepted by the CAS, and Aitken, thinking the matter finished with, asked Ede to report back to the Treasury and tie up all loose ends. Ede must have thought long and hard about this collection, as some months passed before he wrote to the Treasury Solicitor asking if he could buy all that remained (nineteen sculptures, thirteen oils and pastels and 1,595 drawings) for £60, a price that he suggested was a fair one, given Wilenski's valuation and the value of the work which the Tate and the CAS had removed from the collection. On hearing of the Treasury rule that government property could not be sold to civil servants without sanction, Ede arranged for a friend, E. McKnight Kauffer, to act as his front and put up the money. He also obtained agreement that Sophie Brzeska's papers, which filled three trunks and five packing cases, should be included in the sale. Finally, again using McKnight Kauffer as his front, he obtained for five guineas such rights as the Crown had in the copyright on her and Gaudier's writings.

With this terrific scoop, Ede began planning a book on Gaudier, while continuing to confront the frustrations attendant on his work at the Tate. He infiltrated the first ever Picasso into the Tate in 1929 by persuading Frank Stoop to lend one from his collection while he went on holiday. 'Great fun the Press View to the Wilson Steer exhibition', Ede wrote to the artist Ben Nicholson, 'I took all the Press to see the Picasso!!'[13] But he could not shift the Trustees' prejudice against Christopher Wood, whose *faux-naif* style they distrusted. The Board turned down a Wood offered as a gift by Sir Edward Marsh, and only admitted one into the collection when Wood's parents donated a picture after his untimely death in 1930.

'I long *passionately* just now to throw over this whole blessed official position. Why can't I make £300 a year in a quiet way – my own master – perhaps I will some day.'[14] So Ede wrote to Ben Nicholson, whose paintings Ede did succeed in getting into the Tate in 1929, but only as far as his office where they were considered a sign of his peculiar taste. 'I have enjoyed all your pictures at the Tate', he told Nicholson, 'will take some flowers down [tomorrow] and what with them and the pictures I shall hardly know I'm at the Tate.'[15] Soon after this he went to Spain for a holiday and on his return suffered a breakdown. Two doctors diagnosed nerve strain. After two months off work, he was examined by a Treasury doctor who weighed up the effects of his war service, the exhaustion and neuritis brought on by the extra work caused by the 1928 flood, and his recent history of exhaustion, headaches and insomnia. Dr A.S. Russell was clearly a little bemused by this tall, thin sunburnt, talkative man: 'He has no idea of conducting himself properly', his report reads, 'but sits lounging in a chair with his head at one time resting sideways on the cushion and the next moment with his chin over the back, looking at the fireplace but all the time giving a long account of his innumerable troubles.'[16] The report concludes that Ede was 'utterly unfit for work at present and that the probability of him ever rendering efficient service is very remote'. Aitken protested that this report seemed overly pessimistic: 'He does not seem to be specially suited to the detailed administrative work which the post of the second assistant here entails, but he has worked here for eight years with regularity, goodwill and fair efficiency until recently.'[17] While his future hung in the balance, Ede admitted to Ben Nicholson that he would not mind leaving the Tate, but did not wish to be pushed out and had a wife and two daughters to consider. In the outcome he was given a further four months leave.

Immediately after this medical Ede felt better than he had felt for months, and it was probably now that he began work on his book on Gaudier, the American edition of which was to appear under the title *Savage Messiah*. He made clever use of the papers he had acquired, for much of the book is a compilation of Gaudier's letters. Ede returned to the Tate in March 1930. His book was published the following year, at first in a large format with collotype reproductions of drawings. Ede had the idea of also producing a single deluxe version which would contain the original drawings and be offered for sale as a collector's item for a thousand guineas. Though the sale failed to materialise, the various editions of his book, both in England and American eventually brought in sufficient funds to enable Ede to resign from the Tate in October 1936.

On his return from sick leave, Ede found that the Director was himself far from well. Aitken had endured censure at the time of the flood, despite the fact that he had drawn attention to the potential danger of unusually high tides, and, according to William Rothenstein, he underwent much distress and strain.[18] 'I am now sixty,' he wrote, informing Lord D'Abernon of his intention to retire in six months time, 'and have been working for nearly forty years without a break … The flood entailed endless worry and poisoning, owing to having to sort germ-soaked archives and collections in unhealthy conditions.'[19]

Earlier, at the time of the opening of the modern foreign galleries in 1926, D'Abernon had written to 10 Downing Street, recommending Aitken for a knighthood: 'He is almost an ideal museum director and brings endless enthusiasm and tact into the discharge of his duties. He has succeeded in making the Tate Gallery the best museum of its kind in Europe. Twenty years ago it hardly existed. All foreign critics who have recently seen it are unanimous in their praise both of the arrangement and the representative character of the collection.'[20] But Aitken, in a letter to D'Abernon, argued that the collections were on a better footing 'chiefly due to the exceptionally fortunate co-operation there has been between the enterprising activity of National Gallery Trustees, such as yourself and the late Lord Plymouth and Lord Curzon and the extraordinarily whole-hearted and disinterested energy of Witt, MacColl, Muirhead Bone and others'. Aitken claimed that his single merit had been to make use of all this goodwill. And with regard to knighthood, he confessed: 'I have an instinctive feeling that it is better for me, personally, to remain a plain individual. I shall be retiring in a few years with only a small income and such an honour might then prove a little unsuitable and even embarrassing.'[21]

At Aitken's final Board meeting, Lord D'Abernon said: 'I have long experience of the public service and I have known no one more capable and devoted – none more modest and self effacing.'[22] It was typical of Aitken that when his successor, J.B. Manson, had a minor accident just before taking over, Aitken agreed to stay on another month without hesitation.

★   ★   ★

When James Bolivar Manson took over as Director in August 1930, progress on the new sculpture galleries had ceased. Work had begun on this project in 1928 and by July 1929 plans and a model had been submitted, which were subsequently modified in the light of criticisms made by Sir Richard Allinson of H.M. Office of Works. A new model was approved by Allinson, the Trustees, Aitken and Alfred Daniel, when suddenly, in September 1929, Duveen announced that his views had changed and he would not now accept either model, nor would he proceed further until he had obtained a design in 'the latest modern American style', and that he was instructing his architects Romaine-Walker & Jenkins to work with John Russell Pope, an American architect renowned for his designs for public monuments in a severe neo-classical style. This summary rejection of all the work so far done displeased many; Aitken and William Rothenstein implied as much to Duveen, but he would not reconsider his decision.

What may have caused this hiatus was Duveen's awareness of America's booming museum industry. The Museum of Modern Art had opened in 1929, and was followed a year later by the Whitney Museum of American Art. The former was to represent a major challenge to the Tate in its pursuit of works of art of the highest quality that would form a historically coherent collection. In 1931 the Frick Mansion was transformed into the Frick Museum and the architect responsible for the conversion was John Russell Pope. Duveen had helped obtain him this job, and also the task of designing the National Gallery in Washington (completed by Otto R. Eggers and David Paul Higgins), on which he began work in 1936. These and other commissions established Pope as a major figure in the development of the twentieth-century art museum. He was to build for Duveen not only the sculpture galleries at the Tate, in collaboration with Romaine-Walker & Jenkins, but also a gallery (destroyed during the Second World War) to house the Elgin Marbles at the British Museum. Before he began work on the Tate sculpture galleries, Pope went with Duveen to see the new barrel-vaulted sculpture gallery that was being built in the Metropolitan Museum of Art in New York. It helped to fire Duveen's determination, as he later admitted to John Rothenstein, to build a sculpture gallery 'which would in itself rank as a work of art comparable to any modern building of its kind'.[23]

Unfortunately for the Tate, this era of rapid museum expansion in Europe and

24 J.B. Manson

25 Frank Dobson's *Truth*, 1930, being manhandled into position
on the lawn outside the Tate Gallery, 1930s

America coincided with its least satisfactory Director. Manson, like Ede, had a
wife and two daughters to support and subsidised his Tate salary by writing books
and art criticism. Monographs by him appeared on Degas (1927) and Rembrandt
(1929), and his *Hours in the Tate Gallery* (1926) must have introduced many visitors
to the collection. Though it betrayed his dislike of modern art, it upheld Aitken's
opinion that Manson had discernment and character. According to Kenneth
Clark, Manson was a man of great charm, 'with a flushed face, white hair and a

twinkle in his eye; and this twinkling eye got him out of scrapes that would have sunk a worthier man without trace.'[24] But was it lack of integrity or maudlin sentimentality that caused him to praise in the *Studio* the drawings of a twelve year old girl called Pamela Bianco? He claimed to find in these drawings 'art as fine in essence as that of Botticelli, Piero della Francesca, Giotto and some other few examples of primitive inspiration. It is as though Pamela Bianco were the mouthpiece of a divine spirit.'[25]

During his early years at the Tate Manson had had a loyal supporter in Aitken who felt that the younger man's abilities complemented his own. At intervals he had been promoted, and his salary had risen accordingly. But his chief desire was to paint and he managed to combine his responsibilities at the Tate with membership of the Camden Town Group, the London Group and the Monarro Group, through which he acquired a reputation chiefly as a flower painter. As late as 1928, he was still havering over his choice of career and asked Roger Fry's advice as to whether he could make a living from painting. Frustrated ambitions, an unhappy marriage and excessive drinking may have contributed to the depression, occasional blackouts and paranoia which troubled him in the 1930s and caused him to be absent on lengthy periods of sick leave.

Yet Manson alone should not be blamed for the Tate's failure to obtain a great collection of modern foreign art during the 1930s: though new funds had accumulated for acquisitions, there was still no annual purchase grant from the government and the Trustees took a conservative view of art. Manson complained of their hostility to modern art to his friend Lucien Pissarro,[26] and had reason to do so as they turned down a Monet and a Renoir. And when Camille Pissarro offered to lend his painting *La Causette* Manson had to decline it as there were no funds to pay for its carriage from France nor for insurance. Yet he himself had a dislike of Post-Impressionist painting and, like Aitken, continued to ignore the quietly unpretentious displays of first-rate art of this kind which Lefevre's and the Leicester Galleries in London mounted during the 1920s and early 1930s, giving solo exhibitions to the work of Cézanne, van Gogh, Gauguin, Picasso, Matisse and many others. In 1929, when the Contemporary Art Society offered to give the Tate Matisse's *Reading Woman with Parasol*, bought three years before by St John Hutchinson, Aitken and his Trustees had declined it, and it did not become part of the Tate's collection until 1938. It is probable that Manson would have kept Matisse out of the Tate during his term of office, had he not been obliged to accept in 1933 the bequest of the stockbroker C.F. Stoop, which included two Matisse oils (*Trivaux Pond* and *Nude Study in Blue*). This major bequest of seventeen works brought into the collection the first two Cézannes, three of the first four Picassos (another was donated that year by the Contemporary Art Society), two Degas pastels and van Gogh's *Landscape at Auvers*.

The situation was a little better with regard to British art. If Sickert, whose portrait of Aubrey Beardsley was acquired in 1932, was now acceptable to a Tate Director, Henry Moore was not: Aitken and the Trustees had declined *Maternity*, when offered on loan in 1928, and Moore remained one of Manson's *bêtes noires*.

He and his Trustees rejected the gift offered by Mr C. Branson in May 1933 of two sculptures by Henry Moore, four oils by William Coldstream, a watercolour by Frances Hodgkins and other items.

There were, however, definite improvements at the Gallery during Manson's term of office. In October 1932 he won the Trustees' approval for the adoption of 'Tate Gallery' as the official name rather than 'National Gallery, Millbank'. The following year the first cherry trees, which became a much-loved feature of the Gallery in springtime, were planted along Atterbury Street. The battle over the need for artificial light was finally won and its installation in 1935 resulted in an alteration in the Tate's opening hours: from now on it shut an hour later, at 5 pm. Two years before, H.M. Office of Works had also agreed a much-needed improvement and the Trustees 'expressed their gratification that lavatory accommodation befitting the dignity of the Gallery should at last be installed'.[27] This same year the first set of sliding wire screens was fitted in the store. In 1934 a new assistant, David Fincham, began discussing with London Passenger Transport the possibility of regular posters on the Underground. And the following year it was decided that in order to improve the appearance of the Boardroom, the library should be re-established on part of the balcony around the entrance rotunda.

The gradual reshuffling of the Board in the early 1930s brought to the fore Sir Evan Charteris, barrister, historian and dandy. He had originally joined as a Trustee in 1927 but left in 1932 to become a National Gallery Trustee. However, between 1934 and 1940 he served again on the Tate Board as National Gallery liaison member, becoming Chairman in 1935. Among those who served under him as Trustees were the Earl of Sandwich, the sculptor William Reid Dick, and the painters William Nicholson, Augustus John and Glyn Philpot, who was reappointed as Trustee in 1935. One positive step taken by the Board was the unanimous resolution in October 1934 to appeal to the Chancellor of the Exchequer for a Grant-in-Aid of £2,000 for the purchase of works of art. It was also suggested by Lord Sandwich that Manson should draw up a list of artists not represented in the collection in order to facilitate the filling of gaps. But, with the purchase grant not forthcoming, and a want of definite interest in French painting, the Trustees declined to buy Henri Matisse's *Interior with a Figure* for £2,000 from Pierre Matisse in July 1935. This same year the loan of a work by Francis Picabia, *Courtyard in France*, was turned down. And it is possible that lingering resentment over the radical effect of his two Post-Impressionist exhibitions in 1910 and 1912 may have turned the Trustees against Roger Fry who had died in 1934: they declined both his oil painting *Arles*, offered as a gift by Sir George Hill in February 1935, and two paintings which his sister, Margery Fry, wanted to donate in his memory in April 1935.

Yet sufficient improvements had been made for the *Sunday Times* art critic, Frank Rutter, to look kindly on the Tate when he reviewed a collection of Chantrey Bequest pictures which went on show in July 1932. 'There is no art institution in London, or in the provinces, which within the last thirty years has witnessed so complete a change, both in contents and character, as the Tate Gallery in Millbank.'[28] He went on to remark that few of the thirty-five Chantrey Bequest works on display would merit purchase under the new regime, and that these paintings and sculptures, which had been bought for over £25,000, would possibly be worth now little more than £5,000. In Rutter's view, time had vindicated Mac-Coll and his campaign.

The publication of Herbert Read's *Art Now* in 1933 cast a different perspective on the Tate's achievement. This book offered a philosophical and critical defence of avant-garde European art, including Surrealism and German Expressionism, which as yet found no representation at the Tate. To those familiar with these and other developments the Tate appeared hopelessly insular. So it seemed to a young man, working as Freddy Mayor's partner at the Mayor Gallery, Douglas Cooper. He assisted Herbert Read with the illustrations for *Art Now*, and he also helped Paul Nash form the avant-garde group, Unit One, which held its first exhibition at the Mayor Gallery in October 1933. When this group published a book, also called *Unit One* (1934), many of the artists' statements contained within it had been obtained with Cooper's help. In time, Cooper was to become the Tate's most belligerent and vociferous critic.

At a practical level the Tate, in Ede's opinion,[29] 'would have been in an awful muck' at this time had it not been for John Lee. This quiet, dedicated craftsman could be found in the basement, making frames, gilding them and labelling them with painted lettering. Lee had gained his position at the Tate by winning the respect of Aitken who had raised him from attendant to technical assistant. Both men helped each other, Lee undertaking work for a museum in Alfriston, Sussex, with which Aitken was associated, and Aitken paying school-uniform bills for Lee's children. Though outside picture restorers were used by the Gallery, Lee himself cleaned and varnished pictures and did basic repairs, such as strip-lining the sides of canvases when they became worn. He not only worked in the basement, where he boiled his eggs in the same pan as his glue, but also lived there during the week, only going home at weekends, as his daughter recalled,[30] for, as was well known, he preferred the company of his beloved Turners to that of his wife. He had been sleeping in the Gallery at the time of the 1928 flood. Found floating on top of the water, he was taken immediately to St Thomas's Hospital, but went back to the Tate as soon as he recovered to see what they had done to his Turners.

Over the years the Tate was to inspire uncommon loyalty in a great many individuals, but in Manson, who was Director for eight years, this loyalty was divided owing to his continuing desire to paint. The exhibition programme during his time of office was patchy and thin. If he had an eye for what was popular (*Cricket Pictures*, an exhibition mounted in 1934, was timed to coincide with an Australian Ashes Tour), he made little attempt to innovate, and the Sickert retrospective proposed for 1935 was replaced by a small exhibition of Professor Tonks's paintings and drawings (and Sickert not honoured by the Tate until 1941). Manson was certainly active in ways that must have rebounded to the credit of the Gallery, serving, for instance, on the selection committee for the British Pavilion at the Venice

Biennale in 1932 and organising exhibitions in Brussels in 1932 and in Bucharest in 1936. But when, in 1934, the Board of Overseas Trade asked if the Tate would accept an exhibition of modern Italian painting and the Board asked Manson to pursue the matter, nothing further happened. The most successful exhibitions in Manson's era were two centenaries, of Edward Burne-Jones's birth in 1933 and of John Constable's death in 1937. As the former coincided with a heat-wave, the Tate restaurant served luncheons and teas outside on the lawns in front of the Gallery, and the bright blue tables and chairs and multicoloured umbrellas made an attractive scene.

In 1935 Kenneth Clark took over the Directorship of the National Gallery and began sitting on the Tate Board as an ex-officio Trustee. Clark was particularly keen to establish good relations between the two institutions and he invited the staff at the Tate to view the Jubilee Procession from the National Gallery. He also recognised that, because of the overlap in their collections, the relationship between the National and the Tate could be vexed. C.J. Holmes had resented the Tate's right to absorb 'modern foreign painting' after the recommendations of the Curzon Report had been implemented: 'Claims to absorb all our "modern" foreign pictures, including Goya and Ingres, drove me to explosion, and to shelter behind my own Trustees from the masterful rapacity of my friends at Millbank. I admired, of course, all the time that I had to oppose.'[31] But by the late 1930s the boot was on the other foot, for Clark was determined to open the doors of the National Gallery to French Impressionism and improve its representation of nineteenth-century French art. The Tate was already vulnerable to loss, as the terms attached to the Courtauld Fund meant that pictures bought with this money had to be available for transfer to the National Gallery in due course. Because of this, and the fact that the Tate's collection was still vested in the Trustees of the National Gallery and therefore subject to their wishes, the Tate felt in some ways like a mere waiting room for the National Gallery.

In 1917 the question of the transfer of pictures from one gallery to another had been left as a matter of adjustment between the Directors of the two Galleries. By 1936 it was felt that clearer guidelines were needed with regard to the purchasing policy of both Galleries. The first serious discussion took place at a Tate Board meeting on 23 June and it was agreed that a sub-committee should be set up to investigate this matter. The outcome was a flurry of memoranda but no clear directive. Much distress and indignation were revealed at the lack of financial support given to the Tate and some suggested this was due to lack of enterprise on the part of its Director. Clark's memorandum focused on the problem of nineteenth-century French painting, for he was irked by the necessity at the National Gallery of having to combine eighteenth-century and nineteenth-century French painting in the same gallery. 'This is open to obvious objections on the grounds that it does not do justice to French painting of either period and that to hang eg. Cézanne and Boucher in the same room shows an amateurishness unworthy of the National Gallery.'[32] Though his paper looked at various alternatives, he was defeated in his attempt to obtain Seurat's *Bathers, Asnières* but was able to solve his problem without the Tate's help by persuading the Home House Trustees to lend paintings from Samuel Courtauld's private collection.

A still more pressing concern at this time was Duveen's sculpture galleries. A new plan had been agreed in 1933, the year in which Duveen was raised to the peerage. Owing to his itinerant existence he had no home base to commemorate in his title, and so chose the area surrounding the Tate, becoming Lord Duveen of Millbank. Two years later, he was pleased to see that construction of his three new galleries was well underway. The first of these, leading out of the existing building, was almost a hundred feet long and was to be divided from the second gallery, the central Octagon, by a screen of Ionic columns with full entablature and a coffered arch overhead. A similar screen divided the octagon from the third and largest gallery, which was to be some 118 feet in length. Combined with the entrance hall and its adjoining rotunda, these new galleries offered a magnificent vista of some 300 feet in length. The Duveens, as they became known, were all built with stone facings and dressings and were paved with dark green marble terrazzo in large squares bordered with Lunel marble. On either side of the first gallery were two additional side galleries for the display of smaller sculptural work. An inscription at either end of the main gallery (sometimes called the Sculpture Hall) read: 'These Galleries were presented to the Nation by Lord Duveen of Millbank, MCMXXXVII.'

Duveen was aware that these were the first public galleries in England designed specifically for the display of sculpture. He had allocated £50,000 to this project, knowing that it would raise the stature of the Tate, making it the most important modern art gallery in Europe. Given the significance he attached to these new galleries, it is not surprising that in the course of their construction his relations with Manson became strained. This may partly have been Duveen's fault as he was capable of creating additional muddle with his high-handed behaviour. He led an American-based British sculptor Tait Mckenzie to believe that his work was being bought by the Tate after Duveen saw it and instructed him to send five bronzes to London. This Mckenzie did, at great expense, only to learn that all five works had been rejected by the Trustees and the Tate had no power to authorise payment of his expenses. The other side to Duveen's high-handedness was his generosity, and shortly before the opening of the new sculpture galleries he paid £500 towards the cost of new pedestals. The Victoria & Albert Museum had sanctioned the transfer, on loan, to the Tate of most of their Rodins, together with a marble torso by Ivan Meštrović, and other works. As King George VI had agreed to open the galleries on 29 June 1937, the Victoria & Albert also lent a tapestry, the Treasury produced the State Inkstand, and a dark-blue morocco-bound visitors' book for distinguished guests was bought from Zachadorf in Shaftesbury Avenue. Duveen now declined to have any dealings with the Director and most of the elaborate arrangements surrounding this highly successful royal opening were undertaken by Manson's subordinate, David Fincham.

Kenneth Clark recalls that Manson was so confident of his charm that he appeared at Board meetings drunk, and on one occasion fell off his chair and had to be carried out wrapped in a blanket.[33] Illness and depression had led Manson into alcoholism during the last two or three years of his Directorate and much of the administration now fell on Fincham, whose passport into the Tate had been marriage to Lord D'Abernon's niece, rather than any interest in art. Following Ede's departure in 1936, a new assistant had been found in Robin Ironside in 1937; but Fincham, wanting to retain control of the Gallery, put it about that Ironside had no gift for administration. Fincham's roguish humour and love of the bottle gave him an easy camaraderie with Manson, to whom he once wrote:

> I am enclosing various letters, and a nine-page report of that glorious Board Meeting held in your absence. There were six pages of Agenda, which by the Grace of God and His Holy Mother Mary were got through in an hour and a half, in spite of the grumblings of Sir William Nicholson, and the thunders of K.K. [Kenneth Clark]. The Chairman was bewildered, Reid Dick was explosive and … Anyhow, Art was served (a difficult mistress), assisted by the consumption of a proportion of fifty perfectos (4/8d), and two or three fifties of Du Maurier (consigned to the Director) scarcely consumed, utilized later by me.
>
>   You will be pleased to hear that the relict of Sir Alfred East was again disappointed. You will notice, if you con these carefully written Minutes which I enclose … that a Red Scene by Kunstoberst Windam Lovis [Wyndham Lewis] vas purechazed by zee Trustees for eighty shiners. Honour is satisfied, Charteris is happy, Lovis has attained his ambition. And where, in the name of the Seven Jews who piped round the bassinette of Moses the night the Old Jew was born, in the name of God, we are going to hang it beats the band. Otherwise, fine and dandy, as the films say, The Show Goes On, Ironside is no mortal help in heaven or hell, but he might find the Absolute in Paris, whither he is being transported willy-nilly for the last corral about the tenth of February.[34]

It was Fincham who got Manson into trouble with Utrillo. When writing an entry on Utrillo for the third edition of the *Modern Foreign School Catalogue*, Fincham had relied on the *Evening Standard* for his information and, without checking its veracity, had stated that Utrillo was 'a confirmed dipsomaniac' who had died in 1934. He had then covered his tracks by giving as his source the *Dictionnaire Biographique des Artistes Contemporaines*. Unfortunately, Utrillo was alive and sober enough to want to sue for libel. Unmollified by offers made by the Treasury Solicitor, he proceeded to do so and Manson, though not the author of the offending words, had to be named as the defendant, as it was under his authority that the catalogue had been published, and he suffered much opprobrium. The action was settled in court on 17 February 1938, on the basis of an apology to Utrillo, payment of his legal fees and an agreement that the Tate would buy one of his paintings.

But the nadir of Manson's career was yet to come. On 4 March 1938 he attended a grand dinner at the Hotel George V in Paris to celebrate the British Exhibition at the Louvre. Kenneth Clark was the organiser and Evan Charteris had chaired the committee. One of the guests was Clive Bell who afterwards wrote to his wife:

> You will probably have heard rumours … of the remarkable scene that brought the fêtes and galas of the English exhibition to an end. How Manson arrived at the déjeuner given by the minister of Beaux Arts fantastically drunk – punctuated the ceremony with cat-calls and cock-a-doodle-doos, and finally staggered to his feet, hurled obscene insults at the company in general and the minister in particular, and precipitated himself on the ambassadress, Lady Phipps, some say with amorous intent others with lethal intent. The papers seem to be trying to hush the matter up, which of course makes people talk the more. It is certain that he succeeded in breaking up the banquet, and the guests fled ices uneaten, coffee undrunk … I hope an example will be made, and that they will seize the opportunity for turning the sot out of the Tate, not because he is a sot, but because he has done nothing but harm to modern painting.[35]

According to Kenneth Clark, it was at the request of the Foreign Office that Manson was asked to resign on the grounds of ill health. But before this became official, Manson had caused further offence. Since 1932 there had existed an obscure law designed to protect British stonecutters against the importation of cheap Italian tombstones. Stiff import duties were imposed on incoming statues and carvings unless they were recognised as works of art and therefore exempt. If the custom inspectors were in any doubt, they called in the Director of the Tate. This they did in the spring of 1938 when Marcel Duchamp selected and shipped from Paris for exhibition at Peggy Guggenheim's gallery in London, sculpture by Henri Laurens, Jean Arp, Raymond Duchamp-Villon, Constantin Brancusi, Antoine Pevsner and others. Manson was called in by bemused custom officials and shown Brancusi's *Sculpture for the Blind*, a large egg-like marble which he pronounced 'idiotic' and 'not art'. His rejection of this work caused a huge controversy, Henry Moore writing heatedly in defence of Brancusi to the *Manchester Guardian* and Peggy Guggenheim's assistant, Wyn Henderson, getting art critics to sign a protest against Manson's verdict. Peggy Guggenheim, who saw that Manson had abused his privilege, recalls: 'As a result my case was brought up in the House of Commons and we won it. Mr Manson not only lost his case, but pretty soon his job as well. I thus rendered a great service to foreign artists and to England.'[36]

Manson, aged fifty-eight, applied for superannuation after twenty-five years service at the Tate, claiming retirement on the grounds of a nervous breakdown. It must have been some consolation that he could now concentrate fully on his painting. He left Hampstead Garden Suburb and his wife Lillian for a studio in Chelsea and Elizabeth (Cecily Haywood), and continued to cultivate his reputation as a flower painter, until 1945, when he observed the simple truth: 'The roses are dying, and so am I.'[37]

5

A New Beginning

An overdeveloped sense of propriety almost prevented John Rothenstein from becoming Manson's successor. His father William Rothenstein, though he had resigned from the Board six years earlier, kept away from his club, the Athenaeum, when he heard of Manson's disgrace, to avoid the risk of mentioning his son's name in conversation with another Tate Trustee. He also told his son, mistakenly, that candidates had to be invited to apply. John Rothenstein therefore did nothing until his wife, Elizabeth, learnt differently from the critic Eric Newton. A telephone call to the Trustee Lord Balniel put the matter right and the following day Rothenstein was interviewed. He wrote his application travelling down to London on the train from Sheffield.

Kenneth Clark afterwards told Elizabeth Rothenstein that her husband had stood out head and shoulders above the other candidates.[1] By coincidence, Rothenstein had lived for ten years as a child two doors away from his predecessor, 'a tall, spare man in light-coloured shabby tweeds, who spoke to us with a rather wintry kindliness', as he later recalled Charles Aitken.[2] More significant, however, was his father's appointment in 1920 as Principal of the Royal College of Art, for it enabled John Rothenstein to become familiar with a whole generation of artists. 'My debt to the painters and sculptors whom I came to know at the College', he wrote in his autobiography, 'is very great. They gave me an insight into the ideas that were of the most urgent concern to the artists of my own generation and they gave me the germ of the idea – that I would be happier in bearing witness to the activities of my own times than in researching into things past.'[3]

He had read Modern History at Oxford and came down in 1923 with a third-class degree. After this inauspicious start to his career, he spent three years in a flat at the top of his parents' house, talking each day with his father, to whom he was deeply devoted, becoming a Catholic convert and writing a book on Eric Gill, with whom he became friends, as well as occasional art criticism. Of crucial importance was an introduction, through his father, to Wyndham Lewis, the former Vorticist who had repented of some of his earlier views. Rothenstein claims it was Lewis who taught him to scrutinise avant-garde art critically and validated his antipathy towards abstract art. 'He clarified my vague comprehension that abstract art – however natural and beautiful a means of expression for certain temperaments – was wholly inadequate as a means of expressing the full content of the vision of others.'[4] He also admitted that Lewis encouraged his propensity to favour 'the concrete, the exactly defined, the rational'.[5]

Close family feeling, his father's authority and influence, and the many famous

26 John Rothenstein, *c.*1938

visitors whom his father entertained, had made it difficult for John Rothenstein to discover his own views on art. In 1926 he had therefore left for America, where he lectured on the History of Art, first at the University of Kentucky and then at the University of Pittsburgh. He returned to England married to an American, Elizabeth Kennard Smith, and read for his doctorate at University College London, writing a thesis on the relation between classical and romantic traditions in nineteenth-century painting. In addition, he wrote a novel, *Morning Sorrow*, and compiled a book of reproductions entitled *British Artists and the War*, which he prefaced with a pugnacious essay attacking both abstraction and social realism. He had earlier published his biography of Eric Gill (1926), but it was *A Pot of Paint: Artists of the Eighteen-Nineties* (1929) which demonstrated his gift for sparkling and informed biographical sketches and proved him to be a serious writer. In the course of his career, much of it given to public administration, he was to write twenty-five books.

Rothenstein also brought to the Tate his six years experience of working in public art galleries in the provinces. He had become Director of Leeds City Art Gallery in 1932, at a time when the character of the Gallery was overwhelmingly Victorian. He set about making it more representative of significant moments in British and Continental painting, but resigned after a year when the councillors failed to honour their promise to raise his salary which had been fixed at almost half that paid to his predecessor owing to economic cutbacks. At the request of a Sheffield business man, Alderman Graves, who had put up money for a new public art gallery, he moved to Sheffield in the autumn of 1933, to take charge of this project. He advised the city architects on the decoration, lighting and equipment for the gallery, and in order to make an impressive opening display he obtained loans from the National Gallery, the Tate, the Royal Academy and the Home House Trustees. He also did pioneering work with schoolchildren and the unemployed and gave talks for adults. But again, his relations with his employers became troubled when he tried to resist hanging some of the less impressive works in the collection that Alderman Graves had given the city.[6] If, in both Leeds and Sheffield, Rothenstein had shown integrity in pursuing certain policies, he seemed to lack the necessary diplomacy to persuade others of his views.

Nevertheless, in both cities Rothenstein had set new standards and parted on good terms with his colleagues. Consequently, his appointment in 1938 seemed to bode well for the Tate. In Kenneth Clark's opinion, most English gallery and museum directors at this time were colourless.[7] Rothenstein, on the other hand, had style, contacts and new ideas. At Sheffield, he had mounted an exhibition of Walt Disney drawings, knowing this would attract children into the gallery. Owing to his family connections, he was also regarded as a supporter of independent artists against the officialdom of the Academy. Moreover, when Sir James Rae, Under-Secretary of the Treasury, with the Prime Minister's authorisation, offered Rothenstein the directorship, there followed a half-hour chat during which Rae let drop that for some time the Treasury had been far from satisfied with the state of affairs at the Tate. A new broom was badly needed, and the thirty-six year old Rothenstein, genial, gregarious and enthusiastic, seemed the man most likely to provide it.

He walked into the Gallery as Director for the first time on 2 June 1938. Climbing the winding marble steps leading up to the floor where the offices were housed, he met a small, pale man coming down. On questioning him, Rothenstein learnt that his name was John Lee, that he did restoring and other other jobs, and that he had had enough and was leaving. Rothenstein asked him to put off his decision to another day, a tactic that preserved for the Tate one of its most useful employees. When Fincham appeared, he offered to show Rothenstein round the building and to introduce him to the staff. This he did, vigorously spinning, on their way round, the turnstile which kept the toll of visitors. He seemed affronted when the new Director said this practice should cease, and gave no apology for the announcement that he was about to depart on his annual leave, thereby depriving Rothenstein during his first weeks at the Gallery of his most senior and experienced member of staff.

These and other memories found at the start of Rothenstein's second volume of autobiography, *Brave Day, Hideous Night*, make vivid the situation at the Tate in 1938. Coming from the provinces, he had, despite the warnings he had been given, expected to find much to admire. Instead, he was appalled at how demoralised the Tate was. The whistling of the shabbily dressed attendants echoed through the galleries; smoking was ubiquitous and chaos reigned in those parts of the build-ing not open to the public. The hanging of pictures followed no logical plan and three galleries were filled with the worst examples of Chantrey Bequest paintings, selected by Manson as a deliberate tease and reproach to the Royal Academy. Rothenstein discovered that Robin Ironside ('a pale, unconventionally elegant young man of twenty-six'[8]) had spent his first year at the Tate reading, after Fin-cham had told him to stay in his room and not interfere. There was a notional filing system but a marked absence of correspondence with the Gallery's major benefactors – the two Duveens and Samuel Courtauld. What he did find among various accumulations of paper were uncashed cheques made out to the Gallery, and reams of obscene verse which had been typed by the Gallery's secretary at Fincham's dictation.

On small points of detail Rothenstein's memoirs can occasionally be faulted.[9] But, overall, there is ample evidence that his account of the Tate's ills is devastat-ingly accurate. 'It has been dead for so long', wrote a former Trustee, Robert Witt, '– since Charles Aitken, who was a vital force, gave up.'[10] At the same time Kenneth Clark, who showed Rothenstein much kindness during his first year at the Tate, wrote that it was a 'relief to have a reasonable being at the Tate who does not envisage the relations of the Tate and National Gallery as a continual guerril-la warfare'.[11]

Rothenstein immediately set about transforming the Gallery. He recognised in Robin Ironside an independent mind, witty and learned, and he appreciated the loyalty and good sense embodied in the Head Attendant. Like Aitken, he found in John Lee ('a man of boundless devotion to the Gallery and of extraordinary ver-satility'[12]) one of the Tate's most valuable assets and he assigned him the task of bringing order and cleanliness to the dusty chaos of the picture store. Meanwhile, Kenneth Clark, unable to believe that Neville Chamberlain and Lord Halifax would be cheated into an agreement at Munich, was looking for places in the National Gallery shelters which could be made into air-raid cellars when he came across some twenty rolls of grimy canvas. These turned out to be Turner's late, near-abstract, chromatic symphonies. As a result of this find, thirty-four previ-ously unseen Turners went on show at the Tate in February 1939, the same year that A.J. Finberg's erudite life of the artist was published.

In the course of rehanging the Gallery, Rothenstein devoted three rooms to modern British art, with telling effect. Several examples of first-rate modern British art had previously been hung at the Tate, but amid such a mass of conser-vative or inferior work that the effect of the best had been muted. Rothenstein's rehang won praise from Herbert Read in the *Listener*: 'For the first time the mod-ern English school (Whistler to Wadsworth) is treated seriously and hung with taste and discrimination.'[13] But praise from one quarter usually meant disap-pointment or anger in another, and these three rooms were seen as a deliberate slight by Academicians, because not a single work was by a member or associate of the Royal Academy.

A similar conflict was stirred by Rothenstein's rearrangement of the sculpture

27 Henry Moore, *Recumbent Figure*, 1938

galleries. These had extended the Tate's remit, by making it a viable home for the national collection of modern sculpture, but they also presented a problem: the great height of the main sculpture hall made the light very diffuse and the colour of the stone walls did not make a good background for sculpture. Moreover, no selection would satisfy all the interested parties. The artist-Trustee Reid Dick, for instance, was angered by Rothenstein's decision to move the equestrian figure for the Wellington Memorial out of the Alfred Stevens room, which had been closed for some years, and into the Sculpture Hall. And the Royal Society of British Sculptors revealed blatant xenophobia when it protested that Rothenstein, in his new display, had filled the Sculpture Hall with foreigners.

If Rothenstein quickly discovered how easy it was in his position to arouse criticism and dissent, he was still enjoying, in his relations with his Chairman, Sir Evan Charteris, and the Trustees, a honeymoon period. An exhibition of Canadian art, to which the Tate had been committed prior to Rothenstein's arrival, proved to be an uninteresting show, but it nevertheless received much positive attention in the press, owing to Rothenstein's keenly developed sense of publicity and the energetic showmanship with which he successfully put the Gallery on much better terms with the public. His attempts to bring to the Tate from Paris an American art exhibition failed, but an invitation to the Museum of Modern Art in New York to hold a similar exhibition at the Tate received an encouraging response. At the same time, the dismantling of the G.F. Watts room began. After his devoted widow died in the autumn of 1938, the Board, arguing that his work would be better shown in with the rest of the collection, freed the Watts room for special exhibitions. And the following year Rothenstein requested permission to have Watt's *Dray Horses* and *The Court of Death* rolled as they were too vast to store in any other way.[14] While these and other Victorian paintings disappeared into the basement, the Gallery was enhanced by two important loans: Rodin's *The Kiss*, which had sat for many years wrapped in sacking in a stable in Lewes, Sussex, after a local schoolteacher had petitioned successfully for it to be removed from public view; and Whistler's *Arrangement in Grey and Black, No.2: Portrait of Thomas Carlyle*, which came from Glasgow City Art Gallery. It was also agreed, at Duveen's suggestion, that Ervin Bossanyi should be asked to design a stained-glass window for the front staircase, leading down to the restaurant. As Duveen was committed to paying for a new gallery at the British Museum to house the Elgin Marbles and this had already exceeded its original estimate, he declared himself unable to give financial assistance with the window. He died the following year, 1939, before the completion of the window, which proved to be a financial and aesthetic embarrassment.

During Rothenstein's first year, attendance figures for the Gallery rose by 100,000. In May 1939 the galleries of the lower ground floor reopened for the first time since the flood with an exhibition of some hundred and fifty photographs, representing mural painting in Britain over the last twenty years. This same month the Alfred Stevens room reopened, with sculptures, paintings, architectural and ornamental designs and a series of working drawings. The central exhibit was the full-size model for the Wellington memorial, with the equestrian figure once again in place. The new mood of confidence and optimism displayed in the Gallery was shared by the Board, which now included the discerning patron and collector Sir Edward Marsh, as well as Lord Howard de Walden and the painter Allen Gwynne-Jones. In this more enlightened period Matisse's *Reading Woman with Parasol* was accepted into the collection, as was Henry Moore's *Recumbent Figure*, which Kenneth Clark had bought for the Contemporary Art Society. An improvement in the Gallery's image helped attract gifts, Thomas Olsen donating Edvard Munch's *The Sick Child*, which remains to this day the only Munch in a British public collection. The number of bequests also increased, Sir Hugh Walpole announcing his intention to leave fourteen works to the Gallery. To these he added, at the request of the Trustees, *Rossetti and his Circle* – twenty-four Max Beerbohm cartoons.

Yet certain prejudices remained in place, one of which was an antipathy to German art. Lord Duveen's attitude – that it was gross and tasteless – was fairly common among English cognoscenti, familiar with the denigration of German art in the writings of Roger Fry and Clive Bell. The list of artists provided by Courtauld in connection with his fund for modern foreign art was entirely French, and since the opening of the modern foreign galleries, scant attention had been paid to German art. There had been a flicker of interest in 1932 when Hildebrand Gurlitt wrote from Hamburg suggesting an exhibition of modern German art. Gurlitt had been Director of the museum at Zwickau in Saxony and had begun to build up an impressive collection of modern art before being dismissed from his post in 1930. He was then appointed Chairman of the Hamburg Kunstverein (Art Association) and eventually established himself in this city as an art dealer. The Tate Trustees expressed interest in Gurlitt's proposal in May 1932 and in October suggested the Director should visit Germany, see the pictures and consult with the experts. Though this instruction was reiterated by the Board in April 1934, Manson did nothing. Further evidence that the Trustees were prepared to consider German art was the acceptance in 1936 of Lovis Corinth's *The Temptation of St Anthony after Gustave Flaubert,* which was presented to the Gallery by Erich Goeritz. But meanwhile the Nazis had begun impounding modern art, their campaign culminating in the *Entartete Kunst* (Degenerate Art) exhibition which opened in Munich in July 1937. The following spring, while the *Entartete Kunst* exhibition was showing in Berlin, Hermann Göring suggested selling confiscated 'degenerate' art for foreign currency. Goebbels wrote in his diaries: 'Paintings from the degenerate art action will now be offered on the international art market. In so doing we hope at least to make money from this garbage.'[15] He established a commission for the disposal of 'degenerate art', and, in addition to the sale, which took place at Galerie Fischer, an auction house in Lucerne, on 30 June 1939 and was attended by museum directors from many countries, four dealers were authorised to sell works of 'degenerate' art for foreign currency. One of these was Hildebrand Gurlitt. Had the Tate pursued his 1932 proposal, it would now have stood a chance of purchasing, if it so wished, major examples of ill-gained twentieth-century art. But interest in German art was now actively discouraged; English critics had hardened against it, and the language of criticism had become tinged with political disgust. When German Expressionism was shown at the New Burlington Galleries in London in 1938, Raymond Mortimer argued that 'the utmost violence of colour and design' was the product of 'a combination of coarseness and hysteria, two of the chief qualities that make the Nazi regime so detestable'.[16]

If antipathy to German art is partly explained by historical circumstances, there were other blindspots which seriously hindered the Tate in its evolution as a modern art museum. Rothenstein, though he would have been familiar through his father with the work of William Nicholson, claimed he had been ignorant of his son Ben Nicholson's work when he entered the Tate; but, living in Hampstead, not far from the Mall Studios in Parkhill Road, he soon became aware of Nicholson and Barbara Hepworth as 'two shiningly formidable professional creative instruments', whose work, he thought, 'showed a decisiveness, a clarity and crystalline purity'.[17] But if he could appreciate the modernist emphasis in Nicholson and Hepworth's art, and in the art of Henry Moore, whom he secured as a Trustee in 1941, he nevertheless remained distrustful of the non-naturalistic tradition within modern art. As Director, he was an ex-officio member of the Board and could not vote on acquisitions, but he was nevertheless in a position to lead and advise.

He was therefore to some extent responsible when the Board rejected an Yves Tanguy offered by Peggy Guggenheim in May 1939. Previously, in October 1938, four Kandinsky oils offered by Peggy Guggenheim's sister, Mrs Hazel King-Farlow (afterwards Mrs McKinley) had been turned down on the grounds that the Board wished to see further examples of his work. The following month the Board did accept one of these works, *Cossacks*, but instructed Rothenstein in his letter of acceptance to inform Mrs King-Farlow that there would be no guarantee of immediate exhibition and that 'this picture might find a place when and if a room of representative abstract painters was formed'.[18]

News of this letter reached Kandinsky who sent Rothenstein a letter of protest, arguing that his work was 'concrete' but not 'abstract'.[19] A general sense of dissatisfaction with the Tate's attitude to non-representative art caused Peggy Guggenheim in 1939 to offer to put up money for a museum of modern art in London, provided Herbert Read would run it. Read agreed to become director of her proposed museum, gave up the editorship of the *Burlington Magazine*, signed a five-year contract with Peggy Guggenheim and began drawing up a list of movements and artists, with a deliberate emphasis on non-figurative art. The press was informed of the scheme and the first exhibition was scheduled for autumn 1939. But it was not only war that terminated this project; there were several snags, chief of which was that Peggy Guggenheim could not afford to endow it.[20] And though support for this idea came from Sir Kenneth Clark, Douglas Cooper was unconvinced and told Read that the proper place for a collection of masterpieces of modern art was a room at the Tate.

A more significant challenge to the Tate in 1939 was the opening of the Museum of Modern Art's new building in New York. It marked a radical break with previous museum design: instead of being grandly situated, it was squeezed between buildings in a modest side street in mid-town Manhattan; instead of classical rhetoric or elaborate ornamentation, it boasted plain steel and glass and a matter-of-fact reception area rather than a lavish entrance hall. Its galleries were flexible and intimately proportioned, none having more importance than any other. It furthered the institutionalisation of modernism which its founding Director Alfred H. Barr, Jr. had already begun. After his dismissal in 1943, he remained Director of Collections and continued to have a determining influence under his successor, Réné d'Harnoncourt, who proved an effective fundraiser. During d'Harnoncourt's tenure, a new lobby, east wing and sculpture garden were built by Philip Johnson, who also converted an adjoining building, thereby adding east and north wings to the Museum. In the post-1945 years its active and intelligent collecting policy was to act as an indictment of the Tate.

Even during his first halcyon year at the Tate, Rothenstein revealed certain limitations. The focus of his interests remained British art, and in his autobiography he confessed himself to be out of sympathy with 'that equality of response to totally disparate stimuli which is the dominant feature of the twentieth-century attitude towards the arts: an attitude of increasingly enthusiastic but also of ever more superficial acceptance'.[21] Working with a tiny staff, and the minimum of

28 Wassily Kandinsky, *Cossacks*, 1910–11

curatorial support, he had to rely greatly on his own judgement. His most useful colleague in relation to the collection was Robin Ironside who had a specialist knowledge of the Pre-Raphaelites and during the war aligned his interests, both as historian and painter, with the Neo-Romantics, a movement given particular attention in his 1947 booklet, *Painting since 1939*. Further help came in the form of voluntary attachés who worked at the Gallery for a period of six months. Those who came to the Tate in this role included Andrew Maclaren Young (appointed October 1938), who did not get on too well with Rothenstein. But another who, like Maclaren Young, later became a prominent figure in the art world – John Russell – was impressed by Rothenstein's kindness and looked back on his time at the Tate as a period of great happiness.

A paper published by the Treasury in 1938, 'Urgent: Savings and Supplementary Estimates', informed civil servants that the need to increase the Defence programme necessitated renewed efforts to economise in every direction. The Tate had never achieved its purchase grant, but ironically, as war approached, it had more money to spend on British art than ever before, owing to the National Gallery's decision to withdraw the Clarke Fund and replace it with the Knapping Fund, which amounted to about £1,170 a year.

Despite Chamberlain's prediction of 'peace in our time' following the Munich Agreement of September 1938, plans were made for the safe-keeping of the Tate's collection in the event of war. Storage space was to be found initially in three houses – Eastington Hall at Upton-on-Severn, Hellens at Much Marche in Gloucestershire, and Muncaster Castle in Cumberland – as well as in the nearby Underground stations. In August 1939 Rothenstein toured northern England and Scotland. In the early hours of 24 August he was woken by a telephone call from a journalist friend, bringing the news that von Ribbentrop, the German Foreign Minister, had signed the German-Soviet Pact. Rothenstein caught an early morning train to London and that same day set in motion the carefully planned machinery to protect the collection in case of war. He gave immediate instructions for the Gallery to close.

> The Attendants, shouting at intervals 'Gallery closed' as they walked slowly through the rooms, shepherded the people towards the entrance. As the last of them filed out the big doors closed behind them. I wondered how many years would pass before these doors were opened to admit a member of the public. Books were obtainable almost everywhere; music could be broadcast, but these doors (and those of the National Gallery, which were closed about the same time) were shutting out the people from visual arts. In a few days, they would be standing only figuratively between the people and their pictures, for none, or only an insignificant few, would remain.[22]

The main part of the collection filled five railway containers and it was rehoused by the time war was declared. While the the last batch of pictures was being packed, King George VI arrived at the Gallery to have a final look. As he took little interest in art, despite the fact that the Queen was an ardent collector, his appearance was both unexpected and, for Rothenstein, 'touchingly symbolic'.[23] Finally, Rothenstein had to decide what to do with the Gallery records, and, as none of the houses providing accommodation for the paintings could offer office space, he took them, and his secretary, to Far Oakridge, his father's house in Gloucestershire, a part of which had been placed at his disposal.

6

The Hidden Tate

Having dispatched the Tate's paintings to safety, Rothenstein assumed that the Gallery had little further need of his services until peace returned. He determined to make himself useful in other ways and applied for a job with the Air Ministry. His plans were foiled when the Treasury refused to sanction his release and he had to ask the War Office to remove his name from the Officers' Emergency Reserve Register. An urge to redirect his energies next turned his thoughts, with his wife's encouragement, to America. Believing strongly in the need for better relations between the United States and Britain, he went to the Ministry of Information and told them of the connections he had made in the United States during his two years' residence there. He had a further reason to go to America: he had been one of four curators responsible for selecting art for the British Pavilion at the New York World's Fair. This had opened in April 1939, afterwards moved to San Francisco, and a smaller version of the exhibition was about to embark on a tour of Canada and the United States. As the British Council, established in 1934, was not then operative in America, Rothenstein volunteered to take responsibility for these works of art. To further his case, he proposed also giving a lecture tour promoting British art. This won Treasury approval: it was agreed that the cost of his passage and travelling expenses in the early stage of his tour would be met from the National Gallery Vote and he would continue to draw his normal salary.

He and Elizabeth sailed for America on 1 October 1939. While his wife visited her family in Kentucky, Rothenstein went first to Ottawa where he was offered hospitality by Lord Tweedsmuir, Governor-General of Canada. From then on he was constantly on the move. He had prepared for this tour four lectures, which he recycled in seventeen different places in the United States and four in Canada. He also broadcast on Canadian radio, gave interviews to journalists and was much fêted by the press. In Toronto, New York, Boston, Baltimore, Chicago, Detroit, Harvard, Washington and other places he met and dined with leading collectors and museum officials, among them Alfred H. Barr, Jr, the Director of the Museum of Modern Art, which Rothenstein described to Frank Tribe, the Principal Assistant Secretary in the Treasury, as 'a new foundation, a very modern left-wing kind of Tate Gallery'.[1] At Christmas he rejoined his five year old daughter, Lucy, who had been sent in July to live with her grandparents in Lexington for the duration of the war. He also found an old friend, Wyndham Lewis, in Buffalo, painting a portrait of the president of the university. Contacts proliferated and Rothenstein accepted further invitations to speak, without, it seems, worrying about his responsibilities in London.

29 Bomb damage to the exterior of the Gallery, 1940

After he had been away five months, a letter from the Treasury informed him that questions about his lecture tour had been asked in Parliament. Rothenstein failed to act on this warning, even though he was aware that the Trustees had been meeting in his absence and that minutes had not been sent to him, perhaps because the Gallery was uncertain as to where he was. (Story has it that Fincham told the press that Rothenstein's whereabouts were entirely unknown.) During his continued absence, Clive Bell made denigratory remarks about Rothenstein's disappearance to America in the *New Statesman and Nation* and by March even his father was advising him to return home: 'Lord de la Warr is encouraging acquisition of contemporary art, and besides Clark, who has become a sort of Dictator, Maclagan, Walpole, Eddie [Marsh] and others are working actively. My own feeling is that you shd. be here: it is the feeling of others less kindly disposed, also.'[2] Meanwhile Rothenstein's continuing absence was proving an embarrassment to Sir Edward Marsh, who had been elected Acting Chairman of the Trustees in January 1940 after Evan Charteris resigned owing to ill health. Finally, in April 1940, after seven months abroad, Rothenstein sent notice of his return. The Treasury informed Sir Edward: 'he proposes to sail on the 20th of this month unless directed otherwise … You should therefore get him back about the end of the month.'[3]

Following a severe reprimand from Marsh, Rothenstein immediately gathered up the reins of the Gallery and had it announced that the Tate would partially reopen at the end of May. This plan, however, was abandoned as it coincided with an escalation in fighting and the end of the 'phoney war'. Rothenstein, having made a tour of all refuge houses where the pictures were in store and having satisfied himself that all was well, once again tried to join the RAF, but without success. Then in September 1940, after a couple of heavy raids on London, he and his wife arranged to have their beds transported to Millbank so that they could sleep at the Gallery, where each night four warders were on duty. The attendants arranged for them a kind of ducal suite by means of screens in one of the galleries,

30 Bomb damage, probably 1940

but after sleeping one night under a glass roof, they wisely moved into the basement. A week later, early in the morning of 16 September, the Gallery was hit.

'Early one morning I was woken by a terrific explosion to feel the massive
building violently shaking and to hear an avalanche of masonry and glass.' So
Rothenstein recalled in an article for the *Museums Journal* in December 1940.
There was no light. A warder lying on a nearby bench had been thrown on to
the floor. As the raid was still in progress, they could not resort to torches, and
Rothenstein and the attendant, William Hudd, made their way through room
after room by the light of the stars. 'All the glass in the roof had been shattered and
an icy wind was roaring through a place normally so warm and so still. We could
hear the drone of German aircraft; every discharge of the nearby guns brought
down a cascade of masonry and broken glass.'[4] Rothenstein could not wait until
morning to discover the extent of the damage and he and an ex-guardsman
warder went on an inspection tour of the outside of the building. On the east side
of the building, where Bulinga Street ran between the Gallery and the Royal
Military Hospital, they found a deep crater in which water was rising, while all
around, obliterating pavement, lawns and flowerbeds, was what looked like a
crudely ploughed field of white dust. The blast had been so violent that large
chunks of road surface and paving stones had crashed on to the roof and in some
instances through gallery floors. The following morning, Sir Patrick Duff, Secretary to the Office of Works, estimated that repairs would take at least three years.

This, however, was only the beginning of the war damage, which even today is
visible in the pitted surface of the Gallery's side walls. The Gallery was hit again

on 22 September 1940 and over the following weeks suffered almost nightly damage from blast or incendiary bombs. On 6 January 1941 two bombs penetrated the main dome and a third crashed through the roof in another part of the building, burning a large hole in the wooden floor. A further direct hit occurred in March that year and in May a bomb fell in the corner of the Gallery's garden, as a result of which Frank Dobson's sculpture *Truth* was temporarily buried. In the wake of bombing came rain, falling through galleries open to the skies, through the heating grills and into the basement rooms, as Rothenstein witnessed: 'It seemed to me that the Tate was most unlikely to survive the conjunction of bomb damage and the now perpetual rain pouring into every corner of it. Nobody would call the Tate a beautiful building, but it is an immensely sympathetic one to work in, and it had come, during its forty-three years' life, to symbolize a spirit at once adventurous, generous and judicious.'[5] But now, with no roof and few doors or windows, the building was impossible to heat and therefore impossible to work in. Rothenstein recommended to the Office of Works that the remaining staff should be evacuated to one of the houses of refuge. A room at Eastington Hall was requisitioned for their use, and for a period artistic activity at Millbank was solely confined to the watchman William Neale, an ex-soldier and self-taught artist, who, when no other duties prevailed, picked up his brushes and went on painting. Meanwhile, the Gallery's gardens were turned into allotments by local residents and at times used for the erection of prototype prefabricated houses.

★   ★   ★

One of the ironies of this grim period in the Tate's history is that its collection expanded more rapidly than it had ever done before. As a result of gifts and bequests from the painter W. Graham Robertson, Miss A.E. Cardew and R. Beresford Heaton, major groups of work by Blake and the Pre-Raphaelites were added, among them Blake's mottled and intricate colour prints produced between 1795 and 1805 and eight Rossetti watercolours, executed between 1855 and 1864, his most affecting period. Whistler's limpid *Crepuscule in Flesh Colour and Green: Valparaiso* entered the collection as part of the Graham Robertson gift, and notable examples of eighteenth- and early nineteenth-century art, came through the National Art Collections Fund. The Contemporary Art Society presented the Tate with a gouache by Paul Klee, while other contributions to the modern foreign collection came through the Frank Hindley Smith bequest (André Dunoyer de Segonzac, Othon Friesz and André Lhote); from Montague Shearman, who bequeathed through the Contemporary Art Society, six pictures, including Matisse's *The Inattentive Reader*; and from Sir Michael Sadler, among whose donations, via the NACF, was Bonnard's *Coffee*. At the same time, purchases of contemporary British art increased under the terms of the Knapping Fund which had to be spent on British art by living artists or those who had died within the last twenty-five years. Gwen John's *Self-Portrait* was bought for £75 in 1942, and works by David Jones, Ben Nicholson, Victor Pasmore, Ceri Richards, John Piper and

Graham Sutherland entered the Tate for the first time. So active was the Tate's buying during the war years that concern was expressed by the Victoria and Albert Museum at the possibility of overlap in the field of watercolours and drawings. Following discussions between the Tate, the Victoria & Albert and the British Museum in 1941, it was agreed that the Tate should have freedom of action with regard to the purchase of drawings or watercolours, but should inform the other two institutions whenever a purchase was under consideration.

These wartime acquisitions formed two exhibitions – in 1942 and 1945 – at the National Gallery, where accommodation had been placed at the Tate's disposal. The first of these was visited by the Queen, no doubt at the instigation of Jasper Ridley who advised the Queen on her picture collection and who had taken over from Sir Edward Marsh as Chairman of the Tate in 1941. In addition to these displays of recent acquisitions, the Tate mounted memorial exhibitions in honour of Walter Sickert and Philip Wilson Steer, as well as masterpieces from the Tate's pre-war collection. All except the last, in either original or abbreviated form, were also shown in the regions under the auspices of the Council for the Encouragement of Music and the Arts (CEMA), an ad hoc wartime organisation which had been set up in 1940 and became the forerunner of the Arts Council of Great Britain.

Together Rothenstein and Robin Ironside did a great deal to publicise the Tate's achievement. An article by Ironside on the wartime acquisitions appeared in the February 1941 issue of the *Burlington Magazine*. He also wrote a book on Steer, one of a series of monographs which Rothenstein commissioned on behalf of Phaidon Press, as well as another on the Pre-Raphaelites. Meanwhile progress was made towards a new catalogue of the collection, the voluntary attaché John Russell completing a recast of the artists' biographies. Owing to his stutter, Russell had frequently resorted to communicating with the Director by writing memoranda. However prosaic the subject, these notes had such aptness and sparkle that Rothenstein had suggested Russell should try his hand at writing. This was already Russell's intention, and in years to come Rothenstein and others at the Tate were to await anxiously his pronouncements as art critic to the *Sunday Times*.

Rothenstein himself wrote an article on the Tate's acquisitions over the previous two years for the May 1944 issue of the magazine *Studio*. He produced a considerable amount of journalism during the war, some of it on church decoration, as he was excited by the possibility of new commissions caused by the devastation of war. He also lectured at the National Gallery, the Courtauld Institute of Art and elsewhere, and assiduously kept up and extended his contacts with artists. It was at his instigation that the Czechoslovakian President-in-exile Eduard Beneš presented to the Tate *Polperro* by Oskar Kokoschka, who, as Rothenstein was aware, was suffering as an emigré in London from isolation and a lack of encouragement. When sent a form asking for biographical details, Kokoschka returned it with a line crossed through the form and the simple inscription: 'Say that he never submitted to tyranny.'

It was during these years that Rothenstein began actively to promote the British

31 Ben Nicholson, *1933 (guitar)*, 1933

School as a varied, original and serious school of contemporary painting. He had a fondness for eccentricity and this was also reflected in his taste: artists such as L.S. Lowry, Stanley Spencer, Francis Bacon, David Jones, Ceri Richards and Edward Burra, who were either unfashionable or did not fit into any direction that art seemed to be taking, were favoured by him. He also argued that the abrupt severance of contact between English and French artists during the war had given British artists an independence: compelled to depend on their own resources, British artists had developed stronger national characteristics.

Between them, Rothenstein and Ironside ran the Tate. Fincham, after a stint at Muncaster Castle at Ravenglass in Cumberland, returned to London and persistently absented himself from the Gallery. When questioned, he claimed that Military Intelligence had engaged him to keep 'fascists' under observation in Chelsea pubs; but when enquiries were made, the Director of Military Intelligence had no knowledge of him. At a Tate Gallery Board meeting in September 1941 Sir Kenneth Clark and Lord Crawford pointed out 'that Mr Fincham's presence on the staff had for many years past hindered the proper functioning of the Gallery'.[6] It was decided that to avoid unpleasantness, Mr Fincham should be recommended for secondment. The following January the Trustees were informed that he had been seconded to the Ministry of Labour at Kingston-upon-Thames. There he may have fared better, but the irregularities he had perpetrated at the Tate continued to surface in years to come.[7]

The greatest administrative headache during the war years were the practical difficulties presented by the refuge houses. For the protection of the pictures, these houses had to maintain a steady temperature of 60 degrees Fahrenheit. As a result, more than one owner became anxious about the consumption of coal and there was endless correspondence about fuel bills. The attendants serving in these refuge houses were often bored, worried about their families in London, found the evacuation allowances did not cover their costs, sometimes had to share beds, and were not properly provided with essentials. One lost his fiancée who, unable to cope with his removal from London, married another man. Others were annoyed when aristocratic owners expected Tate attendants, when off-duty, to help in the garden or do odd jobs.[8] There were also numerous practical problems. Muncaster Castle proved an ideal refuge, but the other two houses, with their long corridors, small windows and low water-pressure, were eventually regarded as unsuitable, given the danger of fire. In July 1941 paintings in store at Hellens in Gloucestershire were moved to Old Quarries, Avening, a house belonging to Viscount Lee of Fareham. A similar transfer took place from Eastington Hall to Sudeley Castle, near Winchcombe, and a further refuge house was found at Abbotsford, Stow-on-the-Wold, in Gloucestershire. Some use was also made of the tunnels at Piccadilly Circus Underground station where one watchman asked whether he should boil kettles of water in order to keep the humidity at the required level.

Sudeley Castle for a while became the Tate's administrative base. While there, Rothenstein and Ironside joined the Home Guard, as they had done previously while based at Eastington Hall, where both had stood guard at night on the railway bridge over the Severn at Upton. A skeleton office was meanwhile maintained in London and Rothenstein travelled back and forth until 1943, when the administration returned to London.

By September 1944 it became possible once more to conceive of peace. Following the liberation of Paris, rumours reached Rothenstein that the Americans, including art dealers and collectors, were taking advantage of the presence of their forces in the French capital to pursue national and personal interests. He discussed the matter with Kenneth Clark and, having gained the Board's approval, made a visit to Paris with Clark in October 1944. There Rothenstein made contact with almost all the dealers but found that works of consequence had been sent abroad, and in view of the current financial uncertainty, dealers were not eager to make sales. He also made a couple of visits to Picasso and tried to secure *Nude with a Musician* for the Tate. Picasso refused to sell at that moment as no exchange rate had yet been fixed, but he promised to keep this picture for the Tate. Rothenstein perhaps did not pursue this promise actively enough, for this famous picture went instead to the Musée Nationale d'Art Moderne in Paris.

When the war ended, the Tate had only one room fit for the purposes of exhibition. Nevertheless, it had emerged from this difficult period with its reputation enhanced, and its outlook for the post-war years seemed promising.

32 Works of art returning from wartime storage in the London Underground.
The work in the centre is *Wake*, by Edward Burra

7

Post-War Revival

In the aftermath of war a new cultural and social climate encouraged museums to change and expand, to open themselves to a broader and increasingly more knowledgeable public. Leigh Ashton, the Director of the Victoria & Albert Museum, set the pace in London by ridding his museum of clutter and exhibiting objects in a way that beautified them and made them a revelation to many. Here CEMA mounted a Picasso and Matisse exhibition which caused an outcry in the winter of 1945–6. Picasso's paraphrasing of appearances, his humane themes and new-found political beliefs impressed many and offended others, Holman Hunt's daughter standing in the exhibition publicly decrying his work. For many artists this exhibition pointed the way forward: it put an end to the inward-looking melancholy and nostalgia that had characterised wartime neo-romanticism and injected English art with a desire for a new formal and decorative strength.

Having spent much of the war working in damp and draughty offices, John Rothenstein ended it with a bout of severe rheumatic illness. He recovered at his cottage at Garsington in Oxfordshire which he had bought during the war. This country foothold proved indispensable to him, becoming a precondition to his ability to cope with the onus of the Tate. It made possible rest and thought, whereas in London he lived in a whirl of activity, meetings and social commitments. In 1951 he exchanged this cottage for a near-derelict rectory, Beauforest House at Newington, Oxfordshire, a predominantly Georgian house with three acres through which ran the river Thame. From then on the poignant beauty of this house and garden formed the background to his increasingly troubled Directorship.

Though it seemed almost impossible that the dark, damp, draughty wreck of a Gallery would ever recover, Rothenstein and Jasper Ridley put persistent pressure on the Ministry of Works to repair it, at a time when domestic buildings were being given priority with regard to materials and labour. Meanwhile, a tarpaulin covered the roof and Tate administration continued. Certain policies began to change. At the Board meeting held on 15 February 1945 it was resolved that 'in view of the continuing vitality of so-called abstract art and of the very great influence it had exercised upon industrial design, it would be proper that a small room at the Tate should be devoted to its representation.'

Nothing, however, could be exhibited at Millbank for the time being; but the Tate still had the right to use the accommodation put aside for it at the National Gallery, and in the spring of 1945 it began to work with Douglas Cooper on a Paul Klee exhibition. After a brief stint in the RAF, Cooper had become Director of the Monuments and Fine Arts Division of the Allied Control Commission for Germany and had been helping to track down works of art looted from Jews and sold to Swiss collectors. In the course of this work, which gave him a taste for hounding malefactors, Cooper had made friends with Lily Klee, then resident in Switzerland. Her collection of her late husband's work had been saved from confiscation by the Allies by Rolf Bürgi, who had clubbed together with a man called Hadorn and bought the entire estate. This was then divided in two; Bürgi dealing in one half while the other formed the Klee Foundation which was vested in the Berne Museum. Bürgi sold a dozen drawings to Cooper, who informed the Tate that Madame Klee was willing to send a group of Klees to London for display at the National Gallery, provided the Tate would arrange transport facilities.

This exhibition, which opened on 22 December 1945, was such a resounding success that by mid-January some thirteen thousand catalogues had been sold. But the Trustees havered about buying any of the drawings, which were on offer for around £150 each. None was acquired when first considered by the Board on 28 February 1946, though four did enter the collection later that year. After the exhibition had closed, but before any decision had been taken on purchasing Klee, Cooper, angry that his own Klees had not been returned to him, went round to the Tate and was told that they were hanging in the Director's office while the Tate decided which ones they wanted to buy. This was usual practice, but it angered Cooper who began to conceive of Rothenstein a high-handed fool.[1]

Cooper had for some time been a critical observer of the Tate. He himself had inherited wealth, a scholarly mind and discerning eye, immense ruthlessness, and an irresponsibility made possible by his freedom, for much of his life, from paid employment. His passion for Cubism made him ready to pounce on anyone who failed to appreciate its merits. When Kenneth Clark berated Cubism for revealing 'the poverty of human invention when forced to spin a web from its own guts',[2] Cooper sent an immediate reply to the Listener, arguing the need to distinguish between the vitality and innovation of the 'real' Cubists – Picasso, Georges Braque, Juan Gris and Fernand Léger – and the deadness of their followers.[3] Cooper held to this distinction all his life and his dedication to the real Cubists made him critical during the immediate post-war years of Rothenstein's failure to buy a single major Cubist painting. Rothenstein's persistent promotion of English art also irritated Cooper, who felt it to be at the expense of modern European art.

His love-hate relationship with the Tate had caused him in 1938 to invite Rothenstein to lunch at his house, 18 Egerton Terrace, after which he had lent a Braque to the Gallery, the following year adding to this loan three works by Gris, three by Picasso and two more by Braque. Even after the Klee débâcle, he continued to show goodwill to the Tate, while privately sharing with others growing dissatisfaction with its management. In January 1946 there was a fresh attempt to establish a Museum of Modern Art in London, Cooper, working on the idea with Herbert Read, Roland Penrose and E.L.T. Mesens, composed a policy statement which baldly stated his desire to make the Tate and the British Council 'look as silly as they are'.[4] When it became clear that others would not support his policies Cooper resigned, and what emerged was not a Museum of Modern Art but the Institute of Contemporary Arts.

The smallness of the art world meant that Rothenstein often sat on committees alongside his detractors. When he proposed at a British Council meeting that 123 paintings and drawings, mostly drawn from the Tate's recent acquisitions and beginning with Sickert and ending with Henry Moore, should form a touring exhibition and be sent round various European capitals, he discovered an opponent in Herbert Read. 'Briefly,' Read afterwards informed Cooper, 'Rottenstone wants to hawk his mouldy collection round Europe, himself as itinerant showman, whilst his gallery is rebuilt or cleaned. I, almost alone, opposed this little plan, and was gratified to find later that K.C.[Kenneth Clark], who was not present at the meeting, strongly backed my point of view – which is that neither Amsterdam nor Brussels and much less Paris want a show in which Sir William R.[Rothenstein], Sir William N.[Nicholson] and the New English generally predominate.'[5]

Despite Read's opposition, Rothenstein succeeded in persuading the British Council to send this exhibition on an continental tour of nine capitals. But before he himself could take off in its wake, he had to oversee the reopening of the Tate on 10 April 1946 by Ernest Bevin, Secretary of State for Foreign Affairs. Six galleries had been repaired and their fresh paint and new wall-coverings were made to look brighter still by the darkness and gloom of the surrounding galleries, as yet unreconstructed. On show was a room full of French nineteenth-century painting, including Seurat's *Bathers, Asnières*. Another contained mostly English Romantics and was dominated by an enormous newly acquired work by John Martin. There were also three exhibitions: an Arts Council show of Cézanne's watercolours; a British Council exhibition of Braque oils and Georges Rouault aquatints;[6] and the collection of British art which the High Commissioner for Canada, Vincent Massey, was about to donate to the National Gallery of Canada

Massey had chaired a committee, and thereby given his name to a report published in 1946, concerned with the co-ordination of the activities of the various national collections. It had attempted to address the confusion of purpose and practice which had developed as the national museums and galleries had gradually departed from their original prescribed functions. One of its recommendations – that the Tate should be divided into two departments, British and Modern, with two specially qualified Keepers under the Director – proved formative, though this advice was not acted upon for another eighteen years. A similar delay accompanied the recommended transfer to the Victoria & Albert Museum of the Alfred Stevens collection, which went on display again at the Tate in 1948. Less advantageous to the Tate was the proposal that it should act as a source of supply of paintings to the National Gallery and of sculpture to the Victoria & Albert. Under this recommendation, all foreign paintings at the Tate would in due course be transferred to the National Gallery, either when they had ceased to be 'modern' or at an earlier date if required by the Director. The Report also stressed that the transfer of pictures should not be hampered: 'such movement is, in our opinion, an indispensable condition of the proper functioning of the two Galleries.'

Just before publication of the Massey Report, Rothenstein had received from Philip Hendy, who had succeeded Clark as Director of the National Gallery in 1945, a letter requesting the transfer of seven French paintings. Rothenstein protested that the loss of these pictures, which included the only remaining Renoir, would severely damage the Tate. He requested that they wait for the outcome of the Massey Report and effect changes in accordance with its terms. But though the Report attempted to regularise the transfer of pictures and to prevent unexpected raids, it left the Tate in a weak position; in years to come transfers became a battle of wills, the cause of much bargaining and of strained relations. Hendy did not get his seven paintings in 1946, nor the nine that he requested in 1949. But he returned to the attack in 1950 and demanded the transfer of fourteen French pictures. On this occasion the National Gallery Trustees declined even to discuss the matter with the Tate Board. Though questions concerning the transfer of works of art from Millbank to Trafalgar Square were asked in Parliament, Rothenstein now had to give way, and the Tate's display of French paintings was broken up. For some time afterwards the galleries were left bare, in protest.

★   ★   ★

The business of recreating the Gallery's administration with minimal staff, and again making it effective as a public institution, was a severe test of John Rothenstein's abilities. His diary records moments of despair: 'Staff position now really bad at Tate: rapidly growing arrears and confusion', he noted on 12 February 1946.[7] Nevertheless, those who remembered Manson's era congratulated him on his achievement. But in the privacy of his diary he continued to monitor unease. On 15 April 1947 he wrote: 'After nine years as Director of T.G., there is so much I seem unable to get quite right. There are wretched consequences from the utterly inefficient keeping of the Correspondence Register, and so forth.'[8]

Attempts to acquire more staff were not always successful, partly because the salary offered was barely above subsistence level. Roderick Thesiger, employed soon after the war ended, resigned in February 1946 on the grounds that his salary was inadequate. The same reason for resignation was given by Robin Ironside in October 1946, although he had never disguised from Rothenstein that his ambition was to become a full-time painter and writer. Norman Reid offered his services to the Tate in 1946 because a colleague in the Army, the publisher Desmond Flower, had told him that Rothenstein was very short-staffed. Reid had an interview on the same day that he was considered for a job at Chelsea School of Art. Offered both posts, he decided to accept Chelsea as the salary there was the same for a two-day week as the Tate was paying for a five-and-a-half-day week. He went back to the Tate to inform the Director of his decision, but Rothenstein was out. Reid therefore returned home to Oxford where his wife said, 'Why don't you give the Tate a chance?' He did, staying in all for nearly thirty-five years.

Reid was thirty by the time the war ended, and, with a wife and two children, needed a job. He had trained as a painter at Edinburgh and came to the Tate as a temporary assistant straight out of the Army. Rothenstein later admitted that he had taken him on chiefly because he felt certain that a former major in the Argylls would know how to 'look after the chaps'.[9] After just two weeks at the Tate, Reid found himself in charge, Ironside having left and Rothenstein having departed on his European tour. He and the Earl of Plymouth, who was doing volunteer work while waiting to go up to Cambridge, donned brown coats and sat in what had formerly been the Refreshment Room while the attendants wheeled past all the paintings that had been returned to London from the refuge houses. It was a salutary start to Reid's career, and possibly the only time that a member of the staff has seen the Gallery's entire collection. Each picture was checked against lists made chiefly by Ironside in the pre-war period. The only item missing was Benjamin Robert Haydon's drawing for *May Day*. Even the three paintings – Steer's *Painswick Beacon* and Turner's *Windsor* and *St Mawes* – which had been on loan to the British Embassy in Paris when war began, had been safely held by members of the Resistance and returned to London in 1945.

Gradually circumstances at the Tate improved. Rothenstein enjoyed his Chairman's genial imperiousness, which, combined with the affectionate esteem he aroused in the Trustees, enabled him to dominate. A Director not only of the National Provincial Bank but also of Coutts, and eventually Chairman of both, Sir Jasper Ridley was to have his Trusteeship renewed in 1948, in order that he might lead the Tate through the preliminary stages of a proposed parliamentary bill dealing with the national collections. He supported Rothenstein's recommendations for artist-Trustees, and in 1946 John Piper joined the Board, followed by Graham Sutherland in 1948, William Coldstream in 1949, Edward Bawden in 1951 and Lawrence Gowing in 1953. These Trustees played an active role in the purchasing policy, which took on greater importance after the official allocation of a purchase grant in 1946. Though it was only £2,000 per annum, and therefore pitifully inadequate given the Tate's remit to look after British painting, modern foreign painting and modern sculpture, an additional supplement of £1,200 was paid between 1950 and 1953, and by 1953–4 the purchase grant had risen to £6,250.

In 1945 Rothenstein and Ridley had attended the War Artists' exhibition at Burlington House in 1945 and had drawn up a desiderata list. When these works, commissioned by the War Artists' Advisory Committee, were distributed to public collections in Britain and in the Commonwealth, the Tate obtained, in the first batch, seventy-three pictures, including eight drawings by Henry Moore, four works by Paul Nash (among them *Totes Meer*), and nine gouaches and oils by Graham Sutherland. Three years later, in 1949, a further ninety war pictures were added to the collection.

Less impressive was the Tate's acquisition of modern foreign painting. The most notorious loss during the late 1940s was Matisse's *The Red Studio*. This painting, one of two Matisses that had hung for some years in the Gargoyle Club in London, was sold by the Redfern Gallery to a private buyer for less than a thousand pounds, and passed eventually to the Museum of Modern Art, New York. There is no record that the Tate Board ever even considered it.[10] MOMA also bought, unopposed, at a London auction in 1948, Gino Severini's *Bal Tabarin* for £200. One person with his eye on this painting in the hopes that the Tate might buy it was Douglas Cooper. 'Of course I am in entire agreement with regard to the desirability of the acquisition of the Severini,' wrote Graham Sutherland to Cooper, 'but I doubt if there is much hope: I have been to four Tate meetings so far: always there is a tendency to buy muck and some awful buys (worse than even *you* could imagine) have been avoided only very narrowly. At the last meeting a Soutine was refused ... there is *no Soutine* in the Gallery and he is *at least* an historical landmark.'[11] At this same meeting the Trustees had declined to purchase three oil paintings by Moholy-Nagy, offered by his widow for unspecified prices.

Sculpture played second fiddle to painting during the immediate post-war years, partly because wartime conditions had impeded sculptural practice and made casting difficult, and partly because the sculpture galleries had been some of the worst hit and did not reopen until 1949. Nevertheless, the Trustees showed interest in the work of Hepworth and Moore, acquiring a series of maquettes by the latter, and at the Venice Biennale in 1948, Rothenstein, with Ridley's approval, bought *Cardinal* by Giacomo Manzu. Rothenstein thought the little figure was 'marked by gravity and style and a devoutness not incompatible with wit', and, because it was the first official British purchase of an Italian artist's work since the war, 'it was accordingly welcomed as having almost symbolic significance'.[12] He took a similar pride in having spotted in Alberto Giacometti's studio in Paris the plaster of *Man Pointing*. Giacometti agreed that a cast should be made for the Tate, and in 1951 Rothenstein wrote of it: 'The spindly Giacometti figure, immensely tall, walking, pointing, in motion at all events, and seeming always remote, however near one approaches, is one of the haunting symbols of our time.'[13]

Having been commissioned many years before, the Ervin Bossanyi stained-glass window was finally completed in 1947. It depicted an angel bestowing upon washer-women the blessing of Heaven, symbolised by an abstract harmony of blues and scarlets with a flame, as the symbol of life, at its centre. Bossanyi, who came from southern Hungary and had been trained at the Budapest Academy, drew inspiration from the windows at Chartres but failed to recreate this inspiration for the Tate. Worse still, the size of the window far exceeded the existing aperture and therefore expensive structural alterations were necessary before it could be installed. The Trustees decided, after much debate, that because the public had subscribed towards its cost, the Gallery had to proceed with its installation. By November 1948 it adorned the wall of the staircase nearest to the Restaurant and seemed even worse than had been anticipated. 'The utmost dissatisfaction and abhorrence of this work was unanimously expressed,' record the minutes of the next Board meeting.[14] Far more acceptable was the stained-glass window by Evie Hone, inspired by an ancient Irish stone carving at Cashel, which Derek Hill presented that same year. It was placed over the door to the annexe on the east side of the Sculpture Hall.

33 Alberto Giocometti, *Man Pointing*, 1947

34 Queues outside the Tate for the van Gogh exhibition, 1947

If success was mixed with failure during these years, the public voted with their feet; during the first year of reopening they came in greater numbers than before the war, despite the fact that only six galleries were open. The Tate benefited greatly at this time from exhibitions which, owing to the shortage of exhibition space in London, were mounted at the Tate by the British Council and the recently formed Arts Council. The latter was responsible for the exhibitions of the works of James Ensor in 1946, of van Gogh in 1947, (for which long queues formed outside the Tate), and of Marc Chagall, Jack B. Yeats (his first major retrospective outside Ireland) and of Jacques-Louis David, all three of which took place in 1948. Meanwhile, the British Council helped develop the Tate's association with Turner and Blake by touring their work around a number of European capitals. But perhaps the greatest success of the period was the *Hogarth – Constable – Turner* exhibition, organised jointly by the Tate, the National Gallery and the Victoria & Albert Museum, and shown at the Art Institute of Chicago and several other venues in the United States and Canada. When it finally arrived in London at the Tate, in August 1947, the exhibition was referred to as 'a display of British genius',[15] and proved so popular that its showing was extended to October.

The Tate celebrated its fiftieth anniversary in 1947 by putting on display a selection of paintings and bronzes from Henry Tate's original gift. It also abolished the small admission charge which had been levied on so-called 'student days'. Growing confidence in the Gallery's achievements led to plans for a Tate Ball in 1948, but this was postponed and finally abandoned, partly because the Trustee Henry Lamb objected, arguing that it represented 'a confusion of aesthetics with theocracies and that the choreobantic element was hostile to the plastic arts'.[16] This same year, a desire to rehang the Gallery with an uninterrupted chronological display of British painting made necessary an approach to the Duveen Trustees, in order to modify the conditions concerning the use of the modern foreign galleries. A change in the terms of use was agreed; but until 1960 the Duveen Trustees continued to insist that the Sargent Gallery should remain exclusive to this artist. (After that date other artists hung alongside Sargent until 1989 when, after further negotiations, the Duveen Trustees agreed that all stipulations regarding the use of this gallery should lapse, provided work by Sargent hung elsewhere.)

Far less satisfactory was the agreement governing the administration of the Chantrey Bequest. The compromise reached with the creation of Recommending Committees, on which both the Tate and the Academy had a voice, was not working well. Though some £2,000 was available to spend each year, only £186 was spent in 1941, £45 in 1942, and £50 in 1946. In this last instance both the Tate and Academy representatives on the Recommending Committee for pictures had approved Tristram Hillier's *Le Havre de Grace*, but the President and Council of the Royal Academy had exercised their right of veto and the painting had not been bought. It was this same year that the Massey Report recommended that an ideal arrangement would be the transfer of the Bequest to the Tate Trustees or, failing this, that the Tate Trustees should be empowered to refuse works of which they disapproved. The Gallery thus felt understandably aggrieved at receiving such high-handed and uncooperative treatment by the Academy. It therefore suggested that this would be a timely moment to honour the Chantrey Bequest with an exhibition of the entire collection at Burlington House.

The Chantrey exhibition opened at the Royal Academy in January 1949, and the critics had a field day. John Rothenstein's article, 'Why the Tate Does not Show its Chantrey Pictures', on the leader page of the *Daily Telegraph* (20 January 1949), drew a reply from the Royal Academy President, Sir Alfred Munnings, and much correspondence. Raymond Mortimer, reviewing the exhibition in the *New Statesman and Nation*, found 'most of it conspicuously dull and vulgar'. It transpired that the artist who had been paid most for a single picture was Frank Cadogan Cowper. His *Lucretia Borgia Reigns in the Vatican in the Absence of Pope Alexander VI* belonged, Mortimer observed, to the 'Cardinal school', which flourished in the Chantrey collection: 'The appetite of a section of the public for paintings of Cardinals drinking the cook's health or bringing their connoisseurship to bear upon a wine or a statuette deserves study by psychologists.'[17] In general, the exhibition made the public aware that by 1949 some £150,000 had been spent mostly on dire works by mediocrities and nonentities. The exhibition nevertheless made a profit, which the Royal Academy generously shared with the Tate.

Shortly after the exhibition opened, Philip Hendy, at a meeting of the Tate Trustees, stigmatised the Chantrey Bequest as 'a very great public scandal'[18] and urged the Board to seize the opportunity created by criticism of the exhibition to expose this waste of public funds, and to press for better conditions in the management of the Bequest. Four months later a senior civil servant, Dennis Proctor, chaired a meeting between representatives of the Tate and the Chantrey Trustees, as a result of which it was recommended that the Tate should have equal representation with the Academy on the Recommending Committees, and that no picture should be finally purchased until the Trustees of the Tate Gallery had indicated willingness to accept it. In the outcome, parity on the Committees was granted, but the Academy refused to allow the Tate to have the final say over purchases. However, the Tate was accorded the right to decline unwanted purchases. It was a negative advance, but one that gave the Tate Trustees greater influence over the administration of the Chantrey Bequest.

★   ★   ★

These were halcyon years, John Rothenstein averred in his memoirs, when he looked back on the late 1940s. Such an assertion required him to turn a blind eye to trouble in the Publications Department, a small issue which became a matter of public scandal. It also contributed to the nervous breakdown which in 1949 afflicted Humphrey Brooke, who had joined the staff two years before. Having previously worked as Controller of Monuments and Fine Art in Vienna for the Control Commission in Austria, he was instrumental in obtaining for the Tate the major exhibition *Art Treasures from Vienna* in 1949. His wife Natalie, the daughter of Count Benckendorf, the last Imperial Ambassador at the Court of St James, was Sir Jasper Ridley's niece.

In 1933 a Publications Department had been set up, funded from a Treasury grant of stock valued at £3,861 and from a private bequest of £2,000 (the Benson Fund). Its activities were revived in 1946 and a young woman was appointed as supervisor, on a salary of £6 per week, plus £2 per week expenses. She was also offered a percentage of the profits and told she could work what hours she liked. In December of that year the Publications Stall reopened in the Gallery, and despite paper-rationing, books and postcards were once more on sale.

Administrative detail was never John Rothenstein's forte, but it seemed to him that the new supervisor had imagination, drive and initiative. When he left in the spring of 1948 for South Africa, in connection with a forthcoming show of contemporary South African art, he felt confident that the relations between himself, the supervisor and Humphrey Brooke were amicable and cordial. On his return, he was surprised to discover that Brooke had developed an intense hostility towards this young woman and now insisted that all was not well in the Publications Department. Rothenstein felt there was a strong element of personal dislike in Brooke's allegations, while Brooke suspected undue personal liking behind Rothenstein's defence of the supervisor. Nevertheless, Rothenstein agreed to request the Board's permission to bring in the Organisation and Methods Division of the Treasury to investigate the finances of the Publications Department. He then went abroad again and returned in time to hear Brooke deliver a violent outburst against the supervisor at the Trustees' meeting on 16 December 1948. She had, Brooke asserted, formed a business connection with a Mr Liversedge, whose activities were part of an enquiry into corruption by the Lynskey Tribunal. He accused her also of lying and of attempting to evade Treasury rulings and Civil

35 Frank Cadogan Cowper, *Lucretia Borgia Reigns in the Vatican*
in the Absence of Pope Alexander VI, 1908–14

Service procedure in the administration of her department. He also drew attention to the fact that she kept such irregular hours that she often did not overlap with other Gallery staff, and that she had annoyed the Director of the Courtauld Institute of Art with an obstructive attitude to the Courtauld catalogue, currently in progress.

This attack obliged the Trustees to appoint a sub-committee to look into the matter, and, before the Organisation and Methods Division had been brought in, the supervisor was given notice in January 1949 – which, however, was not to take effect until July. Her continuing presence at the Gallery had a disturbing effect on Brooke's mental health. In February it became known that she would not leave until her percentage of profits had been calculated and that she was backed by a solicitor who specialised in litigation against government departments. Ridley warned Rothenstein that the position was becoming awkward. In March 1949 Rothenstein, having taken instruction from the Treasury medical officer regarding Brooke's health, forbade him to attend the opening of the *Art Treasures from Vienna* exhibition. Some ten days later Brooke underwent a complete, but temporary, mental breakdown. When he began to recover in April, he learned that at the April Board meeting the supervisor had been reinstalled at Rothenstein's request, on the grounds that Brooke had been ill when he made his attack against her. The following July the Organisations and Methods Division began their investigation into the Publications Department. Its report, published in October 1949, was severely critical and upheld Brooke's allegations. When its conclusions were brought to the Trustees' attention, they instructed the Director to dismiss the supervisor immediately. The report had made various criticisms, chief of which was that at a time when paper was still rationed, the supervisor had obtained large quantities of paper by misrepresenting the department's export capacity to the Raw Materials Department. It was also noted that paper obtained under licence for export purposes had been sold to printing firms in this country soon after purchase.[19]

This minor episode had lasting repercussions. Brooke was transferred to the Ministry of Town and Country Planning but in 1952 he became Secretary of the Royal Academy, a job that he had always wanted and which gave him a platform from which to let off salvos at the Tate. More sinister was the way in which this conflict began a period of disturbing incidents, half-explained crises and alleged scandals which cumulatively rocked the entire art establishment.

8

Iago

The complete reopening of the Tate was formally celebrated on 24 February 1949, with the Chancellor of the Exchequer, Sir Stafford Cripps, performing the necessary ceremony. His interest in the visual arts had been stimulated by Dennis Proctor, Third Secretary in the Treasury, who was charged with oversight of the national galleries and museums. In 1950 Proctor, a frequent visitor to the Tate, left the Civil Service in order to work for the Danish shipping magnate A.P. Moeller. He also became a Trustee of the Tate in May 1952. When he returned to Whitehall in 1953 it was as Deputy Secretary at the Ministry of Transport. As this job did not in any way overlap with his work for the Tate, he remained a Trustee, becoming Chairman in 1953, and was to steer the Tate through the worst period of its entire history. It was unfortunate for Rothenstein that Proctor did not take up this post a little earlier, for the successor to Sir Jasper Ridley, who died suddenly in 1951, was Lord Jowitt, a former Lord Chancellor who was less well suited to the task.

For its new display in 1949 the Tate received from the National Gallery a collection of eighteenth-century British paintings. But a year later, at the request of the National Gallery, William Hogarth's *Marriage à la Mode* series was returned to Trafalgar Square. Hogarth had formerly been the starting point of the British collection, but Rothenstein now wanted to extend further back in time, an idea supported by the Massey Report. Help came from two private collectors, Francis Howard and Loel Guinness, who loaned a small but choice collection of Tudor and Stuart portraits. However, the Trustees at first showed little enthusiasm for sixteenth-, seventeenth- and eighteenth-century British painting, and it was not until 1960 that there were sufficient works in the collection to justify the allocation of an entire room to Hogarth's predecessors. Only after 1965, when Paul Mellon's collection of British art was shown at Burlington House, did this aspect of the Tate's collection begin to receive adequate attention.

In February 1949 Graham Sutherland drew the Trustees' attention to the need to acquire works by Picasso and Braque. This stirred a determined attempt to look seriously at the gaps in the modern foreign collection. Later that month Rothenstein went to Paris where he visited artists and dealers, often in the company of Douglas Cooper who, having momentarily put aside his anger over the Klees found in Rothenstein's office, was brimming with goodwill towards the Tate. Rothenstein readily conceded that Cooper's knowledge far exceeded his own and, as a result of this visit he was able to put before the Trustees in August some thirty works by Picasso, Gris, Raoul Dufy, Matisse, Rouault, Braque, Léger, Maurice de Vlaminck, Giacometti, Jacques Lipchitz, Emile-Antoine Bourdelle,

Charles Despiau and Renoir. This meeting was one of the high points in Rothenstein's career, for not only did the Trustees acquire two Cubist Picassos (*Seated Nude* and *Bust of a Woman*), Matisse's *Notre-Dame*, a Rouault, a Léger and two Giacometti paintings, all for around £9,000, but eight more Blakes were also added to the collection, as a gift from the executors of Graham Robertson's estate.

Nevertheless, the Tate was acting somewhat belatedly: by 1950 it owned only one Fauve picture, whereas the Copenhagen Museum owned fifteen; Douglas Cooper grumbled to his friends that the Tate's Léger acquisition was a 'tardy act of recognition'; and Rothenstein's enthusiasm for Cubism was far from wholehearted.[1] In 1949 the Curwen Press published Rothenstein's *100 Modern Foreign Pictures at the Tate* in which he repeated views that he had first expressed in his 1943 *Studio* article, 'European Painting 1893–1943': that Cubism lacked imagination and that although it was the product of an architectural conception of painting, it had produced 'not the equivalent of cathedrals or railway stations, but bijou "follies"'.

Cooper remained highly critical of the Tate, blaming the weaknesses in its collection on ignorance and a constant fear of being fooled. The climate in Britain was still very hostile to modern art and there was widespread suspicion that much of it was a con, and Picasso merely a subject for derision. Cooper repeatedly castigated the Gallery for buying uninteresting, second-rate work. But he failed to acknowledge the pragmatic aspects of the situation, which involved not only the limitations in the taste and knowledge of the Director, but also the rarely unanimous opinions of strong minded Trustees, and the small amount of money available from trust funds and the purchase grant. Cooper himself had begun collecting Cubism in the early 1930s, when the booming demand for this art in the 1920s had turned into a long-lasting slump. He was also the first scholar to study Cubist paintings with the kind of attention accorded Old Masters. His systematic chronicling of the development of Picasso, Braque, Gris and Léger enabled him to acquire a high-quality, tightly focused collection, which made the Tate collection by comparison seem hotchpotch and weak. Cooper's impatience with Rothenstein can be glimpsed behind a letter he wrote in 1950 to Philip Hendy who, as Director of the National Gallery, sat on the Tate Board in an ex-officio role. Apropos Derain's *Two Sisters*, currently at Gimpel's and on offer for £1,200, Cooper asked: 'Can you do something about getting it for the Tate? I don't want to put it in an American museum unless I must.'[2]

In May 1950 the Tate Trustees considered commissioning Cooper to write a catalogue of the Modern Foreign School for the Tate. He was currently at work on a catalogue of the Courtauld Collection and was well suited to the task. But the Trustees decided not to proceed with this proposal, perhaps because of Cooper's acerbic reputation and the fact that he had a rabid dislike of most manifestations of modern art other than Cubism. He could not abide Surrealism. He had given short shrift to Peggy Guggenheim's idea for a Museum of Modern Art in London, had resigned as a sponsor of the ICA, and held the Euston Road School in deep contempt – a prejudice that helped worsen his attitude to the Tate when Coldstream and Gowing became Trustees.

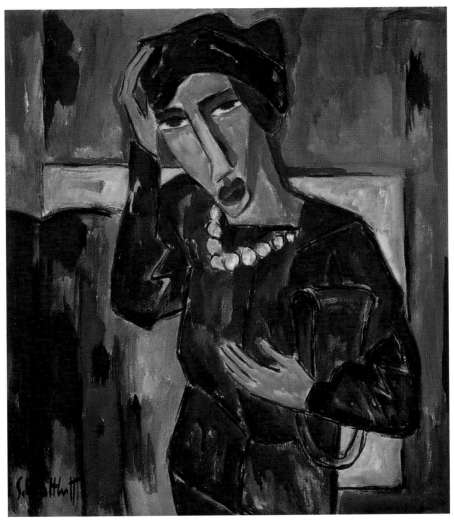

36 Karl Schmidt-Rottluff, *Woman with a Bag*, 1915

In June 1950 the Trustees considered Cooper's proposal for an exhibition of European art from 1900 to 1914. Rothenstein at first welcomed the suggestion but later told Cooper the Gallery did not have the resources to make it feasible. However, it is possible that the Trustees failed to see the significance of such a project. Also in June, Dr Rosa Schapire, an art historian and an early supporter of Die Brücke, offered to give three works by Karl Schmidt-Rottluff to the Gallery. The Board provisionally declined them, but expressed interest in seeing other examples of this artist's work in Dr Schapire's collection and the following month they accepted *Woman with a Bag*. Dr Schapire, who had been a close friend of Schmidt-Rottluff and had come to England in 1939 as a refugee from Nazi persecution, bringing with her a treasured collection of paintings, sculpture and prints, sensed a grudging attitude behind the Tate's acceptance of just one work and was angered by it. Three years later the Tate turned down three works by Otto Dix, offered for sale by Dr Hermann Ganz – despite the fact that Mary Chamot, who was appointed Assistant Keeper at the Tate in 1949, had established contact with Dix's son while he was studying picture restoration in Bristol. Ronald Alley, appointed Assistant Keeper in 1951, witnessed over the years many missed opportunities with regard to German art. But the Tate's failure to respond to German art did not prevent Alley from making friends with Rosa Schapire, whom he invited to lunch early in 1954 so that she might see the Raoul Dufy exhibition which the Arts Council had mounted at the Tate. Awareness of her grievance against the Tate will always colour the fact that, on arriving that day at the Gallery, she collapsed in the entrance hall and died in the ambulance on the way to Westminster Hospital.

★   ★   ★

In the 1939 Tate exhibition of photographs illustrating mural painting in Britain over the previous twenty years, there was a reproduction of the recently completed Zulu mural in South Africa House. The two painters responsible for it, both aged twenty-four, were, one journalist reckoned, the youngest living artists to have had photographs of their work shown at the Tate. Their names were Miss Esmonde-White and LeRoux Smith LeRoux.

When Rothenstein went to South Africa in 1948 to advise its government on a contemporary South African art exhibition which was to be sent to the Tate, he found himself guest of honour at a large reception and dinner given by LeRoux Smith LeRoux, who in the intervening years had become Director of the Pretoria Art Centre. He was a big, flamboyant man and had been deputed by the South African government to be Rothenstein's guide-companion during his visit. They travelled widely together, visited a game reserve and conversed easily and sympathetically on many subjects. But perhaps what clinched their friendship was the fact that LeRoux had studied painting under Rothenstein's father and it had been Sir William who had secured for LeRoux the commission for the South Africa House mural. After Rothenstein left South Africa, he and Le Roux remained in correspondence.

Following the 1949 general election, at which the Nationalists replaced the United Party, LeRoux found his institution criticised for being too liberal, and there was an attempt to bring it under Christian Nationalist 'educational principles'. LeRoux, who was writing a novel at the time, thought of going into seclusion in order to paint and write. Instead he came to London, en route to Holland, and spent a weekend with Rothenstein and his wife in Oxfordshire. Again, he proved convivial and talked, often movingly, of his experiences with animals. It was therefore rather surprising that the Rothensteins's Alsatians showed more hostility to LeRoux that weekend than they ever showed to any other guest.

After he had returned to South Africa, LeRoux sent Rothenstein ever more despairing letters: intrigue was rife, not only was the withdrawal of government support for the Art Centre imminent, but the Provincial Administration was threatening to close it down. Rothenstein must have suggested to LeRoux that he come to work at the Tate, as the younger man expressed gratitude for this 'second chance'. But he said that he could not afford to come for an interview 'on spec'. Could the Tate's Board delegate their powers so that he could be interviewed in South Africa? This proved unnecessary, as LeRoux had been on friendly terms with Lord Harlech, now a Tate Trustee, when Harlech was British High Commissioner in South Africa. The combination of Rothenstein's recommendation and Lord Harlech's support obtained LeRoux the offer of a Temporary Deputy Keepership in December 1949. He accepted it in January and by March he was in post. One thing that recommended him was the fact that he looked the strong, outdoor type which, following Humphrey Brooke's breakdown, was a welcome qualification. He had held important posts in the art world in South Africa and represented himself as a person of integrity who had fought apartheid and had lost his job because of his liberal stand.

At first Rothenstein congratulated himself on having secured the services of this man. Among LeRoux's administrative and general duties were the preparation of the agenda for the Board meetings, the keeping of the minutes and the organisation of the correspondence. He was capable of writing excellent letters – informed, closely reasoned and, when the occasion demanded, forceful. He took pains over detail, was thorough and energetic; and when in January 1951 he was put in charge of the Publications Department, he swiftly turned a shambolic, loss-making organisation into a profitable, well-run business. He also gave a large amount of his time to editing the new Modern Foreign catalogue. Rothenstein informed Lord Jowitt that LeRoux, after eight months in office, had discharged his various duties 'with marked diligence and enthusiasm', and that his relations with his colleagues were excellent.[3] But despite these recommendations, the Selection Board which interviewed LeRoux at the end of his first year was less impressed: he was ratified as Deputy Keeper and Manager of the Publications and Information Departments, but placed on probation for another year. What doubts remained about him concerned the size and scale of his outside interests. He wanted everything to be big, from his desk to his car; and whereas Rothenstein, who did not drive, had the benefit of his wife's cheap Ford, LeRoux drove a second-hand Jaguar.

During these first twelve months LeRoux had also revealed certain alarming propensities. Though he showed Rothenstein respect and congratulated him when, in the spring of 1952, he became the first Tate Director to be knighted, LeRoux assumed the right to open all correspondence, even personal and confidential letters that arrived for John and Elizabeth Rothenstein, who now had a small flat in the Gallery. Norman Reid, with his military experience, observed that LeRoux asked for all the responsibilities which could be regarded as key positions from a standpoint of power. And Rothenstein began to notice that tasks entrusted to LeRoux disappeared behind an administrative iron curtain of secretiveness.

Having instituted daily eleven o'clock meetings with his Deputy Keepers, which were conducted on an open and friendly basis, Rothenstein was disturbed by LeRoux's tendency to view his duties as a form of administrative property.

When Ronald Alley went to Paris in October 1951 on a six-month French scholarship, Judith Cloake was appointed a temporary assistant in his place. On her first day at the Tate, LeRoux told her she must never go near Rothenstein as he was a difficult man. She was sent to work with Mary Chamot on the concise catalogue of the British collection and in time discovered for herself that Rothenstein was not at all the ogre that LeRoux had suggested. After a while Cloake, realising that her interests lay more in administrative than academic work, asked LeRoux if she might instead assist Norman Reid, whose administrative responsibilities included the conservation and display of the collection, its custody, and the building itself. LeRoux told her she would find little to do as Reid was incapable of delegating anything. Again, this proved to be untrue and Judith Cloake (who became Judith Jeffreys) remained at the Tate for many years (first as a volunteer, then as Assistant Keeper and eventually as Assistant Director). But LeRoux's critical innuendoes gradually swelled into a familiar refrain: Rothenstein knew nothing about administration, was hopeless at managing staff, and the Tate was in a terrible mess.

If Rothenstein had a serious weakness, it was an ability to misjudge people and situations. His handling of Humphrey Brooke's anxieties over the Publications Department had been inept. In 1951 Paul Hulton's brief period as Assistant Keeper at the Tate was terminated by Rothenstein. Hulton appealed to the Board which saw no reason to alter Rothenstein's decision and Hulton transferred to the British Museum. LeRoux, aware of Hulton's resentment, was later to use this and other instances of poor staff-relations as evidence against Rothenstein. Nowhere was proof of this charge more evident than in Rothenstein's dealings with LeRoux.

LeRoux, who had come to London with his wife Philippa, knew how to exert charm on others, especially female colleagues. He soon had working for him at the Tate Jane Ryder, a young woman who had formerly assisted Reid but now became LeRoux's secretary. She was introduced by him into the Board meetings to take minutes and eventually became Information Officer.

While LeRoux was abroad on holiday in August 1952, the Assistant Manager in the Publications Department, E. Hockaday Dawson, went to Rothenstein to express his concern over LeRoux's instruction that he should pay any account that LeRoux authorised, including those concerned with travel for himself and Miss Ryder. Hockaday Dawson claimed LeRoux had threatened him with dismissal if he refused. Rothenstein sent Hockaday Dawson to speak with Jowitt, and as a result Jowitt drew up stringent regulations concerning expenses in the Publications Department. When LeRoux returned, he was angry to learn that Rothenstein had drawn this matter to Jowitt's attention in his absence. Rothenstein had himself by then gone away, and on his return, instead of trying to have a friendly talk with LeRoux to explain what had happened, he fired off a list of complaints, mostly about quite trivial matters. The following day, 8 October 1952, LeRoux

37 Zsa Zsa Gabor photographed in the Gallery for *Illustrated* magazine,
25 October 1952

read out a statement at a Trustees' meeting that contained a vigorous attack on Rothenstein and the Tate administration. He also threatened to resign, saying he did not see how he could go on working with a Director who manifested such a palpable lack of trust.

In the turmoil this created, Rothenstein, who could justifiably claim credit for having brought new life to a formerly war-damaged and almost staffless institution, was deeply hurt to realise that some of the Trustees had lost confidence in him. The situation was immediately exacerbated by three minor scandals – concerning Zsa Zsa Gabor, a film called *The Fake* and the purchase of a work by Degas – all of which were stirred by LeRoux's machinations; for, still angered by the way the Director had abused his reputation to Jowitt, LeRoux now began working determinedly to bring about Sir John Rothenstein's downfall.

On 25 October 1952, less than three weeks after LeRoux's public attack on Rothenstein, the magazine *Illustrated* published an article entitled 'Zsa Zsa Gabor Plays to the Gallery'. It reported a visit Gabor had made to the Tate Gallery in order to see its Toulouse-Lautrecs, as she was about to play Jane Avril in a film on Lautrec by John Huston. It had also been arranged that she would meet the Director, whose father had been a friend of Lautrec. If few in England at this time knew much about the background of this actress, they would have learned from this article that she had been expelled from six schools, had married three times, had been charged with spying, had spent a brief spell in a Middle Eastern jail, before becoming a household name as a film star. She was also adept at courting publicity, and knowing that she was to be entertained by Rothenstein in his flat she asked what colour the walls were. On learning they were burgundy, she chose to wear an ivory-shell pink cocktail dress and a mink coat. Once inside the Gallery, despite her imperfect English she was in complete command of the situation. In one room she paused beside Maillol's *The Three Nymphs* (often referred to as *The Three Graces*) and, while giving her autograph to two soldiers, announced her wish that Maillol had sculpted herself and her two sisters. '"The Three Gabors" he would call it. Maybe you give us a special place in the gallery, eh, Sir John?' The visit ended with her sipping sherry in Rothenstein's flat while the late afternoon light filtered through the heavy brocade curtains. On leaving she clutched her voluminous mink around her and promised a return visit. '"When you are changing the programme?" she demanded, poking Sir John in the ribs. Settled at ease in the the enveloping folds of the elegant Rolls for that long trek back to the Savoy, she remarked, "What an inspiring place. Must be worth millions."'[4]

What made this article particularly *piquant* was one of the photographs of Gabor, which Rothenstein later insisted must have been taken while he was called away to the telephone. It showed her posing provocatively with her foot resting on one of the waist-high pedestals in the Sculpture Hall. 'Its deplorable and blatant vulgarity is really shocking', fulminated Lord Harlech to Lord Jowitt, arguing also that Rothenstein was 'temperamentally unfitted to continue as Director and ought to be replaced'.[5] Harlech, like other Trustees, had been sent a copy of the magazine anonymously in the post, as had other dignitaries. It caused such an uproar that questions were asked in Parliament and the wife of the Chancellor of the Exchequer, Mrs R.A. Butler, who was also the daughter of the Tate's great patron, Samuel Courtauld, wrote a protest to Jowitt. Even Douglas Cooper, who had that year moved to the Château de Castille at Argilliers in the South of France, saw the article. He sent Rothenstein a quote from *Paris Match*, referring to the fact that the prisoners in Sing-Sing had designated Gabor 'la femme avec qui ils souhaiteraient être enfermés'. Alongside this he quoted from the recent *Illustrated* article: 'When the tour was over, Miss Gabor … went down the stairs, through a secret door, across a cold sub-basement into a courtyard, and, finally, to the lower depths of the Tate Gallery and the luxurious, though tiny, flat Sir John calls home.' To this Cooper added a single comment: 'From cellar to cell. Now you'd better be careful.'[6]

It seemed to Rothenstein especially hard that, having over the years attracted thousands of favourable notices for the Gallery, he should be so berated for this unfortunate article. But worse was to come. On 1 November 1952 the *Daily Mail* carried a short notice on the film *The Fake*, which said that Sir John Rothenstein, who had written the filmscript, and the Trustees, had given permission for short scenes to be shot in the Sculpture Hall and one other gallery. After reading this, LeRoux called for the appropriate files and, behind Rothenstein's back, sent all the correspondence pertaining to this film to Jowitt. Rothenstein had brought the film and his script to the attention of the Board, but in the minutes no mention had been made of the fact that he was to receive payment for his script – though Rothenstein later claimed, and Reid confirmed, that he had mentioned this. LeRoux drew Jowitt's attention not only to the Director's remuneration, but also to the discrepancy between the terms agreed concerning the use of the Gallery, as recorded in the minutes of the Board meeting, and those agreed by Rothenstein in his correspondence with the film company. LeRoux pointed out that Rothenstein's contract seemed dependent on him getting permission for the use of the Gallery. He was also going to be in Paris at the time of the filming, and therefore LeRoux would be responsible for the Gallery in his absence. This gave LeRoux the opportunity to express a civil servant's grave disquiet at the thought of hordes of film technicians in the building.

In the row that ensued, Rothenstein pointed out that he had in fact written his script long before any film company had shown interest in it. But Jowitt was sufficiently disturbed by LeRoux's insinuations to arrange for Rothenstein to be interviewed by the Treasury Solicitor, Sir Thomas Barnes. The senior civil servant Edward Playfair was also present, and both he and Barnes expressed dislike of an arrangement whereby a Director of a public gallery could make a profit for himself by reason of the shooting of a film in the Gallery of which he was Director. Rothenstein immediately saw their point, and agreed that his fee and any profits that might come to him should be paid directly into the Tate Trustees' account, as a contribution towards the purchase of future works of art.

Meanwhile a brouhaha over the purchase of Degas's *Little Dancer Aged Fourteen Years* had rumbled alongside these two other alleged scandals. In June 1951 David Somerset at Marlborough Fine Art had offered Rothenstein a complete set of Degas's seventy-three bronzes, which Puvis de Chavannes's son wished to sell. The asking price was £18,480. The largest and most important work in this group of sculptures was the *Little Dancer*, a cast of which had been sold by the London art dealers Wildenstein's before the war for £4,000. Given this evaluation for the *Little Dancer*, the price for the remaining seventy-two sculptures was very low. With its insufficient resources, the Tate could not consider spending such a disproportionate amount on sculpture by an artist who was better known for his paintings; but it did express interest in the *Little Dancer*, which was not at first available separately. However, the Chairman of the National Art Collections Fund was very insistent that the Tate should have this, and eventually telephoned Rothenstein in the summer of 1952 to say it was now available. The Tate was advised to act promptly as the Fitzwilliam Museum, Cambridge, was also interested in it. Therefore, at the Board meeting in June 1952 the Trustees agreed to purchase the *Little Dancer* for eight million francs (approximately £8,000), on the understanding that the National Art Collections Fund had promised to contribute £6,000.

When the account arrived from Marlborough Fine Art, the total price, owing to the gallery's commission plus an introduction fee, had increased to £9,076. The

Daily Telegraph got to hear of this and drew attention to the fact that it was the highest price ever paid for a Degas bronze. At the September 1952 Board meeting Graham Sutherland, John Piper and even Henry Moore expressed disquiet at the price paid for the Degas, and the Director was asked to look into the matter and to obtain objective valuations from outside authorities. Accordingly, Rothenstein wrote to Curt Valentin, an American dealer, who replied that he had sold a cast of this sculpture in 1945 for $4,300 to the Virginia Museum of Fine Art in Richmond, but he did not know of any other currently on the market. *Little Dancer* was then thought to have been cast in a smaller edition than the rest of the seventy-two surviving sculptures which, with one exception, were each cast in an edition of twenty-two. The lack of certainty over the number of *Little Dancers* in existence, and the absence of one on the current market, made valuation very difficult and a matter of speculation. The Tate had succeeded in acquiring the largest and most important sculpture made by one of the greatest masters of modern times, but it was generally thought that it had paid far too much.

In mid-November 1952 LeRoux presented Jowitt with a seven-page chronological analysis of the negotiations and events concerning the purchase of this Degas bronze. The pressure he put on Rothenstein over the price of the Degas contributed more than anything to the deterioration in their relationship. Yet, as Rothenstein pointed out to Jowitt, it was LeRoux who had taken the minutes at the June 1952 Board meeting, and the letter concerning the sale, which mentioned the 10 per cent commission and introduction fee, had been given to him beforehand and placed in the Board box. Yet no mention of this commission had appeared on the agenda or in the minutes.[7]

With his fellow Trustees angered and in revolt, Jowitt was by now at his wits end. 'If you ask my opinion as to what ought to be done,' he wrote to Sir Thomas Barnes in the Treasury, 'it is clear – both Rothenstein and LeRoux ought to go … I am greatly disturbed about the whole thing and wish to God I had nothing to do with it. A word from you would be a great help to me.'[8]

Asked to submit a Chairman's report, Jowitt concluded that Rothenstein and LeRoux could no longer work together. However, the Treasury was determined that they should. The Trustees were informed that the imminent National Art Collections Bill, the aim of which was to enhance the status of the Tate, together with an anticipated increase in the Grant-in-Aid, would be jeopardised by public unpleasantness. Sir Edward Ritson, Deputy Chairman of the Board of Inland Revenue, was given the task of writing a report on the so-called 'staff troubles' at the Tate. He did so, bringing to his task the traditional view that no subordinate should be proved right at the expense of his superior. 'To sum up,' he concluded on LeRoux, 'he has shown himself completely unaware of the sort of conduct required from a subordinate Government Servant.' In December, after the appearance of the Ritson Report, LeRoux wanted to resign. Had he done so, it was rumoured, some of his colleagues and at least one of the Trustees would have left with him. Jowitt had the difficult task of reconciling the Ritson Report with the wishes of the Trustees, who at first refused to accept it. Eventually an appeal was made direct to LeRoux by the Chairman; he was offered a further probationary period of one year and received a severe reprimand. The Director was also given a warning and the instruction that he should formulate a scheme for administrative reorganisation in order to create a happier situation at the Tate. And both men were now expected to accept compromise and work together. In the course of this heavy-handed peace-mission, Sir John Rothenstein and LeRoux, like irresponsible schoolboys, were made to shake hands in the Chairman's presence.

38 Edgar Degas, *Little Dancer Aged Fourteen*, 1880–1, cast *c*.1922

9

The Tate Affair

The Ritson Report, far from terminating troubles at the Tate, effected only an uncomfortable compromise. It had been preceded by rumours that Rothenstein was to be summarily dismissed and LeRoux put in charge. When this did not happen, the tense atmosphere lessened slightly but the staff remained nervous and apprehensive.

The following March the Tate Gallery hosted the *Unknown Political Prisoner* exhibition. In June 1951 the Institute of Contemporary Arts had been given the opportunity by an anonymous patron to sponsor a world-wide competition for a piece of sculpture to commemorate or symbolise the theme of the unknown political prisoner. An application form was printed in seven languages and twelve thousand brochures sent out. Some three thousand five hundred applications were received from fifty-seven countries. As it was impossible to bring all the maquettes to London, preliminary contests were arranged in certain countries, visited by Anthony Kloman, Director of Planning at the ICA, Rothenstein, who sat on the committee, and others. Finally an international jury met in London on 7 March 1953 and after four days chose eighty sculptors, each of whom received a £25 award. From this group a further twelve were eligible for prizes and honourable mentions, and the £4,500 prize for the winning artist went to Reg Butler. His working model, a wire and stone construction, successfully evoked allusions to the cage, scaffold, cross, guillotine and watch-tower. Six weeks after the exhibition opened to the public on 14 March, thirty thousand people had visited it, then a record attendance for a sculpture show in Britain. One of these visitors was a Hungarian refugee who, protesting against what he saw as a lack of humanism, damaged Butler's maquette beyond repair.[1] Six other maquettes were bought for the permanent collection, and in time the Tate also acquired Butler's working model for his winning sculpture.

In the lead up to this event Anthony Kloman, the organiser, saw a great deal of both LeRoux and Rothenstein. At first, when LeRoux began denigrating Rothenstein behind his back, Kloman put it down to petty museum rivalries and temperamentalism. But in January 1953 he noticed that LeRoux's antagonism to Rothenstein had become a deep-seated, brooding hatred. In the weeks that followed, both at social gatherings and at official meetings, Kloman realised what a dangerous and emotionally unstable man LeRoux was, and he wrote to Rothenstein warning him of LeRoux's 'capacity for making trouble by deliberate misrepresentations'.[2]

Rothenstein sent a copy of the letter to the Treasury civil servant, Edward

Playfair, as he did also a communication that he received from Douglas Cooper, who the year previously had been enraged by Rothenstein's dismissive remarks about the School of Paris in the first of his three-volume *Modern English Painters*. The fact that so prejudiced a view should originate from the Director of the Tate, where Cooper had himself unsuccessfully applied for a post in 1947, only exacerbated his ire.[3] Formerly, Cooper had directed alternating bouts of geniality and hostility towards Rothenstein, but from now on his attitude was one of unremitting belligerence. Cooper's letter arrived soon after the closure of *Mexican Art from Pre-Columbian Time to the Present Day*, a highly successful Arts Council exhibition organised under the auspices of the Mexican Government, which had brought many people to the Tate for the first time. Though he had not been directly involved with the making of the exhibition, Rothenstein was honoured by the Mexican President and made a Knight Commander of the Aztec Eagle. Cooper then wrote:

> Dear Rothenstein,
> Now that the Mexican President has provided you with the beak and claws of an Aztec eagle you may perhaps feel better equipped to face me in an open contest. But do not deceive yourself into thinking that, because your continual disservices to art bring you in knighthoods and ribbons, I shall in any way weaken in my attack. There are still more than ten years in which to hound you out of Millbank – and it shall be done.[4]

The previous month the composition of the Board of Trustees had changed: Dennis Proctor, who had been abroad for three months and did not attend Board meetings between July 1952 and January 1953, took over from Jowitt as Chairman in July 1953, and Sir Colin Anderson, the shipping magnate and collector with a long-standing interest in art, design and architecture, became Vice-Chairman. Though both gave invaluable service to the Tate, neither carried the same authority in the art world as Sir Kenneth Clark, who, having sat on the Board as an ex-officio member while Director of the National Gallery, could now act as a Trustee. Certain artist-Trustees blamed the fact that Clark was not invited to join the Board on Rothenstein, whose relations with Clark had soured during the war.[5] Rothenstein at first believed he had Proctor's ear. The day after Proctor took over, he and Rothenstein, together with Edward Playfair, lunched at the Reform Club. Afterwards Miss Butcher was asked to stand in for Miss Ryder in the taking of the minutes, and that evening Rothenstein left for Paris. On his return, he found Miss Ryder reinstated, LeRoux in high favour and Proctor in close partnership with another Trustee, John Fremantle (later Lord Cottesloe). Suspicion and intrigue were once again rife. When LeRoux was cited in the divorce case of a certain Noel Langley in September, he told a Tate employee that the Director was a friend of the petitioner and had put him up to it. Rothenstein, hearing of this, protested, as he had never met Langley. LeRoux blithely turned his protest aside by saying there had been some misunderstanding and that the director he had intended to implicate was a film director. Meanwhile, Humphrey Brooke was spreading a rumour that Rothenstein was to be dismissed once the Coronation had taken place.

Brooke was an honourable, intelligent man, but his disaffection with Rothenstein following the mishandling of the Publications Department scandal now made him a key player in what became known as 'the Tate Affair'. Brooke's house, 8 Pelham Crescent, became the meeting place for a small but powerful cabal, plotting to remove the Director of the Tate. Here Douglas Cooper occasionally dined when he was in London, as did his friend, Lord Amulree – a geriatrician prepared to use his position in the House of Lords to further the cause. Graham Sutherland was a good friend of Brooke, as was Denis Mahon, collector and authority on Italian Seicento art, who took an active interest in the progress of the National Art Collections Bill through Parliament. So did Denys Sutton, art historian, editor, critic and, like Cooper, a disappointed man in that he had applied for a post at the Tate and been rejected. Another sympathiser with Rothenstein's opponents was Benedict Nicolson, editor of the *Burlington Magazine* which kept a critical eye on the Tate. Anti-Rothenstein gossip also flowed at the parties given by the fashionable picture-framer Alfred Hecht who worked for, and was a friend of, Graham Sutherland. All were waiting for the next scandal.

At a second reading of the National Art Collections Bill in the House of Lords on 24 November 1953, which aimed to give the Tate legal independence, Lord Kinnaird argued that the clause transferring the Knapping Fund from the National Gallery to the Tate should be dropped as Miss Knapping had specifically left it to the National Gallery at a time when the Tate already had its own Trustees. Two weeks later he raised the Knapping Fund again, having by then examined the donor's will and discovered that certain purchases made with her money did not fit the terms of her bequest. This began a series of investigations into the Tate's allocation of trust funds which uncovered many small and well-intentioned irregularities. Cumulatively, they created the impression of gross carelessness and maladministration.

As both Reid and Rothenstein were away on Friday, 27 November when, according to LeRoux, Kinnaird rang up demanding information on Knapping purchases, LeRoux himself supplied it. In the weeks to come this damning list proved to be inaccurate,[6] perhaps not surprisingly as it was difficult to establish what exactly had been bought with the Knapping Fund – the ledger sometimes listing a quantity of paintings rather than individual titles. It is possible that LeRoux had spotted inconsistencies in the use of trust funds before this date and may have been responsible for drawing Kinnaird's attention to those connected with the Knapping Fund. But what is certain is that in the weeks that followed he and Jane Ryder leaked remarks made by the Trustees to outsiders. As Sir Colin Anderson recalls: 'It began to be noticed that figures and facts from past files were becoming impossible to find when wanted by the Trustees to enable them to answer accusations. They were evidently being removed, and with the purpose of causing maximum nuisance.'[7]

This turmoil had only just begun when Douglas Cooper heard that Lord Jowitt, speaking to the House of Lords in favour of deaccessioning, had instanced the sale by the Tate Trustees of a Sisley in order to buy a Monet, with the acquiescence of the donor Samuel Courtauld. In a letter to *The Times* (21 December 1953), Cooper pointed out that no mention had been made of Renoir's *Nu dans l'eau*, which, he had discovered in the course of cataloguing the Courtauld Collection, no longer belonged to the Tate. This picture, he claimed, 'has silently disappeared from the walls (and cellars) of the Tate Gallery since 1939, no statement about its going has ever been made, and requests to see this picture (which figures in the last edition of the modern foreign schools' catalogue) are met by Tate Gallery officials with an evasive answer.' This letter, with its scatter of further questions, was disingenuous, as Cooper had already been informed by Humphrey Brooke that the Renoir had been sold to Tooth's in 1944 for £5,300. The Chairman of the Trustees hastily published a rejoinder stating that the Renoir had been sold with Courtauld's permission and that two other works, Picasso's *Seated Nude* and Matisse's *Notre-Dame*, had been bought in 1949 as replacements.

The issue of deaccessioning was exacerbated by clause 6 of the National Art Collections Bill: modelled on a a similar provision in the National Gallery Act of 1856, it gave Trustees of national collections the right to sell works of art in their care. The Trustees had been discouraged from doing this in the past because the proceeds from such a sale had to go to the Treasury. But the new Bill would permit the proceeds to be retained by the Trustees, in which case the Trustees would have far greater power over the nation's pictorial heritage. This worried many and gave rise to correspondence in the pages of the *Spectator*. Denis Mahon, realising that the maladministration of funds could have a direct bearing on the Bill, began to uncover damaging evidence against the Tate as part of his campaign against deaccessioning. A mere hint of his findings appeared in the *Spectator* (8 and 15 January 1954). In the second of these letters he drew attention to a statement Rothenstein had made in the *Listener*, where he claimed that the Picasso and Matisse which had replaced the Renoir in 1949, together with Picasso's *Bust of a Woman*, had been purchased 'out of a recent bequest'. But the Courtauld Fund was neither recent nor a bequest. Which fund, therefore, had been used? 'I enclose cuttings from the *Spectator*,' Humphrey Brooke wrote to Douglas Cooper:

> Denis Mahon and I think we are now hot on the trail to the unmasking of all the Tate's recent fund shufflings. These involve violation of two wills (Cleve and Kerr) in addition to the Knapping and Courtauld irregularities. We have most of the documentary evidence but the *Spectator* are reluctant to publish – scared stiff of the stink … and have only allowed the insertion of these mild-looking queries.
>
> Mahon and I both think it important that you should write *immediately* to the *Spectator* giving all the facts you know about the purchase of Pic.[asso] Mat.[isse] and Giac.[ometti] in 1949. *Please* bear in mind that the *Spectator* will definitely not publish anything conjectural or in *any* degree abusive.[8]

Without further prompting, Douglas Cooper sent a letter to the *Spectator* (22

January 1953). Why, if a Matisse and a Picasso had been bought with Courtauld money, had the Director of the Tate not honoured Courtauld and included them in his lists for the memorial catalogue which Cooper was compiling? Cooper could only agree with Mahon that a certain amount of confusion covered the Tate's finances and cataloguing. Though Cooper did not raise any mention of Giacometti, it soon came out that the Courtauld Fund money had also been used for the purchase of two Giacometti paintings and a Léger, although these two artists were not on Courtauld's prescribed list. Nor was the Fund available for sculpture; yet two Degas bronzes had been bought with Courtauld money. As a result, the Trustees now had to reimburse the Courtauld Fund, in all £742 19s. 3d. At the same time labels on picture frames, some of which acknowledged the wrong trust fund and others of which failed to show any acknowledgement, were hurriedly changed, as the *Evening Standard* observed.

The Trustees were made acutely aware of the need to overhaul the administration of these funds and to tighten up administration in general. They discovered further defalcations: £1,000 drawn from the Kerr Fund, which was restricted to 'oil paintings of merit by British artists', had been used towards the purchase of a Henry Moore sculpture; and the Cleve Fund, which the donor had wanted used for British art but had imposed no legally binding restrictions, had been regarded as a source of money for the recent purchase of Picasso's *Nude Woman in a Red Armchair*. Although this Fund had only come into existence in 1949, at which time Rothenstein would have been clearly informed as to the donor's wishes, he had failed to impart these to the Trustees. It was shocking to discover that, whereas £9,000 from this Fund had been spent on British works, some £5,800 had also been spent on foreign works; and if the cost of the new Picasso was added to this, more Cleve money would have in fact been spent on foreign than on British works of art. In order to put the situation right, the Board hurriedly agreed to complete their purchase of the Picasso not by using Cleve money but, because no other fund was available, with a bank loan arranged by Sir Colin Anderson from Coutts. He was careful to make it clear that they could not pledge next year's Grant-in-Aid as a security, as this depended on a vote by Parliament. Nevertheless, Coutts agreed the loan on the good faith of the Trustees and expectation that a Grant-in-Aid for 1954 would be forthcoming. This arrangement was then leaked to the press, and the Gallery and the Trustees were severely reprimanded by the Comptroller and Auditor General.

In order to clear the air, on 26 January 1954 the Trustees published a list of trust fund errors. Thirteen were given and a general admission made of failure to take into account the donor's wishes in relation to the Cleve Fund. 'What is at stake', wrote Denys Sutton in the *Daily Telegraph* (29 January 1954) 'is no less than the sanctity of testamentary wishes.' Nevertheless, this public acknowledgement might have passed without too much fuss had the Trustees been able to present an unanimous front. But four days earlier Denis Mahon had written to Douglas Cooper: 'We are doing everything we can to keep things going here and we have a good deal of high explosive up our sleeves. But Graham Sutherland is *at the moment* a key figure who could play a decisive role.'⁹ It was Mahon's suggestion, as conveyed first to Cooper, that Sutherland should resign as a Trustee, thereby adding greatly to the Tate's bad publicity.

Sutherland was at this time, and earlier, genuinely aggrieved with the Tate administration, despite the fact that it had given him a major exhibition in 1953. But he was also a friend of Cooper's, and beholden to him, in that Cooper had agreed to write a monograph on Sutherland's art, which was tantamount to being elected into Cooper's pantheon of the great, alongside Picasso, Braque, Gris and Léger. Against this, Sutherland's debt to Rothenstein, who had made available (at Reid's suggestion) Poynter's studio at the Tate, when Sutherland was painting his large canvas *The Origins of the Land* in 1951, counted for less. Thus three days after the trust fund errors had been publicly announced, Sutherland issued a press statement at Roquebrune announcing his resignation. The fact that he did so in close proximity to Beaverbrook's villa in the South of France may explain why it was one of Beaverbrook's newspapers, the *Evening Standard*, which first picked up this news. Two days later the *Sunday Times* quoted Sutherland as saying that the Trustees had been misled over funds, several breaches of trust had been committed, and testators' wishes disregarded. His other criticisms included the hesitant purchasing policy and the missed opportunities to purchase works of art at a reasonable price.

Simultaneous with his statement to the press, Sutherland sent a letter of resignation to the Prime Minister, Winston Churchill, setting out his views. Luckily, Rothenstein was well regarded by Churchill and, with the encouragement of the Trustees, he now went to see him and spoke with him confidentially. As a result, Sutherland's letter was quietly accepted by the Prime Minister and allowed to fall flat.

Nevertheless, Sutherland's resignation touched off an uproar. Elizabeth Rothenstein became convinced that the Beaverbrook press was running a concerted campaign against her husband. This may have been true, as Sutherland had painted Beaverbrook's portrait, and the *Sunday Express*, which was also part of his empire, ran a full-page spread of the story as soon as it broke, using for a headline Douglas Cooper's comment: 'I feel the time has come for a thorough judicial enquiry into affairs at the Tate. Thousands of pounds have been lost to the nation altogether.'¹⁰ Criticisms of the Gallery became headline news, questions were asked in Parliament, and demands were made for public enquiries.

To some extent, Sutherland's resignation was to Rothenstein's advantage, for it was seen to be part of a concerted personal attack on the Director and therefore created for him a wave of sympathy. This made it much more difficult for the Trustees to reach an objective assessment of his merits or lack of them. Had Sutherland remained on the Board, he would now have been a powerful voice among others who wanted Rothenstein dismissed. Ironically, as Proctor observed, Rothenstein owed much to his enemies, for their campaign of vilification 'tipped the scales of justice so heavily in the Director's favour that a balanced verdict was well-nigh impossible'.¹¹

39 *Millbank Resurrection*, cartoon by Nicholas Mawbridge
for *Punch,* 1954

A meeting of the Trustees was held late at night on 8 February 1954 in the Pre-Raphaelite room at Admiral's House, Hampstead, the home of Sir Colin Anderson. It was a dramatic moment in the Tate's history, as they had met to decide on whether or not to sack the Director – watched over by Holman Hunt's *The Awakening Conscience* which hung on one wall. All the Trustees agreed that LeRoux should leave the Gallery, but on Rothenstein they were divided. Four of the Trustees felt it would be giving in to a disgraceful campaign to ask for his resignation. Yet all four also agreed that he was a poor leader, an inadequate organiser and administrator, and maladroit at staff relations. When one Trustee said it was unthinkable that Rothenstein should be dismissed by a divided Board, the others concurred. But as a result of this meeting, the entire Board agreed to attend the Gallery on Saturday, 13 February 1954 in order to interview as many members of staff as possible. In all they saw eleven staff, the interviews beginning at ten in the morning and lasting until nine at night. A conclusion was to be reached at a further special Board meeting, arranged for 18 February 1954, but before this took place five of the Trustees met informally in Hampstead and agreed that Lawrence Gowing, who was unable to be present on 18 February, should put in writing the 'half-fantastic suggestion', as he called it, which he had proposed as the kind of official letter Rothenstein should now receive. Though Rothenstein never saw it, this letter remains the most concise and damning assessment of his part in the affair.[12] What Proctor eventually wrote, in his position as Chairman, was severe, but lacked the pungency and particularity of Gowing's summary.

While Rothenstein was admonished, LeRoux learned that his employment had been terminated. As soon as this became known, several members of staff wrote a letter of protest, and further support for LeRoux came from the Lords Kinnaird, Harlech, Jowitt and Methuen, as well as Sutherland and Mahon. As a result, Le-

Roux was not sacked, but allowed to resign. He was also permitted to work out three months notice. Immediately on leaving, he went straight into the employment of Lord Beaverbrook, first in London, where in April 1955 he organised the *Daily Express Young Artists' Exhibition* and was convenor of the judges – Herbert Read, Anthony Blunt and Graham Sutherland. Afterwards he acted as buyer for Beaverbrook, who was establishing an art collection in his native Fredericton, in New Brunswick, Canada. In 1956 LeRoux resigned hurriedly, partly it seems for medical reasons. Later he joined Wildenstein's, and was on the point of being dismissed when he died suddenly, at the age of forty-seven. Despite his hale and hearty appearance, he had during much of his time at the Tate been an ill man, prone to blackouts. The suddenness of his death led to rumours that he had committed suicide, but the coroner's verdict at his inquest was 'coronary occlusion'.

Right up until the final weeks of the Tate Affair, LeRoux was behaving in a duplicitous manner, writing letters to Rothenstein that suggested he was trying to do all he could to improve the situation. Despite LeRoux's energy, competence and drive, there was something clumsy, wild and pathological about his vendetta against Rothenstein. Of all the many aspects of the affair, Rothenstein in retrospect admitted that he found LeRoux's personality and influence most baffling.[13] 'One thing however he did achieve for me,' wrote Sir Colin Anderson, 'he made me able, for ever more, to believe in Iago.'[14]

★   ★   ★

While LeRoux worked out his notice at the Tate, Henry Lamb, a former Trustee, called for an inquiry. This resulted in a report by the Tate Trustees, published by the Stationery Office on 11 March 1954. It admitted that at Board meetings no systematic procedure had been followed whereby a purchase was debited to a particular fund. This and other statements led to the decision 'to revive the custom … of issuing an annual report in which due publicity is given both to their purchasing policy and to the state of the funds which they administer'. At the previous month's Board meeting John Fremantle had asked his fellow Trustees to ignore the financial statement circulated with the agenda and to substitute for it the one laid before each Trustee on the table. Under the name of each fund, information was provided on the restrictions governing its use, its balance and commitments. The Board approved Fremantle's financial statement and resolved that from then on a statement of this kind should be incorporated into the minutes and circulated with the Agenda. It was also recognised that the problems presented by a Victorian system of files and registers was aggravated by the lack of an accountant at Millbank. An innovation was therefore agreed – the appointment of a Higher Executive Officer – and for the first time in its fifty-seven years of existence the Tate finally had its own accountant and Accounts Department.

LeRoux departed the Tate on 1 June 1954. A fortnight later Jane Ryder resigned. As she was by then a senior member of the Publications Department, her departure caused Mr Eric Fletcher, Labour MP for Islington East, to ask the Chancellor of the Exchequer to order another enquiry into the Tate's administration. R.A. Butler turned this down with the remark that the present Trustees enjoyed the full confidence of the government and the administration of the Gallery must be left to them.

In the aftermath of LeRoux's departure the Beaverbrook press went silent, making very probable Rothenstein's claim that Proctor told him Churchill had intervened and prevailed on Beaverbrook.[15] But further acrimony was stirred by the *New Statesman and Nation* which carried, on 28 August 1954, an article more venomous than any that had so far appeared. Titled 'The Tate Gallery Affair', it reopened all the earlier crises, criticisms and alleged scandals, and denounced the Ritson Report for having hushed up staff problems in order to maintain the prestige of the Gallery. Not until the appearance in October of the Tate Gallery Report for 1953–4, together with the *Review of the Years 1938–1953*, could it be properly answered.

Rothenstein's drafting of the Report disappointed Proctor: 'It seemed to me weak and equivocal in tone, ambiguous in phrasing, defunct in various important matters of fact and quite inadequate as an exposition of the major policies of the Gallery.'[16] Earlier that year, in March, after the publication of the Trustees' Report, Proctor had spent ninety minutes with Rothenstein at the Reform Club and told him frankly that he had no confidence in his ability to produce a tranquil gallery; and that he thought it best if after a year or two Rothenstein should quietly resign and seek a post in America. Rothenstein thought this a cruel and unjust suggestion.

The Report and the *Review* were published on 5 October 1954 and were well received. The most significant article to appear was that in the *Spectator* on 8 October 1954. Its title, 'The End of the Tate Affair', was also emblazoned on the cover of the magazine. It was a deliberate riposte to the *New Statesman and Nation* and ended with a call for an expression of confidence in the Director.

This was what Rothenstein and his wife now felt was urgently needed. Throughout this affair Elizabeth Rothenstein had never lost her belief in her husband's 'scrupulosity for justice'. Her very clear and determined view of Rothenstein's innocence and other people's guilt had never wavered. She had many supporters, for Rothenstein had a gift for making loyal friends, and, like his father, was kind and generous to artists. When later in October the National Gallery and Tate Gallery Bill (as the National Art Collections Bill was now called) reached the House of Commons on its second reading, the Rothensteins both attended, as did several members of Tate Gallery staff. The Bill was taken by the Financial Secretary, Henry Brooke, and debated on 29 October 1954. Brooke was repeatedly asked to express the government's confidence in the Director of the Tate. One Member of Parliament pointed out that as the Director was a civil servant and unable to speak for himself, the Financial Secretary now had an opportunity to put the record straight. Various tributes to Rothenstein came that afternoon from other sources; but Brooke refused to be drawn on the controversies that had raged over the Tate, nor would he express confidence in the Director. Instead he announced that it was better to let a period of silence fall over the Tate, in the hope that harmony would prevail. Rothenstein went home a deeply disappointed and bitter man, feeling that he was as much exposed to calumny as he had ever been.

The effect on Rothenstein of these years of persecution was mitigated by his Catholic faith and the constancy of his wife's support. But he had nevertheless suffered greatly and at one point, in February 1954, had been obliged to take leave on doctor's orders as he was in a condition of nervous exhaustion. In November, shortly after the debate in the House of Commons, he invited the new Assistant at the Contemporary Art Society, Pauline Vogelpoel, to accompany him to a preview of the Diaghilev exhibition at Forbes House. As he had earlier that evening dined at the French Embassy, Rothenstein was in evening dress. His guest was startled to hear, as they climbed the staircase at Forbes House, a man's voice mockingly referring to Rothenstein as 'that poor, persecuted man'. It was Douglas Cooper, who began to follow them around, provoking Rothenstein with ostentatiously loud, disparaging remarks. Others remonstrated with Cooper but he would not desist. At one point Pauline Vogelpoel turned away to talk to a friend, and when she looked back it was to see an extraordinary sight. The small, dapper Rothenstein, mindful of the months of misery that Cooper and others had caused him and members of his family, suddenly punched Cooper twice in the face with such force that Cooper was visibly stunned and his glasses flew off. Soon afterwards Rothenstein found his hand was being shaken with approval by a curator from Versailles, and over the next few days a sheaf of congratulatory letters and telegrams arrived. 'It was', Colin Anderson has written, 'a great surprise, not only to Cooper. We had none of us dreamt that John had it in him to do anything so refreshingly direct. We only knew him as a master of the oblique.'[17] Some dire reprisal was expected, but nothing followed – not even a claim for assault.

10

An Independent Tate

On 14 February 1955 the National Gallery and Tate Gallery Act came into operation and the Tate became legally separated from the National Gallery. From now on the Tate Trustees took full responsibility for the Tate collection. The chief advantage of this long-awaited event was financial independence: no longer was the Tate subordinate to the National Gallery's Accounting Officer, for the Tate Director took on this role.

During the lengthy discussions preceding this Act, the subject of greatest concern had been the division of the pictures. The two Directors, Rothenstein and Hendy, had drawn up lists of French and British paintings, but, at the wish of the Treasury, these had been abandoned in February 1953 and it was decided that those works of art in the Tate's care at the time of the passing of the Act would be vested in the Tate's Trustees. Certain transfers took place to ensure that the right pictures were in the right Gallery; and in addition the National Gallery Trustees sought to retain the ownership of fifty-eight British paintings (later reduced to twenty-seven) which would be physically in the Tate's possession on vesting day. Nevertheless, anxiety remained over the likelihood of future transfers or loans; and on 19 August 1954, after further negotiation, Dennis Proctor and Colin Anderson signed an agreement on behalf of the Tate Trustees: the Tate Trustees promised to transfer 'from time to time … such British pictures as the National Gallery Trustees may require for exhibitions', and in turn the National Gallery Trustees promised to relinquish any picture not needed for exhibition. Following advice from the Treasury Solicitor, the agreement was signed over a sixpence stamp and was legally binding, though it has been argued that its validity was nullified by the subsequent passing of the National Gallery and Tate Gallery Act.

This new Act acknowledged the close relationship between the two Galleries by making the provision that each Board should nominate one of its members to serve as a liaison member on the other. The Act also dealt with the issue of transfers, and upheld the need to secure 'that each picture is in that collection where it will be available and on view in the best context'. Throughout, the Act treated the two Galleries as equals, but its ambiguous criteria permitted the senior institution to maintain the upper hand when it came to requests for tranfers or loans. The Act did, however, establish a machinery for arbitration should a dispute arise. In such a situation, a committee was to be formed, composed of both Directors and two nominees from each institution, with a Chairman chosen by the Treasury.

An inherent anomaly remained: whereas the Tate housed the national collection of historic British art, the National Gallery had a right to the very best British pictures. The older institution had suffered badly during the war, and by 1954 still had nine of its galleries out of use. In 1947 it had collaborated with the Tate and the Victoria & Albert Museum on the *Hogarth – Constable – Turner* exhibition, which, shown at the Tate, had proved very popular. In 1949, when the Tate fully reopened, the National Gallery had allowed most of its British paintings to be sent to Millbank. In the National Gallery's view, however, this was only a temporary measure. It did not want to regain as many British paintings as it had in 1939, but was certain of its right to withdraw the best.

Now the biggest gallery in the Commonwealth, and with a collection almost twice the size of that of the National Gallery, the Tate no longer wished to be regarded as merely a supply collection for the older institution; and it resented the suggestion that it was inferior to the National Gallery. Yet it was still vulnerable to raids on its collection, not only of British art but also of late nineteenth-century French painting. Moreover, a certain ambiguity hovered over the purchasing boundary between the two Galleries, the Tate clinging, with justification, to its interest in French Post-Impressionism. What was wrong with this situation was not the overlapping of interests, but the lack of principle. If the National Gallery so desired, it could assert its identity as 'a collection of pictures of established work or significance' (National Gallery and Tate Gallery Act) and demand pictures that broke up the Tate's carefully gathered collection.

The untidiness of this arrangement affected the Publications Department. When transfers to the National Gallery took place, the Tate not only lost valuable revenue through the loss of best-selling postcards and Christmas cards, but the usefulness of catalogues, which had often taken many years to produce, was immediately impaired. A further argument against the transfer of French Impressionist and Post-Impressionist paintings was that both movements were so sparsely represented in the national collections that they suffered badly when split between two institutions. This was Rothenstein's argument in 1955 when the National Gallery, which now opened all but two of its rooms, attempted to improve its holding in late nineteenth-century French art. Now, and in years to come, fairly persistent negotiations regarding transfers went on in various places, over dinner parties or at the Athenaeum, and at least one agreement was reached in the back of a taxi. At another moment the National Gallery lost patience and simply sent round to Millbank a removal van. Such was the way in which this aspect of arts policy was conducted.

Under the terms of Courtauld's deed of gift, French paintings bought with money from his fund were destined ultimately for the National Gallery. When Douglas Cooper published *The Courtauld Collection: A Catalogue and Introduction* in 1954, he quoted Courtauld's desire 'to see the French Impressionists and their immediate followers exhibited as the true heirs of the Old Masters and to break down the artificial barrier between the old and modern'. What made the Tate additionally vulnerable was the understanding that the French paintings on loan to the Tate and the National from Courtauld's personal collection, now under the management of the Home House Trustees, would eventually be withdrawn and given to London University when the Courtauld Institute Galleries opened.

Rothenstein and his Trustees had put up a hard fight, but nevertheless lost 139 foreign paintings to the National Gallery between 1945 and 1959. Then suddenly, in January 1960, following the withdrawal of the Home House pictures to London University and a recent agreement which sent half of the Hugh Lane pictures on loan to Dublin for the first time, Rothenstein informed Hendy that his Trustees had decided to make available for transfer to the National Gallery thirty-four Impressionist paintings. As the National Gallery's Reconstruction Scheme was not then complete, nothing was resolved until the next year, when the National Gallery argued that in order to present a balanced representation of nineteenth-century French painting, they needed to ask for a further seventeen Post-Impressionist pictures, making a total of fifty-one transfers. The Tate responded with a passionate protest: contemporary work would no longer be seen in the context of work by recognised founders of modern art; the modern collection was still too weak to stand on its own and needed a stiffening of great Post-Impressionist pictures. These and other arguments were accepted, and in his lengthy reply John Witt, Chairman of the National Gallery Trustees, stated that thirty-five of the fifty-one pictures originally requested should remain with the Tate. In addition, though the Courtauld Fund pictures were now to be united at Trafalgar Square, the National Gallery would lend van Gogh's *Chair and Pipe*, to add to the single van Gogh that remained in the Tate's collection. It was a rare moment of unanimity, despite the fact that the Tate now lost Seurat's *Bathers, Asnières*, which Kenneth Clark had tried to obtain for the National in the late 1930s without success. Such was the accord between the Tate and the National Gallery in 1961 that they issued a joint press release, outlining their differing responsibilities with regard to acquisitions. Yet behind this co-operation lay a history of resentment and frustration. The following year the Tate's Publications Manager drew up a claim for compensation from the National Gallery, resulting from the recent transfer of Impressionist and Post-Impressionist paintings.

In 1951 the Tate had offered to relinquish its right to acquire prints, in favour of the British Museum and Victoria & Albert Museum. This seems to have been part of a tidying-up exercise, for after two years of intermittent discussion, the arrangement broke down: the Tate's offer to transfer all its prints and lithographs was rejected by the British Museum, which only wanted to accept a proportion. The steady increase in size of the Tate's collection was beginning to cause problems; shortage of space – particularly office space – impelled the Chairman, Dennis Proctor, to write in 1955 to the Ministry of Works about the possibility of a further extension. But though the Tate now had control over its financial affairs, it did not have control over its building. No further extension on the Millbank site, the Ministry replied, would be considered within the next ten years. The Contemporary Art Society had office space in the Tate, and that was therefore, it was agreed, reason to suppose that this could be used for Tate staff.

All the adverse press attention given to the Tate between 1952 and 1954 had obscured the fact that this was also an exciting period in its history. Much benefit had accrued through acquisitions, gifts and bequests. Mrs Benson, who before the war had given £2,000 which helped to set up the Publications Department, was discovered by Norman Reid to be living in the Grand Hotel in Eastbourne. He arranged to visit her and continued to do so at intervals. When in 1954 her husband died, Mrs Benson announced that she was making a £30,000 bequest to the Tate. (She died in 1971 and the bequest that the Tate received in 1972 had risen to £50,000.) Though Mrs Benson had stipulated that two watercolours by her late husband, A.H. Benson, should be permanently on view, there were no other restrictions on the use of the gift, which was, at this time, the largest unrestricted gift that the Tate had so far been promised or received.

The Gallery also continued to run a lively and varied exhibition programme, thanks to the Arts Council, and in particular to Philip James and Gabriel White, who used the Tate as the Arts Council's major London venue until the Hayward Gallery was built. Each year a major Arts Council exhibition was shown first at the Edinburgh Festival and then at the Tate, and in this way Degas, Renoir and Cézanne had come to Millbank. After the showing of the Pleydell-Bouverie collection in 1954, its owner, Mrs A.E. Pleydell-Bouverie, was so satisfied with the way it had been exhibited that she offered to bequeath the Tate six paintings – four of the best and two minor works – and left it to the Director to choose. In this way Cézanne's *The Avenue at the Jas de Bouffan* entered the collection after her death in 1968. In 1954 the Tate also accepted from the executors of Rosa Schapire a portrait of her and a head in wood by Schmidt-Rottluff, together with another painting by him the following year. This same year the Tate was successful in obtaining at auction, for 6,700 guineas, Matisse's *André Derain*.[1] Douglas Cooper had suggested its acquisition. He had also advised Proctor to raise a subscription by writing to private individuals and had himself donated £250. Only a very small part of the price was raised in this way, but further contributions came from the National Art Collections Fund, the Contemporary Art Society and the Knapping Fund.

One surprising development in the Tate Affair had been the friendship which Proctor suddenly extended to Cooper. It had enabled him to ask Cooper to call off the vendetta against Rothenstein, and Cooper had subsequently urged Denys Sutton and Benedict Nicolson to join him in a 'campaign of silence'. Proctor himself was to remain Chairman of the Trustees for another five years, and during that time he frequently consulted Cooper over purchases. There was good reason for this, as Cooper – a brilliant art scholar if an irresponsible journalist – was the foremost authority in his field, and planned, selected or procured numerous exhibitions. In 1957 he was elected the Oxford University Slade Professor. But he also occupied a role not dissimilar to that which Peter Fuller later filled: that of a scourgeful, watchful, outspoken critic, given to intemperate abuse. In appearance, as Bryan Robertson has said, he looked 'like something half way between Mae West and the Baron de Charlus'[2]; and in 1956, when he arrived at the Tate for the Arts Council Braque exhibition, for which he had written the catalogue introduction, he sported a green, cream and fawn dogtooth check to match the Tate's new colour scheme. But he had not forgotten his vendetta against Rothenstein; on the rare occasions when their paths crossed at the Tate he made rude gestures or remarks in Rothenstein's presence and had to be reprimanded and sometimes removed. His friend John Richardson explained to the lawyer Anthony Lousada: 'I think he is quite unbalanced in his feelings about Rothenstein, who has become a lightning conductor for the enormous resources of aggression that he is constantly generating.'[3] This unbalanced behaviour did not prevent Cooper from exercising, mostly through letters penned in green ink, an important influence on the Tate from his Château de Castille, where he held annual parties timed to coincide with the Easter bullfight at Arles.

It must have been galling for Rothenstein to discover at Board meetings that Cooper had either secured a loan for the Tate or had been putting Proctor in touch with dealers and collectors. Cooper drew the Tate's attention to the Braques on show at the Galerie Maeght in 1957, and when this gallery offered to sell to the Tate Braque's *Reclining Woman* (1930–52), together with Léger's *Two Women Holding Flowers*, for thirty-seven million francs, it was Cooper who bargained them down two million francs. The Trustees were divided over the Braque, which although a large, ambitious work, was a curious throwback to the Cubist period. However, as the Trustees were determined on filling gaps in the foreign collection, they decided to ask the Treasury for a special grant of £40,000 in connection with this Braque and the Léger, together with Picasso's *Goat's Skull, Bottle and Candle* and a painting by Nicolas de Stael. In recent years a special grant of £7,500 had made possible the acquisition of Constable's *Old Chain Pier, Brighton* in 1950, and though the £5,500 requested for Matisse's four bas-reliefs, *Backs*, had been turned down in 1955, an increase in the Grant-in-Aid had been agreed over two years which made possible this purchase. But in 1957, on seeing photographs of the Braque, Picasso, Léger and de Stael, the Chancellor Sir Alexander Johnston refused to ask the House of Commons for a special purchase grant for such 'controversial' work.

The Trustee and company chairman, Colonel (later Sir) Robert Adeane, immediately offered to buy the £24,000 Braque and to give the Tate the option to purchase it from him at a future date for the price he had paid for it. This scheme was subject only to Adeane's liking the picture as much as he expected when he saw it for himself. Arrangements were made for him to travel to Paris with Rothenstein. 'I know it was a risk sending the Director over to Paris with him,' Proctor wrote to Cooper, 'but it was a risk I had to take. I had to bring the Director into the transaction somehow and I thought that, after the tremendous build-up at our two Board meetings in favour of the Braque, it would be impossible for him to deflect the Board from its course.'[4] As it turned out, both Adeane and Rothenstein decided against the Braque, but fell in love with the Léger, and it was this picture which Adeane, in his generosity,[5] bought, on the understanding that the Trustees could buy it from him over the next twelve months at cost price. 'I must pay a tribute for this to the Director,' Proctor told Cooper, 'who had previously led the opposition to my claims for a Léger.'[6]

If, since the Tate Affair, the balance of power had shifted more towards the Trustees, Rothenstein remained a potent figurehead – a small, dapper, knowledgeable, vital and mildly notorious figure. Gradually, during the late 1950s, owing partly to the contribution made by the Arts Council exhibitions and the elegant previews mounted by the Contemporary Art Society in the Sculpture Hall, the Tate's image changed; it was to become, in Alexander Dunluce's memory, 'a showroom, a talking shop … a social whirlpool of the artistic world. It was an era of exuberance and John enjoyed being ringmaster.'[7] But this took time to achieve. When Corinne Bellow had been appointed Rothenstein's Personal Assistant in May 1954, she had initially found the Tate a puzzling and slightly sinister place. She was astonished by the number of dogs, both small and large, brought in by members of staff and allowed to wander in and out of offices, or, like Pauline Vogelpoel's pug, put out of a basement window on a long lead. A certain lack of trust prevailed and Corinne noticed that Rothenstein insisted on answering all press calls himself. It took some months before Rothenstein placed his trust in her. When he did so, his entire manner changed.

The Gallery was gradually strengthened by an increase in staff. In 1954 Ronald Alley had been promoted to Assistant Keeper Grade I and Dennis Farr appointed Assistant Keeper Grade II. The following year Martin Butlin joined the curatorial staff and was soon singled out by Rothenstein for the task of cataloguing the William Blake collection. He subsequently worked with Rothenstein on a book on Turner's watercolours. Meanwhile, Mary Chamot, who was associated primarily with British art, published a concise catalogue of the British School in 1953. There was generally an increase in the sophistication of scholarship, and when Ronald Alley published a new *Modern Foreign School Catalogue* in 1959 it was received with widespread respect.

Still more of a landmark, given the greater size of the collection, was the catalogue of modern British paintings, drawings and sculpture produced by Chamot, Farr and Butlin in 1964. It drew on many interviews with living artists, some of whom had been entertained by Mary Chamot – for she dispensed tea from a samovar in her office and fascinating stories to all whom she came across in the course of her work. A White Russian, she recalled that when the Kirov Theatre changed the plush on the seats, her entire family wore new outfits in keeping with the new colour. Having lived through the Russian Revolution and worked for the Allied Control Commission in Vienna, she was forthright in her convictions and manner and also an exceptionally good linguist. She also had the Slav ability to ignore requests to do things she did not wish to do, and was often in conflict with Rothenstein as a result.

Two floors down, in the former Boardroom, which boasted the only open fire in the building, Norman Reid ran the administration, with the dedicated assistance of Judith Cloake. Since June 1954 Reid had been Deputy Director, a role that gave him complete responsibility for the internal workings of the Tate, in addition to deputising for the Director when he was away. In 1954 Research Days had been introduced – the Assistant Keepers and Director being allowed one a week – as was the practice at the National Gallery. This enabled Rothenstein to disappear to Oxfordshire on Thursday evenings, in gentlemanly fashion, in order to have a long weekend in which to write. Reid, on the other hand, belonged to a different and more professional generation of museum curators. He was, as Rothenstein observed in a letter to Proctor, 'popular with the staff and has a very good touch with them, although neither the time nor inclination for over-intimacy'.[8] This capacity to make links with people yet remain his own man may explain why Reid had managed to survive the Tate troubles without being drawn into unequivocal support of any party. He had, like other staff, been interviewed by the Trustees during the course of their all-day session at the Tate on 18 February 1954, when their aim was primarily to assess Rothenstein and his effect on the staff. Sir Colin Anderson made some acute notes on Rothenstein's character, also on Reid's strengths and weaknesses, noting his candour, honesty and apparent lack of ambition among other things, but concluding that he was, 'all the same, Gold all through'.[9]

★   ★   ★

Shortly before the tenth anniversary of Rex Whistler's death, the Board had authorised the spending of £720 (the actual cost rose to £1,200) on an edition of 50,000 brochures illustrating the murals he had painted for the Refreshment Room (now the Restaurant). These were illustrated in their entirety alongside an account of the story they told. A further £200 was spent on a booklet containing the full story by Edith Olivier, 'In Pursuit of Rare Meats', which had been written as a narrative to the murals. In addition a plaque had been put up with wording by Sir Osbert Sitwell:

> This room, which was painted by Rex Whistler, is dedicated to his memory; that of an artist multifarious in aim and accomplishment who excelled in the several arts he practised, and of a man of delightful and endearing personality. He was born in Eltham, on June 24th, 1905 and died fighting for his country at Demouville, in Normandy on July 18th, 1944.

The delicacy of these sentiments, though permanently associated with the Restaurant, did not always match the service it provided. In May 1950 the Board had approved the change to self-service catering, in order to effect staff economies. But in the months that followed this system evoked such criticism that in 1951 a change of staff was recommended and the existing contract was terminated. Mrs Tondi Adams took over and made such improvements that the Restaurant became popular with people from all walks of life. It also became a regular lunching and trysting place for MPs. At one period the distinguished MP for Coventry, Maurice Edelman, was seen lunching almost daily at the Tate with one or another of his lady friends, one of whom would spend every lunchtime in a romantically tearful state. Here Sir John Rothenstein would entertain Augustus John, Jacob Epstein, Stanley Spencer, Matthew Smith and other artists. On the third Thursday of every month a table would be reserved for those Trustees wishing to lunch before the Board meeting.

Running a restaurant on lines that were not entirely commercial proved difficult, and by 1954 Mrs Adams was full of complaints. Owing to the terms of her contract, the meals her staff served and the prices charged were controlled by the Trustees and she had little room to manoeuvre. Unlike commercial restaurants, she had to remain open during hours when custom was slight. Moreover, the lighting and ventilation were inadequate and that year her chef resigned on the grounds that the kitchen conditions made his work impossible. It further upset her and her staff that outside caterers were brought in whenever a banquet or special entertainment took place. The Tate Trustees took a percentage of Mrs Adams's gross profits, whereas, she argued, a much fairer agreement would be if they took a percentage of net profits, after she had deducted wages and overheads. Despite these difficulties Mrs Adams – or Tondi Barr, as she became known, for she married three times – reigned successfully over this nether region. Some people came to the Restaurant in order to have a chat with her, for she was a well-dressed, strikingly good-looking woman with dark hair. She had various friends in the theatre world – among them Fenella Fielding – and they too formed part of her clientele.

Inevitably the Restaurant had to respond to the changing social climate and by 1960 it was once again self-service. By then it was also apparent that Rex Whistler's murals required cleaning and restoration. The lower part of the murals suffered badly during self-service periods and eventually plate-glass protection was put in place. Through subsequent changes of management, the Restaurant veered an uneasy course, its standards at times deteriorating and at others becoming almost too elitist. However, it was neither the food, nor the service, that angered the American Richard L. York in 1970, but the 'racialist' character of the murals, for he pointed to the section in which, as the story describes, Gilabia 'captures a little Negro boy who proved a useful acquisition to the party'. This, York argued, should have no place in a public restaurant. After an altercation with the Information Department which only angered York further, Norman Reid replied:

> I am afraid … no custodian of works of art can entertain the proposition
> that those works of art in his care should be censored, let alone destroyed,
> because they are no longer fully in accord with the moral principles that
> had developed since they were created. In addition, I think it only requires
> a small amount of emotional detachment to see these so-called offensive
> works as what they are, the reflection of a bygone and less happy age. In
> other words, tolerance should be extended even to works of art.[10]

There are many ways in which works of art need protection, and one of the Tate's concerns remained the close proximity of the river. Although the river wall at Millbank had been rebuilt and strengthened by the London County Council after the 1928 flood, the LCC was not convinced that the existing structure was satisfactory, and it pressed Westminster City Council to rebuild the entire parapet

40 Paintings being moved from the lower ground floors
as a protection against flooding, 1953

at a different height. This proposal was abandoned when the recession set in, and
the Tate continued to be at risk during exceptionally high tides. One night in February 1953 Reid received a warning of high water which would reach its peak at
3.07 am. He and his wife, together with Denis Matthews, the Secretary of the Contemporary Art Society, and the night staff at the Tate cleared 250 paintings from
seven of the lower galleries before danger hour arrived and passed without
mishap. The continuation of occasional flood warnings led eventually to the tank-
ing of the lower galleries in 1968–9 and the raising of the Embankment wall; but
it was not until the completion of the Thames Barrier in 1982 that the likelihood
of flooding was finally removed.

The physical care of any art collection is of primary importance, and when Norman Reid joined the staff in 1946, his training as a painter led him to take a particular interest in the condition of the collection. He discovered that straightforward
repairs and cleaning were done by John Lee, a master gilder – also a talented and
cautious craftsman – but that anything requiring more complex attention was
sent out to private restorers. During the war some of the Tate's pictures had been
cleaned by Helmut Ruhemann, Head of the National Gallery's Conservation
Department, from whom John Lee had received some instruction.

The Trustees gave Reid the responsibility of keeping a check on those paintings,
which were entrusted to four of the most prominent private restorers. It soon
became clear to Reid that this work should be done within the Gallery so that it
could be supervised more effectively, and to enable discussion with other specialist curators. In addition, though pictures were periodically examined for visible
signs of deterioration, these sporadic checks left unaltered an urgent need for a
systematic survey of all the paintings in the Tate collection, in order to detect

more precisely, and at an early stage, the causes and extent of their deterioration, so that preventative treatment could be applied.

This development became possible after Stefan Slabczynski came to see Reid in the hope of getting more work. Slabczynski had studied painting at the the Academy of Fine Art at Cracow, history of art at the University of Montpellier, and, after the war, the restoration of pictures at the Courtauld Institute of Art. He was then working as a freelance restorer for the National Maritime Museum and the National Gallery.

The Tate Trustees approved the proposal to test his ability on two pictures, the work to be done at the Tate. He proved to be a first-class restorer and as he was looking for a permanent post, Reid began negotiations with the Treasury. There was a long battle about the grading of the post but in the end the Treasury agreed that it should be for a Chief Restorer.

As soon as Slabczynski was appointed he began designing much of the technical equipment needed, including a vacuum hot-table which he used in wax-relining of paintings.[11] In 1955 he began training two craftsmen in some of the primary techniques of conservation, so that they could assist him with the huge backlog of pictures requiring attention and so that he could concentrate on processes that required specialist skills. He also instituted the systematic keeping of conservation records. The Treasury approved the appointment of a Restorer in 1956 and, two years later, an Assistant Restorer. In 1957 Slabczynski – whose concept of conservation involved the art historian, the scientist and scientific instruments – went on a tour of conservation departments on the Continent and afterwards wrote a report. Although certain places, notably the Louvre, were much better equipped – with laboratories that had x-ray apparatus, microscopes and facilities for making chemical analysis – he was confident that the Tate, which had access to the scientific laboratories at the Courtauld Institute, was 'not behind but, in some respects, in advance' of other places.[12] He was referring especially to the method of wax-relining under vacuum pressure in which he took great pride and was undoubtedly one of the pioneers. His electrically heated table, combined with the infra-red heating unit for the wax impregnation of panels and for 'marouflage' (the sticking down of a canvas onto a rigid support), designed and built by himself and his men and due to be installed in August 1957, would, he claimed 'constitute one of the finest relining equipments in existence'.[13]

Where the Tate's Conservation Department was deficient, Slabczynski pointed out, was in the absence of in-house photography – for he was alert to the importance of photography for conservation records – and in the need for larger and lighter accommodation. The second of these two needs was rectified in March the following year when his department was moved into a group of three rooms in the basement which received light from a courtyard in the north-west quadrant. As well as the workshop that housed all his equipment, there was a special varnishing room with temperature and ventilation control and a large carpenter's workshop for making and repairing frames, stretchers and panels. In July 1958 the Conservation Department was officially opened and visited by the press and delegates from the Museums' Association International Conference. Slabczynski, a respected figure within his profession, became a member of the International Council of Museums in 1962 and from then on attended that institution's international conferences as a representative of the Tate in the field of conservation. Slabczynski also proved to be an outstanding organiser and teacher whose contribution to the re-emergence of the Tate Gallery cannot be overestimated.

A rapid provisional review of the majority of old paintings in the Gallery's possession in 1956 had revealed that out of 1,800 some 200 were in need of urgent repair. Among these were 105 Turners, many of which had recently been transferred from the store rooms of the National Gallery where they had been since 1851. In November 1956 the Chief Restorer's report estimated that it would take the existing staff approximately five years to complete the restoration of these Turners. The Conservation Committee agreed that the Turners should be given priority, and by 1964 some 159 Turners had been treated – sixty-two of which had been relined, most cleaned, then retouched and varnished. These included some of Turner's unfinished paintings and oil studies on millboard which then went on view, having never before been available for exhibition to the public. In addition, 193 paintings by other artists had been restored, of which fifty-three had been relined. By the time Slabczynski retired he had himself restored some 208 Turners, and he told a reporter: 'In my twenty years here I have grown to know and love Turner – show me ten square inches of any canvas and I'll show you whether it is a Turner. I know every brushmark, every type of pigment [that he] ever used.'[14]

If Slabczynski ever hoped to reach the end of his Forth Bridge, he was rapidly disillusioned by his department's ever-increasing involvement with the examination of paintings in connection with loans and exhibitions. This work increased year by year, and by the 1960s frequently interrupted, and delayed completion of, the restoration work on paintings in long-term conservation programmes. Slabczynski made several protests, causing the Trustees periodically to review their loans policy.

At the time of the official opening of the Conservation Department, Rothenstein had paid tribute not only to the organising ability, skill and inventiveness of his Chief Restorer but also to Norman Reid who had proposed this new venture and been responsible for seeing it through all the stages of its development.[15] There were many improvements and alterations that Reid steered through committees and brought to fruition. The Sculpture Hall, for instance, had long been recognised as unsympathetic to many displays. Henry Moore had suggested at the March 1954 Board meeting that some kind of paint could be applied that would not alter the character and texture of the stone cladding, but would change its colour. Lady Duveen gave her consent to this idea, but the Ministry of Works opposed it on the grounds that if the paint ever had to be removed it would be a costly and laborious job. Not until 1962, by which time internal screens and rooms within rooms were becoming a fashionable part of museum display, was agree-

41 John Rothenstein by the new staircase, c.1959–64

ment obtained to line the Sculpture Hall so that paintings could be hung on its walls. Equally slow to arrive – for it was initially asked for in 1953, promised in 1958 and finally built in 1962 – was the staircase in one gallery in the Turner wing which made circulation through the lower galleries possible, as previously the lower-ground floor could only be reached by a stair at the far end of the building. This new staircase disrupted the space in the gallery and was removed in 1990 because it made looking at certain pictures awkward, as can be seen in the above photograph of Sir John Rothenstein, taken towards the end of his directorship.

★   ★   ★

In 1957, when the Trustees considered buying Braque's *Reclining Woman*, the request for a special grant of £40,000 for this and three other pictures brought home to the Treasury the sort of prices the Tate Gallery would from now on have to pay in order to fill the gaps in its Modern Collection. The cost of the Braque alone (£24,000) was more than three times the value of the purchase grant.

This same year the economist and Tate Trustee, Lord Robbins, wrote to Douglas Cooper: 'I think that the drumfire of propaganda in the last three years has begun to make an impact on the Treasury attitude.'[16] He was proved right in 1959 when the Tate Gallery's annual purchase grant was raised from £7,500 to £40,000. However, neither this year, nor in 1960, did the Chancellor of the Exchequer grant the Tate Trustees' request for a lump sum of £100,000 to help fill the major gaps in the Tate's collections. These were becoming more and more difficult to fill because, in addition to the world-wide boom in the art market, the number of modern art collections, both private and public, was on the increase. The Trustees often faced agonising decisions, as they tried to assess the need for one work of art against a possible commitment to another in the months ahead. In May 1957 the Tate declined Brancusi's *Fish*, offered by H.S. Ede for £7,000, in order that priority could be given to Henry Moore's *King and Queen*, bought the following year with help from the newly founded Friends of the Tate Gallery.[17] Committee-buying also proved cumbersome: whereas some organisations had delegated their purchasing powers to one or two individuals who could make a decision on the spot, the Tate often had to wait several days or three weeks before reaching a decision. Discretionary purchasing power was given to the Director, but on a very small scale: in 1963 Rothenstein could spend £200 without the authorisation of the Trustees and £500 with the agreement of two Trustees.

The Trustees continued to apply for special grants in connection with specific works and in this way acquired an additional £7,500 towards the purchase of Stubbs's *Mares and Foals in a Landscape* in 1959, and £16,000 towards the purchase of Matisse's *Standing Nude* in 1960. But the problem with special grants was that aesthetic considerations became blurred by politics; for if the Chancellor thought the work of art 'controversial' he was reluctant to take the request for a special grant to Parliament.

A way forward, in some instances, was made possible by the acceptance of compromise. After the Treasury refused to give a special grant for a major Cubist painting, Braque's *Bottle and Fish*, in 1961, the Tate Trustees renewed their appeal and the Chancellor agreed to advance £19,000 from the following year's Grant-in-Aid to make this purchase possible. The same was done a year later, when the Trustees wanted to buy the papier collé brought to their attention by Roland Penrose, Matisse's *The Snail*. The treasury turned down a request for a Special Grant but authorised the Tate to spend £10,000 of the next year's grant. This was matched by the Friends of the Tate Gallery and the remaining £3,000 was provided out of the Gallery's own funds. But as a result, for two years running, the Tate started its financial year with depleted funds.

A need to look beyond the government for help with purchasing had led to the founding of the Friends of the Tate Gallery. This scheme had first been mooted in 1956 and came into being in 1958 under the Chairmanship of Colonel Robert Adeane (of whom Sir Colin Anderson had said when Adeane was first appointed to the Board, 'I think we've got room for one buccaneer').[18] His Midas touch was guided by the solicitor Anthony Lousada, who sat on the council of the Royal College of Art, drew up the Friends of the Tate Gallery charter and became its first Treasurer. Among the first patrons of the Friends were Queen Elizabeth the Queen Mother and Associated Rediffusion, for the scheme attracted both private and corporate members. Its main aim was to raise money to make up the deficiencies in the government's purchase grant, which in 1958 still stood at £7,500. 'A scheme to alleviate the economic difficulties of the Tate Gallery was launched informally at the Tate last night,' announced *The Times* on 23 April 1958. Within a year the Friends had raised £18,775, which proved vitally important in helping the Tate to achieve certain purchases. On 4 February 1959 Adeane (who two years later was knighted) ceremoniously handed over to the Tate Trustees, as

42 Henri Matisse, *The Snail*, 1953

represented by Sir Colin Anderson, the Friends' first purchases, among them Henry Moore's *King and Queen* and paintings by Constant Permeke, Robert Delaunay and William Roberts. The press gave the event a very favourable reception and the Friends continued to play a crucial role in the growth of the Tate collection. Between 1958 and 1963 they contributed over £85,000 towards the acquisition of thirty-seven works of art. Among these were some major purchases, notably Matisse's *The Snail* and Stanley Spencer's *Swan Upping at Cookham*.

The Friends also received some remarkable gifts, including £21,000 from an honorary American Friend, the food manufacturer Henry J. Heinz, a portion of which later enabled the Tate to purchase its first two Jackson Pollocks in 1960 and 1961. With the prospect of further gifts of this kind, Rothenstein and Adeane went to New York in order to set up an office for American Friends of the Tate Gallery. Soon afterwards the Kennedy administration brought in a law that said no more offshore charities were allowed to register. This meant that the office which had been established in New York, and the money collected by it, were left in limbo.

The situation was to be resolved as a result of Norman Reid's visit to America in 1959. He visited principal art galleries and dealers in New York, Montreal, Boston, Washington and Chicago. Even more importantly for the Tate, he met Roy Neuberger, then President and Director of the American Federation of Arts, who became a personal friend. As a result, American Friends wanting to offset a 'tax situation' by making a donation, were able to give to the Tate through the American Federation of Arts. In this way the Tate received a significant part of its collection of American art.

Officially established in New York on 29 March 1960, the American Friends, whose Honorary President was John Hay Whitney, then American Ambassador in London, was a timely development. Not only did America at this time set the model for an expanding industrial economy, but it was also culturally in the ascendant. Interest in American art had been growing in London as a result of Bryan Robertson's pioneering exhibition programme at the Whitechapel and two epoch-making shows at the Tate: *Modern Art in the United States* in 1956 and *The New American Painting* in 1959, both of which had been organised by the International Council of the Museum of Modern Art, New York. In the wake of these shows young artists in England began looking to New York rather than Paris as a source of innovation in art. Awareness of this sent the Assistant Keeper Ronald Alley, by means of a Ford grant, on an exhaustive study tour of American galleries and museums in 1960. It also opened the Tate's doors to American art. One of the earliest gifts via the American Friends was Louise Nevelson's *Black Wall*.

Given these developments, Rothenstein's final years at the Tate should again have been a halcyon period. He abandoned the flat in the Tate basement and made a pied-à-terre for himself in a small Chelsea house. This move may have been caused by the upgrading of his job, for his responsibilities had been more precisely defined as a result of a comprehensive review of galleries and museums in 1959. Previously he had been called Director and Keeper, and as a result had been paid on a Keepership level. But now he was put on a par with other Directors of national museums, though not paid as much.

During these last years he presided over certain improvements to the Gallery. As well as the new staircase in the Turner wing, the lower galleries were redesigned, with screens which obscured radiators and projected out into the room, making small bays down one side. Venetian blinds were fitted over the windows so that light from outside was reflected up on the ceiling, the lighting of the galleries as a whole being a mixture of daylight and fluorescent. The decoration, lighting and re-equipment of these rooms was undertaken by the Ministry of Works, in liaison with Norman Reid, who also oversaw the improvements to the Tate's two stores. These introduced temperature and humidity control as well as sliding screens.

Rothenstein was relieved of much responsibility by Reid's quiet and effective administration and by Corinne Bellow, his personal assistant, whom he praised in his autobiography for her 'organising capacity, her sense of proportion, her benevolent, reassuring presence'.[19] The paranoia which LeRoux had stimulated in Rothenstein gave way to respect and trust. At the January 1960 Board meeting Rothenstein expressed extreme satisfaction with the work of his curatorial staff. Of Mary Chamot, he said that 'he doubted whether there was a more accomplished linguist than she on the staff of any national museum'. He praised, too, the work done by Slabczynski, with his assistants Percy Williams and John Bull, who were joined in 1964 by Alexander Dunluce. The last appointment especially pleased Rothenstein, as his daughter Lucy, who had trained as a restorer, had for a period worked in partnership with Dunluce.

Rothenstein remained very much the public figure with whom the Gallery was identified. ('He was Mr Tate,' Alexander Dunluce recalls.)[20] He presided over memorable exhibitions, among them *Stanley Spencer* (1955), *Wyndham Lewis and Vorticism* (1956), which drew from the artist William Roberts three pamphlets angrily protesting at Lewis's interpretation of Vorticism, and a major Picasso show (1960) arranged by the Arts Council, to which the artist himself made generous loans. These and other exhibitions proved the occasion for grand parties and the customary display of jewels. But perhaps Rothenstein's proudest moment came when his daughter married in 1959, and a nuptial mass at Westminster Cathedral was followed by a reception at the Tate for some six hundred guests.

In his role as Director, Rothenstein made a visit to Paris in March 1959 in the company of Anthony Lousada. He attended principal exhibitions in private and public galleries, called on Giacometti, Max Ernst and S.W. Hayter in their studios, and paid a special visit to Frantizek Kupka's widow, as a result of which the Tate obtained *The Waterfall* – an uncharacteristic early work by a pioneer of abstract art. Nevertheless, he was congratulated warmly by the Trustees on his return for having secured options on so many outstanding works, especially those by artists on the Trustees' 'A' Priority List. But there was another Board meeting at which Rothenstein failed to present any potential purchases, and the Chairman ordered the Trustees to disperse in taxis to various West End galleries and to reconvene later that afternoon in order to report on what they had seen. Rothenstein was further humiliated by the Trustees' tendency to seize the artistic initiative and to arrange for works of art to be sent to the Tate as potential purchases. Not only was this embarrassing, because the advice of the Director and his staff had not been sought, but the dealer was often angered when the work was rejected and had to be returned. Looking back on this period, Lawrence Gowing remarked that the Trustees operated like 'a dozen directors', romping off in all directions, each with ideas of his own.[21]

In his arrangement of the Gallery Rothenstein had confined foreign art to the lower galleries, for he wanted 'to show the development of the national school from the time of the Tudors to the present day with such regard to chronology, logic and proportion as to make it intelligible to a perceptive visitor without special knowledge of painting'.[22] He was noticeably less interested in certain aspects of contemporary art. In Paris in 1959, he viewed a Jean Dubuffet exhibition in the company of his brother, Michael Rothenstein, and his second wife, who was very aware, despite the elaborate courtesy with which they were received by the

43 Piet Mondrian, *Composition with Red, Yellow and Blue*, c.1937–42

gallery owners, that John Rothenstein disliked this artist's work. Nor did his negative attitude towards abstract art, which he voiced freely after leaving the Tate,[23]
encourage purchasing in this field. Moholy-Nagy's widow returned to the Tate in
1955, offering two of her late husband's pictures for 200 guineas and a third for 125
guineas. The Trustees declined all three. In 1962 the opportunity to acquire a
Mondrian from the Galerie Beyeler in Basle was turned down owing to financial
difficulties; and the following year, a 1920 Mondrian, offered by Marlborough Fine
Art for £15,000, was also turned down on the grounds that the Trustees were concentrating their attention on a different period of this artist's work. They perhaps
already had in mind *Composition with Red, Yellow and Blue*, which in 1964 became
the first Mondrian to enter the Tate.

Rothenstein's affection for and loyalty to the Tate remained steadfast and is evident in his *Brief History of the Tate Gallery*, published as part of the Pitkin 'Pride of
Britain' series in 1958. He also wrote another book on the Tate Gallery for Thames

& Hudson, providing not only an introduction for the sixty-eight tipped-in colour plates but also accompanying notes. Two years before, he had published the second volume of essays in his series, *Modern English Painters*, which, like other books of his, testifies to his capacity for friendship with artists, from which the Tate undoubtedly benefited. He was, for instance, an early supporter of Lucian Freud, and his arresting catalogue introduction to the Tate retrospective which he gave to Francis Bacon in 1962 had a determining influence on the public perception of Bacon's art.[24] During the final years of his Directorship, a new wave of artists entered the collection. In 1963 the Tate acquired Bridget Riley's *Fall*, R.B. Kitaj's *Isaac Babel Riding with Budyonny*, David Hockney's *The First Marriage* and Peter Blake's *On the Balcony*, as well as works by Leon Kossoff and the Constructionists Gillian Wise Ciobotaru and Anthony Hill.

There had been no scandals at the Tate since 1954, other than the stealing of a Berthe Morisot by a young Irishman in 1956, in protest at Britain's retention of the Hugh Lane Bequest in spite of Ireland's claims. Earlier that day the thief had informed a photographic agency that there was to be an Irish demonstration at the Tate that day. A photographer was standing outside and happened to take a picture of the young man who ran down the steps carrying a painting between two pieces of board. His suspicions aroused, the photographer also photographed

44 David Hockney, *The First Marriage (A Marriage of Styles I)*, 1962

the car in which the young man made his getaway. Soon afterwards, the Irish National Students' Council announced that the aim of the theft had been to give the picture to Dublin Municipal Art Gallery. When the Corporation of Dublin declared they could not accept a stolen picture and the theft was condemned by the Irish Ambassador, the painting was returned unharmed to the Irish Embassy in Eaton Square.

Rothenstein rode the alarm this caused without fuss. He had never lacked tenacity and wanted to remain Director of the Tate until 1966 when he would have reached the age of sixty-five. But in 1964 the Trustees decided he should go. Sir Colin Anderson, who had returned to the Board as Chairman in 1960, asked Anthony Lousada, now a Trustee, to inform Rothenstein of their decision.

His last five months at the Tate were spent in what he called 'an eerie limbo',[25] for although his retirement was announced in April, he did not leave his post until 2 October 1964. He did so oppressed with regret at his loss of public position. Ten days later a dinner was held in his honour. The Earl of Crawford and Balcarres sent apologies for his absence to Sir Colin Anderson, with the following opinion: 'What has happened to the Tate is really remarkable: and I think that we owe a great deal to John (as well as the Board) for having, against awful odds, created something living and new and rich out of the shifting and really intolerable days of Manson.'[26] Rothenstein himself cherished an image of the Tate at night, its interior candle-lit and embellished with flowers for receptions, and of himself wandering among the crowd of artists, writers, collectors and friends, 'happy at having played some part in bringing into being this life, so engaging a blend of the serious and sociable, in a place once redolent of decay ...'[27]

45 Man stealing one of the paintings from the Lane Bequest,
in action by Irish Nationalists, 1956

II

Whaam!

Long before Rothenstein's retirement was publicly announced, the Trustees began discussing the question of his successor. According to a memoir by Anthony Lousada, Lawrence Gowing announced he would like to be a candidate if he was assured of his co-Trustees' support. As a result, a dinner party was held at Sir Colin Anderson's house in Hampstead, for all the Trustees except Gowing. There was much discussion and little certainty. But, in spite of the considerable hesitation voiced by Lionel Robbins, agreement was reached.[1] Afterwards, Sir Dennis Proctor records, Anderson told Norman Reid that the Trustees wanted Gowing if he could be persuaded to accept, and failing him, Alan Bowness, then a thirty-five year old lecturer at the Courtauld Institute of Art, specialising in nineteenth- and twentieth-century art.[2] Anderson went on to assure Reid that his own claims to the post would also be considered.

This was in 1963, and towards the end of this year Gowing approached Reid as a fellow painter and asked how much opportunity he would have to paint if he became Director. Reid gave him all the necessary information concerning 'research days' and other regulations, and Gowing informed the Trustees he would accept the appointment. From then on, until the later stages of the Selection Board, it was assumed by many that Gowing would be the next Director. Gowing, himself, with a certain lack of diplomacy, began making plans as to which room he would occupy at the Tate. He also gave in his notice as Principal of Chelsea School of Art and, after submitting a formal application, resigned, as was necessary, from the Tate Board.

In the Boardroom Gowing's vital responsiveness to art had impressed his fellow Trustees. 'It is one of the very few great classic works of the twentieth century not yet in captivity,' he once wrote to Sir Colin Anderson of Kokoschka's portrait of Herwath Walden, then on offer to the Tate. He continued: 'It is like Francis Bacon *avant la lettre*, but finer of course – with a miraculous chalky iridescence spread across the bare canvas.'[3] His brilliant, original mind, combined with his ability to articulate the sensations art aroused, made him a persuasive advocate. He could also be extremely funny, despite the fact that his severe speech impediment often delayed his punchlines. Willing to listen to others and, if need be, change his views, he could nevertheless be tactless, also clumsy, both physically and in his relations with colleagues.

The Trustees had intended to appoint Gowing without further ado, but the Treasury, arguing that the Director was a civil servant and therefore should be independent of his institution's elective representatives, insisted on holding a public competition under the auspices of the Civil Service. The job was advertised in April 1964 and applications had to be submitted by 24 June. At this stage many people still thought the competition merely a cynical device to clothe with decency the Trustees' choice, and it remained a foregone conclusion that Gowing would be the next Director.

Concurrently, between 22 April and 28 June, there was a major exhibition at the Tate Gallery, *Painting and Sculpture of a Decade, 54–64*. It was the biggest exhibition so far mounted in the Gallery, filling the entire central spine as well as further galleries to one side. Though officially the product of a triumvirate – Lawrence Gowing, Alan Bowness and Philip James of the Arts Council – Gowing had ruthlessly cut James out of any part in the choice of the work. The seedbed of this exhibition had been the friendship between Gowing and Bowness.

Soon after Bowness had married one of the daughters of Barbara Hepworth and Ben Nicholson in 1957, he and his wife moved into a top-floor flat in Percy Street which Gowing had found for them. He himself had a pied-à-terre at number 17, and the arrangement was made that the Bownesses would provide him with breakfast when he arrived in London for Trustees' meetings. This arrangement continued until 1959, when Gowing exchanged his professorship at Newcastle for the Principal's post at Chelsea School of Art. In the course of these breakfasts some interesting discussions took place as Bowness felt challenged to convert Gowing to modernism. The end result was a wish to mount a ten-year survey exhibition which would mix different generations and place British art in an international context, giving particular attention to recent American art. Gowing persuaded the Calouste Gulbenkian Foundation to fund it, and Philip James was brought in because of his enormous experience in arranging exhibitions for the Arts Council. Intended to be a major statement on the current state of art, the exhibition was architect-designed by Peter and Alison Smithson and the catalogue made radical by Edward Wright's typography. The selection captured the new liveliness of British art, and it was hoped that its impact would be as dramatic as that made by Roger Fry's Post-Impressionist exhibitions in 1910 and 1912. The exhibition also contained the kind of art that both Bowness and Gowing thought the Tate ought to be showing, presented in a way appropriate to a museum of modern art.

Soon after this exhibition opened, Lord Bridges was appointed Chairman of the Selection Board for the new Tate Director. This was unfortunate for Gowing, since Bridges, together with Sir Dennis Proctor, was a member of the Fine Art Advisory Committee of the Gulbenkian Foundation which had promoted and financed the *54–64* exhibition. As the leading member of the triumvirate commissioned to organise this exhibition, Gowing had grossly overrun the estimated expenditure and had done so in an overbearing, high-handed way without expressing any regrets. Moreover, when asked for an explanation, he had attempted to cast blame on the staff of the Foundation. Having observed the way in which Gowing had expanded the exhibition without regard for cost, Bridges concluded that he had a *folie de grandeur*. As a result, when Bridges became chairman of the

46 Installation view of the exhibition *Painting and Sculpture of a Decade 54–64*, held in 1964

Selection Board, the outlook for the other short-listed candidates – Alan Bowness, Norman Reid, Graham Reynolds (Prints and Drawings, Victoria & Albert Museum), Bryan Robertson and Hugh Scrutton (Director of the Walker Art Gallery, Liverpool) – brightened.

In sharp contrast with Gowing's irresponsibility was Norman Reid's reliability, which Proctor praised at length in his reference.[4] He described how Reid had been in charge of the Tate's administration ever since the Trustees had made him the cornerstone of their planned reorganisation. This swung the Selection Board in Reid's favour. Having worked for eighteen years at the Tate in Rothenstein's shadow, Reid emerged as the new Director and months of speculation ended. The *Daily Telegraph* announced: 'Mr Reid's appointment is a triumph for moderation and will be widely welcomed. One of the least flamboyant of the candidates who have been much discussed, he has won a reputation as a sound museum man.'[5] He took up the post on 1 October 1964 on a salary of £4,335.

Neither a drum-beater nor a publicity seeker, Reid introduced a scholarly, sympathetic and sensitive approach to the running of the Tate. He had, as Gowing has put on record, 'a genius for good personal relationships',[6] and as a result during the period of his Directorship certain artists – notably Hepworth, Moore, Ben Nicholson, Mark Rothko, Giacometti and Naum Gabo – made generous gifts of their own work to the Gallery. With his 'softly lambent humour',[7] Reid also injected a note of realism into the heady world of high art. Even Rothenstein, who had done little to promote Reid's organisational wizardry, praised his 'versatile practicality and his pervasive good sense'.[8] But perhaps Reid's greatest asset in relation to the Tate was his concept of a work of art as a living thing. When interviewed by Nigel Gosling in the *Observer*, he admitted: 'I think of even the oldest pictures as being in a real sense alive. Perhaps this is a new attitude and rather an important one. A museum is no longer thought of as a dead repository where things never change.'[9]

The possibility of change was further enhanced in 1964 by a rise in the purchase grant to £60,000. At the same time, Sir Colin Anderson succeeded in finally persuading the Treasury to acknowledge the need to fill gaps in the modern foreign collection, and the Tate was promised an additional £50,000 each year for the next five years. This 'gap' money made possible the acquisition of Picasso's *The Three Dancers* which Roland Penrose negotiated with the artist (who rarely answered letters) on behalf of the Tate. It was, with Matisse's *The Snail*, the Gallery's most important purchase since the acquisition of Seurat's *Bathers, Asnières* through the Courtauld Fund. Of further benefit was the decision in November 1964 to raise the Director's discretionary spending power to £2,000. This same year the Treasury also granted the Tate the right to charge an entrance fee for their own exhibitions.

In April 1964 Douglas Cooper had sent a letter to *The Times* arguing that the Tate collection should be separated into a British collection and a museum of modern art. This suggestion had been voiced before and was clearly in Reid's mind when he took over. The division he instigated led to the advertisement of two new posts: a Keeper of the British Collection and a Keeper of the Modern Collection. Ronald Alley succeeded to the second of these, winning by a head over Alan Bowness, whose request for a reference from Lawrence Gowing caused Gowing to consider applying for the Keepership of British Art. He asked Reid if it was acceptable to him if he applied. Reid concurred without hesitation, but was amused by the twist Gowing gave this in his interview: when asked why he had applied, Gowing replied, 'because Norman asked me to'.[10]

Soon after Gowing joined the Tate's staff in March 1965, Sir Colin Anderson wrote to Proctor: 'This produces a strange alignment of personalities, which, if it works, could be splendid. It heralds a retreat of the Trustees from the position in which they have found themselves far too much making the pace.'[11] Gowing did not naturally fill the position of second-in-command, but Reid was good at delegating and let Gowing have a hand in spending the Director's discretionary purchase money. Too big a personality to confine his powers to the Historic British Collection, Gowing occasionally infuriated Ronald Alley by rehanging the Modern Collection. Nevertheless, the Assistant Keeper, Martin Butlin, learnt much from Gowing, who was an immensely stimulating presence in the Gallery. To be invited to join him at lunchtime in the basement, where he cooked his own lunch on an old stove, was to share in conversations that were often exhilarating. But after two years Gowing left to take over from Quentin Bell as Professor of Fine Art at the University of Leeds, where he was more able to pursue his interests in writing and painting. His successor as Keeper of the British Collection was Martin Butlin.

Gowing saw the absurdity inherent in the situation that had arisen with regard to the cataloguing of Turner's work. Whereas Martin Butlin had taken over responsibility for cataloguing the oils in the national collections, Evelyn Joll, of

47 Pablo Picasso, *The Three Dancers*, 1925

Agnews', was quite separately compiling information on the Turner oils elsewhere. It was largely due to Gowing that the Tate Trustees overcame their doubts
about a member of the Gallery staff collaborating with a dealer and that *The Paintings of J.M.W. Turner* by Butlin and Joll received financial support from the Paul
Mellon Foundation, which had links with Yale University Press. In 1978, the year
after it was first published, it won a Mitchell Prize for the history of art.

When Mary Chamot retired in October 1965, the Assistant Keeper, Leslie Parris, appointed the year previously on a temporary basis, became a permanent member of staff and took over responsibility for Constable, inheriting the files of correspondence which Chamot had exchanged with various collectors, experts and members of the Constable family. But it was Turner rather than Constable who was in the ascendant at this time – owing to the *Turner* exhibition that Gowing selected for the Museum of Modern Art, New York, in 1966. To coincide with the exhibition and to uphold his interpretation of Turner as the first abstract painter, Gowing published *Turner: Imagination and Reality*, which remains a high point in the modernist appreciation of this artist. The following year, the Turner rooms at the Tate were rehung and redecorated, Gowing working with Reid on a complete transformation of the Edwardian galleries. The walls and the marble dados were covered with white-painted plywood screens to break up the space, and high-vaulted roofs were hidden by false ceilings made of butter muslin through which the light was diffused. The aim behind these temporary galleries-within-galleries was to get away from the grandiosity of the architecture and to create very simple, peaceful spaces in which to show paintings.

Under Reid, alterations were not confined to the Turner rooms. Elsewhere he introduced new wallpapers, brighter lighting, in some places lower ceilings, and a redesigned entrance hall. He brought the modern foreign collection upstairs and rehung the entire Gallery so that the visitor, on entering, had three clear choices: the British Collection on the left, the Modern Collection on the right, and special exhibitions straight ahead in the sculpture halls, and sometimes also into the lower galleries. Reid also abandoned the rigid separation of modern British and foreign artists, arguing that 'the highly international character of much of the art being produced today makes purely national divisions of this kind illogical'.[12] He also claimed in the Annual Report that the new arrangement represented 'a gain in lucidity'. Certain critics accepted this view, but added that this very lucidity made glaringly apparent the gaps in the collection. Nevertheless Guy Brett in *The Times* wrote: 'Nobody can miss the new air of confidence and efficiency there is about the Tate. The bringing of clarity to the confused jumble of the Tate's inheritance of modern art has been a neat job, and it is echoed in the new official guide which sorts out the history of modern art in an unruffled way.'[13] Finally, to celebrate the rehanging of the collection, a reception was held on 15 February 1967 which was attended by the Queen.

The following year the Hayward Gallery on the South Bank came into operation as the Arts Council's London venue for major exhibitions. The Tate, no longer able to benefit from Arts Council exhibitions, from now on had to take full responsibility for its exhibition programme. This made still more urgent an increase in curatorial staff. Reid made exceptionally good appointments: as well as Leslie Parris, who had initially joined after Dennis Farr left to become Curator of the Paul Mellon collection in the autumn of 1964, Michael Compton and Anne Seymour came in 1965, and Richard Morphet in 1966. Compton arrived with considerable experience, as he had formerly been Director of the Ferens Art Gallery,

48 Sir Norman Reid, *c.*1965

Hull, but was so determined on a job at the Tate that he had already applied twice before. He was soon asked to draw up a paper on exhibition policy and in 1970 became Keeper of the newly created Exhibitions and Education Department.

The creation of this department represented a major bureaucratic development in the history of the Tate. It was helped by the fact that the Gallery was no longer directly responsible to the Treasury. In 1964 the Robbins Report had recommended that national galleries, museums, universities and learned societies should be placed under a new Minister for the Arts and Education, so that they could have a voice in the Cabinet and play a greater part in the political life of the nation. Harold Wilson was responsible for appointing the first Minister for the Arts and he chose Jennie Lee who remained in office until she lost her seat with the Labour defeat in 1970. She was not a great intellect and claimed to have no profound knowledge of the arts, but she became a tireless visitor to arts events up and down the country, and achieved a great deal. Under her regime the National Theatre came to be built, the National Film School was contrived, and the Tate Gallery was to obtain the Queen Alexandra Military Hospital site. A friend of the Gallery and a personal friend of Norman Reid, Jennie Lee persuaded the Tate to lend modern pictures to the House of Commons where they hung in the Harcourt Room. The intention was to familiarise, and in this way convert, MPs to contemporary art; but the paintings were the object of such persistent philistine sniping that the arrangement ceased in 1971. Difficulties also arose when Jennie Lee pressed for Sunday morning opening at the Tate. To her surprise, the unions, instead of welcoming additional working hours, refused to co-operate.

In 1968 the Tate had informed the Department of Education and Science of its need to create the following: special exhibitions and an exhibition programme; an archive for twentieth-century British art; and public access to the Reserve Collection. The paper outlining these needs had been welcomed by Jennie Lee and her Department, but, though a £31,000 grant for these purposes was made available for 1969–70, the Tate was simultaneously told that no new staff could be appointed owing to a standstill on the number of people in government employment. An increase in the Tate's programme therefore applied still more pressure on the already overburdened staff.

Nevertheless, from now on exhibitions and education were to become an important part of the Tate's remit. Michael Compton took over responsibility for education at a time when the library had only one member of staff, and Simon Wilson was the only official lecturer in the Gallery. After the appointment in 1971 of a Deputy Keeper, Terence Measham, who made a lively, innovative contribution to the education side of the department, Compton spent more time working on exhibitions with Ruth Rattenbury, who came to the Tate from the British Council in 1970 and proved to have great flair for organisation. Unlike American museums, where exhibitions are often used to boost a particular curator's career, the Tate adopted an approach closer to the pattern that had evolved in the Arts Council, whereby exhibitions were selected and catalogued by specialist scholars, with the institution providing a small team of people responsible for negotiating with lenders, compiling lists of works, arranging loans, insurance or indemnity, and for the design and editing of the catalogue. This method left the Tate curators free to concentrate on the permanent collection which remained at the centre of the Tate's activities. In these early pioneering years Compton and Rattenbury worked in tandem on all the Tate's shows, with help from Judith Jeffreys (formerly Cloake) if a legal question arose.

Under Reid, Judith Jeffreys retained key administrative responsibilities, was promoted to Deputy Keeper (and later Assistant Director), and took responsibility for all the business relating to the Board meetings. Stefan Slabczynski was upgraded from Chief Restorer to Keeper of the Conservation Department and his craftsmen were reclassified as Museum Technicians. Corinne Bellow had been promoted to Press and Information Officer and soon proved herself as crucial to Reid as she had been to Rothenstein. By 1973, when she was awarded an MBE, she had become Head of Information Services, in which role, as *Arts Review* commented (21 April 1973), her 'special combination of tact and determination' had made a significant contribution to the Tate's success over many years.

Up until now no professional art historians or critics had been invited on to the Board, both Gowing and Adrian Stokes having been taken on as artist-Trustees. But when a vacancy came up and Jennie Lee asked for Reid's advice on who should fill it, he replied emphatically that it must be Herbert Read. Lee accepted

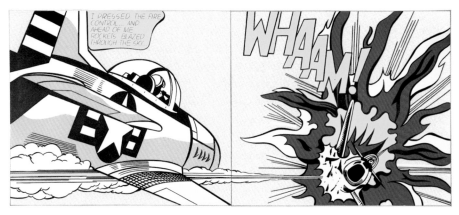

49 Roy Lichtenstein, *Whaam!*, 1963

his recommendation, though insisted that the next vacancy must be filled by someone younger; and so, very belatedly, Read joined the Board in place of the financier and collector Lionel Fraser in 1965, the same year as Barbara Hepworth, who was pleased to be the first woman Trustee and to find herself working with Read and Adrian Stokes (two of her earliest friends), as well as with a Director she respected. Though she was suffering, like Read, from cancer of the tongue, she still sat at the Board table with a box of a hundred cigarettes near-to-hand and a large glass of whisky to help numb the pain. She often passed no comment on potential purchases, but when she did speak her tiny voice obliged the other Trustees to lean forward with complete attention. Like Hepworth, Read was something of a spent force, if also a quiet, authoritative presence. The man who had once been a vital spokesman for the avant-garde was now ill-at-ease with much contemporary art. He had a strong objection to Pop art and tried unsuccessfully, with Hepworth, to oppose the acquisition of Roy Lichtenstein's *Whaam!*, which, based on comic strip imagery, made an ironic comment on American militarist attitudes, and in 1966 became one of the Tate's most spectacular purchases. Read died on 12 June 1968. Eight days later, at the next Board meeting, the Trustees stood in silence around the table in tribute to his memory. His friends Gabo, Hepworth, Moore and Ben Nicholson each presented one of their works to the Gallery as a memorial to him.

Following the requirements set down by the 1954 National Gallery and Tate Gallery Act, the Board of Trustees could not exceed ten in number. The term of service was seven years and after this period a person could not be immediately eligible for reappointment. However, a very short time elapsed before the reappointment of Anderson, Coldstream, John Piper, Robert Sainsbury and Henry Moore, all of whom served for two terms.

In 1967 Anthony Lousada, for the last two years of his office, took over as Chairman from Sir Colin Anderson – an arrangement with which Robert Sainsbury, the more senior Trustee agreed, as he was planning to retire from his family's firm in 1969, when the Chairmanship would suit him better. By this time the sculptor

Phillip King (aged thirty-three at the time of his appointment) had become the youngest artist-Trustee ever to sit on the Board. The critic and exhibition organiser David Sylvester also joined in 1967, but resigned two years later owing to pressure of work. The least happy Trustee appointment was Victor Pasmore who resigned after three years. Temperamentally unsuited to committee work and inclined to extreme views, he was, according to Lousada, 'jerky, unpredictable but with deep feelings'; when a picture by Lucio Fontana came up and no one voted for it other than him, Pasmore 'slammed down his papers and stalked out not to return for over a year until I remonstrated with him'.[13]

Lousada, who never missed a meeting in all his seven years, ceded the Chairmanship in 1969 to the equally conscientious and deeply committed Robert Sainsbury, who, with his wife Lisa, formed the remarkable art and ethnographic collection which was eventually given to the University of East Anglia. Sainsbury once admitted that the day he became Chairman of the Tate was the proudest day of his life. Living nearby in Smith Square, he was often in the Gallery and could walk into any department without causing embarrassment or difficulty. Under his Chairmanship one of the most influential Trustees was Howard Hodgkin who usually sat on the Chairman's left, and so, when Sainsbury went round the table asking for opinions on potential purchases Hodgkin was often the first to speak. With his immense knowledge of art and the art market, Hodgkin had a unique gift for either promoting or killing a potential purchase. He might merely lower his eyes and begin to doodle, but it had devastating effect. He was usually supportive of historic British purchases, but at one Board meeting a Conversation Piece by J.F. Nollekens was so completely destroyed by Hodgkin that Martin Butlin, who had initially presented it with great confidence, felt he never wanted to see the picture again. A more benign, if less influential, presence on the Board was the landscape architect Geoffrey Jellicoe, whose expertise was thought useful in a period when the prospect of a further extension became a reality.

During the mid-1960s the Friends of the Tate went from strength to strength, and in December 1967 its membership topped two thousand. The Gallery was specially opened for the Friends between ten and one on the first Sunday morning in every month. A programme of talks and discussions had begun and the *Sunday Times* collaborated with the Friends over a fashion show at the Tate. At the far end of the east corridor, in a room adjoining the Friends' office, a Friends' sitting-room, where magazines were available and smoking allowed, had been instituted in 1966. In 1969 a Young Friends began at a reduced rate of subscription and with a membership of 750. They established their separate identity by taking a building in Pear Place, just south of Waterloo Bridge, and there set up a programme of lectures as well as painting classes for local children on Saturday mornings. When they began to mount their own exhibitions, and to apply to the Arts Council for a grant towards an exhibition, the Chairman and Trustees grew worried that the public would think they had the backing of the Board. They were asked to desist from holding exhibitions, and, angered by this, the Young Friends committee, together with its Chairman – the future Tate Director Nicholas Serota – resigned and the organisation collapsed, the building at Pear Place afterwards becoming a venue for National Theatre rehearsals.

Despite this rebuff, the Tate continued to attract a young audience. Ever since the Contemporary Art Society exhibition, *British Painting in the Sixties*, which had been followed the next year by *Painting and Sculpture of a Decade 54–64*, and by *Recent British Painting: Peter Stuyvesant Foundation Collection* in 1967, the Gallery had been closely identified with contemporary art. This was further emphasised by its willingness to show the student exhibition *Young Contemporaries* in 1967 – the same year that it hosted the biennial modern European art competition, the Marzotto Prize. Three other shows that had been particularly stimulating for a young audience were the Arts Council's Marcel Duchamp exhibition in 1966, the *Picasso: Sculpture, Ceramics and Graphic Work* exhibition, organised by Roland Penrose in 1967, and the Roy Lichtenstein retrospective in 1968, which caused long queues to form around the Tate. Whereas in 1962 the acquisition of Matisse's *The Snail* had caused a storm of controversy,[14] by the late 1960s there was great excitement about modern art and a new optimism, typified, for instance, by the opening of the Hayward Gallery, the move of the ICA into premises on the Mall, the *New Generation* exhibitions at the Whitechapel Art Gallery, Princess Margaret's attendance of the 1967 Picasso exhibition, the appearance of the 'new' *Studio International*, edited by Peter Townsend, and other glossy art magazines, and the willingness of the *Evening Standard*, in 1969, to appoint as its art critic the twenty-two year old Richard Cork.

Relations between certain artists and the Tate were carefully cultivated. Louise Nevelson's *Black Wall* formed the centre-piece of a room devoted to recent American painting and sculpture when the artist visited the Tate on 2 June 1965. Impressed by what she saw, Nevelson announced her intention of giving to the Gallery an eighteen-foot long 'Gold Wall'. It arrived later that year, with the title *An American Tribute to the British People*. Still more productive was the attention given to Giacometti during the course of his exhibition at the Tate in 1965. Not only was he given a working space in the Tate basement where he made *Four Figurines on a Base* but, at the urging of the Trustee Andrew Forge, £20,000 was put aside for purchasing his work. When Giacometti was informed of this and given a list of works in which the Trustees were interested, he generously assured the Tate they could have the lot for £10,000, on the condition that he could be free to present as a gift another work. This he did, the Tate acquiring in all eight sculptures and two paintings, which went on view in October 1967.[15]

Less successful was the Tate's long love affair with Peggy Guggenheim. Her dislike of her Guggenheim relatives made the eventual destination of her outstanding collection of modern art, housed in a Venetian palace, the subject of much speculation. John Rothenstein had first drawn attention to it in 1951, by suggesting to the ICA that it should sponsor the bringing to England of a selection from her collection to be shown at the Tate. Nothing had come of this, but in 1962 while attending the Venice Biennale, Rothenstein visited Peggy Guggenheim, having heard from Herbert Read that she was disillusioned with the municipality of Venice and had raised the possibility of leaving her collection to the Tate. She wanted to do so without incurring American death duties, as she intended leaving her fortune to her daughter intact. However, by then she had been made an honorary citizen of Venice and had to be careful what she said to the press (even though the citizenship was for what she had done for Venice in the past and did not bind her to any future action), for she did not want to make difficulties for herself there. The tax situation was also problematic: though she had hoped to present the collection through the American Friends of the Tate Gallery, she soon learnt that though the American Federation of Arts, acting for the Friends, was empowered to secure tax remissions on gifts, it could not do so on bequests. As a result, Anthony Lousada was asked to look into ways of overcoming legal impediments, and, meanwhile, plans went ahead to exhibit 187 of her pictures, sculptures and tribal carvings at the Tate.

The exhibition opened at the Tate on 31 December 1964. Before this, Slabczynski had gone out to Venice to prepare the pictures for their journey and to attend to those in need of restoration after fourteen years exposure to salt breezes from the Grand Canal. Much was done to please Peggy Guggenheim. She was allowed to hang the Tate exhibition, was Guest of Honour at a private dinner in one of the galleries before a Friends' evening party, was given a leather-bound edition of the catalogue and an impressive opening. This took place on New Year's Eve, with the Tate steps red-carpeted and canopied. Peggy Guggenheim walked round on Norman Reid's arm. While in London, she was besieged by interviewers who found that, despite her silver fingernails, this woman, who loved to surround herself with outrageous and talented people, was rather mundane, despite her gift for repartee. 'The show was a terrific success,' she recalled in her memoirs, 'with people queuing up all the way down the steps of the Tate and along the Embankment. My only rival was Churchill's funeral. After the show, which was prolonged two weeks, they restored lots of paintings for me.'[16]

The Tate continued to restore works for Peggy Guggenheim and to pursue the matter of her bequest. By January 1966 it had been agreed that she would donate her collection – arguably the greatest private collection of early twentieth-century modernist art in Europe – to the Tate through the Contemporary Art Society. Yet various factors served to undermine this agreement. One of these was the death in 1967 of her daughter Pegeen, which raised problems of possible claims from Peggy's grandchildren, whose rights to her estate under Italian law could well be pursued by their father. A further problem was that the Italian authorities had discovered that Peggy Guggenheim's collection had initially entered the country irregularly, undeclared and without import papers, during or immediately before the Second World War. When it became clear that the collection could not leave Italy, Peggy Guggenheim asked Reid if the British government would accept her Palazzo Ca' Venier dei Leoni with her collection and maintain both. Reid had to reply that there was no possibility of this happening. She then addressed this offer to the Trustees of the Guggenheim Foundation, who accepted it. It was, after all, a solution that best suited her needs, maintaining her home and collection in Venice, and probably bringing her substantial tax concessions under US law. At the time of her Tate exhibition, she had told Robert Sainsbury that she did not think her pictures looked at their best in a public art gallery and she was longing to get them home again. There, to this day, they remain. But, as Sainsbury pointed out to her at the time, they had made a very fine and popular exhibition at the Tate, and this had made all their efforts worthwhile.

★   ★   ★

Various events continued to keep the Tate in the public eye. At a time when 'happenings' and performances were making a lively contribution to contemporary art, the Board agreed that the French sculptor César could make 'instant sculpture' in the Gallery at a party hosted by the Friends in 1968. It was a rather grand evening-dress occasion, with an introductory talk by the French critic Pierre Restany, and with the French ambassador and his wife among the guests. César poured a mixture of plastics into a container, added some red and yellow colouring and a catalyst and then inserted an electrical mixer. When the mixture began to bubble and rise, he poured it on to black vinyl sheeting covering the floor. The mixture frothed and heaved like an advancing flood of lava, causing the spectators to back away. It quickly cooled and set in large discs. Towards the end of the evening two artists who had dined too well rolled some of the plastic down the front steps and made a bonfire between the front gates. It burned fiercely (although César had assured the Director that it was not flammable). A fire engine with crew in full kit arrived suddenly and asked who was in charge. Reid confessed he was, whereupon the fireman said mildly, 'Please don't do these things'.[17]

The Tate steps became the setting for many events. Here the Conceptual artist John Latham burnt books. Here the Queen greeted King Faisal of Saudi Arabia at the start of his state visit on 9 May 1967, after which they both – not stopping to look at the pictures – drove off to Buckingham Palace in an open horse-drawn carriage. It was here too that Reid, with the help of eighty-nine schoolchildren, released ninety white homing pigeons as a tribute to Picasso's ninetieth birthday on 25 October 1971. Afterwards each child was given a card showing Picasso's *Girl Holding a Pigeon*, painted when he was twenty. The event was celebrated on the news, but was followed by a sour postscript: over the next few days batches of dead pigeons were left on the Tate steps in protest at the Gallery's treatment of 'living British artists'. Sigi Krauss, whose gallery had closed owing to financial problems, explained to a reporter that there were about one hundred young artists who wanted to see fewer retrospectives and more 'actual' art at the Tate.[18]

Sigi Krauss was part of the short-lived International Coalition for the Liquidation of Art which in October 1970 had held demonstrations in New York, Amsterdam and London in protest at the present systems of art production, consumption and manipulation. On 20 October one of its sympathisers – Felipe Ehrenberg, a notable Fluxus artist and founder of the Beau Geste Press – arrived at the Tate dressed in a brown corduroy suit and a Ku Klux Klan-type hood, with an opening for one eye, and with a tape recorder hanging from his shoulder. He was stopped by an attendant and denied entrance and the conversation that followed, caught by his tape-recorder, was later published in *Studio International*.[19]

During Reid's directorship, the Tate held a number of highly successful artist's dinners, usually timed to mark the opening of an exhibition. Silver and gold table-cloths enlivened the dinner in honour of Barbara Hepworth at the time of her ret-rospective exhibition in 1968. Two years before, another had been held in honour of Duchamp and his guest, Man Ray, who looked a little eclipsed by Duchamp's celebrity. When his turn came to make a speech, Duchamp stood up and said, 'Prenez-garde à la peinture fraîche!' (Beware wet paint), and sat down. 'It's just like living art history,' said one awe-struck guest to Norman Reid.[20]

By the time the Tate's seventy-fifth anniversary arrived in 1972, Reid, who had been knighted in 1970, was confident of the need to celebrate. As well as mount-ing a display of Henry Tate's pictures, the Gallery held a party for artists and bene-factors on the lawn. Inside the Gallery kites designed by Richard Smith, Robyn Denny and Gordon House hung over the postcard stall. Outside on the lawns were large, colourful banners which later reappeared on the cover of the October 1972 issue of *Studio International*. Designed by Margaret Traherne, without charge to the Gallery, they were suspended between masts and created a cluster of forms responsive to air and movement and changing light. 'Alas!', Reid recalls. 'They proved too tempting and all were stolen during the night.'[21]

50 Sir Norman Reid and schoolchildren releasing
the first of ninety pigeons in honour of Picasso's
ninetieth birthday, 25 October 1971

12

The Fourth Quarter

By the end of the 1960s the Tate Gallery had been transformed by an increase in professionalism at all levels. Its former isolation, which had made it difficult in Rothenstein's era to raise gifts and bequests for modern art, was a thing of the past. From now on the Tate was regarded as the centre and pinnacle of modern art in England. In the eyes of some, this seemed detrimental to the Historic British Collection. In a letter to *The Times*, Humphrey Brooke pointed out that the 1964–65 Report rested on the assumption that the Tate's primary concern was with modern international art. This, he argued, went against the original objective of the Gallery, which was to display British art – including the Chantrey Bequest and the Turner Bequest. Would it not be better, he concluded, to build a new museum of modern art elsewhere?[1] In his riposte Norman Reid pointed out, among other things, that a separate staff had been appointed to look after the British Collection which was in fact receiving more attention than it had for many years.[2] But every now and then Brooke returned to his charge – 'Humphrey's campaign', as Reid privately termed it.

The opportunity to experience Blake and Matisse in the same building continued to be a vital, if eccentric, aspect of the Tate. Since 1937 there had been no increase in gallery space, despite the fact that the collection had doubled in size. The need to enlarge the Tate first became apparent in the early 1950s. The Standing Commission on Museums and Galleries voiced support for this development, but years passed before the idea received government approval. The plan of the Tate which appears in the *Tate Gallery Review 1953–1963* shows a large question mark over the north-east quarter of the original site which remained empty except for a few makeshift huts. This, 'the final quarter', was to become the site of the 1979 extension, the only part of the Millbank conglomeration to be built with public money. The complications that arose in connection with this development set the background to the last ten years of Norman Reid's directorship, during which time he maintained the Gallery's manifold responsibilities: 'The Tate with its collections, special exhibitions and increasing educational activities, aims to provide a bridge between the present and the immediate past, to be a major organ of propaganda and encouragement to the fields in its care.'[3]

In 1969 it was decided to switch from annual to biennial reports in which, from now on, all new acquisitions were to be illustrated. They remained, however, a vital exercise in public relations and a platform from which arguments could be voiced regarding the need for an increase in the purchase grant (Grant-in-Aid). In 1968, when the quinquennium 'gap' money came to an end, the Trustees asked the Department of Education and Science for a £500,000 purchase grant. With this amount, it was argued, they could prevent desirable works of art going abroad and in general play a more positive role as purchaser, instead of, as so often happened, fighting against time to find money. Having just paid £63,000 for one picture and seen Stubbs's *Cheetah with Two Indians* enter Manchester City Art Gallery, with assistance from the National Art Collections Fund, at a cost of £200,000, the Trustees were disappointed when the purchase grant for 1969–70 was set at only £75,000. However, the following year the Labour Government decided to make purchase grants of £2 million to national museums and galleries, and of this the Tate received £265,000. But even this amount, given the Tate's responsibilities with regard to both the British School and the Modern Collection, was inadequate. In 1975 the Trustees asked for £1,555,000 annually, and backed this request with a carefully reasoned and well-documented paper. They received £570,000 for the next three years. But despite the continuing gap between the sum asked for and that given, the government was now listening and responding to the Tate's arguments.

The Gallery continued to have the right to request special grants in connection with specific, outstanding works of art. However, these grants were often unforthcoming if the work in question was twentieth-century. When Roland Penrose decided to sell a Cubist construction, Picasso's *Still Life*, of 1914, a unique work of prime importance, the government refused the Tate's request for a special grant of £16,000 at the very moment when a special grant of £200,000 was provided so that the National Gallery could acquire a ceiling painting by Tiepolo.

Inevitably, the limitations upon the purchase fund meant that acquisitions were often the object of tense dispute. One issue that periodically came up was whether the Tate was right to spend money on relatively inexperienced, often experimental and newly fashionable artists as opposed to more established names. In 1965 Andrew Forge had expressed his concern that the Tate was buying too much too prematurely. However, an alternative point of view, voiced on one occasion by Sir Philip Hendy, was that the Tate would have far greater buying power and more funds at its disposal had the Trustees, or their predecessors, followed a more progressive acquisitions policy in the past.

Gifts and bequests of works of art added significantly to the estimated value of the total acquisitions in any one year. In addition, large and small gifts of money further attested to the affectionate regard the Gallery inspired. Among these was the substantial sum of £50,000 from Mrs Beatrice Benson, also the £4,000 given by Mrs Mara N. Savic, in memory of the many happy hours her husband had spent in the Gallery. Benefits of this kind increased after the 1972 Finance Act which made the Tate and fifteen other institutions exempt from Estate Duty on bequests of money. This relief was in addition to the exemptions from Estate Duty and Capital Gains Tax which applied when works of art were given, or sold by private treaty, to the Gallery.

Some outstanding acquisitions entered the Tate during the early 1970s. Among them was Gabo's *Head No.2*, which was a 1964 enlargement of a 1916 construction.

51 Francis Danby, *The Deluge*, ?c.1840

Made out of Cor-ten steel, its elegant planes slice into and thereby activate the space within a head. The deep pockets of shadow add to its hieratic presence and for many years it sat on the front lawn, becoming as intimately part of the Tate as Francis Danby's *The Deluge*, a huge *tour de force* involving immense turmoil, bolts of lightning, fiery comets and a blood-red setting sun, all of which were intended to re-establish the artist in the public eye after his eleven-year absence in Switzerland. Equally impressive are the atmospheric effects caught by Philip James de Loutherbourg in his *The Battle of Camperdown* and *The Battle of the Nile* and such effects readily explain why this artist became a model for Turner. With the help of the Friends and a special grant, the Tate also acquired Stubbs's *A Couple of Fox-hounds*, at a reduction from the original price as the painting was badly damaged at Heathrow Airport when a fork-lift truck drove into the packing case and tore the picture. Restored by John Brearley, the picture's tear was made invisible, but this did not prevent Douglas Cooper, when he returned to the attack, from accusing the Tate of wasting public money on a wreck.

The more usual criticism was that the Tate was slow off the mark in buying from living artists. In 1968 the Trustees had declined to buy David Hockney's portrait of Don Bachardy and Christopher Isherwood for £2,500. Three years later they paid £5,400 for Hockney's *Mr and Mrs Clark and Percy*, a painting that was to become one of the most popular in the Modern Collection, but which perhaps lacks the bite found in his etching series, *The Rake's Progress*, a set of which the Tate acquired in 1971.

A considerable number of American gifts, among them work by Willem de

Kooning, Robert Motherwell and Ad Reinhardt, continued to come to the Tate via the American Federation of Arts. By making gifts to the Tate through this organisation, American artists were able to obtain tax relief until late 1969, when the US tax law changed. This alteration did not, however, affect private collectors from whom the Tate still benefited.

Among those needing to make a gift against tax was Mark Rothko, and the impending change of law in 1969 gave additional urgency to the negotiations between Reid and himself. Over a period of five years, Reid, every time he had visited New York, had called on the affable, laconic, almost silent Rothko and a friendship had developed. The Tate had purchased one painting by Rothko in 1959, two years before a critically acclaimed exhibition of his work at the Whitechapel Art Gallery. In 1966 Rothko spoke with Reid about the possibility of giving a group of works to the Tate. At that time he had in mind some thirty-two paintings. He said that he liked the idea of his work being shown in the same building as Turner; but when Anthony Lousada asked him why he felt so generous to a British gallery, Rothko spoke, not of Turner, but of his affection for Shakespeare, Herrick, Thackeray and Dickens.[4] The following year, 1967, Rothko was still keen to present a group of his paintings to the Tate, but he had recently learnt that his gift of paintings to Harvard had used up all his tax remission until 1969.

In the spring of 1968 Rothko suffered severe illness, after which he separated from his wife and began living entirely in his studio. In 1958 he had been commissioned to paint a series of murals for the Four Seasons Restaurant in the Seagram Building in New York, some of which had been shown at the Whitechapel Art Gallery in 1961. He had come to feel that these paintings, with their smouldering maroons and tenebrous browns, were inappropriately grave for their proposed location and had withdrawn from the commission. He was also becoming increasingly obsessed by what he called 'a deep sense of responsibility for the life my pictures will lead out in the world'.[5] And he remained confident that, in the right setting, they would find an audience. 'If I must place my trust somewhere,' he wrote to Katherine Kuh, 'I would invest it in the psyche of sensitive observers who are free of the conventions of understanding. I would have no apprehensions about the use they would make of the pictures for the needs of their own spirit. For if there is both need and spirit, there is bound to be a real transaction.'[6]

On 7 January 1969 Reid went to New York at Rothko's request in the hope of making final decisions about the long-promised gift. To Reid's disappointment, he found the studio in a state of chaos as every single work in Rothko's possession was being photographed. In addition, Rothko, much altered by illness, had changed his views about giving works to galleries, and had, at the suggestion of his legal adviser, Bernard Reis, set up a foundation to help artists over fifty-five who had not experienced commercial success. He still intended pictures to come to the Tate, but as permanent loans for as long as the Tate needed them. Owing to the muddle and confusion, Reid subsequently wrote to Bernard Reis, requesting clarification of the new proposals. Two months later the negotiations became even more complicated with Rothko requesting assurance that his paintings

52 The Rothko Room in 1997

would be on permanent exhibition, wanting also to ship more paintings over than he intended to give, so that he could make a final selection in London, and asking to have some of these paintings repaired in America at the Tate's expense.

Just as negotiations seemed on the point of breaking down, news came of the impending change in the US tax law which was to exclude artists from giving their work and off-setting the value against tax. The law was to change in December and Reid flew to New York in November in the hope of clinching the promised gift. Rothko abandoned the demand that the works should be exhibited continuously, and in the final arrangement the only condition which the Board had to approve was that no work by any other artist would be exhibited in the same space as this gift. On this, his last visit to Rothko's studio, Reid, taking a model of the gallery in which the paintings were to hang, spent many hours discussing arrangements, selecting eight works which, with the one already in the Tate's Collection, made a group of nine related works. He was also shown by Rothko a series of near-monochrome gouaches in grey and black in which he felt the artist had reached an emotional cul-de-sac.

When the paintings reached the Tate Gallery on 25 February 1970, many of the curatorial staff went down to the unloading bay in order to watch as these large, darkly glowing canvases were lifted out of huge crates. At that very moment the Director's assistant came in with a cable announcing that Rothko had been found dead. Ever since his aneurism, Rothko had continued to smoke and drink, and had in effect been committing a kind of slow suicide, but his decision to take his own life was still shocking and tragic. Three months later a luncheon was held at the

Tate to celebrate the opening of the Rothko room, hung according to the arrangement which Rothko had indicated on Reid's model. The artist's widow was present and, in the memory of those present, the atmosphere that prevailed was religious in mood.[7]

★　　★　　★

Not until 1958 was further action taken on the plan to extend the Gallery into the remaining quarter of the original site, an idea that had first been mooted in 1953. Mr Kendall, a Ministry of Works architect, produced some designs for a proposed extension which the Trustees thought needed amending. A lack of confidence in these designs is reflected in John Piper's suggestion at the 19 November 1959 Board meeting that the Trustees should by-pass the government architects and obtain the advice of a really first-rate architect, such as Richard Llewelyn-Davies. This was an unprecedented step for a national museum, but an agreement was reached with the Ministry of Works that a consultant architect could be approached. However neither Llewelyn-Davies, nor his alternate, Sir Leslie Martin, wanted to act as consultant, but Llewelyn-Davies indicated he would be willing to act as architect. He submitted a preliminary report which took eighteen months to pass through the offices of the Ministry of Public Buildings and Works. Sir Edward Muir, then Permanent Secretary, was entertained to lunch at the Tate in an attempt to clarify the reasons for this delay. Still nothing happened and the Chairman, Sir Colin Anderson, decided to adopt a policy of relentless charm. At subsequent meetings with Sir Edward Muir he discovered that considerable delay had been caused by the Treasury. There had been criticism of the 'extravagance' of appointing an outside architect and a preference for consultancy on a limited basis. This had been strongly opposed by the Ministry of Works on the grounds that the project was too important to be a matter of divided responsibility. Then came a period of financial stringency and the Treasury had fallen back on the suggestion that the project should be postponed. However, a comprehensive review was underway of all the building projects which would come under the auspices of the Ministry of Works over the next few years, and until these had been scrutinised in accordance with the government's general objectives, no decision could be taken. Bureaucratic and civil service procedures continued to put a brake on the project: by April 1963, some two years after Llewelyn-Davies had submitted his preliminary report, the Treasury still had not authorised his appointment.

All this was merely an overture to the labyrinthine delays and complications that were to dog this project. Once Llewelyn-Davies had officially been appointed architect, he was given a brief for two projects: Project 'B' involved the completion of the north-east quarter; Project 'A', which was far more contentious, was a plan to remove the Tate steps and portico and to mask completely the original Gallery by building across the front and over the existing garden a three-storey International-Style extension. It was estimated that the two projects would

53 Maquette of proposed façade, 1968

increase the space at the Tate by 50 per cent and would make possible a lecture theatre, a new conservation studio, better facilities for the Photographic Department (temporarily housed in a far corner of the existing building) and a new restaurant with a view over the river. There was, in addition, an even bolder idea for a front extension with a restaurant cantilevered over the road and reaching down to the river front, but this remained a pipe-dream.

The Trustees had agreed that the Tate's existing facade had no architectural importance. It was nevertheless a familiar focal point and a feature that dominated a large span of river, therefore objections to Project 'A' were expected. However, in February 1965, Llewelyn-Davies's plans were approved by Mr Bedford, Chief Architect in the Ministry of Public Buildings and Works. But there were other hurdles to overcome, namely committees attached to the Royal Fine Arts Commission, Westminster City Council and the Greater London Council. The last of these had two planning committees, one of which was a Historic Buildings Committee, chaired by Lady Dartmouth (later the Countess of Spencer and now Comtesse Raine de Chambrun), which took advice from Sir John Summerson, John Betjeman and others. This was the only committee that objected and it did so noisily, arguing that a landmark was to be sacrificed to the needs of the Tate. Lady Dartmouth said the front extension would 'completely destroy' the building aesthetically and would leave the dome sticking up behind like a pepperpot. 'This plan is really frightening,' she told the *Daily Telegraph*. 'The members of my board, which includes six experts, were absolutely unanimous in objecting to it.'[8] She asked the Ministry of Works to make public details of this plan. As a result the plans and model were exhibited at the Tate in January 1969, 20,000 people went to see them, and *The Times* and the *Evening Standard* opened their pages to comment. The *Architects' Journal* came out in support of Lady Dartmouth and her

Committee. There was also considerable public support for the retention of the portico, with its idiomatic bravura – for it had become an irreplaceable symbol of the Tate – and Project 'A' was eventually abandoned. The fact that the Tate's 1968–70 Report carried a picture of Britannia on its cover, to celebrate her survival, together with the rest of the Tate portico, suggests that the failure of Project 'A' was met internally with a certain relief.

While the front extension remained under discussion, a small controversy arose over funding. The main source of funds for the Tate enlargement was the £775,000 allocated by the government, on the advice of the Standing Commission for Museums and Galleries. In addition, the Trustee Anthony Lousada, who was also Chairman of the Royal College of Art Council, had sat next to the Director of the Gulbenkian Foundation at a RCA convocation and had asked him to consider giving towards the Tate extension. The following Monday a telegram arrived at the Tate announcing that the Gulbenkian were donating £250,000, which at that time was the largest single grant the Foundation had made in the United Kingdom. In total, the Tate now had £1,025,000. The following year, 1967, Henry Moore proposed making a gift to the Tate of twenty-six major sculptures, plaster casts, working maquettes and the contents of what he called his 'thinking studio'. The Tate used this to put pressure on the government to grant adequate funds for the Gallery to be able to show this gift properly. There was talk of adding a special Henry Moore gallery to the new building scheme, for the Tate already possessed the largest Henry Moore collection in the world and was planning a major retrospective for 1968 in celebration of the artist's seventieth birthday. The point was taken: in April 1967, at the first Royal Academy banquet to admit women guests since its inception in 1770, Harold Wilson announced that the Government was willing to donate £200,000 towards the housing of Henry Moore's sculpture, on the condition that the Tate Trustees matched this by raising a similar amount from other sources.

A controversy arose when forty-one British artists, including Moore's former assistant, Anthony Caro, got together in the offices of *Studio International* and composed a letter to *The Times* objecting to the Tate Gallery's plan to spend £400,000 on a new building to house exclusively the works of Henry Moore. 'The radical nature of art in the twentieth century is inconsistent with the notion of an heroic and monumental role for the artist and any attempt to predetermine greatness for an individual in a publicly financed form of permanent enshrinement is a move we as artists repudiate.'[9] Among the signatories were Howard Hodgkin, Elisabeth Frink, Eduardo Paolozzi, David Annesley and Gillian Ayres.

Anthony Lousada, by then Chairman of the Tate Trustees, replied in *The Times* the following day: only the government's £200,000 was intended to go towards the housing of Moore's work; the equivalent sum raised by the Gallery would be to complete the new wing of the building which would house the Modern Collection.[10] If a misunderstanding had been corrected, a distrust of an individual artist's desire for aggrandisement remained. *The Times* kept the issue alive by printing Myles Murphy's rejoinder to Lousada: 'A museum of modern art must be

... radical ... a permanent gift such as Mr Moore's by its very massiveness and generosity is in the end self-defeating.'[11]

One irony in this controversy was that Moore himself had once been too radical for the Tate. When Robert Sainsbury, in his early days as a collector had been approached by Manson for the loan of a Degas bronze, he had agreed to lend on the condition that the Tate also borrowed his 1932 Henry Moore of a mother and child. Manson immediately refused and went on to say that no Henry Moore would ever be exhibited at the Tate while it remained under his directorship.[12]

In 1968, however, Moore's work was the subject of a highly successful Tate exhibition, curated by David Sylvester, at Moore's request, as Sylvester had curated Moore's first retrospective, in 1951, for the Festival of Britain. Sylvester's catalogue for the 1968 exhibition remains one of the definitive texts on this artist; and at the dinner held at the Tate in celebration of Moore, the American millionaire Joseph Hirshhorn and his wife presented the Gallery with $30,000 (£12,480) as a mark of admiration for the artist. With Moore's approval, this was put towards the cost of the new extension. Two months later Moore reiterated his desire to give a large collection of his work to the Tate. After further discussion a deed of gift was signed by him on 17 July 1969. It contained a clause to the effect that the works of art would only pass to the Tate if and when an extension had been completed which provided an increase in gallery space of not less than 50 per cent of that currently existing. This clause effectively put his deed of gift on hold.

Moore's initial idea for a memorial to himself had been to have his house and studio preserved. He had told Norman Reid of this on one of his visits to Perry Green in Hertfordshire. Reid argued that the cost of upkeep would be enormous and that it would be better to augment his representation at the Tate. Moore knew that at this time Sir Kenneth Clark was thinking of bequeathing to the Tate (he later changed his mind in favour of the British Museum) the Henry Moore drawings in his possession. Moore was also visibly pleased by Reid's suggestion that space should be put aside for his work in the new extension, so that he would have similar treatment to Constable, Turner and Blake – all of whom had rooms to themselves. Reid's timely suggestion had led to Moore's deed of gift. But in time Moore was to return to his original idea and to embroil the Tate in further complications.

★   ★   ★

One of the attractions of the front extension was that it had been planned so that an area for temporary exhibitions, a lecture theatre and restaurant could be opened independently, at times when the permanent collection was closed. But the most decisive factor in favour of the front extension had been Jennie Lee's initial failure to persuade Denis Healey, Minister of Defence, that one of the two adjacent sites, occupied by the Royal Army Medical College, the Barracks and Queen Alexandra's Military Hospital, should be made available to the Tate. Left without the prospect of additional space or a front extension, the Tate's only solution was to conceive of a four-storey extension on the final quarter. This would be unacceptable to Westminster City Council as it had recently imposed conservation regulations on the Millbank area. The situation changed dramatically in July 1969 when Harold Wilson announced that, owing to the decision to build a new military hospital at Woolwich, the Queen Alexandra site would become available to the Tate in 1975. *The Times* commented: 'The way is now clear for the trustees to draw up revised plans to develop the north-east corner of the present site and the Government are prepared for building to start as soon as the trustees are ready.'[13]

One primary objective favoured by Norman Reid in the new extension was daylight. His views on lighting had changed after walking through the galleries with Giacometti who had regarded the old Victorian galleries with delight, owing to the volume and quality of the light. By comparison, he accepted reluctantly those galleries which had been modernised and on which a good deal of time and money had been spent trying to produce good artificial light. Another primary objective was flexibility; for there was an awareness that, owing to changes in the artistic and social climate, certain categories were beginning to dissolve: already criticism had been levelled at the Museum of Modern Art in New York for its rather rigid emphasis on historical display. At the Tate the idea was that the new extension would house the Modern Collection, leaving the older part of building available for the British School, but a certain fluidity would govern modern British art which could be shown in either section. It was also thought advisable to open up entrances in the Sculpture Hall (in the 'North Duveen'), giving access to the far galleries in the new extension, so that at times they could be used as a separate unit for special exhibitions.

Michael Compton was asked to draw up a brief for the architectural partnership Llewelyn-Davies, Weeks, Forestier-Walker. The firm was primarily associated with the building of hospitals and was thought to be capable of dealing with complex lighting and air-conditioning. With hindsight, Compton now thinks his brief was too prescriptive, for it was his idea that the extension should be based on a grid-like scheme, divisible at certain points that related to its roof structure. Working to this scheme, Lord Llewelyn-Davies and his job-architect, Michael Huckstep, produced a cell-like structure of twenty-one modules – not unlike squash courts and each nine metres square. These could be combined to form layouts of varying size and character. Each module was to be regarded as a separate unit with its own air-conditioning and controls which enabled natural light to be enhanced, if need be, by artificial light. Each module was to be covered by a pyramid of clear glazing incorporating an ultra-violet filter to exclude radiation at wave-lengths damaging to paintings. The volume of light was to be controlled by a set of triangular roller blinds to be pulled up on the outside of the roof and diffused by a further set inside the roof structure. This meant that each bay would have eight blinds. The Tate questioned the viability of these and asked for a full-scale mock-up. This was not requested loudly enough and the architects went ahead with these blinds which, once installed, were to be subject to a maintenance contract, on a weekly basis. When the first ones installed failed to function correctly, Judith Jeffreys insisted on a demonstration. This took place at the Tate's Gorst Road store where it was found that the testator – the device which kept the blinds under tension – made a noise like a pig having its throat cut every time a blind moved. In July 1974 the architects recommended with regret that work on the blinds should cease and an alternative remedy be investigated.

They found a solution in a double layer of aluminium louvres, one adjusted on a seasonal basis and the other to be activated by a photo-electric cell in each bay. These kept natural light within the limits required for conservation and they reduced solar heat to a manageable level so that temperature and humidity limits could be maintained. The louvre installation nevertheless added a further two years to the delays already incurred. The Tate had repeatedly to revise its announcement concerning the date of opening. Screen installation caused additional delay, but the final straw was the discovery that the air-conditioning was not functioning properly: the amount of air drawn in by pumps at either end of the plant room – a corridor-like space attached to the side wall of the North Duveen – did not match the volume of air which, after being pumped through a complicated system of filters, de-humidifiers and heaters, emerged into the galleries. It was discovered that the Tate was, in effect, air-conditioning much of Millbank as the air was leaking through the porous breeze-block walls of the plant room. Attempts to make the walls air-tight caused the flat roof to bubble up with pressure. Next, paving slabs were placed on top of the roof to keep it in position. When these too began to lift off, the Ministry of Works stepped in and persuaded the architects that the scheme was not working. The entire roof of the plant room had to be taken off, all its machinery lifted out by crane and put in store, and the walls lined with zinc. This caused another two-year delay and put an end to hopes of opening, as planned, in 1976. The Queen's Silver Jubilee in 1977, an apt event to celebrate with a new building, came and went and still the extension hung fire.

13

The Fierce Light of Publicity

In an article entitled 'Collecting for the Tate Gallery' John Rothenstein once observed that 'the fierce light of publicity beats upon the genius, the charlatan, and even the plodding journeyman alike'.[1] Norman Reid, recognising the need to deal carefully with indiscriminate press interest, instructed that no press call was to be taken by a member of staff unless it had been vetted first by Corinne Bellow. But the Tate had become increasingly outward-looking in its ambitions and was now far more active in its attempts to court the press. Even bad publicity, it discovered in the 1970s, did not always go amiss, for it increased attendance figures.

Reid involved the press in his battle to improve the public transport systems affecting the Tate. From the Director's office, which overlooks the river and Atterbury Street, he noticed with concern the ever greater queues of people, many of them tourists, waiting for the erratic No.88 bus which passed the Tate on weekdays. On 15 May 1972 the *Evening Standard* reported Reid's suggestion that there should be a special weekend bus linking museums and art galleries – a 'museum special'. A year later he and Corinne Bellow were still trying to get a bus to pass the Tate at weekends. Finally, on 8 March 1973, London Passenger Transport Committee announced that Route 77 would be diverted via Millbank instead of along the Albert Embankment between Vauxhall Bridge and Lambeth Bridge.

The Tate became much less isolated when Pimlico station was added to the Victoria Line in the autumn of 1972. Reid had hoped that the London Underground authorities could be persuaded to name the station 'Tate Gallery', but this was thought not sufficiently representative of the area, and at first the authorities even refused a notice saying 'Alight here for the Tate Gallery'. Nor did the tiles chosen to ornament this station offer much help, as they bore a rather unexciting abstract design by Peter Sedgeley. And problems of security eventually defeated the notion that sculpture should be placed in the relatively spacious ticket hall. Unlike the Metro station in Paris which serves the Louvre, Pimlico still today gives little welcome to the Tate visitor, despite the fact that certain Tate works are now depicted in murals on the passageway walls.

Once out of the station the visitor has to negotiate a route to the Gallery. It soon became obvious that signposts were needed. Not long after these were put up, one Pimlico householder, puzzled and apologetic, rang the Information Department to ask why a large number of people kept knocking on her door to ask if they had arrived at the Tate Gallery.

Among other often small but significant improvements affecting the visitor's experience of the Tate was the opening of the Coffee Shop on 2 August 1972. Intended as a place where a quick snack could be obtained, it offered a limited menu and was soon serving daily around 500 people who spent on average 19p per head. Its chief problem was excessive heat for its temperature was rarely below 80 degrees Fahrenheit. This was thought to be a factor behind the rapid staff turnover, for by March 1973, twenty-eight staff had come and gone. As a temporary solution a 'heat bonus' was added to the standard wage. Difficulties had also been caused in 1972 by the government-enforced 'three-day week', which closed two galleries on the lower floor and kept lights in galleries and offices down to the minimum.

The appointment of Iain Bain to the Publications Department in 1972 proved a significant development. Both a scholar (with a specialist knowledge of Thomas Bewick) and publisher, he set high standards and achieved a marked increase in the quality of Tate publications. At all levels the Gallery now had many excellent members of staff, among them William (Bill) Wellstead, the Head Attendant, whose natural dignity enabled him to exert authority in a quiet, restrained manner. He had entered the Tate in April 1937, returned after the war, and was promoted to Head Attendant in 1947. His wife sold catalogues for the Arts Council during the period when they held exhibitions at the Tate. After she died, Wellstead's deep sadness was evident to many. But he eventually remarried a lively widow, who was also the Tate telephonist, and retired in May 1976, after thirty-nine years of service.

The early 1970s saw an increase in staff numbers and in professionalism in every aspect of the Gallery. The Education and Exhibitions Department was strengthened by the appointment of Robert Cumming and Caroline Odgers. In 1970 the Tate acquired its first trained librarian, Antony Symons, formerly Liverpool City Libraries' Art Librarian. He pursued an active policy with regard to the catalogue

54 Left to right: Michael Compton, Richard Morphet, Anne Seymour, Sir Norman Reid, Ronald Alley, Martin Butlin, 1973

collection which soon became a resource without parallel elsewhere in the field of modern and contemporary exhibition catalogues. Symons inherited Elisabeth Bell as Assistant Librarian, and he appointed Beth Houghton, who was eventually to succeed him as Librarian. Meanwhile the consolidation of the curatorial staff resulted in the promotion of Leslie Parris and Richard Morphet to the Deputy Keeperships of, respectively, the British and the Modern Collections. Elizabeth Einberg, Ronald Parkinson and Judy Egerton joined the British Collection, while in the Modern Collection Anne Seymour took temporary leave in order to select the first Hayward Annual, which became the seminal *The New Art* exhibition in 1972. Penny Marcus filled her place, remaining on the staff until 1976 when Sandy Nairne arrived, first as a Research Assistant but becoming Assistant Keeper in 1978 when Anne Seymour left in order to marry the dealer Anthony d'Offay. Three others appointed to the Modern Collection were Teresa Newman, Pat Gilmour (who was given special responsibility for prints) and David Brown who had changed career in mid-life, having formerly directed the Technical Department of Veterinary Research for Nigeria.

The Conservation Department not only increased in size during the 1970s, but also underwent a dramatic increase in status and scientific respectability. Though this was part of an international development, the Tate's Conservation Department benefited from the Director's keen interest. Reid, a council member and Vice-Chairman of the International Institute of Conservation, also served for eight years on the Council of the Rome Centre and for two years was its President. He had been concerned with the physical well-being of the Collection since his arrival at the Tate; and of the many projects he initiated, the setting up of the Conservation Department remained the one which gave him the most satisfaction. In 1964 he had sent a paper to Jennie Lee on the need for a Central Institute for the Conservation of Works of Art, as he was worried by the serious shortage of skilled restorers. With higher fees available on the commercial market, there was also the ever-present danger of losing trained restorers to the trade. Commercial restorers, with one or two honourable exceptions, had a different outlook and standards to those adopted by national collections: whereas a commercial restorer had to see that the job in hand covered overheads and his or her salary, a conservator in a national institution gave each work the necessary time that its importance, or the necessary treatment, required. Also, a Conservation Department serving a national collection tried to keep up with research in new and safer methods of treatment; while the commercial restorer tended to stay with outdated methods which were quicker, but in the long-term less sound.

Reid's initiative had been taken with the approval of Sir Philip Hendy, Director of the National Gallery. Both were dismayed by the slowness of the government's response to this demand for a Central Institute. They therefore joined with the Director of the Victoria & Albert Museum and in 1966 put forward a provisional scheme for training a small number of restorers, in collaboration with the Courtauld Institute of Art. Two years passed before even this modest proposal was taken up and the Tate took on five students. Although these students spent 40 per cent of their three years at the Courtauld, they still placed an extra burden on the Tate conservation staff and studio space, and initially took time from the prime responsibility of the department – namely to conserve the collection.

The Gulbenkian Foundation, aware of the seriousness of the problem, set up a committee, under the chairmanship of Sir Colin Anderson, to report on 'Training in the Conservation of Paintings'. They published their recommendations in 1972 and gave unequivocal support to the idea for a central Conservation Institute, which many other countries now had. The Foundation also offered £150,000 towards the equipping of such an institute, but the idea was still not supported by the Paymaster General, who favoured the proliferation of small centres. The only positive proposal that finally emerged was that the Courtauld Institute of Art should be elevated to the Central Institute.

During 1974 the work of the Tate's Conservation Department had been dominated by Turner in preparation for the two-hundredth anniversary of his birth the following year. This major exhibition (mounted at the Royal Academy, not the Tate, as it was felt that its permanent display would blunt the impact of a special exhibition) enabled Slabczynski to fulfill his ambition: to see the majority of the Turner collection put into safe and exhibitable condition. Just as this work was coming to an end in the spring of 1975, the restorers became aware that the floor of the main studio was gradually sinking beneath them, owing to subsidence. An immediate evacuation took place to nearby galleries on the lower floor. At a press conference for the 1972–74 Report, the journalists showed more interest in the dramatic collapse of the studio floor than in delays to the extension, signalled in the Report by an essay entitled 'A Growing Concern'.

The Conservation Department's abrupt change of surroundings more or less coincided with Slabczynski's retirement. His successor, Alexander Dunluce, though he had at one point left the Tate for eighteen months, was from the ranks of the existing staff. Therefore there was more a change of emphasis than a dramatic redirection. Dunluce put the Condition and Treatment files on to a comprehensive system, and during the first year that he was in charge a survey was done of all the paintings in the collection. Eighty-five were found to be in need of treatment in the near future. Conservation concerns were becoming increasingly complex as artists turned to new media, approaches and methods. It was no longer always the case that physical durability and constant appearance were inherent properties to all works of art. Rapid changes of appearance and structural degradation might be a part of the artist's intent and therefore intrinsic properties that were in no way detrimental to the work of art. The conservator's job was to consider the work of art from many points of view – including material, structure, technique and intent – before reaching conclusions on preservation. At the same time there was a shift in emphasis – akin to the move from curative to preventative medicine – from restoration to conservation.

One of Slabczynski's first appointments in the Conservation Department had been Percy Williams, who personified the qualities associated with his profession – chiefly the self-effacement necessary to restore with due care and attention another's work. Two younger members of staff, Roy Perry (who was to provide specifications for the Conservation Studios in the new extension) and Christopher Holden, had learnt much from Slabczynski, despite the fact that the strict, elderly Pole had sometimes announced that the young men were finally ready to learn a certain method long after they had, in fact, acquired it. With the appointment of Katarzyna Szeleynski in 1971, the department gained a restorer with a specialist knowledge of paper. In time, with the establishment of a Print Department and the Archive, paper conservation became increasingly important and caused the appointment of two additional restorers in 1975. However, the Tate did not acquire a purpose-built paper conservation studio until the mid-1980s, and sculpture was still at this time sent to the Victoria & Albert Museum sculpture studio for treatment.

★   ★   ★

One of Sir Norman Reid's strengths as a Director was his readiness, once he felt confidence in a member of staff, to accept and approve, in a non-interfering way, what she or he wanted to do.[2] Nowhere was this licensed initiative more firmly grasped than in the Exhibition and Education Department during the early 1970s. Michael Compton, its Keeper, recollects that Reid was determined that the exhibition programme should not be an expression of the Director's, nor anyone else's, personality; and that it should mirror, enrich and extend some aspect of the Tate's Collection.[3] As a result, Tate exhibitions, many of which enjoyed a high profile, helped define the character of the institution and conveyed to the public a feeling that the Gallery had a clear sense of purpose. They also provided staff with research opportunities, generated income through admissions and (indirectly) through increased sales in the shop, restaurant and coffee bar, and eventually attracted sponsorship.

Michael Compton wanted the cycle of exhibitions to have a certain rhythm: usually major shows devoted to artists such as René Magritte, Barnett Newman, Ben Nicholson or Roy Lichtenstein alternated with retrospectives of artists in mid-career (Eduardo Paolozzi, Robyn Denny, William Turnbull and Richard Smith), and with thematic or historical displays. Owing to the need for advance planning, Compton often planted an also-ran in the programme which could be dropped or suppressed if need be, to make possible opportunistic shows. Having worked with local government in Hull while running the Ferens Art Gallery, he was adept at getting his proposed schedule of exhibitions approved by the Exhibitions Sub-Committee. This had been set up in the early 1970s and normally consisted of relevant staff and three or four artist-Trustees, the most senior one taking the Chair. Because the Chairman was shown the agenda only a short while before the meeting began, he had little time to rally the troops; and the committee – except much later when Patrick Heron joined it – often did little more than rubber-stamp the proposals.

For many visitors, memories of the Tate are often linked with specific exhibitions. One outstanding year was 1970. Continuing from the previous year into the first week of February was Roy Strong's spectacular *The Elizabethan Image: Paintings in England 1540–1620*. Overlapping with this and lasting until May was a show based around a single picture, *Endymion Porter and William Dobson*, organised by William Vaughan, which was followed by a display of the work donated in memory of Sir Herbert Read. Next came *Richard Hamilton*, which chronicled the artist's entire output up to that date and made transparent the highly intelligent, teasing awareness behind his various processes of image-making. Richard Morphet, the organiser, wrote a 30,000-word catalogue which supplied, John Russell noted, 'insights of his [Morphet's] own with extensive Eckermannising of Hamilton's own writings and table talk'.[4] Then for three weeks in May the Tate moved into environmental art for the first time and showed three separate installations dependent on small variations of colour, surface and light, designed by three Los Angeles artists – Larry Bell, Robert Irvin and Doug Wheeler. The major summer exhibition this year, *Claes Oldenburg*, was also the last exhibition at the Tate organised by the Arts Council of Great Britain (in collaboration with the Museum of Modern Art, New York). It included Oldenburg's soft typewriter, his stuffed canvas hamburger and his vinyl wash-basin, about which the critics were undecided whether the humour was viciously cynical or generous and fond.

The two following exhibitions reflected the input of Tate Trustees, for it was Phillip King who suggested the display of work by Julio González – the Spanish sculptor who taught Picasso how to weld; and it was Andrew Forge who proposed the ground-breaking *Léger and Purist Paris*, and David Sylvester who suggested that it should be curated by John Golding, who also took on board Christopher Green. The exhibition focused on the decade 1918 to 1928 – the period characterised by the 'call to order' (Cocteau's phrase) – and it took a fresh look at not only neo-Classicism but also the interest in the modern – machinery, aeroplanes, cars and consumer goods. Not the least remarkable aspect of this show (which contained 120 paintings, half by Léger and the rest by Picasso, Braque, Gris, Mondrian, Delaunay, Purist and De Stijl artists) was its design by Neave Brown, for the sculpture halls became translated into an ocean liner of the 1920s or 1930s. Robert Melville, in the *New Statesman*, called it 'the best exhibition of his [Léger's] work ever held in this country', but he also argued that the attempt to represent Léger as the most representative artist of his generation 'resulted in a distortion of his role in the modern movement'.[5]

Rich contrasts of experience continued the following year, particularly in February, when *Shock of Recognition* – which underlined the debt British artists of the eighteenth and nineteenth centuries owed to Dutch landscape painting of the seventeenth century – overlapped for one week with *Warhol*, which reconstructed five of Andy Warhol's major themes, and was the first exhibition in London devoted solely to his work. Visitors entering the former show were immediately confronted with Turner's *Dordrecht: The Dort Packet-Boat from Rotterdam Becalmed*, which took its chief inspiration from Aelbert Cuyp's *View of Dordrecht* hanging

55 Installation view of *The Elizabethan Image: Painting in England 1540–1620*, 1969

nearby. Alternatively, visitors joined the queue for *Warhol*, whose work impressed with its clarity, resonance, and what Caroline Tisdall called 'his unfailing ability to touch and capture the nerve centre of his time'.[6]

To deal selectively with the 1970s exhibition programme is invidious, but among the many shows that deserve mention are *Caspar David Friedrich* (1972), *The Age of Charles I* (1972–3), *Paul Nash: Paintings and Watercolours* (1975) and *George Stubbs: Anatomist and Animal Painter* (1976). Another landmark exhibition – *Landscape in Britain, c.1750–1850* (1973–4) – was intended to provide a stimulating introduction to the Turner and Constable bicentenaries in 1975 and 1976, for it showed how the aping of the Classical tradition gradually gave way to the feeling eye. It was curated by Leslie Parris, who, with Conal Shields and Ian Fleming-Williams, was also responsible for the 1976 Constable show. This, the biggest display of his work ever staged, caught what made him popular and what he said he wanted in painting: 'Lively and soothing, calm and exhilarating, fresh and blowing ... Silvery windy and delicious; all health and the absence of anything stagnant.'

Some exhibitions inevitably proved more successful than others. One disaster was the 1971 Robert Morris exhibition. Michael Compton and David Sylvester had negotiated this with the American artist, whose work followed a minimal and conceptual approach. Wanting to avoid ponderous museum-type planning, Morris had refused to submit advance guidelines for his installation and simply announced he would build everything himself within a month of his arrival in London. His intent was in keeping with a current desire for art without permanent material basis. When the show opened visitors were invited to climb

wooden ramps, swing down ropes, inch their way up fifteen-foot wooden chim-
neys and also walk a tightrope. There was also a steel structure which was intended to be hit with tethered lumps of concrete. Morris's desire was for the audience
to explore their own bodily reactions. What the Tate had underestimated was the
over-zealous enthusiasm of the audience and the readiness with which competition and aggressive instincts came to the fore. When the lumps of heavy concrete
were swung round and dropped they made a shattering noise. After five days
some of the exhibits had disintegrated and enough minor injuries had been
caused for Michael Compton to ring Norman Reid at home during the weekend
and request his permission to close the show. It was eventually reopened in a non-
interactive form, with examples of Morris's sculpture, drawings, a film, and photographic documentation of the short-lived participatory event. Though Richard
Cork thought this had been 'a lightweight affair that leaves no lasting impression',[7] Reyner Banham experienced it very differently: 'It was intoxicating, irre-
sistible, completely deafening and fabulous; by the end of the private viewing the
place was a bedlam in which all rules of decorum had been abandoned as liberated aesthetes leaped and teetered and heaved and clambered and shouted and
joined hands with total strangers.'[8]

During the whole of 1973 one gallery was put aside for educational installations
and other events organised by the Education team. Terry Measham, who published *A Child's Guide to Looking at Paintings* in 1979, was often the instigator, but
his ideas required the help of others in order for them to take form. The policy at
this time was to expand and diversify educational activities, also to begin a collec-

56 Installation view of *Warhol* exhibition, 1971

tion of films on art and artists, so that a regular programme of these could be added to the daily lectures. One instance of an educational installation was the display of large-scale British abstracts which were hung in Gallery 15 between February and April 1973, where, looked at from the point of view of 'process, mark-making, structure, space and scale', they became the subject of a series of talks and lectures. The highlight of this year, from a child's point of view, was *Kidsplay*, which ran during the summer vacation and was designed by three art college tutors – John Gingell, Diane Setch and David Wightman – committed to Herbert Read's concept of 'education through art'. By creating environments that played on illusion and reality, the exhibition introduced children to the use of perspective to control our perception of space. Kids queued to get in, and in the words of one national newspaper, the Tate was 'swamped by little children'. Different in scope but similar in intention was *Kidsplay II*, run the following year in a canvas dome on the lawn, owing to shortage of gallery space.

The Education Department liaised not only with schools but also the Open University and London University, collaborating on specific courses. It also edited, and in some cases wrote, short guides to special exhibitions. But the backbone of its educational efforts remained the lecture programme. Each year this included Laurence Bradbury's children's Christmas lectures which catered for a very young audience. Bradbury became one of the longest-serving of a rota of lecturers whom the Tate employed on a freelance basis. He had himself learnt much from listening to Alan Bowness lecture at the Tate, and went on to become a skilful communicator, capable of dealing with all kinds of audience and talking about art in a serious but light manner. Norman Reid used to say that if laughter could be heard in the Gallery, you knew that Laurence Bradbury was lecturing.[9] Initially these talks took place in the galleries, in front of certain pictures, and with the audience sitting on collapsible stools provided by the Gallery. On one occasion a visitor came rushing back in from the Embankment, with the apology that she had been so enthralled by what she had heard that she had walked out, with her handbag over one arm and unaware that the Tate Gallery stool was over the other. After a lecture room was created, Bradbury and others often worked with slides, but would afterwards invite the audience to go and find the relevant works of art in the Gallery.

Certain educational activities featured in the thirty-minute film 'Beyond the Frame', made by the Royal College of Art Film School in collaboration with the Tate. It showed, for instance, the physical exercises done with primary school-children among examples of New Generation sculpture produced by students and followers of Anthony Caro. This large, abstract and often brightly coloured work frequently relates to bodily experience, and to the act of balancing, leaning or supporting. Over a period of some six or seven years, Alistair McAlpine had collected sculptures by David Annesley, Michael Bolus, Phillip King, Tim Scott, William Tucker, William Turnbull and Isaac Witkin, and in 1973 he gave fifty-nine of these to the Tate, making the largest gift from an individual so far received, with the exception of the Turner Bequest. It was too big a collection to be exhib-

57 Upside-down room in *Kidsplay* exhibition, 1973

ited in its entirety, and after a selection had been shown at the Tate in the summer of 1971, further selections were displayed in a former drill hall in Chenies Street, off Tottenham Court Road. It was here, in response to the physical cheerfulness and robust vitality of this sculpture, that young children were encouraged to make with their bodies similar shapes, rhythms and movements to those found in the works of art. The Chenies Street Gallery, as it became called, was leased from Camden Council and ran from May 1972 for two years, after which it had to be closed as its fire precautions did not meet GLC regulations.

Alistair McAlpine proved a generous benefactor in another way. His original idea was to set up an art library of nineteenth- and twentieth-century books, documents, archival material and prints in St Mary of Lambeth after its deconsecration. This project became too costly for the money available and instead, with the help of Stewart Mason, formerly Director of Education for Leicestershire and a Tate Trustee, McAlpine set up the Institute of Contemporary Prints. Registered in 1973 as a charitable trust, with Reid, Bowness and Morphet sitting on the Council of Management, it initially operated as a reference library of post-war prints, which was to be housed at and eventually given to the Tate Gallery. With a combination of vision and diplomacy, Mason suggested to artists, printers and dealers that they should donate work on a principle similar to that which obliges publishers to donate one copy of every book they issue to copyright libraries. In this way, Marlborough Fine Art, Editions Alecto, Christie's Contemporary Art, Clarendon Graphics, The Tetrad Press, Annely Juda and others were encouraged to give generously – though the three largest gifts came through Stanley Jones and the Curwen Press, Rose and Christopher Prater of Kelpra Studios and from Leslie Waddington. In all, some 2,500 prints came to the Tate through the auspices of the Institute of Contemporary Prints.

In the past, responsibility for collecting prints had been left to the British Museum and the Victoria & Albert Museum. The Tate now felt that distinctions made according to media were too rigid. Many artists, such as Eduardo Paolozzi and Joe Tilson, used prints as a means to link with and feed into their work in other media; while others, such as Robert Rauschenberg and Richard Hamilton, defied compartmentalisation by deliberately blurring the boundaries between painting and print-making (problems that the Tate likewise confronted with photography at a later date). But the addition of the Institute of Contemporary Prints multiplied the Tate's modest print collection overnight by ten times, making necessary the creation of a Print Department. Pat Gilmour, already widely acknowledged as an authority in this field, was put in charge assisted by Jill Howarth, and set about this new venture with seemingly inexhaustible energy and invention. The special furniture which she designed for the storage of prints proved to be most effective and was later taken up by the Victoria & Albert Museum. Gilmour and Howarth also mounted 'thank you' exhibitions which acknowledged the donors. Further contributions arrived from Anderson-O'Day, Bernard Jacobson, Andrew Dickerson and Patrick Seale Prints, as well as from artists. Eventually, at the Board meeting on 17 May 1979 the Trustees started to question the Print Department's policy of more-or-less automatic acceptance of prints, for by then the British Museum and the Victoria & Albert Museum had also begun to collect contemporary prints. The introduction of a more selective approach also put an end to young artists claiming representation at the Tate on the basis of a print given to the print collection.

In 1976 the Print Department began a series of small exhibitions linking paintings and prints. This integration of prints into the Modern Collection in an effective and involving way came to an end when the Conservation Department began to tighten regulations concerning light levels. But if integrated displays were no longer possible, the Tate continued to benefit from gifts such as Henry Moore's presentation of 160 lithographs and etchings (in effect a copy of every print he had made), which helped widen and deepen perception of post-war art.

So, too, did the establishment of the Tate Archive. The intention to set up an Archive Department had first been announced in the 1965–66 Annual Report. In fact the Gallery had begun keeping certain records of artists, art dealers and art societies since 1957, but this beginning had not been followed up systematically. A grant from the Robert and Lisa Sainsbury Charitable Fund enabled Michael Compton to set up an Archive in earnest and its existence was publicised by a letter from Sir Norman Reid in the July 1970 issue of *Studio International*. Four years later Sarah Fox-Pitt was appointed to oversee both Library and Archive but even-

58 Joseph Beuys at the Tate, March 1972
(Richard Hamilton second from right)

tually took charge solely of the latter when it became evident that the Archive required a separate administration, owing to the value and variety of the work collected. The original aim – to provide a home for documents and photographs relating to twentieth-century British art – remains the core concern, though the collection has expanded to include material relating to pre-twentieth-century British art and modern foreign art. A wide range of items is collected, among them artists' letters, notebooks, sketchbooks, records of sales, photographs, posters, slides, collections of press-cuttings, tape-recordings, transcripts of interviews, video-recordings and assorted memorabilia. A number of leading artists – notably Dame Barbara Hepworth, Henry Moore and Naum Gabo – expressed themselves willing to present or make available material for the Archive, at a time when a number of American universities had begun actively collecting and paying substantial sums for archival material. Among the first major purchases made by the Archive were Stanley Spencer's papers and Paul Nash's papers, the latter including 1,267 negatives, only 99 of which had been used in the popular and intriguing Tate Gallery exhibition of his photographs in 1973.

By this date the Tate was also having to take into account the various activities loosely accommodated under the umbrella label 'Conceptual art'. The first instance of this was the *Seven Exhibitions* mounted at short notice in February–March 1972, when Robyn Denny's retrospective was delayed a year. The decision had been to ask seven artists each to make a separate exhibition that would fill all or part of the four-week gap. Bruce McLean opted for twenty-four hours and mounted a display he called 'King for a Day'. Keith Arnatt made a work based on photographs of every single worker in the Tate Gallery to point up how many people are required to mount an art exhibition. Owing to staff protest, this work was never shown. The other participants in this stop-gap event were Bob Law,

Michael Craig-Martin, David Tremlett, Hamish Fulton and Joseph Beuys.

Beuys contributed an exhibition of films and videotapes of his past performances. He also agreed to appear at the Tate on a Saturday in order to give one of his live-action pieces. This was his first public appearance in England, though two years before, one of his performances had been the sensation of the Edinburgh Festival. His marathon discussion, which took place in the octagon in the Sculpture Galleries, lasted six-and-a-half hours. Wearing his famous grey trilby hat and his many-pocketed waistcoat, he brought with him an immense, almost mythical reputation, owing to the catalytic nature of his teaching at the Kunstakademie in Dusseldorf. 'All I do', he was quoted as saying, 'is inform people of their own possibilities.'[10]

But if the Tate was now ready to accept Beuys in person, it was less certain about his art objects. It bought his bronze sculpture *Bed* in 1972, but on 18 July 1974 the Board rejected four pieces by Beuys because of the unstable nature of some of the ingredients. The most important of these was *Eurasia* which consisted of items that had been used by Beuys in a piece performed twice in October 1966, in Copenhagen and Berlin. For ritualistic and symbolic purposes it had become part of Beuys's method to include in his work both dead and living materials, and *Eurasia* incorporated a wedge of fat, a blackboard and chalk, and a stuffed hare. Despite a persuasive letter from the Beuys expert Caroline Tisdall, assuring Reid that it was an ideal representative work, bringing together many of the themes in Beuys's thought, and that the artist had taken care to use a good taxidermist, that the fat had been bonded with beeswax and the chalk fixed with three layers of polyurethane, Reid was not convinced. It remained for him less a complete work of art than 'an interesting remainder of a performance piece'. As he explained to his Chairman: 'For me what remains of *Eurasia 1966* has no greater significance but for imagination than, say, the costume of the pantomime horse in 'Parade' after the cleaners have gone.'[11] He also thought that it presented conservation problems that were unanswerable and therefore he could not advise the Trustees to acquire it. Earlier the Trustees had rejected Beuys's *Fat Battery*, again because of the unstable nature of its ingredients, and it was bought instead by the art collector and Tate Trustee, E.J.(Ted) Power.[12]

Reid has admitted that for him decisions concerning some contemporary art during the 1970s grew increasingly hard.[13] He could not always see the point of certain works of art which his Modern Collection staff put forward as potential purchases. But he listened to his curators, and in many instances supported their views at Board level, even when the work was not to his personal liking. At a Board meeting held 15 February 1973, he reported that he had asked the Modern Collection staff to carry out a survey of Conceptual art, in an attempt to pinpoint those works they thought the most important available. This had now been done and a sub-committee, composed of Sir Robert Sainsbury, Ted Power, Howard Hodgkin and the Director, was formed to consider their recommendations. The following month it was reported that this sub-committee had approved the acquisition of works by Victor Burgin, Jan Dibbets, Dan Graham, John Hilliard, Sol

LeWitt, Richard Long, Bruce McLean and Klause Rinke, as well as documentary material by Beuys for the Archive. The only item on the list of recommendations that had been withdrawn was a socio-political work – Hans Haacke's *Manhattan Gallery Goers*. The total cost of these purchases, it was estimated, would come to approximately £15,545.

The Tate's commitment to Conceptual art was also affirmed in the 1972–74 Biennial Report which contained an intelligently argued and persuasive essay by Richard Morphet. This not only placed Conceptual art within the context of past art, but it also underlined the richness of interpretation which its complexity, ambiguity and use of deliberately objective methods of presentation invited. In order to demonstrate this further, the Tate embarked on a series of displays of recent Conceptual acquisitions. These included Sol LeWitt's *Wall Drawing / Four Basic Colours (Black, Yellow, Red and Blue)* which had to be drawn each time it was exhibited on the gallery walls, the Tate owning no material object other than the written instructions, incorporated into a signed certificate by the artist.[14]

The prevalent myths, misunderstandings and prejudices about modern art became the subject in 1973 of a Tate exhibition, entitled *A Child of Six Could Do It!* It contained over two hundred cartoons which looked at a period of modern art that coincided with the life-span of the Tate and effectively formed an anti-history of twentieth-century art. Subsequently these cartoons became the subject of a book produced by the Publications Department with an introduction by George Melly. Ironically, this willingness to acknowledge the humour associated with modern art gave little pause to the journalists who leapt on the bandwagon once the uproar concerning 'The Bricks' began to roll.

14

Brickbats and Bouquets

The optimism that had accompanied developments in the arts during the 1960s waned as a period of affluence gave way to the economic crises of the 1970s. In the wake of the collapse of the fixed exchange rate, the take-off of inflation, the rise in oil prices, a world recession, growing unemployment and an increase in industrial unrest, there followed a period not of expansion but restraint. Arts Council grants now rarely matched the needs of the companies and organisations they supported. And soon after the Conservative government took over in 1970, the principle of free entry to national collections came under scrutiny. Wanting to reduce the dependency of national museums on the state and the government's own expenditure, the Conservatives proposed the introduction of entry charges. Although Mrs Thatcher, State Secretary for Education, was fiercely in favour, this proposal was opposed by all the national museums and galleries, with the exception of the Imperial War Museum.

Nationalistic sentiment had been a vital force in the making of the Tate Gallery, many donors giving generously in the belief that they were contributing to an aspect of the nation's cultural life that was available to all, and thus also to the nation's health, owing to the vital connection between art and society.[1] Over the years the Tate, like other national museums and galleries, had depended largely on taxpayer's money, and this reinforced the feeling that these collections belonged to the nation and should be freely accessible.

The Heath government had wanted to introduce charges in 1971 but practical administrative difficulties delayed their imposition. When Princess Anne visited *Shock of Recognition* on 22 January 1971, a demonstration against charges was taking place and a blue bus, parked outside the Tate, bore the slogan 'Keep Museums Free'. Despite much lobbying on the part of campaigners against admission charges, the government proceeded with their plans, and the Trustees of the Tate and the National Gallery fought hard for one free day a week and concessions for children, pensioners and the disabled. At first the government steadfastly refused to consider a free day, and the Sainsbury family, anxious to preserve a time when entry would be without charge, offered to defray the cost of opening the Tate Gallery free on two evenings a week for one year. This proved unnecessary when in July 1973 the Government suddenly reversed its decision and granted the request for a free day.

Though opposed to charges, the National Gallery and Tate Trustees were in a difficult position, for they were responsible to the government and had no wish to drive an wedge between Lord Eccles, who had replaced Jennie Lee as Arts Minister, and themselves. The effect of inflation on wage demands and the growing economic crisis was affecting all the arts. But, ironically, the wage increases, which helped make charging necessary, eroded potential profit, as did the new value-added tax. Shortly before he was replaced by Norman St John-Stevas in December 1973, Lord Eccles did, however, agree a reduction in the amount to be charged – from five to two shillings – but even so, when charges were introduced in January 1974, all the museums and galleries involved experienced a drop in numbers. At the general election the following month Labour was returned to power as a minority government and by 30 March museum charges were formally revoked. On Norman Reid's instructions, fifty coloured balloons were flown from the flagpole, and a banner saying 'FREE' was hung outside the central front window.

Art's role in the political arena came to the fore again that year when Moscow police and plain-clothes agents used bulldozers, dumpers and sprinkler wagons to thwart attempts to hold an exhibition of abstract art in a field on the outskirts of the city. Hearing of this, Reid cancelled his official visit to the Soviet Union in connection with a Turner exhibition which was to take place in Moscow and Leningrad. This was the first time that the arts had stood so overtly at the centre of protest in the Soviet Union and the event was widely reported. Subsequently, the authorities modified their harsh views, and in January 1975, Reid, together with Gerald Forty, Director of Fine Arts for the British Council, made his trip to the Soviet Union. He returned there in October, to be present at the official opening of the Turner exhibition at the Hermitage in Leningrad, after which he reported to his Trustees that the rooms devoted to Turner had looked splendid.

In 1976 the Tate again became a focus for criticism of the Soviet government – this time voiced not by a Gallery official but by the Women's Campaign for Soviet Jewry. A small group of demonstrators stood outside the Tate, wearing striped replicas of prison clothes, with skull caps and with balls and chains attached to their feet. They directed a barrage of protest about the treatment of Jews in the Soviet Union at Andrei Gromyko, the Soviet Foreign Minister, when he viewed the Constable exhibition during the course of a three-day visit to London.

Another visitor to the Constable exhibition was Mollie Panter-Downes, who afterwards filed, as she had done for almost forty years, her 'Letter from London' to the *New Yorker*. Renowned for her 'stubborn egalitarianism', she took her readers around the Constable show, 'where it's nearly always summer and most of the day is afternoon',[2] and then went in search of the work which was causing uproar in the press. She noticed that Tate visitors, on finding a neat, low arrangement of bricks, were predictably horrified or scandalised.

The row over 'The Bricks' blew up in the wake of the Chancellor's recent announcement of cuts in government spending. An editor at the *Sunday Times* had noticed in the January 1976 issue of *Books and Bookmen* Douglas Cooper's review of the Tate Gallery Biennial Report for 1972–74. Cooper did not mention Carl Andre's brick sculpture, but he did cite examples of what he called 'stupidly experimental or temporarily smart rubbish', instancing work by Gilbert and

George, Victor Burgin and Barry Flanagan. He also made far more serious allegations concerning the authenticity of the Tate's recently acquired cast of Umberto Boccioni's *Unique Forms of Continuity in Space* and the value of the damaged *A Couple of Foxhounds* (then called *Hound and Bitch in a Landscape*) by Stubbs which the Tate had to refute in the press.[3] But what caught the attention of the *Sunday Times* was the vitriol Cooper poured over the contemporary art purchases. 'Why is it', he asked provocatively, 'that nobody can yet hear the shrill mocking laughter with which future generations will greet the freaks and follies which are being passed off as creative art during the last decades of the capitalist era?'

Following this, the journalist Colin Simpson was asked by the *Sunday Times* to write a provocative piece on Conceptual art. Drawing on the catalogue of new acquisitions in the Tate's Biennial Report, he focused on Accession Number T1534, a Carl Andre sculpture then listed as 'Untitled' but which has since been given its correct title, *Equivalent VIII*. When first exhibited, this had been one of eight sculptures, each involving 120 bricks, which, playing upon the various mathematical possibilities, had been arranged in different rectangular configurations. Because all occupied the same amount of space in cubic inches, the show had been called *Equivalents*. What intrigued Colin Simpson was that none of these works had sold when first exhibited in New York in March 1966, and Andre had returned most of the bricks to the brickyard in order to get a refund. The Tate had expressed interest in buying one of these works in 1972 after seeing a photograph of the exhibition, whereupon Andre, unable to buy back the original sand-lime bricks, had instead reconstituted the work with firebricks, which likewise have no 'frog' (the space left in an ordinary brick to carry mortar). The *Sunday Times* put a large picture of T1534 on the front page of its Business Section and ran the article under the by-line, 'The Tate Drops a Costly Brick'.[4]

With its unerring knack for the common touch, the *Sunday Times* had seized on the one work among all the Tate's recent acquisitions that would catch the imagination of a wide public. Controversy could have been aroused, for example, by David Tremlett's *The Spring Recordings* (eighty-one tapes of spring noises made in eighty-one different counties) or Keith Arnatt's photographic sequence *Self-Burial (Television Interference Project)*, but neither would have sustained the interest that Andre's work generated, simply because it involved one of the most basic units in the building trade. It was the humble ordinariness of the brick in the costly world of high art that created a rumpus in the national and local press and on television. Moreover, the fact that the bricks were pre-made added to the outrage, for it was concluded by many that Andre himself had made nothing.

The *Daily Mirror* jumped in first, the day after the *Sunday Times* article appeared, with a repeat of its terrible pun: 'What a load of rubbish. How the Tate dropped 120 bricks.'[5] Because it was the Tate's policy not to disclose the price of a work, there was much speculation as to how much it had paid for 'The Bricks', most of the estimates far exceeding the actual cost, which, owing to the advantageous rate of the pound against the dollar, was £2,297. The *Daily Mail*, determined to go one better than other newspapers, asked three artists what they would do

59 Carl Andre, *Equivalent VIII*, 1966

60 'The repose and calm of this work reflects the simplicity and restraint
of my earlier period, the symbolism remains personal and eludes exact
interpretation'. Cartoon by Giles, *Daily Express*, 19 February 1976

with 120 bricks, and ran the headline: 'The Tate paid £4,000 for it … But the *Mail* proves you can do it cheaper. Brick-a-brac art.' One of these artists, Graham Dean, was photographed building a wall on the pavement opposite the Tate, while John Bratby made a brick improvisation which ran out of his drive into the road, along the pavement and around a drain. 'The drain, of course, is the integral part of this work,' he told the reporter. 'Once I had established the strength of the drain, with its symbolic teeth of steel, I could then move on to the rest … I was really concerned with assessing the bricks in relation to the gutter, the cobblestones and the concrete.'[6] The mockery came from all levels, from the tabloids, with their photographs of bricklayers and the repeated question 'is this art?', to *The Times*, where Bernard Levin categorically stated: 'Art may come and art may go but a brick is a brick for ever.'[7] A joking reference to Andre's work even appeared in a stock-market report: 'On a lighter note, trading men watched *London Brick* with more than usual interest, but the price shaded to 59p on the absence of orders from the Tate Gallery.'[8]

Since its acquisition, Andre's *Equivalent VIII* had twice before been on show at the Tate, alongside other works of a Minimal or Conceptual nature, and had aroused no comment. Moreover, a year before the furore over 'The Bricks' broke out, Andre's poetry had been the subject of exhibition at the Museum of Modern Art, Oxford, and at the Lisson Gallery in London, and had been accorded a respectful review in *The Times*. He was, by this date, an artist of considerable stature who exhibited internationally and was represented in many contemporary art collections. After the row started in 1976, Reid had bravely put 'The Bricks' on show so that the public could see what the fuss was about; but when a visitor threw blue food-dye over the work on 23 February 1976, it was withdrawn from view (and the stain successfully removed). But public scorn remained, partly because the Director gave instructions that no member of staff except himself should communicate with the media about this work; and though he defended the work in principle by reference to the Tate's adventurous purchasing policy, no article appeared, justifying the work, that met the needs of the general public. When a *Burlington Magazine* editorial pointed out that 'to go on talking about principles, without constantly relating them to actual examples, is a sure way of encouraging a form of academic art',[9] Reid recognised that a reply was needed and he asked the Deputy Keeper of the Modern Collection, Richard Morphet, to write it. The result was a major article, published in the same magazine the following November. This not only acknowledged Andre's debt to Brancusi and analysed the conceptual and expressive richness of *Equivalent VIII*, but it also addressed various criticisms of the Tate that had occurred in the course of the furore. However, this scholarly magazine reaches a specialist readership and what was still needed in the popular press was the kind of persuasive argument that John Russell produced for the *New York Times*: 'The thralldom of a sculpture by Mr Andre is owed to the clarity of his intention, to the frank and unambiguous way in which the materials are assembled and to the way in which a specifically American gift for plain statement has been applied to situations that in ordinary life are confused and contradictory. An Andre "is what it is", as a seventeenth-century philosopher said, "and not another thing".[10]

In April of the following year, the Tate exhibited Andre's brick piece together with about a dozen other pieces of Minimal art, in Gallery 19. To coincide with this, a forty-eight page booklet was compiled which was primarily intended to give wider circulation to Richard Morphet's *Burlington Magazine* article, but which was to be preceded by a generous selection of cartoons and hostile press comments. When presented to the Board of Trustees in February, it was vetoed by the Chairman who thought its combination unworkable and unwise.[11]

The Chairman at this time was Lord Bullock, who had joined the Board in this role in 1973. The senior Trustee who had been expected to take over from Sir Robert Sainsbury was Lord Harlech, but he felt it would be difficult for him to maintain the chairmanship of his television company and take on the Tate. Bullock, though an experienced committee man, was an unusual appointment, as the role of Chairman of the Tate had never before been filled by an academic. Author of books on Hitler and Ernest Bevin, Bullock had spent the past thirty years at Oxford, and during four of those years had been simultaneously Master of St Catherine's College and Vice-Chancellor of Oxford University. He had chaired the Friends Committee for the Ashmolean Museum, had been President of Oxford's Museum of Modern Art, a Member of the Arts Council of Great Britain, and had helped save the Ruskin School of Art by bringing it into Oxford University at a time when critical opinion had wanted it closed. He had a strong Yorkshire accent and a firm conviction that no committee is much good after it has sat for two hours. The first meeting that he chaired at the Tate was conducted with such dispatch that the staff were astonished to see the Trustees emerge before tea had been served. An additional incentive was always Bullock's determination to catch the five o'clock train back to Oxford.

When in 1975 the National Gallery wanted to extend its purchasing into the twentieth century, Lord Bullock argued that an agreement between the National and the Tate on collecting was urgently needed. This issue came up just as the Army moved out of the Queen Alexandra Military Hospital and there seemed a reasonable prospect of a Gallery of Modern Art being built on this site. At such a moment it was crucial that the Tate's identity as the National Gallery of Modern Art should not be undermined by the decision on the part of the National Gallery's Trustees and its Director, Michael Levey, to advance the purchasing limit to 1915 with the idea that in time it would extend to 1925. Simultaneously the Victoria & Albert Museum was intending to move into the field of twentieth-century sculpture and the British Museum was already collecting watercolours of this period. Also worrying was the old-fashioned view of the Tate held by Sir Arthur Drew, the new Chairman of the Standing Commission for Museums and Galleries, who stated in one paper that the National Gallery should have a voice in the Tate's purchasing policy, since they would eventually be taking over works bought by the Tate.

The issue of transfers led Sir Richard Attenborough to suggest, soon after his appointment as Trustee in 1975, that the National should be asked for an unequiv-ocal statement on the matter. In the following debate the Tate Trustees came close to obtaining from the National Gallery an undertaking that there would be no further transfers. But had such an agreement been reached, it would have required further legislation to alter the 1954 Act which provided for transfers. In order to facilitate these discussions, Bullock hoped that Sir Ernst Gombrich, who in 1976 was appointed government representative for the National, Tate and National Portrait Galleries on the Standing Commission for Museums and Gal-leries, would chair a joint committee selected to deal with the issue of purchasing responsibilities. Gombrich, however, proved unable to accept, and instead Isaiah Berlin acted in a non-partisan role at a meeting of representatives from the two Boards and the two Directors. The Tate became increasingly agitated about the chronological division between the two collections when the National Gallery bought Matisse's *Portrait of Greta Moll* (1908) in 1979, and still more so when in February of the same year a 1914 Picasso (*Fruit Dish, Bottle and Violin*) was offered by Marlborough Fine Art to the National Gallery (who bought it) rather than to the Tate. No fixed and final policy emerged from all these discussions, but there was an acceptance of the National Gallery's wish to purchase into the twentieth century, combined with an awareness that the entire national holding of early twentieth-century art was still seriously thin.

Public attention focused on the Tate each time a Biennial Report, heralded by a press conference, was published. While these usefully logged significant devel-opments, their readiness to inform was curtailed by diplomacy and restraint. Of the 1972–74 Report Bernard Denvir wrote that 'it combines opaque discretion with revelatory prolixity, and promotes reactions of hilarity, depression and respect in almost equal proportions'.[12] It was not easy for journalists to compare the Tate with what was being done elsewhere, as there was no other museum or gallery that was identical in its remit and method of funding. But there was an awareness at this time that the Stedelijk Museum in Amsterdam, under the Direc-torship of Eduard de Wilde, was making an ambitious attempt, both in its exhibi-tions and purchasing, to represent art as it happened. The Stedelijk's purchasing policy also upheld an alternative to New York's Museum of Modern Art in that it did not attempt to be fully representative or to fill gaps, but instead it often bought large groups of works by a single artist who was to be deliberately 'over-repre-sented'. By comparison, the Tate's recent acquisitions, as shown in the Biennial Report, reflected a broader commitment and a more cautious approach.

In the early 1970s, encouraged by the Chairman Robert Sainsbury, who can be credited with helping to enlarge the foreign sculpture collection, the Tate became determined to acquire a Brancusi. A *Bird in Space*, offered by the Feigen Gallery, was turned down after it was discovered that it had been illegally exported from India. Instead the Tate acquired *Maiastra*, based on the legendary bird of Ruman-ian folklore supposed to speak with a marvellous voice, to work miracles and to help people overcome the forces of evil. Other outstanding acquisitions for the Modern Collection in the course of the 1970s included Salvador Dalí's *Autumnal*

61 David Des Granges, *The Saltonstall Family*, c.1636–7

Cannibalism and *Metamorphosis of Narcissus*, both of which had been on loan to the Tate for many years from the Edward James Foundation; Kasimir Malevich's *Dynamic Suprematism*; Arshile Gorky's *Waterfall*; Magritte's *The Reckless Sleeper*; Stanley Spencer's *Double Nude Portrait*; Braque's *Clarinet and Bottle of Rum on a Mantelpiece*; George Grosz's *Suicide*, painted after his discharge from the army in 1916, as he said, 'to convince the world that this world is hateful, sick and lying'; and Max Ernst's *Celebes*, which was sold by Sir Roland Penrose in order to set up the Elephant Trust, and first shown at the Tate alongside other Ernsts lent by Penrose. These and other acquisitions enriched and deepened the Tate's representation of twentieth-century British art. The number of works by women artists also increased, with, for instance, the acquisition of Mary Potter's *Bonfire*, Vanessa Bell's *The Tub* and *Studland Beach*, as well as work by Eileen Agar, Wilhelmina Barns-Graham, Ithell Colquhoun and Prunella Clough. One overlooked artist at this time was Dora Carrington, although in 1977 her brother, Noel Carrington, expressed his intention to bequeath her *Farm at Watendlath* – a work that he finally presented to the Tate in 1987 shortly before his death.

The British Collection also benefited from outstanding acquisitions. Five sixteenth- and seventeenth-century portraits, including Marcus Gheeraerts the Younger's famous likeness of the bare-legged *Captain Thomas Lee*, which had been on loan since 1949 from Loel Guinness, finally entered the Tate's Collection in

1980. Four years before, it had also gained a large painting by the miniature artist David Des Granges, *The Saltonstall Family*, in which the father leads his two children by his first wife to meet their new sibling by his second wife, who is seated with her baby beside the bedside of the first wife who had died some six years previously. The patterning of the figures and their gestures contributes to the psychological unity of the work, which, as the Biennial Report observed, makes the picture 'a joy to look at'.[13] The Tate's increasingly rich holding in Romantic narrative landscapes already included John Martin's *The Great Day of His Wrath*, one part of a huge triptych bought in 1945. The other two parts were later acquired by the gallery owner Robert Frank and were bequeathed by his widow to the Tate in 1974. One of these, the centrepiece of the triptych, is *The Last Judgement* – a fantastic panorama extending to Elysian fields as well the vicissitudes of hell and including, among the sea of faces who compose the ranks of the blessed, many recognisable likenesses of famous historical figures.

Another benefactor was Miss Ethel Hodgkins, a former ballet dancer who had taken up residence at Carbis Bay, near St Ives, shortly before the Second World War. Her near neighbours during the war had been Ben Nicholson and Barbara Hepworth, who encouraged her to collect modern art and give her support to local artists. As a result, she acquired an extensive collection by St Ives artists during the first half of the 1950s. At Barbara Hepworth's suggestion, Reid visited Miss Hodgkins and encouraged her to bequeath her collection to the Gallery. She did so, and when she died in 1977, aged ninety-one, twenty-one works from her collection entered the Tate. A further outstanding bequest resulted from Reid's long friendship with Naum Gabo, whom he had first met in 1964. Late in 1975, Reid stayed with Gabo at his home in Connecticut and together they repaired a number of the models for his sculpture which had been in Gabo's attic for many years. Gabo agreed to a Tate exhibition in which he would show thirty-two models, seven completed sculptures, seven miniature carvings and an important group of drawings. This took place in the winter of 1976–7. Gabo was too ill to come to London in order to see it, but shortly after the exhibition closed (and a few weeks before he died) Gabo gave virtually the entire exhibition to the Gallery, thereby making the Tate's holding in his work more comprehensive than that of any other museum or gallery. Among the sculptures in this gift was the model for a fountain, *Torsion*, which Gabo said he had always hoped to enlarge to six feet. On returning to London, Reid persuaded Alistair McAlpine to pay for the making of *Torsion* at full scale, and he also spoke to the architect Eugene Rosenberg, who was in the process of enlarging St Thomas's Hospital. Rosenberg enthusiastically took up the idea and at his suggestion the Special Trustees of the Hospital agreed to defray the cost of installing the fountain in front of their Hospital, opposite Big Ben. The fountain itself remained the property of the Tate – though on loan.

When Sir Colin Anderson had retired as Chairman in 1967, the senior Trustee Adrian Stokes had remarked on his combination of talents, 'such as sensitivity with practical imagination, firmness with tolerance and elasticity and great kindness with dispatch.'[14] In turn, Anderson continued to hold a deep affection for the

62 Naum Gabo, *Torsion (Project for a Fountain)*, 1960–4,
in the grounds of St Thomas's Hospital, London

Tate, and when, four years before he died, he resigned from public life and moved
to Jersey he gave to the Gallery, through the Contemporary Art Society and the
Friends of the Tate Gallery respectively, two works: Robert Colquhoun's *The
Fortune Teller* and Holman Hunt's *The Awakening Conscience*, the latter being such
a classic example of the Pre-Raphaelites' interest in modern-life subjects that it is
often forgotten it entered the Tate as late as 1976.

In April 1977 the Trustees expressed great interest in two paintings by Stubbs,
Haymakers and *Reapers*, which were offered by a private vendor through Peter
Johnson and Hugh Leggatt for £800,000. As a result of Capital Gains Tax remission, the cost of this pair of pictures was reduced to £774,000. It was still some
£200,000 more than the whole of the annual purchase grant, but, encouraged by
the reaction of the Friends of the Tate who immediately promised £25,000, the
Trustees put forward a request for a special purchase grant. This was turned down
as the Callaghan government had imposed cash limits on museums and galleries
which meant no special grants were available. In recompense, the Department of
Education and Science said that, out of its own resources, it would match, pound-
for-pound up to the sum of £190,000, whatever the Tate managed to raise by
means of a public appeal over the next three months. In addition, the government
agreed to underwrite the transaction, if the appeal did not make its target, by
advancing money as a debit against next year's purchase grant. On hearing this,
the Tate was able to proceed with the purchase, as it had in addition obtained the
vendor's agreement to wait until April 1978 for the second half of the purchase
money.

The success of the Stubbs Appeal owed much to the quiet dignity of these two lyrical paintings – each containing seven figures portrayed in rhythmic yet seemingly natural, frieze-like groupings. Soon after the Appeal had been launched, the Pilgrim Trust put up £30,00 and the National Art Collections Fund gave £20,000. (Because the Department of Education and Science agreed to match these two amounts immediately, the Tate, juggling its funds, was able to continue with the

63 William Holman Hunt, *The Awakening Conscience*, 1853

64 George Stubbs, *Haymakers*, 1785

purchase of a Mondrian – one of his Cubist-influenced tree paintings which hovers on the edge of abstraction.) Meanwhile, two lotteries were set up, one run by the Friends, the other by the Publications Department. At this time, the first prize in a lottery was not allowed to exceed £2,000 in value, but a Mini car cost just less than this. Reid, on the radio, mentioned this fact and that same day a telegram, signed Algy Cluff, arrived offering to donate a Mini. The Information Services Department thought it was a hoax until they discovered that there was a company called Cluff Oil and that A. Cluff was its Managing Director. He telephoned Reid that evening. A second Mini was donated by the Lex Service Group. When, in connection with the Appeal, both cars went on show in the Sculpture Hall, they aroused some comment; but the Appeal, which had the support of the *Evening Standard*, was by then generating such goodwill that the unusual nature of the exhibits was overlooked. Thompson Travel contributed five holiday prizes for the lotteries and sold tickets for one of them at travel agents throughout the country. The Post Office auctioned three rare stamps and various other activities took place, including appeal letters to individuals, charities, private and public companies; a leaflet campaign financed by the printer Gordon Fraser; an appeal poster; and competitions. Finally, an evening auction organised by the auctioneers Bonhams and conducted by Nicholas Bonham himself was arranged. Paul Mellon, who had hoped to purchase the two Stubbs paintings for the gallery of British art which he had presented to New Haven, with characteristic generosity (and wry humour) donated two paintings by Vuillard and one each by Bonnard and Giacometti. He also offered to make up any remaining difference when the Appeal had closed, as did Mr and Mrs H.J. Heinz. The final event, which took place on 15 December 1977, was the conclusion to the lotteries, Glenda Jackson drawing the prize-winning tickets and Lord Bullock making a speech which contained the cautionary remark that, despite the success of the Appeal, this was not an ideal way to raise money.

Perhaps it was Bullock's speech combined with the success of the Stubbs Appeal, but more likely it was the long-pursued policy on the part of the Director and Trustees regarding the purchase grant, that caused the Labour government to increase it by 77 per cent at the end of 1978, thereby bringing it up to £1,012,000. The following year it was raised again, by another 55 per cent, and reached £1,570,000; though set against this sum was the £309,000 which had been advanced towards Braque's *Clarinet and Bottle of Rum on a Mantelpiece*, and the £100,000 final advance for Malevich's *Dynamic Suprematism*. The purchase grant rose again, for the third time in succession, at the end of 1980 by another 20 per cent, reaching £1,888,000. But set against the optimism created by this improvement in purchasing funds was the awareness that in 1978 the Paul Getty Museum had entered the purchasing field with an annual spending budget of $30 million. There was also, by now, widespread anxiety over Britain's economic decline. Callaghan's 'winter of discontent' was followed in 1979 by a General Election which led to a government under Mrs Thatcher dedicated to the market and to the creation of an 'enterprise culture'.

With hindsight, the Stubbs Appeal represents a watershed in regard to the Tate's attitude to fundraising and sponsorship. Four years before, in 1973, the Gallery had sent an exhibition, *Henry Moore to Gilbert and George: Modern British Art from the Tate Gallery*, to the 'Europalia' festival in Brussels, with the co-operation of the British Council. Reid had assumed that the event was to be financed jointly by the British and Belgian governments. At a late stage he discovered the funding was only partial and he was told, without consultation, that the Commercial Union Assurance Company was sponsoring this Tate Gallery exhibition. Though he was angered by this, it was too late to protest or withdraw, and, he was assured, the sponsors wanted no more that a discreet mention in the catalogue. But at the next Board meeting Reid informed his Trustees: 'He [had] made it quite clear to Count d'Ursel, the Chairman of the joint Anglo-Belgian fundraising committee ... that he felt it entirely inappropriate that a national collection should be sponsored by a commercial enterprise.'[15]

A similar principle concerning the use of the Tate for entertainment purposes was likewise undermined by a change in political and economic climate. When, in October 1977, the Chairman of Midland Bank had asked if a dinner could be held at the Tate to which leading European bankers would be invited, the Trustees had felt unable to agree to this request. 'They decided that they saw no reason to change their policy of permitting receptions in the galleries only for art societies and official government hospitality.'[16] However, two years later, another request was received from a Mexican Bank which wanted to hold a reception at the Tate. Again, this was said to contravene the Gallery's policy; but when Lady

Airlie, Chairman of the Friends of the Tate Gallery, said the bank was willing to donate a sum of £10,000 to the Gallery, the Trustees agreed.[17] In the face of the oncoming tide, the Trustees opted not for Canute-like obstinacy, but for an alteration of the rules in relation to a changed climate and changing needs.

★　　★　　★

The Tate Gallery received over a million visitors between 1 April 1975 and 31 March 1976. Attendance figures dropped by 19.5 per cent the following year, but the year after that they again exceeded a million. With such a growth in audience came a commensurate growth in demand for services. There had been a terrific increase in the sale of postcards, Dalí for many years remaining a chart-topper with his *Metamorphosis of Narcissus* and *Autumnal Cannibalism*. Three counters had been set up to cater for this demand, one of them situated in the centre of the rotunda that abuts the entrance hall. But in 1972 all three were removed and a shop, designed by the Conran Design Group, opened in a gallery to the left of the rotunda.

When Corinne Bellow suggested to the Director that the Information Department should publish a calendar of events, Reid replied, 'Do you think there's enough going on?' But when these calendars were unfolded, as they were designed to be, and stuck like a poster on art-school notice boards and elsewhere, they made visible at a glance the Tate's continuous programme of changing exhibitions, talks, lectures and films. By 1976 the Education Department was receiving a hundred school parties a week at peak times, and though not all made use of the services provided, they had to be monitored by the Gallery.

Shortly after the Friends of the Tate had been founded, the Countess of Airlie – who worked closely on the Friends Committee with Sir Robert Adeane and his niece Penny Allen – had the idea that the Tate should benefit from voluntary guides. An American herself, she brought back from the Metropolitan Museum of Art in New York information relating to this idea; but as education at the Tate was then run by a skeleton staff, and the Exhibitions and Education Department had not yet been founded, the scheme could not be implemented immediately. It did, however, find support from Norman Reid, after he spent a month in the summer of 1965 visiting galleries in America as the guest of the US government. He and his wife were so impressed by the widespread use of gallery-trained volunteers that on his return to London he resolved to begin training a group of guide-lecturers for the Tate.

Eventually an advertisement was placed, and Lady Airlie, Cynthia Fraser and Penelope Allen undertook the task of interviewing 125 of 400 applicants. Twenty-four were chosen and then underwent a year's training – the Education staff effectively giving them an education in art history in return for their commitment. Their remit was not so much to acquire an impressive body of art-historical information, but to talk clearly and with enthusiasm about the works of art in the Tate. So successful was this scheme that many of these guides remained working at the Tate for considerable periods of time, some also eventually joining the official list of Tate lecturers. The guides immediately laid siege to the library which was at this time receiving a steady increase in use by outsiders.

With the continuous turnover of Trustees, the character of the Board changed from one period to the next. The artist Rita Donagh, the second woman Trustee, joined in 1977, as did Lord Hutchinson, QC (his celebrated cases included the defence of *Lady Chatterley's Lover*), who took over the Chair from Lord Bullock in the summer of 1980. The arrival in 1979 of Peter Palumbo, the property developer, and Peter Moores, at that time Chairman of the Littlewoods Organisation – though similar to their predecessors, Colin Anderson and Robert Sainsbury, in that both were businessmen and collectors – was seen with hindsight to represent the start of a new era in which a closer relationship was to be sought between the private and public sector. Then, in October 1978, Sir Norman Reid privately informed the Trustees that he would be retiring at Christmas 1979.

There was no lessening of activity in the lead-up to Reid's retirement. The issue of the Queen Alexandra Military Hospital site was very much to the fore. In April 1978 Reid had met with Mr Ellis, Chief Architect to the Department of the Environment, and had told him of the unanimous wish of the Trustees and senior staff to see a new building created on the Hospital site. This received a discouragingly negative response, but encouragement was given to the idea which the Trustee Colin St John Wilson, proposed – namely to develop the site in stages. Professor of Architecture at Cambridge, and himself the architect of the British Museum infill project and the new British Library, St John Wilson took a leading role in these discussions and suggested that the Tate could now demonstrate the need to close Bulinga Street, which ran between the Gallery and the Hospital site. Meanwhile agreement was obtained that alterations to the existing buildings on the Queen Alexandra site should proceed. The intention was to house part of the library, the prints and archives, together with the Contemporary Art Society and the National Art Collections Fund (which had been asked to leave the basement of the Wallace Collection), on this site. It was also hoped that some of the old wards might be converted into galleries. Half-a-million pounds spent on improvements to these existing buildings would not, it was thought, in the long term jeopardise a larger scheme. And in the meantime, five architectural firms were to be interviewed by a buildings sub-committee with regard to plans for piece-by-piece development of the Hospital site.

Another dominant issue at this time was the housing of the Turner Bequest. At his bicentenary exhibition, held at the Tate's suggestion at the Royal Academy in 1974–5, 600 works, spanning the artist's development from pedestrian topography to the imaginative transcription and elevated visionary mood of his late work, had been seen by some 450,000 visitors. While people queued to get in, a young art-gallery assistant from Manchester called Selby Whittingham gave away leaflets promoting the idea of a Turner Society. Whittingham had looked at Turner's will and was determined to stir in the public a desire to honour Turner's request – for a gallery to house his bequest to the nation. Simultaneously, there was talk of Turner's work being reunited – for since the 1928 Thames flood his watercolours, drawings and sketchbooks had been in the possession of the British Museum and only a select number lent to the Tate. 'Moonshine!' exclaimed the British Museum's Director, John Pope-Hennessy, when told of the Tate's desire to repossess Turner's works on paper.[18] With these two issues very much to the fore, the Turner Society quickly mustered a significant membership. The New Yorker Al Weil became its lead spokesman and Henry Moore, its president.

In 1977, after years of bureaucratic occupation, two top-floor rooms within Somerset House, which had once housed Royal Academy exhibitions, became vacant, and a demand arose that Turner and Somerset House should be permanently united. The Strand wing of Somerset House had begun to house the Royal Academy in 1779. Turner, born in nearby Maiden Lane, had enrolled in the Academy Schools in 1789 at the age of fourteen, and was elected an RA at the young age of twenty-six; he had himself taught perspective there and had exhibited his art annually at Somerset House until 1837 when the Academy moved to larger quarters. To some, the match therefore seemed perfect: Sir William Chambers's elegant and historically apt rooms and England's greatest painter. Sir Hugh Casson, President of the Royal Academy, and William Allen, an award-winning museum architect, were commissioned by the Department of the Environment, to report on the suitability of these rooms as a picture gallery. Both had large areas of glass and were like hot houses in summer. The only access to them was by a small lift that held two people, by a curved staircase, made famous by a Rowlandson drawing, or by narrow service stairs. Yet despite the fact that temperature and humidity-control factors did not conform to art conservation standards, and the restricted access meant that in the event of fire paintings would have to be lowered out of third-floor windows, Casson nevertheless argued that scholarship must be tempered with commonsense and 'both buildings and artefacts must be allowed to live a little dangerously'.[19] This scandalously reckless conclusion was unacceptable to Norman Reid. As well as pointing out that the Somerset House rooms offered Turner less space than he was currently given at the Tate, and far less than what he would have once rooms in the Military Hospital had been turned into galleries, Reid told his Trustees that 'it would be irresponsible to place part of the nation's collection of Turner in a building that was demonstrably less satisfactory than the existing housings'.[20]

The Keeper of the British Collection, Martin Butlin, pointed out that if Turner went to Somerset House the result would be 'a further dispersal of Turner's work to yet another building rather than a concentration towards a study centre'.[21] Because the issue of the Turner Bequest involved the Tate, the National Gallery and the British Museum, all three institutions spoke out forcibly against Somerset House, but the Tate bore the brunt of the attacks relating to this issue. 'With their scholastic prissiness being decried publicly and often by men like Sir Hugh Casson,' announced the *Evening News* when the Prime Minister announced support for the scheme, 'Lord Bullock and his obdurate colleagues the Tate Trustees – the people primarily responsible for the hoarding of Turner's magnificent bequest – were already in a corner.'[22] On the 126th anniversary of Turner's birthday, Sir

Hugh Casson handed to the Arts Minister, Lord Donaldson, a petition to the Queen, signed by many prominent names, asking her to back Somerset House as a permanent home for the Turner Bequest.

In December 1977 the National Gallery and the Tate made a joint statement which again rejected the proposal to use part of Somerset House to display Turner's paintings. An uncomfortable deadlock had been reached. But the issue was kept boiling, partly because in 1979 talks began about the vesting of the Petworth Turners in the Tate Trustees – Reid having pressed the Treasury for the transfer of these Turners for many years, so that they could receive expert conservation, one or two having been permanently damaged by an incompetent freelance restorer. In June of that year the Turner Society published two booklets, 'The Study of Somerset House as a Turner Centre' and 'The Case for a Turner Gallery'. These added little to the debate but they helped keep it alive. Two things then dramatically altered the situation. Lord Annan, Vice-Chancellor of London University, appealed to Norman St John Stevas, who had again become Arts Minister, with the request that Somerset House should house the Courtauld Institute's art collection. This had recently been enhanced by a bequest – the most magnificent bequest to an art institution since the war – of Old Master paintings and drawings valued at £30 million from the art historian Count Antoine Seilern. Secondly, at a dinner given by Jacob Rothschild, Lord Hutchinson found himself seated next to Mrs Vivien Duffield, daughter of Sir Charles Clore who had recently died. Mrs Duffield, mindful of her late father's interest in the matter, asked what the Tate was doing about the Turners. The conversation that followed led, soon after, to her offer, on behalf of the Clore Foundation, of between five and six million pounds for a building to be erected to house the Turner Bequest in memory of her father. Initially referred to as the Turner Museum, then the Turner Centre, it became known finally as the Clore Gallery at the suggestion of the Tate Trustees.

Another major achievement in the late 1970s, owing chiefly to Reid's skill as negotiator and tactician, was the acceptance by the Tate of the Barbara Hepworth Museum. Reid had been a regular visitor to St Ives for a number of years in connection with the Penwith Society, of which he had been elected President on the death of Sir Herbert Read. He was also a Trustee of the Porthmeor Studios. In 1964, soon after Reid became Director of the Tate, Adrian Stokes had suggested that it might be a good moment to visit Barbara Hepworth as he sensed that she was considering making a gift to the Tate. Reid went down to St Ives in November 1964, and, as a result of his visit, Hepworth offered to present four sculptures to the Tate on the understanding that the Trustees would buy two more at a specially reduced rate. In addition, she persuaded the collectors Mr and Mrs Marcus Brumwell to offer as a gift one of her early carvings, *Three Forms* (1935). In 1967 Reid visited Hepworth again in Cornwall. On this occasion she had a broken leg and so Reid was sent on his own to the nearby Palais de Danse, a former dance hall where Hepworth stored her work and had another studio. She gave Reid the back of a large cigarette packet on which to make a list of works relating to the

65 Barbara Hepworth's studio, St Ives, in 1976

gaps in the Tate's collection. On his return, he read out the list of nine works and asked if the Tate might have one of these. 'No,' Hepworth replied, explaining that instead she wanted the Tate to have the entire list.[23] At Sir Colin Anderson's suggestion, the public announcement of this gift was delayed, until the controversy concerning the housing of Henry Moore's own generous gift had died down.

In addition to the retrospective Hepworth was given at the Tate in 1968, a display of her work from the Tate's own collection was mounted in celebration of her seventieth birthday in 1973. Two years later a small memorial display went on show in the Sculpture Hall after Hepworth died tragically in a fire in her studio.

Reid attended her funeral in St Ives. Afterwards, he and Alan Bowness, both executors of Dame Barbara's will along with Sir Anthony Lousada, selected and installed an impressive group of her work in her studio, chosen to complement the Tate's holding. They did this as a preliminary move towards fulfilling the wish Hepworth had expressed in a memorandum to her will: that her house, which consisted mostly of one large, light-filled studio room, and its garden, which she had designed, with help from Priaulx Rainier, as a showcase for her work and to demonstrate its close relationship with landscape, should become a permanent museum of her work. By February 1976 the Department of Education and Science had made it clear that they were not prepared to support the project and pay for the necessary staff. Despite this, the artist's family and in particular, Hepworth's son-in-law Alan Bowness, decided to go ahead and the Hepworth Museum opened to the public in April 1976, with Brian Smith, formerly Hepworth's assistant, as its first curator. The family, however, was not prepared to sell sculptures from the artist's estate in order to endow the museum, for they felt that their offer to the nation of the artist's studio, garden and a selection of twenty-seven sculptures was generous enough. The evident success of the venture encouraged Reid to go back to the Department of Education and Science, pointing out that the running costs were very low and could be found from within the overall vote. He had the full support of his Trustees, one of whom, Robert Sainsbury, offered to underwrite any loss in the first year. The Trustees agreed with pleasure to annex the Barbara Hepworth Museum, and Reid also obtained official approval for this development from the Minister of Arts before Hepworth's son-in-law, Alan Bowness, arrived to take up his appointment as Reid's successor. The museum was formally accepted on behalf of the nation by the Rt Hon. John Nott, Secretary of State for Trade and MP for St Ives, on 30 October 1980.

Reid also discussed with Henry Moore, over many years, the composition of a group of his work which the sculptor wanted to give to the Tate. The group was added to from time to time. When this gift had first been announced, there had been talk of setting up a Moore Sculpture Park in Regent's Park. After this project fell through, Moore proposed the creation of the Henry Moore Trust, to be governed by the Director of the Tate, its Chairman, two other members of the Tate Board, and his daughter Mary. Moore gave to this Trust all the land and buildings at Hoglands, his home at Perry Green, Much Hadham, and all the sculpture sited there. In this way the artist hoped to achieve a permanent open-air setting for the display of his work, and also the site for a study centre. As an initial investment, he also gave to the Trust a sum of £250,000.

Some five years later Moore telephoned the Director and said that he did not wish to change any of the existing arrangements, but forewarned him that he was thinking of creating another trust which would run parallel with the first trust. His interests had slightly changed and he now wanted to set up the Henry Moore

66 1979 extension under construction

Foundation, a charitable trust for the development of education in the fine arts in general, and sculpture in particular. Now that his daughter was married, there was also to be more family involvement in it. When this conversation was reported to the Moore Trustees they decided that the simple course would be to return all the Trust property to Henry Moore, together with the original £250,000 (which had grown to £500,000, thanks to the skill of the accountant who advised Lord Bullock at St Catherine's College, Oxford). Henry Moore accepted the Trustees' recommendation, and, with the approval of the Charities Commissioners, the original Trust was dissolved.

This alteration did not prevent the Tate from receiving in May 1978 the collection of work Moore had promised to the Gallery in a deed of gift signed in 1969. The thirty-six sculptures, along with other Moores in the collection, went on show in the summer of 1978. His work was also prominently displayed when the new extension opened in 1979, though Moore is said to have been disappointed not to have had a room permanently identified with his name, as had at one time been suggested. Nevertheless, still more ambitious plans for the representation of his art at the Tate were to surface in the following decade.

★   ★   ★

Owing to the hiatus over the air-conditioning in the Llewelyn-Davies extension, the opening display of the Modern Collection had to be shelved for two years. In its place the Tate mounted a series of stop-gap exhibitions, drawn from the Gallery's collections. These allowed the curators to bring out of the stores works that in other circumstances might have been held back. David Brown, for example, for the exhibition *Whistler and his Influence in Britain*, dipped into all kinds of forgotten corners of the collection in order to demonstrate how far-reaching Whistler's influence had been. Richard Morphet conceived the exhibition *Art in One Year: 1935*, which attempted to subvert accepted hierarchies by showing the whole spectrum of art activity in one year. He followed it with *Artistic Licence,* in which works were hung in pairs, each pair consisting of two very disparate works united by their choice of subject matter, again in a subversive attempt to shift attention from style to content.

Unfortunately there was no exhibition of this kind on view in March 1979 when David Hockney visited the Tate, talked with the Director, and was shown round the Modern Collection display in the as yet unopened extension. Despite the courteous treatment he received, he afterwards wrote a piece for the *Observer*, lambasting Gallery officials for 'trying to find work to fit in with their theories instead of looking at what is being done'. He instanced the neglect of Lowry, Patrick Proctor and Euan Uglow over the last fifteen years and the fact that the two paintings by himself in the collection did not give a fair idea of the range of his work during this period. At the same time he noted that the Tate owned nine works by Richard Smith and eight by Robyn Denny, and, after being given thirteen by William Turnbull had purchased three more. 'This is fine … I am not criticising individual artists … But … you see the results of a very unbalanced choice. What it suggests above all is a very deliberate bias in favour of non-representational art.'

In relation to contemporary art, he detected an attitude that was, he claimed, 'so narrow, so biased in favour of joyless and soulless theoretical art'. He was angry that the Tate had turned down a Leon Kossoff painting of a swimming pool for £3,000 and complained that it had no David Oxtoby portrait of a rock-and-roll star. 'Why is it that they have this idea of modern art as something basically puritanical, abstract, conceptual. I've got a little theory which may partly explain it. Bureaucrats, sensing that theoretical art involves the destruction or rejection of other kinds of art, welcome it because it appeals to the philistine in them.'[24]

Hockney scored some hits – he criticised the Tate for ignoring the strong school of realism in American art – but many of his criticisms were rebutted by Reid in his published reply.[25] He argued, for instance, that major examples of figurative art *had* been acquired during his term of office, among them works by Freud, Bacon, Kossoff, R.B. Kitaj, Roger Hilton and Patrick Caulfield. Nevertheless, Hockney had voiced a frustration shared by some of the Tate's curators, namely that the emphasis on European Modernism was too narrowly focused, favoured abstract art and tended to rule out a more pluralistic attitude to figurative work. There was also an unintended irony in the title of Hockney's article, 'No Joy at the Tate', for, as Reid pointed out, 'the capacity of a work of art to be warm and life-enhancing is a prime consideration in my selection'.[26] Hockney's attack received a surprising degree of support from London's artistic community. It made apparent frustrations with the Tate that were perhaps an inevitable consequence of the delayed extension. Reid himself had wanted to retire before this date, but had stayed on in order to oversee the opening of the extension. The hiatus it had caused, the consequent crowding of the galleries and entrenched attitudes with regard to the hanging of the collection drew criticism, such as the diatribe Bryan Robertson delivered in the *New Statesman*:

> Lack of space has been no excuse for over-crowded, poorly lit galleries in which good works of art have been jostled by would-be *chic* jokes, expensively purchased, and flaccid exercises in basic design, also costly, by untalented practitioners. Many fine English painters and sculptors are still unrepresented in the collections; others are inadequately represented …[27]

Further dissatisfaction surfaced with Anthony Caro's and Tom Phillips' request for a discussion at the ICA about the Tate, the role of its Director and its collecting policy. Chaired by Leslie Waddington, this was intended, primarily, to be a forum for artists' views, but as only about a dozen were in the audience the event lacked urgency and conviction.

The opening of the new extension in 1979 created a chance to show the breadth and richness of the Modern Collection. When planning this event, the curators, led by Richard Morphet, had first conceived of two exhibitions, the second gradually replacing the first in a rotational display. This idea had been abandoned

67 Banners designed by Margaret Traherne to celebrate
the opening of the 1979 extension

when it was realised that the Tate's Modern Collection would be judged by the
impression it made on the public at the initial opening. There was already, too, a
need to suggest that despite the new extension still more galleries were needed to
do justice to the collections. As a result the hang was deliberately crowded. Out
of sight to the public were the new service facilities – conservation and photographic studios and workshops, storage rooms, boilerhouse and loading bay. As a
whole, the extension fitted in well with the older building: its galleries, though
modern in character, contained echoes of the older parts of the building in their
rhythm and structure. Moreover, the additional storage space on the floor below
meant the Gallery could now forego two of the four warehouses in use as stores.

A royal opening was planned for the new extension. As the day approached,
Reid found himself lacking a sponsor for the firework display which was to be part
of the celebration. Therefore, when Dr Armand Hammer of Occidental Petroleum Corporation visited the Tate, Reid informed Dr Hammer of his plight. 'How
much do you need?' asked Hammer. 'Only £5,000,' Reid replied. Hammer turned
to his young assistant. 'Can we manage that?' 'Sir,' came the reply, 'I think we have
that much in petty cash.' Hammer then turned to Reid with the remark, 'Do you
know, my wife has never met the Queen.'[28] On 24 May Mrs Hammer met the
Queen and the Tate had its dramatic firework display, designed by John Piper,

which took place over the river. The police had closed off the Embankment between Vauxhall Bridge and Lambeth Bridge so that the guests could swarm on to the Embankment while the Queen, surrounded by her entourage, sat on a throne-like seat under a blue canopy constructed by the Department of the Environment at the top of the steps.

One of the finest encomiums for the 'New Tate' came from Lawrence Gowing. Writing for *Encounter*, he caught the sense of surprise that the Tate ('a source of dependable pleasures and familiar controversies') had suddenly doubled in size and now presented its collection in such a way that it seemed twice as rich. His only lament was that the new building 'is not an absolute masterpiece'. The spaces he found logical and beautiful, the total provision ingeniously lavish. 'But, looking up at the ceiling ... we find ourselves looking at the sky between no less than three superimposed systems of ribs, each with a different character, with its own residuum of unresolved detailing and its slightly excessive ponderousness, each seeming to have been drawn by a different hand.' The result, as he observed, was that daylight had frequently to be supplemented by tungsten light. 'Moreover, the daylight falls at too steep an angle to get the best visual return out of oil paint.' Nevertheless, Gowing was convinced that, through Norman Reid's persistence and perceptiveness, the Tate now had 'a unity of purpose and a consistent intelligence that is not noticeable in any other museum anywhere'. He concluded: 'I envy the next Director; Norman Reid has left an instrument and a resource with an incomparable potential. I pity the next Director; British culture makes its authorities bear the brunt of the oedipal antagonism that infest[s] it – and he (though perhaps not *she*) will surely suffer.'[29]

68 View of the first installation in the 1979 extension

15

Brinkmanship

On 1 January 1980 Alan Bowness took over as Director of the Tate, having been appointed from a shortlist of six the previous June.[1] It was an uncontroversial decision, for many had considered Bowness to be the heir-elect. He had applied four times for a position at the Tate,[2] and had been shortlisted for the Directorship when Rothenstein retired in 1964, but at the age of thirty-six had been thought too young for the job. Instead, he had watched Reid's developments with interest, meanwhile himself rising within the Courtauld Institute of Art to the position of Deputy Director and receiving a personal chair in the history of art from the University of London. Descended from two generations of teachers, he was happily ensconced in the educational world but saw the Tate as an exceptional challenge that could not be ignored.

There were many reasons why Bowness seemed well suited to the Tate. Before joining the Courtauld staff, he had worked for two years as a Regional Arts Officer for the Arts Council and in 1960 joined its Art Panel, which eventually he chaired. He identified strongly with the spirit that had led to the creation of the Arts Council – especially its commitment to the regions and its missionary attitude to art – which in Bowness was combined with an unrepentant élitism. He did, however, recognise the importance of accessibility which made him a keen proponent of educational activities. He was also well versed in art politics, having sat on many international art juries, the executive committee of the Contemporary Art Society and the Fine Arts Advisory Committee of the British Council. He had been very actively involved with the making of exhibitions in the 1960s and 1970s, and had helped form the Association of Art Historians in 1973, recognising a need for a formal organisation to replace the family network of art historians which was disappearing owing to the enormous growth of the subject. When he took over at the Tate, he found himself working with a number of art historians whom he had once taught.

Bowness came to the Tate with a deeper historical knowledge of modern art than any of his predecessors. He was determined to use this to benefit the Collection, but he also had high regard for the curatorial staff and wanted to give them more responsibility. Although he tended to reserve the pursuit of major acquisitions to himself, he directed his curators to look for work of a certain kind and placed much trust in them, particularly when it came to work by younger artists which he felt was better judged by those who were contemporary with it. His buying policy was to be helped, not only by the sudden large increase in purchase grant that had been achieved in the late 1970s, but also by further rises that

69 Alan Bowness in front of Turner's *Light and Colour (Goethe's Theory) –
The Morning after the Deluge – Moses Writing the Book of Genesis,* exh. 1843

took the grant to its peak in 1984–5, when it reached £2,041,000. This sum of
money made the Tate the envy of several world-class museums, including the
Pompidou Centre in Paris.

With regard to acquisitions, Bowness's aim was two-fold: to increase the historical breadth of the collection – especially in relation to British art – and to
acquire major works of art in the modern field. He believed there was still time to
emulate New York's Museum of Modern Art in making a comprehensive collection of twentieth-century art. This notion was shared by the Keeper of the
Modern Collection, Ronald Alley, who had for many years persistently and
knowledgeably argued for accessions that would fill gaps. Bowness, partly
because he felt Reid had bought well in the abstract field, and partly because Surrealist and German Expressionist paintings were under-represented in the Tate
(and cheaper than Russian abstraction), concentrated attention on the figurative
side of international Modernism – including Pop art – and achieved a great deal
on a broad front. Among the outstanding additions were Ernst Ludwig Kirchner's
Bathers at Moritzburg, Max Beckmann's *Carnival,* Duchamp's *Coffee Mill,* Picasso's
Nude Woman with a Necklace and Léger's *The Acrobat and his Partner,* as well as
works by Brancusi, Joan Miró, Ernst, Dalí, Paul Delvaux, André Derain, Oskar
Kokoschka, Jacques Lipchitz, and artists associated with the multi-national group,
Cobra. The Historic British Collection gained work by Blake, Collinson, Gains-
borough, Millais, Ramsay Wilson and Constable's magisterial *The Opening of
Waterloo Bridge.* Bowness also felt that Victorian painting had not been collected
with much enthusiasm in the 1970s and that buying work by Leighton (his *Lieder*

70 Marcus Gheeraerts II, *Portrait of Captain Thomas Lee*, 1594

Ohne Worte was acquired soon after Bowness arrived) and Albert Moore would tell people that the Gallery was again interested in Victorian painting. It also gained key works within the history of twentieth-century British painting, among them Mark Gertler's most ambitious picture *Merry-Go-Round* and Hockney's *A Bigger Splash*. The Tate's acquisitions in the 1980s were also quick to register a change in artistic climate. In 1981 the exhibition *A New Spirit in Painting* at the Royal Academy, organised by Norman Rosenthal, Christos Joachimedes and

71 Max Beckmann, *Carnival*, 1920

Nicholas Serota, achieved something similar to Bowness and Gowing's 1964 Gulbenkian *Painting and Sculpture of a Decade, 54–64* exhibition in that it proposed a new view of contemporary art which won a large measure of acceptance. Soon after this, work by Jasper Johns, Frank Stella, Jannis Kounellis, Arnulf Rainer, A.R. Penck, Francesco Clemente, Georg Baselitz and Anselm Keifer was purchased. In addition, a younger generation of sculptors – Bill Woodrow, Tony Cragg, Antony

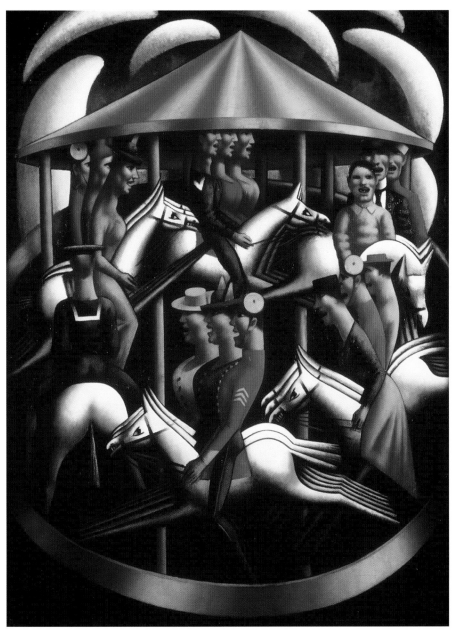

72 Mark Gertler, *Merry-Go-Round*, 1916

73 Pablo Picasso, *Weeping Woman*, 1937

Gormley and Shirazeh Houshiary – found representation at Millbank. Bowness was helped by the fact that, like previous Directors, he had a discretionary amount that he could spend without seeking the approval of the Trustees. In general, however, the Trustees were supportive, particularly under Jeremy Hutchinson's Chairmanship.

By the mid-1980s a number of factors began to inhibit such bold purchasing. These included the big art boom, the reduction of the 1985–6 purchase grant by 11 per cent, the effect of inflation, the loss in the exchange rate between the pound against the dollar, and the need to go for a few very expensive works – in particular, two major paintings that had been in the Penrose collection – Giorgio de

Chirico's *The Uncertainty of the Poet* and Picasso's *Weeping Woman*. As a result, during the latter part of Bowness's Directorship there was a reduction in the number of acquisitions and a slowing down of the earlier impetus towards building the collections across the full range.

There were, however, many other ways in which Bowness and Hutchinson effected far-reaching changes, transforming a rather tight, inward-looking institution into something more international and European. Hutchinson achieved an increase in travel and research funds for curators. He also encouraged evening receptions and made sure that artists were invited. And whereas Reid had kept the Friends of the Tate Gallery at arm's length, Hutchinson brought them closer to the organisation by obtaining for their Chairman, Lady Airlie, a place on the Board of Trustees.

Board meetings were now preceded by agenda meetings, on either side of which would be meetings between the Director and relevant staff. In recognition of the important role played by the Conservation Department, Alexander Dunluce was now invited to attend Board meetings. Whereas Michael Compton thought that in the interests of decision-making, Trustees should have less information, Bowness wanted them to have more – his Quaker-socialist mind making him a believer in industrial democracy.

He made an increased distinction between the active and contemplative sides of curatorship, took away certain responsibilities from the Keepers, made the Library and Archive into two separate departments under Michael Compton, who now became Keeper of Museum Services, leaving Ruth Rattenbury in charge, as Deputy Keeper, of Exhibitions and Technical Services, the latter now headed by Peter Wilson. Bowness was keen to have more curator involvement in exhibitions and wanted both major group and one-artist shows, as well as small-scale British and contemporary exhibitions, with a short gestation period, which could draw on a particular enthusiasm of one of the curators. He made new appointments, among them Richard Calvocoressi in the Modern Collection, Richard Humphreys who joined the Education Department, and research assistants who were usually so bright that they quickly gravitated towards the interesting work and rose to Assistant Keeperships, leaving the dogsbody work still unattended. The appointment of Richard Francis, formerly of the Arts Council, as Assistant Keeper in the Modern Collection, was made with the hope that his experience of mounting exhibitions would have a salutary effect on the way the Modern Collection was hung. Though Bowness intended to strengthen the staff, he also added to their work by insisting that the Tate should now be working towards a complete catalogue of its collection. This decision grew out of his belief that biennial reports were an inappropriate place for scholarly information which was better placed in biennial catalogues of recent acquisitions and in a series of specialist catalogues. The first of these full-scale catalogues, devoted to Hogarth and his circle, appeared in 1988. At the same time Tate exhibition catalogues improved, and now carried bibliographies compiled by the library staff.

Having brought with him from the Courtauld his personal assistant, Edwina

Sassoon, Bowness had in her a very competent and authoritative administrative ally. This proved timely as Judith Jeffreys, who had commanded the administration of the Gallery for many years, took early retirement in 1983. Michael Compton, who had made a major contribution to the translation of the Tate from a small into a major international institution, also found his scope dwindled under Bowness, though he stayed on until the day before his sixtieth birthday. But more problematic than the disruption change brings was the political climate, for in a Thatcherite age Bowness, though excellent at negotiating with civil service and other official bodies, was to find himself constantly wrong-footed in relation to government and to some of his Trustees. As his time at the Tate progressed, he found the job, which had seemed such an exciting challenge, very different to what he had expected. Under Thatcher's government the sum of money set aside for the Tate did not grow at the rate it had done before 1980 and it bore less relation to the Tate's needs or ambitions. The issue of funding was fundamental to the dynamism of the Tate and was to be a major cause of change.

★   ★   ★

The decision to talk with five architectural firms in connection with the Hospital site took on a more specific focus after Mrs Duffield indicated that the Clore Foundation was willing to fund the building of a Turner museum. In the conclusion, which was reported at the Board meeting in November 1978, the runners-up were Evans and Shalev ('their buildings were well planned, elegant but not ostentatious and often meeting difficult requirements and strict financial controls').[3] But the winner, unanimously recommended by the buildings sub-committee, was James Stirling, Michael Wilford and Associates. Stirling, who had achieved international status as a daringly avant-garde architect, had during the 1970s received more commissions from abroad than in England, and was currently involved in two gallery extension projects; for the Staatsgalerie in Stuttgart, which when it opened in 1984 brought him immense acclaim, and the Sackler Wing of the Fogg Art Museum at Harvard. He proved particularly adept at creating an 'informal monumentality' which contained reminiscences of the past within a language that was undeniably modern. The choice of Stirling, who had been proposed by Reid, especially pleased Bowness, for he had long admired this architect and had made his Engineering Block at the University of Leicester the final illustration in his Thames & Hudson book, *Modern European Art* (1972).

Meanwhile, work had begun on the renovation and alteration of the Hospital buildings which, when taken over by the Gallery, were in a very dilapidated condition. The lifts were repaired, the heating system renovated, the floors in the ward blocks strengthened and the nurses' wing gradually transformed into pleasant office space – all under the auspices of the Property Services Agency. There was also talk at this time of the Tate making use of space in the base of a 500-foot forty-storey tower block and its attached five-storey block of luxury flats which European Ferries wanted to build on the opposite side of the river – on the east side of Vauxhall Bridge – and which became nicknamed the Green Giant, as the intention was to sheath it in green glass. As it was a requirement that the public should benefit from a scheme of this size, European Ferries offered to lease 60,000 square feet to the Tate for a nominal rent, knowing their project would be more favourably received by planning committees if it included arts and leisure facilities. Aware that they were being used as sprat to catch the mackerel, the Trustees nevertheless were attracted by the space and by the fact that European Ferries were prepared to run a ferry every ten minutes between the Tate and the new site. But the mammoth size of the tower block aroused strong opposition; Lambeth Council objected to it and the Green Giant, as originally planned, was never built.

The flurry of excitement and dispute aroused by this offer was soon replaced by the more serious issue of the new Turner museum. A position had to be agreed that would not disadvantage future developments on the Hospital site. Requests for planning permission had resulted in the City of Westminster Planning Department's conclusion that, though two ward blocks could be demolished, the central administrative block of the Queen Alexandra Military Hospital had 'substantial townscape merit' and could be considered a 'building of character'. But despite this, and the fact that some years before *The Times* had deplored the suggestion of its demolition, the building had not been (and still is not) listed. In discussion with Westminster planners, James Stirling offered to preserve it, as a way of securing their agreement to other demolitions. The central administrative block therefore remained a feature of the site, as did the Lodge on the south-east corner, which at the time still housed a major-general and two other high-ranking officials. Stirling decided to use these two buildings as an architectural source for his designs, and the stone grid of squares which eventually became such a feature of the outside of the building was employed as a 'bridge' between the new museum and the older classical buildings. Wisely the Trustees decided at this stage not to press the Tate's case for the Lodge since objection to Stirling's plans from this quarter would have been unhelpful.

A brief was hurriedly drawn up by Michael Compton, which assumed that the Turner Bequest watercolours and drawings would eventually be transferred to the Tate and therefore made a print room one of the objectives. Another was a paper conservation studio, which Alexander Dunluce said should be north-lit. Martin Butlin stressed that it was essential that the galleries should be traditional in their proportions and shape. They were also to be air-conditioned, top-lit and built at the same level as the older building so that where the new and old met, the visitor could move easily between the two. Stirling conceived of a two-storey 'L'-shaped building, the gallery floor divided into a sequence of rooms, both small and large, thereby allowing for changes in scale and grouping of Turner's pictures. The paper conservation studio was to be on the lower level, as were other non-exhibition facilities such as the entrance hall, cloakroom, lecture theatre, reading room and plant room. A new 'schools entrance' at the back of the building was to serve both the Clore and the education facilities in the old building, while at the front, in the short leg of the 'L' and facing the old building, was the main entrance – its pediment containing an abstracted reference to the Tate's Victorian portico. Another subtle connection was the decision to allow the parapet of the new building to match in level the lower parapet of the central block, rather than the higher parapet of the pavilioned corner, as a result of which the symmetrical balance of the Tate frontage remains undisturbed.

Stirling's initial ideas were formally presented to the Board in December 1979, with the Director-Elect present. Director, Trustees and senior staff then had until the January Board meeting to consider the design, after which Stirling and Department of the Environment staff worked very fast to produce plans, a brochure and a model for a feasibility study, all in time for the Board meeting in February.

The reason for such haste was that the Stirling, Wilford feasibility study had to be agreed by the Clore Foundation by March, before the end of the 1979–80 financial year. The formal announcement of the Clore gift was made by the Minister for the Arts on 6 May and two days later the Working Party for the Clore Gallery met for the first time. Two of its members were Turner specialists from among the Historic British Collection staff, a fact which indicates that a continuous central issue was the need to ensure the best possible display of Turner's art. The Working Party had the job of formulating a detailed brief. Because each tranche of Clore Foundation money had to be spent within a certain period of time, Stirling had to proceed with his plans, which were being finalised while the brief was still being refined at a series of meetings; the final brief did not exist until the project was well on its way. After Judith Jeffreys' retirement responsibility for this brief passed to Robin Hamlyn, Assistant Keeper in the Historic British Collection, who had originally trained as an architect. Effectively working alongside the Property Services Agency as project manager for the Tate, he was to encounter difficulties in obtaining agreement with Stirling's office over certain details, owing to a conflict of interests between design requirements and curatorial needs. For instance, decisions were made about the profile of the ceiling before the lighting had properly been discussed. Stirling also had to respond to a demand, on which Lord Hutchinson insisted, that at some point the visitor to these top-lit galleries should have contact with the outside world and a view of the river. The idea for a viewing balcony, however, gave way to a narrower, vertically emphasised, angled window in one side gallery.

The amount offered by the Clore Foundation was now understood to be £5.4 million. Initial costings suggested that a paper conservation studio and a print room could not be achieved within this budget. The Trustees proposed to forego a million pounds of the purchase grant, but this proved unnecessary when in April 1980 the Office of Arts and Libraries agreed to take responsibility for the addition of these two features. (In the final reckoning the government contributed not £1 million, as was initially agreed, but a sum that matched, if not surpassed, that provided by the Clore Foundation.) Once the outline plans had been costed in November, the contract figure (£4,912,410), combined with the cost of demolition of two hospital wards, came to £6,850,000, which was still too much, and in order to bring it within the funds then available, the project was slightly but permanently trimmed, two metres being cut off one side of the building with the result that the central corridor gallery was narrower, all the galleries a little smaller and the seating capacity of the lecture theatre was slightly reduced.

Work on the site started in the autumn of 1982, and on 5 October Bulinga Street closed. This year the Petworth Turners, which had been offered in lieu of tax, were at last vested in the Tate Trustees, but negotiations concerning the transfer of Turner's watercolours and drawings, despite a change of Director at the British Museum in 1977, still had not reached a satisfactory conclusion. The British Museum clung to the argument that these works were best shown alongside their unique collection of comparative work by British watercolour painters and engravers. In addition, their Conservation Department was in the process of mounting and treating the Bequest and they had appointed an Assistant Keeper to work specifically on it. Bowness had, however, established a good personal relationship with David Wilson, the Director of the British Museum, and was able to persuade him of the desirability of respecting Turner's wishes. In time, as it became evident that a Turner museum existed not merely on the drawing board but was in the process of being built, the situation changed, and the transfer, when finally agreed, more than doubled the number of works in the Tate collection. The future of the Clore was publicly affirmed on 19 April 1983 when the Queen Mother unveiled the foundation plaque, set in a circular area of York stone paving, at a point where steps would lead down to a sunken terrace in front of the Clore entrance. Champagne, tea and cucumber sandwiches were served in one of the tents, which had been put up on the front lawn the previous year by Winsor & Newton for the *Paint and Painting* event. A great deal of activity went on in these tents over a two-year period, and they contributed to the sense of excitement and increased informality which marked the early 1980s.

★   ★   ★

It had not been possible to conceive of the Clore Gallery without thinking about the Hospital site as a whole. During his first month at the Tate Bowness informed the Trustees that he envisaged the Clore as the beginning of a large-scale development. He had in mind the 'New Museums', a collective term for developments that were to be linked but able to function separately. He proposed a documentation centre, a sculpture museum or wing overlooking a sculpture garden, a museum of twentieth-century art and a museum of new art. The distinction between the two latter museums, Bowness claimed, 'is fundamental to my thinking about the future of the Tate'. He continued: 'In the new design, the existing Tate building would become the Museum of British Art. It would display only British art, up to the present day – this was always the founder's intention and we should revert to it.'[4]

James Stirling was entrusted with the task of planning the New Museums, and in time he was to present an outline scheme to the Trustees. Though Stirling had become the Tate architect, he did not concern himself with smaller schemes, such as the redesigning of the dark, dingy and uncomfortable Coffee Shop which sat in the basement immediately below the building's dome. Its shady corners had made it popular as a trysting place, and Bowness, not wanting it to lose its social function, hoped it could be transformed in a way that would still encourage the chance encounter. He also wanted to balance the Restaurant, which was said to be elitist, with a really good Coffee Shop. A small, two-stage competition was held in which five architectural practices were involved. The winners, Jeremy and Fenella Dixon, chose to develop a scheme which, in its main circulation routes, echoed the shape of the circle imposed on the ground plan by the dome above. The four curved, communal tables which filled each quarter of the main seating space, created another circle over which hung a plaster dome with inset mirrors. Further use of mirrors on the walls helped create spatial complexity, while the use of natural materials in the furnishings added to the crisp effect.

Bowness also effected change with regard to the Chantrey Bequest. He had inherited an awkward situation following a breakdown in relations between the Royal Academy and the Tate Trustees which had occurred at the annual Chantrey Recommending Committee before the opening of the Royal Academy Summer Exhibition. On several occasions Tate representatives found themselves unable to choose any works, nor would they support those put forward by the Royal Academicians. As a result, Norman Reid had suggested that the Tate should give up its right to influence the choice of works so that the Academy might buy whatever it wished. But in turn it was also agreed that the Tate would have the right to receive only those works that it requested, and the rest would remain the property of the Royal Academy. This proposal had been welcomed by the RA representatives at the time, but by 1980 they had accumulated seventy-eight works which they had to either loan or store. They had also begun to realise that they had lost the back-door into a national collection and were unhappy at the way things had developed. Bowness, who had excellent relations with Sir Hugh Casson and Piers Rodgers, the Academy's President and Secretary, felt a new *rapprochement* was timely. This proved correct and a Recommending Committee was reinstated, chaired by the Secretary of the Royal Academy, to ensure that only those works were bought which were acceptable to both institutions. From now on the annual sum available through this Bequest, which had risen to £10,000, could once again only be spent by mutual consent. Between 1981 and 1988 all recommendations were bought, but in 1989 the Academicians vetoed John Lessore's *Sunday*. It subsequently entered the Tate collection as a Director's purchase.

Back in 1974 the Tate had for three weeks in May run films made by David Hall, formerly a sculptor, in collaboration with the film-maker Tony Sinden. This was the first time that film as an art form had been shown at the Tate during the day, when gallery visitors could experience them. Two years later Simon Wilson, advised by David Hall, had organised the Gallery's first video show, which, though tucked away downstairs in a lecture room, nevertheless treated video as a primary medium rather than as a secondary means of communication. Eight British artists were shown over four weeks. The growing interest in time-based media was reflected in the 1981 Tate exhibition *Performance, Installation, Video*, which included work by Marc Chaimowicz, Charlie Hooker, Tim Head and Chris Welsby.

This formed part of a schedule of exhibitions which followed Bowness's policy of mixing group and solo-artist, large and small exhibitions with contemporary displays. A run-away success was the reduced version of the Pompidou Centre Salvador Dalí exhibition held in 1980. Another show dedicated to Meredith Frampton's art proved almost as disturbing, in that the extreme clarity of every detail created a brittle stillness. To find such an intensely academic artist hallowed by an exhibition at the Tate was a surprise and an indication that the modernist agenda was being undermined by a widespread distrust of master narratives, and a desire to look beyond the accepted canon. The audience for art became more volatile, and the Exhibitions Department found it became less easy to predict correctly attendance figures for the various shows. Tate exhibitions in the 1980s brought to the fore the gore and lustful cruelty of Edwin Landseer; presented Stubbs as a figure to be reckoned with; lucidly explained the genesis of abstract art and the emergence of Cubism; and put a left-wing slant on Richard Wilson – David Solkin arousing a furore by showing how the serenity in Wilson's art upheld the 'myth of social harmony', which, he argued, was little more than a confidence trick played by the ruling classes on the rural poor. There were one-off innovative shows, such as *Sculpture for the Blind* – devised and carried through by Terry Measham and Ruth Rattenbury – which had a catalogue and title plates in Braille and ingenious changes in matting which indicated to blind visitors when they had reached the next exhibit; and the *Paint and Painting* event, sponsored by Winsor & Newton, which combined an exhibition on the history of colour and painting techniques with an opportunity for members of the public to learn how to paint. In 1984 the popularity of *The Pre-Raphaelites* exceeded all expectations, and over a hundred thousand people visited the Francis Bacon retrospective held in 1985. Like his first show at the Tate in 1962, which overnight established him as a major figure in British painting, Bacon's 1985 exhibition proved another landmark in his career.

Perhaps most outstanding of all in the 1980s was *The Essential Cubism*, selected by Douglas Cooper and Gary Tinterow. Not only did this achieve loans from private and public collections all over the world, but it was also a major feat of diplomacy, and Bowness and Lord Hutchinson were congratulated by the Trustees for 'healing the long-standing rift between Mr Douglas Cooper and the Tate'.[5] Sir John Rothenstein, on his visit to the show, was so impressed that he expressed a desire to congratulate Cooper who was in the Gallery with Bowness. When told of Rothenstein's expressed wish, Cooper would have none of it, and no reconciliation between the two men was effected.

Six months before Bowness had taken over as Director, the Property Services Agency's budget for the Gallery had been cut by £60,000. Soon after he took office, the extent of the deterioration of the building became evident. A piece of masonry fell from the cornice in the North Duveen shortly before a dinner party was to take place in connection with the Gainsborough exhibition. Bowness hoped it proved to the Secretary of State for the Environment, Michael Heseltine, who was attending the dinner, that it was not practical to cut funds for the maintenance of national museums and galleries. The next month part of the balustrade round the side of the main steps collapsed. When this was brought to the Trustees' attention, it was also noted that 'Mrs Jeffreys had received a letter from the Property Services Agency secretariat giving the most depressing view of the current financial situation and a rather worse forecast for 1981–2'.[6]

Consistent underfunding now forced museums to look beyond the state to the private sector, actively to seek sponsorship and to place more emphasis on marketing. In November 1980 Lord Hutchinson suggested that a small committee should meet 'to try and generate some ideas of how money from the private sector could be channelled into the Gallery'. He chaired the initial meeting attended by Alan Bowness, Corinne Bellow, and two Trustees, Peter Moores and Peter Palumbo, both of whom had experience of fundraising – Moores having been involved in opera sponsorship and Palumbo being a member of the Visiting Committee of the Museum of Modern Art, New York. But little consensus was reached, and though a sponsorship sub-committee was set up, its chairman Peter Palumbo reported to the Trustees six months late, in January 1982, that it had made little progress and the Gallery 'must now look to individual sponsors on an ad hoc basis.'[7] This failure of initiative was observed by Corinne Bellow, who asked Lord Hutchinson if she might herself attempt to raise sponsorship for the Tate. Hutchinson replied, 'Yes, please do.'[8]

The first business with which Corinne Bellow had success was the Tate's near neighbour, S. Pearson & Son, which at the eleventh hour agreed to help sponsor the Landseer exhibition in the spring of 1982. Though the sum given was a small one, and the time available too short to allow for an effective advertising campaign, it established a relationship between this firm and the Tate which led to further support for other major exhibitions of British art, including *The Pre-Raphaelites*.

After this initial success, Corinne Bellow took the lead in the obtaining of sponsorship. Commercial sponsorship of exhibitions was at this time relatively new and it aroused considerable suspicion. Its appropriateness was questioned and fears were expressed about potential censorship. Mobil Oil sponsored the John Piper exhibition in 1983–4 and went on to become a regular sponsor, despite the fact that, three days after the Piper show closed, a Hans Haacke show went on view in which Mobil was indicted by three of the works and in the interview with the artist published in the catalogue. Haacke, whose work is profoundly critical of capitalist systems and corporations, and especially of the duplicity of many multinationals to the situation that pertained in South Africa under apartheid, drew attention to the vast holding Mobil had in the South African petroleum market and to the fact that they supplied the South African police and military with about

20 per cent of their fuel needs. The oil company charged that its property rights had been violated by the use of their logo in the works of art. It threatened to take further legal steps if there was further distribution of the offending material and as a result the catalogue was withdrawn.[9] The fact that the Tate, having allowed Haacke to criticise Mobil on the walls of its Gallery, went on to accept further money from this company, is a reflection on the 'institutionalisation of dissent' and the peculiar, sometimes perverse, relationship between money and art.

Although the Trustees vetoed sponsorship from cigarette companies, they accepted a very substantial sum of money for the Stubbs exhibition (1984–5) from United Technologies Corporation. The fact that the Tate was receiving support from a manufacturer involved with US Defence contracts aroused a good deal of angry debate in the press, though when demonstrators outside the Gallery began collecting signatures, some people mistook them for Animal Rights supporters, given Stubbs's interest in drawing horses in extreme circumstances. When the *Guardian* art critic Waldemar Januszczak suggested that the matter should be openly discussed, Corinne Bellow organised 'What Price Arts Sponsorship?', a public debate which took place in the cinema in nearby Millbank Tower.[10]

During his involvement with the short-lived sponsorship sub-committee, Peter Palumbo had expressed grave fears over the financial outlook for the Gallery. In a paper delivered in July 1981, he pointed out that not only had the Grant-in-Aid been cut by 5 per cent, but if 12 per cent inflation was taken into account, the shortfall amounted to about £340,000. In the present climate, he warned, there was the likelihood of increasing pressure on the part of the vote that covered salaries and administration. The Trustees needed to protect the assets over which they had responsibility; a failure to act now would result in a long-term lowering of the standards and would in effect be a dereliction of duty. In Palumbo's view, the Tate had no alternative but to adopt a more uncompromising, businesslike attitude to fundraising. He outlined ways in which this was done in America, instancing various activities, the success of which depended on a massive public-relations exercise. Bowness, in his reply, stated categorically that this was impossible to sustain. Such emphasis on fundraising also ran contrary to his belief that the government had a moral obligation to fund and maintain its national collections.[11]

This marked the onset of an uneasy relationship between Palumbo and the Director, despite the fact that Palumbo seemed at this time full of goodwill towards the Tate. In 1983, when the Property Services Agency was suffering a cutback and was unable to find the money to finance Stirling's design-study for the New Art and Sculpture Museums, Bowness asked Palumbo for help, because if £30,000 could be raised from a private source this financial year, they could authorise the design-study and hope to complete payment for it the following year. Palumbo agreed and asked his gift to be treated anonymously. Later that year he told Bowness that he also wanted to make a substantial contribution towards the refurbishment of part of the Sculpture Hall (the 'South Duveen'). When the estimated cost of this exceeded the budget, the idea was shelved and Palumbo redirected his offer towards the Restaurant – also in need of refurbishment. This project survived the cuts, and Jeremy and Fenella Dixon's redesign of the Restaurant in 1984 introduced, among other things, bench-seating around the walls and concealed lighting behind the slightly scalloped edges of the new ceiling.

Of Italian descent, Palumbo had been educated at Eton and Oxford. His father Rudolph Palumbo had started with almost nothing, and had created the family firm, City Acre Property Investment Trust, which, holding the deeds to four acres of the City of London, had become one of Britain's richest private companies. At Eton Peter Palumbo had become fascinated by the extreme simplicity of Mies van der Rohe's Farnsworth House. Later he went to Chicago in pursuit of Mies, persuaded him to become his youngest daughter's godfather, and to design the 290ft high Mansion House Square tower which Palumbo wanted to build on the site of some existing Victorian buildings. Since 1968 a man-size model of this project had sat in his office, but the planning permission it had received from the Greater London Council in the 1970s had been revoked by the City Corporation who thought the design inappropriate and overbearing. Among Palumbo's supporters were the Tate Trustee Richard Rogers, James Stirling, and other eminent architects and historians, including Sir John Summerson, many of whom spoke on behalf of the tower at a public inquiry which began in June 1984. The long history of this obsession, and the amount of time and money that it had cost Palumbo, left him convinced that 'the more worthwhile something is, the harder you have to fight for it'.[12]

Palumbo's forceful personality had made an impression on the Tate Trustees, particularly the artists Anthony Caro and Patrick Heron; and when it came to considering Lord Hutchinson's successor, Palumbo, asserting his seniority as Trustee, was chosen over Sir Rex Richards, Warden of Merton College, Oxford, and became Chairman-Elect in February 1984. He began to see a great deal more of Bowness and travelled with him in March to the opening of the Staatsgalerie in Stuttgart. He announced that he had a lot of time to give to the Tate, wanted to speak with the staff, and needed an office on site. This last request was turned down by Bowness. Palumbo was also informed that Trustees were not expected to approach the staff except through the Director's office. Palumbo already felt that recommendations made by the Trustees were largely disregarded, and that private sector intervention was not welcomed. Looking back on this period, he has admitted that in many ways he found the Tate 'a dispiriting experience'.[13]

Bowness, meanwhile, felt that Palumbo's attitude towards him had changed, that he began to regard him more as a Manager rather than a Director, and that he was trying to take over the Director's function – rather as the Trustees were doing at the Victoria & Albert Museum, to the dismay of its Director, Roy Strong. This change became noticeable at an informal meeting of Trustees and the Director, held on 16 February 1984, for which Palumbo drafted the minutes. He put on record the feeling that the various abilities of individual Trustees had not been optimised; that the Trustees wanted greater participation, in order to advise and help the Director where appropriate; and that there might be times when the

Trustees would wish to discuss certain matters without the Director being present. Despite the advice he had been given, Palumbo began to see staff without reference to the Director, and on one occasion, while Bowness was abroad, took a Swiss printer into the Publications Department to discuss with Iain Bain the possibility of Tate catalogues being designed and printed abroad.

Intent on introducing new ideas into what seemed to him a cumbersome and slow-moving institution, Palumbo found himself thwarted by civil service procedures. He brought into the Tate an American lighting consultant, despite the fact that the Tate had a lighting committee and the legal responsibility for the building, which was Crown property, rested with Property Services Agency who did not welcome consultants and had accepted Jeremy Dixon after some difficulty. Whereas to those outside the administration of the Tate, such as Patrick Heron, who remains an 'immense admirer',[14] Palumbo seemed a man of action, generosity and imaginative ideas, to those inside the institution he seemed inexperienced, brash and naive. Never before had a Trustee volunteered to take the Director and an artist-Trustee to New York for the weekend, so that they could see a Picasso exhibition and visit galleries with an eye for potential Tate purchases. Patrick Heron accepted the invitation, and Anthony Caro agreed to meet them there, but Bowness declined to go. During this visit Palumbo and Caro began negotiations to buy a David Smith for the Tate from the artist's two daughters and son-in-law; and after seeing a de Kooning and a Cy Twombly, both of which were to be sold at Christie's, New York, on 10 May 1983, they vetoed Bowness's desire to bid for them. Palumbo, himself a collector with a penchant for 1960s art, was determined the Tate should go only for the best and was instrumental in the decision to acquire works by Ellsworth Kelly and others.

In March 1984, at a dinner given at the Tate for the Prime Minister, Palumbo had to stand in for Lord Hutchinson who, owing to a last-minute change of arrangements, was unable to attend. There were two speeches, one by Mrs Thatcher, the other by the Chairman-Elect. Palumbo delivered a prepared speech which was deliberately political. He also announced private funding (his own) for the Restaurant and offered Mrs Thatcher the loan of paintings from the Tate. His energetic pursuit of new ideas continued unabated. In April he proposed that a film should be made about the Tate for publicity and television purposes. He also offered to sponsor it. By now Bowness had had enough, and, in a carefully worded letter to Palumbo, he laid down the correct procedures governing the Trustee/Director relationship. To Bowness's anger, this letter, which had been marked confidential, was circulated to the other Trustees.

That same month the journalist Deyan Sudjic asked Bowness if he could speak with him about an article he was writing on Peter Palumbo for the *Sunday Times*. Bowness refused. On 29 April 1984 the article appeared, and though it was primarily concerned with Palumbo's involvement with the Mansion House scheme, on which an inquiry was to begin the following week, it led on to the fact that he was about to become Chairman of the Tate. In conversation with Sudjic, Palumbo had outlined his ideas for its future.

I want to change the style at the Tate. I get depressed when I go there now … It's dull, it's turgid, it's unimaginative and it's badly done: all very British. The staff at the Tate have power, but no responsibility. I'm desperately unhappy at the way the place is run. I want to change all that. Either the Trustees let the Gallery get on with it or, if we have the ultimate responsibility, which legally we do, we assume it …

I think Bowness has been buying too much fashionable work at very high prices … The first thing that I will institute is a private meeting of the trustees which the director will not attend. That's when we will be discussing policies without him.[15]

The article represented an unprecedented attack on the Tate. In the brouhaha that followed, Palumbo claimed he had been speaking off the record and was deeply shocked to see his views on the Tate made known to the public. But now that they were generally known, the Tate found itself in a very serious situation, politicians concluding that it was in a state of complete chaos. Palumbo's opinions represented a personal blow, not only to the Director, but also to the staff, the Chairman and Trustees. Bowness immediately sent a letter to Lord Hutchinson asking the Trustees to disclaim publicly the outrageous indiscretions and allegations. He also made it clear that he could not work with a Chairman capable of such a gratuitous attack and such a breach of confidentiality. He then flew to New York, with the expectation that by the time he returned Palumbo would have resigned.

The Trustees held an emergency meeting in May while Bowness was abroad. Palumbo was present throughout. He offered sincere apologies and agreed to make a personal statement to Bowness. The Board, in spite of some diversity of mind, voted that Palumbo should not resign. Finding the situation unchanged on his return from America, Bowness reiterated his position to Lord Hutchinson and told him that if Palumbo did not resign, he would. He then explained his position to the senior staff, many of whom had already sent him letters of support. Nine of them afterwards signed a letter to the Chairman, expressing deep concern at the situation which had arisen. Consequently, the Trustees came behind the Director, Palumbo stood down, not as a Trustee but as the Chairman-Elect. A press release went out stating that owing to the pressure of 'other current commitments' he had asked his fellow Trustees not to proceed with his appointment. (And simultaneously he withdrew his offer to pay for the refurbishment of the Restaurant.)[16]

Later that month the art-historian and painter John Golding attended his first Board meeting as a new Trustee and found the atmosphere very tense.[17] It should have been Lord Hutchinson's last appearance, but he was asked to stay on until the question of his successor had been decided. Unfortunately Sir Rex Richards, having just agreed to take over as Director of the Leverhulme Trust the following year, felt unable to accept the Chair. Though Lady Airlie, one of the senior Trustees, was considered, the Chair passed in October to Richard Rogers, a former pupil of James Stirling at the Architectural Association, architect of the Pompidou Centre and the Lloyds Building in London, holder of the Saarinen Chair of Design at Yale University and an enthusiastic supporter of Palumbo's Mansion House project. Though the choice of Chairman rests with the Trustees not with the Prime Minister, Lord Hutchinson had to negotiate Rogers's appointment, as he was technically one of the artist-Trustees, who were not usually considered for the Chair.

One of the ironies of this débâcle was that, whereas there was general feeling that Palumbo wanted to turn the Tate Gallery into an American-style museum of modern art, supported by rich patrons, it was Bowness who went some way towards achieving this by establishing in 1982 the Patrons of New Art. Because the membership of the Friends of the Tate Gallery had become large and rather anonymous, Bowness wanted the support of a smaller body of people specifically involved with contemporary art. By June 1983 the Patrons had nearly 100 supporters, each of whom had pledged more that £1,000. Within four years it had 200 members, who each covenanted between £250 and £1,000 for four years. These subscription fees were directed towards the purchase of contemporary art which was being offered to the Tate, and in time also contributed towards some educational and exhibition projects, while all administrative costs were funded by tax reclaimed on covenants. The Patrons of New Art were also a means by which Bowness broke down the fortress-like mentality at Millbank which had formerly discouraged open discussion. He was keen to fulfill his intention of permitting greater involvement from dealers and collectors. As a result London dealers made up about 20 per cent of the Patrons' membership. So successful was this venture that its twin, the Patrons of British Art, was founded in 1986.

It was also Bowness who in 1982 persuaded Charles and Doris Saatchi to lend their collection of work by Julian Schnabel for a small exhibition of this American artist's large, crockery-encrusted paintings, as part of a series of shows dealing with the latest developments in contemporary art. The second exhibition in this series was devoted to Jennifer Bartlett, who had been recently commissioned by the Saatchis to design a dining room for their house. The press noticed this coincidence. There was much speculation at this time as to how influential the Patrons of New Art would be on the Tate's purchasing policy, and a fear that it could be manipulated by a few powerful dealers and collectors. The fact that Charles Saatchi was already on the Patrons' steering committee (also a Trustee of the Whitechapel Art Gallery) and, with his brother, a principal in the advertising firm which had played a large part in Mrs Thatcher's 1979 election victory, added to the suspicions of those critics who, having noticed at the Schnabel exhibition that almost every picture had been lent by the Saatchis, concluded that the Tate was being used to validate not only the artist but also the Saatchi collection, which was daily growing in fame. Such adverse criticism was aroused that the Saatchis withdrew from the Tate, and in 1985 they opened their own gallery in a converted paint warehouse in north London.

16

Tate in the North

Palumbo's withdrawal from the Chairmanship was interpreted by some as a blow to Conservative strategy for a new approach to museums. However, though Richard Rogers was, like his predecessor Lord Hutchinson, politically to the left, and also a long-standing personal friend of Bowness who had suggested him as a Trustee, his policies as Chairman were similar to Palumbo's. He also felt that the position of leading museums was changing; that the Trustees needed to play a less passive role; and that the huge rise in the price of art and the increase in the number of well-funded museums in Germany and France meant that the Tate now had to compete to maintain its identity. Rogers, like Palumbo, was certain the Gallery had to go out and find business patrons. And he was keen for it to develop a more dynamic image in the field of public relations. His hopes for the Tate were similar to those that had inspired his conception of the Pompidou Centre:

> It is my belief that exciting things happen when a variety of overlapping activities designed for all people – the old and the young, the blue and the white collar, the local inhabitant and the visitor, different activities for different occasions – meet in a flexible environment, opening up the possibility of interaction outside the confines of institutional limits. When this takes place, deprived areas become dynamic places for those who live, work and visit; places where all can participate rather than less or more beautiful ghettos.[1]

Ambitious and far-sighted, Rogers did not, however, make a natural Chairman and seemed uncertain as to how to give leadership to other Trustees. His first move was to initiate a series of strategy meetings, the first of which lasted two days and took place at the Bear Hotel in Woodstock, Oxfordshire, in January 1985. All the Trustees (except Patrick Heron, who sent apologies) attended, as did the Director. Palumbo was nominated Vice-Chairman, and the resolutions included a request for more information about potential purchases, comparative pricing of each work, and the means of sale, i.e. whether at auction or through a private treaty. One significant decision at Woodstock was that the Gallery needed a higher profile so that money could be raised by a parallel, independent fundraising body, headed by a director of development.[2]

The Tate Gallery Foundation came into existence in October 1986 and took over the ground floor of the Lodge on the south-east corner of the Millbank site. Its purpose was to raise money for improvements to the existing Tate building, for new developments and for major purchases. Palumbo became its first Chairman. The refurbishment of the Lodge by Colquhoun, Miller and Partners – a firm that had recently won high praise for the skill and subtlety with which they had redesigned and slightly enlarged the Whitechapel Art Gallery, was paid for by Peter Palumbo and two other Trustees – Sir Mark Weinberg and Gilbert de Botton. Alexander Gilmour began work as Executive Director, somewhat uneasily because, though he was answerable to Palumbo, he was charged with raising money for a venture directed by Bowness who was never invited to Foundation meetings. Still more discomforted by the Foundation was Bowness who repeatedly asked at Board meetings for clarification of the Director's role in relation to the Foundation, for he was aware that a certain faction was intent on keeping him out. Initially, the Foundation had five Trustees, all drawn from the Tate's Board of Trustees, but this was soon felt to be restricting and independent Trustees were gradually added, among them John Botts, Felicity Waley-Cohen, Sandra Morrison and the Hon. Janet Green. The Duchess of York was invited by her daughter's godfather, Palumbo, to be the Foundation's patron, and a few glittering events were held, not all as profitable as was hoped. In an attempt to encourage other artists to do the same, all three artist-Trustees (Caro, Heron and Golding) gave three of their own works to the Foundation. But the most successful aspect of the Foundation in its early days was its International Council (set up on lines similar to that associated with the Museum of Modern Art, New York), which aimed to enhance worldwide awareness of the Tate. Its first fruit, obtained by its Chairman, Gilbert de Botton of Global Asset Management, was a gift of £1.5 million from the Japanese investment bank, Nomura Securities.

Meanwhile, the fundraising initiative had already been seized by the Director and his personal assistant Edwina Sassoon, with some advice from Corinne Bellow, in order to realise Tate Gallery Liverpool. The concept of a 'Tate in the North' had come into existence long before it became linked with Liverpool. Back in 1968, when a desire for more space had led to debate about the proposed front extension, Stewart Mason had said 'he personally thought that it would be necessary to disperse parts of the collection as temporary exhibitions to various sub-museums belonging to the Tate in the provinces'.[3] On his retirement as a Trustee in 1973, he returned to this issue at his last Board meeting. 'Mr Mason … wished to leave the idea for an outstation for the permanent collection as a possible project for future Trustees to consider. He had long considered a project for a building in the north of England … Here he envisaged displays of first-class works from the Tate's permanent collections which would be a real joy to those who lived so far from London.'[4]

The concept of a new outstation had been resisted by the staff in the Modern Collection, who feared that its duty to display the principal developments in twentieth-century art would be compromised by the needs of a regional gallery. But the idea did not go away, partly because succeeding governments of both political parties favoured artistic developments in the provinces as part of an attempt to end London's monopoly on culture. In keeping with this policy the Railway Museum had opened in York in 1975, followed by the National Museum of

Photography, Film and Television in Bradford in 1983, both under the auspices of the Science Museum in collaboration with the local authority; and for a while it was also proposed that the Victoria & Albert's Asian Collection should move to Bradford – an idea that was eventually terminated during the early 1990s while the Museum was under Elizabeth Esteve-Coll. In his role as Chairman of the Arts Council Art Panel, Bowness had supported regional expansion and, as Director of the Tate, he saw it as both desirable and politically expedient; for, following the 1979 extension, further building at Millbank would be much more likely to receive government support if the Tate could demonstrate that it had expanded into the regions. Even before he arrived at the Tate, Bowness went to Oxford to discuss with the Chairman, Lord Bullock, his ideas for the Gallery, including an outstation in the north. Lord Bullock wholeheartedly endorsed the notion of a 'Tate in the North' and himself hoped that a site might be found in a converted West Riding mill.

Having proposed a 'Tate in the North' to his Trustees in 1980, Bowness visited Leeds, Manchester, Sheffield, Newcastle and Liverpool, talking in each place with local politicians, museum people and Arts Council officers. One outcome of his visit to Manchester, where he visited potential buildings in the company of Bob Scott, a local councillor, was that Scott himself seized the initiative and helped bring into existence the independent centre for contemporary art, Manchester's Cornerhouse, in 1985. But of all the cities Bowness visited, Liverpool seemed the best choice, for it had a lively artistic life, a strong local culture and an audience for contemporary art which had been developed over many years by the biennial John Moores exhibition. In addition, two Merseyside county councillors, John Last and Ben Shaw, took up the idea enthusiastically and helped interest the Merseyside Development Corporation which, set up in an attempt to halt accelerating decline in the area, came into existence in March 1981. One of its first actions was to use government money to acquire some 120 hectares of the South Docks, which had been derelict for ten years. Among these was the outstanding Albert Dock. Built by Jesse Hartley between 1841 and 1848 out of brick and stone over a cast-iron colonnade of squat Doric columns, the Albert Dock, in its monumental simplicity, is one of the grandest examples of industrial architecture in Europe. However, although Bowness was now convinced he had found the site, it required a real act of faith to conceive of a 'Tate in the North' in Liverpool. The Tate Trustees were at first resistant to the idea, worried in part by the militant council and by the gloomy reports of relevant economic enquiries. The city was very run down, suffering chronic unemployment and showing no signs of rebirth. The Mersey ferries no longer had to duck and weave to avoid the shipping to get to Liverpool's Pier Head, and whereas slumps and depressions had been a recurrent aspect of Liverpool's history, the present slump seemed destined to last, owing to the switch of trading patterns from the western seaboard eastwards to Europe. It was also ironic that while plans for the 'Tate in the North' went ahead, the closure of Tate and Lyle's Liverpool refinery in 1984 seemed to slam shut the coffin-lid on the corpse of the city's manufacturing base.

In the summer of 1981 the Toxteth riots played an indirect part in making a Liverpool outstation feasible, for they shook the government and secured the Merseyside Development Corporation's sense of purpose. These riots had been the result not of unemployment in Liverpool, though this was clearly a factor, but of an ultimate collapse in relations between the police and the mainly black residents of Toxteth, who were sick of what seemed to be officially tolerated harassment. A chain of events was set in motion which began with the appointment of Michael Heseltine, Secretary of State for the Environment, as Minister for Merseyside, with the instruction to offer a 'package' to help the city. Bowness, who had already shown his Trustees slides of the complex of warehouses, now seized the opportunity to approach Heseltine with Lord Hutchinson, after Michael Compton had to some extent prepared the ground by talking to one of Heseltine's assistants. First the Director and then the Chairman spoke, each for no more than ten minutes. Heseltine said nothing until both had finished, then without hesitation pronounced it a wonderful idea and made it a part of his fourteen-point package.

In November 1981 the Tate Trustees visited the Albert Dock. They were shown round by representatives of the Merseyside Development Corporation and afterwards lunched in the MDC offices in the Royal Liver Building. Though another four years passed before government approval for the scheme was officially announced, it was agreed that Sir Richard Attenborough should mention it that year in his opening speech at the Peter Moores exhibition, a biennial contemporary art event which for a while alternated with the John Moores exhibition. The MDC, meanwhile, agreed to make the Albert Dock building structurally sound and the Tate invited James Stirling to take an interest in the project. Having been brought up and educated in Liverpool, Stirling welcomed the idea of a new gallery in the Albert Dock and visited the site in March 1982, in the company of Lord Hutchinson and Michael Compton. The weather was appalling and the tremendous force of the wind sent salt spray right up the full height of the building. Local opinion maintained it was a freak phenomenon, but Stirling's plans were to take into account the fact that the building looks down the Mersey to the sea and is exposed to wind-chill factors of minus twenty on the exposed seaward corner. In time eight inches of fibre-glass insulation was to be placed between the yard-thick exterior walls and the interior timber walls.

In May 1982 the Property Services Agency agreed to commission a feasibility study on the conversion of the north-west corner of the Albert Dock, originally a seven-storey warehouse, into a five-storey modern gallery. This study was completed in January 1983, but the following year the Tate lost the support of Merseyside County Council when all these metropolitan councils were abolished by Mrs Thatcher's government. One result of this was the Arts Minister's proposal that the Tate should increase its presence in Liverpool by also taking on the Walker Art Gallery, a suggestion Bowness turned down.[5] Meanwhile, the choice of site was helped by the fact that a museum presence in the dock had already been established by the Maritime Museum, which at that time was open only during the summer months. This museum wanted to expand and Richard Foster, Director of Liverpool Museums, suggested that it might share a unit with the Tate. But Bowness was already determined that the Tate should be housed in Block C, which stretched along the north front of the dock. The estimated cost of the Tate scheme was £9.5 million, but it was to be built in two stages, and £6.5 million was needed for the first. The Merseyside Development Corporation gave £4.5 million, £500,000 was promised by the Minister for the Arts, and £1.5 million had to be raised by the Tate from the private sector. Government approval for the scheme, officially announced on 8 March 1985, came with the conditions that the Tate would find the funds necessary to complete the building and that it would not expect a commitment of extra funds for the running costs. Given the amount of money being offered, Bowness and the Trustees were prepared to accept these terms, in the hope that in time the government might become more generous in regard to running costs.

While the restoration of the Albert Dock went ahead, with the creation of shops, penthouse flats, restaurants and a marina in the nearby warehouses, Bowness opted not for a public appeal, but a more private pursuit of funds from individuals, national bodies, companies and trusts. He had the notion of finding some twenty founding patrons, who would each donate, or covenant over four years, £100,000. Several outright donations came in, not all for the full amount, from the Sainsbury family, the Henry Moore Foundation, the new Moorgate Trust Foundation, the Wolfson Foundation and the Pilgrim Trust; but in addition some philanthropic businesses, such as the John Lewis Partnership and Royal Insurance, made donations, and by November 1986 £1,258,001 had been already been raised. Subsequently almost £2 million was found.

Richard Francis and Michael Compton began writing the brief and liaising with Stirling and the two young architects, Peter Ray and David Turnbull, who became part of the team. During 1984 and 1985 Francis spent two days a week in Liverpool setting up contacts; talking with artists, the engineers (the Steenson, Varming, Mulcahy Partnership) and the Property Services Agency, who managed the project along with the Merseyside Development Corporation; and all the while continuing to work with the architects on the design of the building. So close was the relationship between client and architect that towards the end of this period, Francis was spending almost half his week in Stirling's office, helping with the choice of every detail, right down to door handles. The decision to leave the existing staircase at the south end of the building in position helped determine the arrangement of the galleries. Stirling also respected the basic architectural character of Hartley's building, making very little alteration to the outside of the building other than a screen under the arcade which, with its bright blue panels and orange lettering, was to draw attention to the entrance. If the drama and playfulness of his Clore Gallery was shortly to horrify purists, Stirling was to opt in Liverpool for reticently detailed, simple and elegant solutions, including a vertical service core between the front and back sections to accommodate ventilation and public access to the galleries. The first phase of the conversion, begun in 1986, was intended to be complete in 1988. In the meantime, the title 'Tate in the North' was replaced by 'Tate Gallery Liverpool'.

★   ★   ★

Had there been a change of government in 1983 the situation facing the arts in the second half of the 1980s might have been very different. But though Mrs Thatcher's government courted much criticism in the early 1980s, she regained popularity in May 1982 during the Falklands War, after which the museum which did best from the point of view of government funds was the Imperial War Museum. Some of Bowness's most ambitious plans, conceived in the early 1980s, had been predicated on hopes of a different political climate. By the mid-1980s he had begun to look enviously at museum developments across the Channel where it seemed President Mitterand was always willing to spend money on the arts.

Nevertheless, Bowness made considerable changes within the Tate and achieved a great deal during the eight years of his Directorship. His acquisition policy remained astute, if ultimately hampered by the government's decision to give more emphasis to conservation than purchasing. In 1977 Roy Strong had closed down the Circulation Department at the Victoria & Albert Museum, thereby putting most of its twentieth-century collection in storage. Seizing an opportunity in 1982–3, Bowness successfully negotiated the transfer to the Tate of all the Victoria & Albert's British and foreign sculpture from the post-Rodin period. The print collection did less well, for though it continued to expand rapidly, with Liz Underhill taking over responsibility after Pat Gilmour left and buying well, the Print Study Room closed in 1985 and the Print Department was absorbed into the Modern Collection. The Archive, on the other hand, continued to be regarded as a crucial part of the whole collection, and as a result its holdings grew increasingly rich and surprising, covering major caches of documents, such as the Charleston Papers, as well as two pairs of overalls that had been worn by Sickert. Where Bowness proved less successful was at staff relations, for, having announced an open-door policy, he soon realised the impossibility of making himself available to everyone and he began to rely on Edwina Sassoon as his intermediary.

Another of Bowness's notable achievements was the creation of the annual Turner Prize, which he hoped would do for modern British art what the Booker Prize had done for the modern novel. The idea had first been mooted by the architect Max Gordon at an executive committee meeting of the Patrons of New Art. It was supported by Felicity Waley-Cohen, then in the Chair, and met with further encouragement from another Patron, Oliver Prenn, who volunteered to donate anonymously the £10,000 prize for the first three years. There was some resistance internally to Turner's name being attached to the Prize, but because prizes for excellence are often associated with an illustrious name and Turner is the best known and loved of all British artists, it seemed the right choice. Moreover, Turner himself had attempted (with only partial success) to institute prizes

74 The Turner Prize exhibition in 1984

to encourage younger artists. Nominations were invited for the person, whether it be artist, critic, historian or curator, who had made the greatest contribution to British art over the last year. A jury of five met twice, to decide the shortlist and, eventually, the winner, the first of whom in 1984 was Malcolm Morley. As Morley had lived for many years in New York, this choice proved controversial. Though subsequent winners (Howard Hodgkin, 1985; Richard Deacon, 1986; and Gilbert and George, 1987) aroused less dispute, the Prize in all its aspects proved contentious – to such an extent that in 1987 the Patrons of New Art recommended reconsidering its terms of reference. At the same time it had to be acknowledged that the extensive publicity which the Prize attracted helped widen the audience for contemporary art. And with the offer from Drexel Burnham Lambert in 1986 to sponsor it for the next three years, it seemed firmly established.

Bowness, while courting the unpredictable publicity attendant on the Turner Prize, also encouraged the habit of small celebrations, marking, for instance, important birthdays of distinguished figures. Lunch parties were given to celebrate Sir John Rothenstein's eightieth birthday, Sir Roland Penrose's eightieth birthday and Josef Herman's seventieth birthday. Hospitality was also offered to visiting artists such as Joseph Beuys, who came to the Tate on 27 July 1984 with the dealer Anthony d'Offay to see two of his vitrines, purchased very belatedly earlier that year. Beuys had been angered by the Tate's neglect of his work and, wishing to improve his representation, constructed a third vitrine in which he placed, as a gift to the Gallery, two early bronze sculptures, *Ofen* and *Tierfrau*, together with *Fat Battery*, which had recently been donated by Ted Power.

By 1987 the Tate Gallery had become the fifth most popular tourist attraction in London, and had displaced the Victoria & Albert Museum. It had suffered a blow, however, in 1984 when the National Gallery demanded the transfer of five British paintings, including Gainsborough's *The Market Cart*, Hogarth's *The*

Graham Children and Joseph Wright's *Experiment with an Air Pump*, owing to its desire to show these pictures in the context of European painting. Four of the five paintings – the exception being Whistler's *Miss Cicely Alexander* – had been specifically given to the National Gallery and this fact lent weight to its claim, though legally it had no right to enforce it. Though an agreement had been reached in 1954 whereby the National Gallery had the right to claim any British picture that had entered either collection prior to the 1954 National Gallery and Tate Gallery Act, this agreement was invalidated by the Act and from then on had no force in law. The Act made clear that the Tate was now totally independent and that any future transfers of British paintings to the National Gallery must be by consultation and agreement.

Technically, the Tate had the right to refuse to transfer these works, but in practice the situation was more complex. There was a moral obligation to recognise the National Gallery's long-standing claim to four of these works, as well as the realisation that if the Tate fought to retain them, the public would support the National Gallery as the rightful home for masterpieces of British art. There was also a disinclination to jeopardise what were, on the whole, good relations with the National Gallery. Nevertheless, the loss of these paintings in 1987 was upsetting – particularly to the Tate's Education Department, now headed by Simon Wilson, which had built some of its activities around several of these works. Beyond that there is no doubt that the loss of the Hogarth and the Wright, in particular, seriously impoverished the Tate's representation of eighteenth-century art.

In contrast with this loss was the enormous gain when, on 7 August 1986, all the Turner Bequest material from the British Museum Print Room arrived at the Tate. Instead of the expected 19,000 watercolours, drawings and sketchbooks, it soon became apparent there were almost 35,000 accessionable items and intensive work began (computerisation coming into use for the first time) on the cataloguing, conserving and photographing of this collection. Because Turner had kept all his working materials and had bought back a number of major works, his Bequest is unique, for the art of no other great artist can be seen in this way. Though the care of his oils had formally passed to the Tate after the 1954 Act, nine had remained at the National Gallery and seven of these (leaving the two that Turner had asked to be hung in perpetuity in the National Gallery next to two Claudes) were lent for six months to the Clore Gallery so that they could be part of the opening display. The troubled history of the Turner Bequest, the long years that many of his canvases had spent in store at Trafalgar Square, many of them rolled up, unattended and covered in grime, combined with the damage and subsequent dispersal caused by the 1928 flood, and the discovery, as late as 1968, in the the National Gallery basement of *Dido Directing the Equipment of the Fleet, or the Morning of the Carthaginian Empire* – a picture on record as having perished in 1917 – all made the opening of the Clore Gallery an emotive occasion.

But in its final stages the Clore was only slightly less fraught with problems than the 1979 extension.[6] By January 1985 it was forty-one weeks behind schedule and in June it had to be publicly announced that the Clore would not now open until the end of 1986 at the earliest. The problem at that point was the leaking roof, caused by the faulty construction of its windows by the sub-contractors. Even after the date of the opening had been fixed for 1 April 1987, there was still work to be done on the refinement of the lighting, for the company responsible for the computerised control of the sunblinds and light levels in the galleries had gone into liquidation the year before.

It was the details that caused the most aggravation. Meeting after meeting was held at which the curatorial staff or the working party gave vent to angry frustration with, for instance, Stirling's insistence on brass lamps in the study room, which would create unwanted reflections, or his desire for bright green paint on the glazing bars and window frames of the paper conservation studio, which would result in some green reflection that might affect the conservators' perception of the true tones of watercolour. In turn, Stirling was equally frustrated by the inability of the curators, Director and Trustees to agree on a concerted client view. Though the brass lamps and the green window frames were abandoned, he refused to budge on the artificial strip-lighting which had been positioned too close to the wall and cast a raking light on the paintings, as Alexander Dunluce pointed out at a demonstration mock-up in the Gorst Road store.

The issue on which the working party and the architect seemed to reach a dead-lock was the colour of the wall-covering in the galleries. Since his appointment as

75 The Clore Gallery

Curator of the Turner Collection in January 1985, Andrew Wilton had joined the working party, adding his voice to that of Martin Butlin and Robin Hamlyn, in an attempt to stand up for what seemed to them right for Turner's pictures. Wilton's career had taken him from the British Museum to the Yale Center for British Art for five years, after which he had returned to the Prints and Drawings Department at the British Museum, with specific responsibility for the Turner collection. Having published several books on Turner, he was able at the height of one argument over the choice of wall colours, to support Robin Hamlyn in his claim that he was 'speaking for Turner'. But Stirling did not want his light, modern galleries filled with the heavy green or red wall colours associated with the nineteenth century. Alan Bowness supported him in this and at one point introduced into the discussion the pale 'oatmeal' fabric which had been used in the Yale Centre for British Art by Louis Kahn. As a result Turner's art was shown against a much paler colour than some of the experts thought suitable.

Turner studies had moved on considerably since Gowing's exhibition *Turner: Imagination and Reality* at the Museum of Modern, New York, in 1966. Gowing, who promoted the view that Turner's art prefigured the future, had drawn attention to the affinities in his work with Impressionism and Abstract Expressionism. Since then, Turner scholars have taken a revisionist view, and have argued that his objective was not consonant with the modern world and that, unlike Constable who created new standards for himself based on his feelings, Turner always judged himself by reference to the past. What was never in doubt was his technical mastery, his ability to create powerful effects of light and to turn any experience, however pedestrian, into serene and Romantic impressions. The opening of the Clore Gallery, with its explanatory and handsome display, made this fully apparent. After the official opening by the Queen on the very wet afternoon of 1 April 1987, an evening party was held for some 1,500 guests. In keeping with the mood of celebration were the fireworks, sponsored by the Electricity Council and again designed by John Piper, which also drew attention to the river that had played a large part in Turner's life.

One irony of the Clore was that although it increased access to Turner's art, the major scholarship on this artist had now been completed. Nevertheless, Andrew Wilton, wanting to stimulate further research and fresh appreciation, began mounting four exhibitions a year of works on paper, such as *Turner and Architecture* and *Turner and Natural History*, which were accompanied by modest catalogues. He also wanted some of these to be selected by outsiders. With Corinne Bellow's help, sponsorship was obtained from various sources, including Volkswagen, who initiated two biennial Turner scholarships for advanced research over a period of two years leading to exhibition and publication. These helped maintain original research as did the periodical *Turner Studies* which, though not strictly a Tate magazine, was published by the Gallery and had two Tate representatives on its editorial board.

Crucial to the use of the Turner Bequest was the study room, which with the reserve collection, was housed on the second floor. Andrew Wilton brought to

76 Firework display designed by John Piper to celebrate the opening
of the Clore Gallery, 1 April 1987

the setting up of this room his familiarity with the internationally accepted principles concerning the handling of prints, drawings and watercolours. But though
its opening hours were deliberately chosen to be as convenient as possible for the
public, it was less used than expected and also staff-intensive. Its high cost in relation to the number of users eventually caused a review of its management and its
opening hours, with the result that for a period in the mid-1990s it was only open
one day a week.

At the initial opening of the Clore it had been thought necessary to put barri-
ers, made out of large posts and brown silk ropes, in front of the pictures; but
these were eventually removed, as was the original carpeting, since this was found
to create a fine grey dust which the air filtration system could not extract. None
of these details detracted from the achievement of the Clore, which won a national award from the RIBA in 1988, the National Art Collections Fund in the same
year giving Mrs Duffield the 'Benefactor of the Year Award'. Yet there is a sharp

contrast between the galleries, with their traditional proportions and muted harmonies, and the entrance foyer, staircase and landing of the Clore, where Stirling
turns his back on Turner, plays to the architectural world with a language that is
both archaic and modern, and uses dissonant colour and sudden changes of space,
height and direction, reminiscent of Mannerism. He intended the entrance to
unsettle visitors, but with the hope that it would 'settle down' and in time become
more acceptable, as it gained 'a certain identity and memory for the public', who
would then 'expect to see these colours when they come again.'[7] But even before
this happened the public voted for the success of the Clore with its feet and came
in droves. Attendance that April doubled and reached a record figure of 12,000 on
Easter Monday.

★   ★   ★

Today few visitors realise that the Clore was intended to be a front-of-house building, the first of a college-like cluster of 'New Museums' on the Hospital site, predicated on the belief that 'the creation of further galleries was essential to the
future of the Tate'.[8] This scheme, which had been announced in the 1982–84 Biennial Report, advanced a step further in February 1986 when Stirling presented, by
means of slides and a model, his firm's outline plans for the first two stages of this
three-phase project. Phase A involved a Museum of Modern Sculpture and a

77 Interior view of the Clore Gallery

Sculpture Court; Phase B included a Museum of Twentieth-Century Art and a Museum of New Art; and Phase C, which was to reflect the growing importance of the Tate's library and archive collection, was to be a Study Centre.

Work on the Study Centre was held back during the winter of 1986–7 while the Trustees considered Mrs Duffield's idea for a Children's Museum. She had looked at various sites in connection with this project and now asked if space could be found for it on the Hospital site. She was keen to extend her connection with the Tate – particularly its Education Department – and was prepared to pay for a feasibility study. But when Jocelyn Stevens, on her behalf, put forward a proposal for a series of environments for children aged between five and eleven, to be independently staffed, financed and run, it was opposed by Patrick Heron; and though Bowness thought it a good idea, he felt it had little to do with the Tate. As a result Mrs Duffield withdrew her offer in February 1987 and took it elsewhere, eventually creating Eureka in a former railway station at Halifax.

Work now went ahead with designs for the New Museums, even though there was little indication that the government would support the scheme. Two private donations had helped pay Stirling's fees for his draft designs for Phases A and B, commissioned by the Property Services Agency, who still had responsibility for the Tate's buildings, but the funding of this project remained hypothetical. Whereas all three phases had been costed at £29–£30 million in 1985, by the following year detailed estimates for just Phases A and B came to £28 million. In March 1986 the Property Services Agency negotiated a fee of £50,000 with Stirling for designs for the Study Centre, but again the Tate had to find part of this sum from private sources. This they did, but when designs were submitted in the summer of 1987, the estimated cost of the Study Centre – £13.5 million – had more than doubled from the original estimate. The July Board meeting minutes record: 'The Trustees thought that the new estimate made the project almost inachievable, and did not wish to spend further money on developing the scheme at this stage.'[9]

One of the most striking aspects of Stirling's scheme was the great bow-fronted window running almost the full length of the modern sculpture galleries. These were to be built on to the side of the 1979 extension, and were to be centred on the same axis as the entrance to the Hospital administration block, situated on the other side of the courtyard which was to become a terraced Sculpture Court. Attached to the north end of the Sculpture Museum, and running parallel with John Islip Street, was to be the Museum of New Art. The main floor, which, as with the Sculpture Galleries, was to match the height of the galleries in the old building and provide access to them, was to have a large suite of galleries, half of them top-lit, while above this was intended to be a large open-plan gallery of 'industrial' character. The remaining buildings – the Museum of Twentieth-Century Art, the Study Centre, Sculpture Conservation Studios and loading, packing and handling bays – were to be built on the east side of the site, and to be so arranged that the visitor could make a complete circuit, through all the new buildings, into the Clore and thence back into the old building, which was to become a Museum of British Painting. The 1984–86 Biennial Report claimed: 'The plan will be seen to be an energetic symbiosis of organisms for the collection, study and display of art, each with its own distinctive character and vivid personality.' Moreover it promised the visitor 'an architectural experience to match the experience of the great works of art within'.[10]

Bowness, who was a Trustee of the Henry Moore Foundation, arranged for several of its Trustees to visit the Tate in November 1986 in order to see the new Sculpture Conservation Studio. Housed (it was thought, temporarily) in one of the old ward blocks, this had come into existence that year with the help of the Henry Moore Foundation, which had given a substantial sum to cover salaries for the first years. In the course of this visit, its Trustees were shown plans for the Modern Sculpture Museum in which the largest gallery had been especially planned to house the Tate's large collection of Moore's work. It was also intended that his large bronzes would dominate the Sculpture Court. Furthermore, as Bowness had indicated in a letter to Lord Goodman, the Foundation's Chairman, the Clore and Turner were nearby, 'so that we shall be showing two of Britain's greatest artists side by side'.[11] Subsequently, the Tate submitted a formal application to the Foundation for money towards the cost of this Museum. Knowing that Mrs Thatcher was an admirer of Henry Moore (Lord Hutchinson having been instrumental in getting some of his work into 10 Downing Street), Bowness wanted pressure to be put on the government to come up with matching funds. Thus when the Foundation approved a £3 million donation towards the cost of building new sculpture galleries, it was conditional on a matching grant of £3 million from the government. This, it soon became clear, was not going to be forthcoming.

Instead, there was a move afoot to change the method of museum funding, by means of devolution. Museums and galleries, now familiar with the tactics of consistent underfunding, were already being forced to embrace the values of enterprise culture, such as marketing and business sponsorship, in an attempt to reduce financial dependence on government-provided funds. From April 1986, in order to bring them into line with other non-departmental public bodies, they had also to accept a switch from a parliamentary vote to Grant-in-Aid. Although the Tate had always been subject to the control of one or another government body – first the Treasury, then the Department of Education and Science, and latterly the Office of Arts and Libraries – it had each year been voted a sum of money by Parliament. Under the new system, Grant-in-Aid would come direct from the Office of Arts and Libraries. Although this change in funding was largely technical and had little visible effect in the day-to-day running of the Gallery, it gave more power to the Trustees. They were now able to retain unspent money at the end of each financial year, not only in relation to the purchase grant, but also in relation to the running costs. In addition, they were allowed to retain all receipts which gave the Gallery an incentive to earn money. This change was the first step towards a larger move which would turn the Trustees of the Tate into a corporate body.

Related to this process of devolution was the 'untying' of the Property Services Agency, which meant that from 1 April 1988, the Trustees were also responsible for the maintenance of the Tate Gallery buildings. It was the intention of the

Office of Arts and Libraries, as soon as an Act of Parliament had been passed giving the Tate Trustees corporate status, to hand over not just funding but also the freehold of the Tate buildings, which would no longer be Crown Properties. Meanwhile, provision was made in the 1988–9 Grant-in-Aid for the upkeep of Millbank. Previously, the range of services which the PSA had supplied covered everything, from major projects and general maintenance to the changing of light bulbs. The 'untying' meant an end to secrecy, as the Tate had never known the extent of the resources available through the PSA, and greater freedom, for under the old system Bowness could not have a gallery refurbished without PSA approval. Moreover, the amount of money involved was considerable: during 1985–6 the PSA had spent a total of £4.8 million on Tate Gallery buildings, £0.8 million of which had gone on Clore Gallery contracts, including staff costs, consultants' fees, payments to builders and maintenance firms, fuel bills, services and a contribution in lieu of rates.

The changeover uncovered problems. One was that, owing to an overlap in time for certain contracts in connection with Tate Gallery Liverpool, the PSA put in a large claim for money owed to them by the Tate which the Trustees refused to recognise except in part. Secondly, as soon as the Tate began employing outside consultants, having decided against setting up its own internal PSA, it discovered that the Millbank building was in a parlous state. The surveyors appointed, Drivers Jonas, examined its fabric and services and found asbestos in the older part of the building, also wiring so dangerous that three galleries had to be closed immediately. In the course of arriving at a planned maintenance scheme, Drivers Jonas estimated that, without allowing for any improvements or new building, the Tate needed a £27 million refurbishment and that some £15 million of this was urgent work. The situation was exacerbated by the fact that the Tate no longer had Crown Immunity from certain regulations. Soon after the consultant architects Colquhoun, Miller were appointed in 1986, they submitted proposals for the restoration and development of the Tate, which by March 1987 had reached the total estimated cost of £33 million. Meanwhile, the level of government grant indicated for the building stood at £2.4 million for 1988–9, rising to £2.5 million the following year. As this would do little more than cover general maintenance, the Trustees announced they were reluctant to take on responsibility for the freehold, and were able to do so owing to a delay over the new legislation. An additional worry at this time was whether or not the Office of Arts and Libraries would recognise the extent of the Tate's need of help with running costs for the Clore Gallery and Tate Gallery Liverpool.

It was estimated that £750,000 was needed to finance Liverpool's running costs in the lead up to its opening by the Prince of Wales on 24 May 1988. This much was requested, and in response the government gave £700,000, but as running costs not only for Liverpool but also the Clore. As work progressed on the conversion of the warehouse, it became apparent that the initial estimate fell far short of actual needs. Begun in August 1986, it had followed a tight schedule, carefully monitored by Richard Francis who had been appointed Curator of Tate Gallery

78 Tate Gallery Liverpool in 1989

Liverpool in October 1986. He set up an office first in the Piermaster's House and then in the Harbourmaster's House, and, while the building alterations went ahead, was helped by John Matthews, formerly the Assembly Plant Manager at Ford's, an efficient organiser and experienced manager who proved especially good with contractors. Francis liaised with local bodies and appointed the staff necessary to run the new gallery, including Lewis Biggs who became Curator of Exhibitions. Instead of modelling itself on the London Tate, the Liverpool Tate was to pioneer new schemes, in effect to become something of a research and development limb of the larger institution, acquiring experience that was later to have a crucial effect on the thinking about design at Bankside. One innovation was the decision not to appoint guards, but trained invigilators, who would be able to answer questions from the public about the work on display. Much work was done in the first three years to set up projects with various community groups and to ensure that Tate Gallery Liverpool became firmly linked with the city's educational infrastructure. But even before the Gallery opened, the growing revenue crisis meant that its programme had to be curtailed. At one point, the Mobile Art Project – a van paid for by Volkswagen, the Merseyside Task Force and the Laura Ashley Foundation, and painted to a design by David Hockney – could not take travelling shows to schools and other centres as intended because there was no money to pay for a driver.

Moreover, although the first phase of this conversion had been achieved on schedule, about 30 per cent of the building still remained undeveloped, including the top floor which was intended to encompass artists' studios and workshops and make possible films, dance, conferences and a restaurant. Without these facilities, the social and artistic potential of the new Gallery was inevitably diminished. There was also a degree of local antagonism to the project which was framed for many by the fact that the initiative for it was London-based. It had also followed in the wake of the 1984 Garden Festival, an eccentric hybrid of theme park and modern art, made possible by the planting of a quarter of a million trees in reclaimed dockland, which was eventually to form a public park. Whereas this had provoked the protest of 'jobs not trees', so Liverpool residents called for 'work not bricks' when in 1989 two brick pieces by Carl Andre formed part of a one-year Minimalism display at Tate Gallery Liverpool.

Nevertheless, Tate Gallery Liverpool got off to a triumphant start. The public was excited by Stirling's treatment of the entrance like a giant hoarding and, once inside the building, two great blue balconies, arched like the bridges on a liner, swung out over the entrance hall and found an echo in the semi-circular benches, commissioned from the artist Scott Burton, which wrapped round the columns below. The vertical stacking of the galleries, on the three available floors, discouraged the showing of survey exhibitions, but the space provided was equivalent to that of the Hayward Gallery. A computer-controlled lighting system, designed by Phillips for industrial use, provided diffuse but effective illumination, and, as a whole, the building added to the scattered greatness of Liverpool, with its two cathedrals, the Cunard and Liver buildings, St George's Hall and the Walker Art Gallery.

Attendance figures exceeded the target of 500,000 per annum after the first seven months. An ingredient in this success was the sponsorship provided by Volkswagen, which not only paid for a launch advertising campaign and the opening week celebrations but also helped make possible an ongoing community education programme. But of vital importance was the choice of displays which began on a populist note with a selection of the Tate's most witty and provocative Surrealist works. These went on show for a year, as did Rothko's Seagram murals, which were carefully hung in the way that the artist himself had devised. Under Richard Francis, Tate Gallery Liverpool was conceived not as a static museum, but as a collection of exhibitions which changed at different rates. Its existence helped attract a grant from the Henry Moore Foundation for the conservation of twentieth-century British sculpture which became the subject of another year-long display. But Tate Gallery Liverpool soon broke away from its parent

79 The *New Realities* display at Tate Gallery Liverpool, 1992

institution in its choice of displays and in the course of a lively programme of one-person, group and theme exhibitions it mounted ground-breaking events, such as *Art from Köln* in 1989, *New Art from the North of Britain* in 1990, *Strongholds: New Art from Ireland* in 1991 and *Africa Explores* in 1994. In its desire to maintain an international profile, it established links with institutions abroad, such as the IVAM Centre Julio González in Valencia, whence came the *Hélion* exhibition in 1990. It also brought to Liverpool exhibitions focusing on the work of Bacon, Giacometti, Freud, Spencer, Hockney, Beuys, Robert Gober, Gormley, Alison Wilding, as well as Gilbert and George's *Cosmological Pictures*. But though it drew audiences from far and wide, it could not sustain the enormous impetus with which it had begun, partly because its ambitions outran the funds available. Certain plans, including a major touring retrospective of the American painter David Salle, had to be shelved, and gradually attendance figures began to drop.

To celebrate the opening of Tate Gallery Liverpool, a free-admission spectacular, *Invention of Tradition*, was devised jointly by the composer Gavin Bryars with Bruce McLean and David Ward for Liverpool's two cathedral organists, members of the Royal Liverpool Philharmonic Orchestra, the Wirrall Schools Concert Band and certain vocalists. Performed three nights running at the time of the opening, it involved five performers, all wearing different-colour boiler suits, making gestural movements which cast shadows on giant sail-like screens standing on rafts secured to the edge of the dock, while the sixth performer, Gavin

Bryars, in red, conducted from a raft at its centre. With the organ music projected from speakers, the brass players in two groups in different parts of the dock and
the rest of the musicians in a warehouse, the whole ensemble was held together
by a video-link on which the musicians could see the conductor's gestures, while
he, owing to the acoustics of the dock and the effect of wind and weather, sometimes heard the sound reflected from the buildings several seconds later. The
performances were timed so that they began in twilight and ended in darkness,
the acoustic effects travelling around the complex of buildings and over the water.
Today, Bryars admits that the music itself has limited interest away from the event.
But he remains proud of the fact that for a long time afterwards, behind the door
in the staff toilets in the Liverpool Tate, hung a red boiler suit with the word
COMPOSER on its back.

★   ★   ★

During the early 1980s Bowness had purchased many American paintings and
sculptures, the Tate now owning the most important collection of American art
outside the United States. It was still possible at this time, given the Tate's funds,
to make major acquisitions of American art, and work by Hans Hofmann (hitherto unrepresented in the Tate), Warhol and Johns, entered the collection. Bowness, however, failed to secure an important group of paintings from the Clyfford
Still estate, owing to tax reasons, but was more successful with the Rothko Foundation. He also established a good relationship with Lee Krasner and, after her
death in 1984, with the Krasner-Pollock estate, which enabled the Gallery to

80 John Constable, *The Opening of Waterloo Bridge*
('Whitehall Stairs, June 18th, 1817'), exh. 1832

spread the $2.5 million payment for three Jackson Pollocks, including *Summertime*, over a period of three years. By then it was becoming more difficult to purchase the kind of works thought desirable. But the situation improved in 1987 when an anonymous private donor (later declared as Sir Edwin Manton) set up an American Fund with an endowment of $6.5 million, the interest from which was to be used for the purchase of works of art. In time, the terms of the Fund were widened so that it could become a channel for additional donations from private benefactors, who under American law could claim these gifts against tax, as had previously been possible with gifts via the American Federation of Arts. The Fund, which had its own Board of Trustees in New York, bought works of art after consultation with the Tate's Director, which were then sent to the Tate on loan, and after a period of time often given to the collection.

Sir Edwin Manton's involvement with the Tate Gallery had initially been fired by his interest in Constable and his correspondence with the curator Leslie Parris. Manton was one of many generous contributors to the appeal for Constable's *The Opening of Waterloo Bridge ('Whitehall Stairs, June 18th, 1817')*. The combination of a panoramic riverscape with the human animation provided by the pageantry connected with this historical event makes this one of the artist's most exhilarating works. It first went on public view at the Tate on 27 January 1987, after which the Gallery had until May to raise £2,945,650 (the price agreed after a tax concession had been deducted from the original asking price which was £4 million). £1 million came from the National Heritage Memorial Fund. The National Art Collections Fund gave £250,000 and £100,000 was put up by the Friends of the Tate. The National Heritage Memorial Fund then additionally agreed to match pound-for-pound all donations, except those from public institutions, to a total of £500,000. This left a balance of £600,000 to raise. Public contribution was slow and insufficient; but at the last moment Vivien Duffield stepped in, the Clore Foundation donated £430,000 and the work was saved.

The Constable appeal convinced Bowness that the price of certain works of art had now far outrun what was possible to achieve by means of appeal to the general public. In 1985 there had been little public support for his attempt to run an appeal for Giorgio de Chirico's *The Uncertainty of the Poet*, though one of the mistakes in this instance had been to run the appeal after the work had been bought. Meanwhile, works that the Tate would have liked to acquire, such as Paula Modersohn-Becker's *Self-Portrait of her Fifth Wedding Anniversary*, which sold for £613,611 in 1986, went elsewhere, and when the Tate went up to £400,000 at auction for Otto Dix's *Der Salon I*, they were outbid by the Galerie der Stadt, Stuttgart, which paid £561,000. Nevertheless, Bowness's acquisition of contemporary artists such as Schnabel, Baselitz and Salle, as well as figurative Europeans, such as Beckmann, Kirchner, Dubuffet, Ernst, Miró and Picabia, made sense to the *Guardian's* art critic, Waldemar Januszczak, who found in the latter a convincing lineage for expressionistic and often nationalistic new art.[12]

Changes in the running of the Gallery meant that by the mid-1980s staff wanting to know the whereabouts of a picture or sculpture no longer consulted 'The

Bible', formerly kept by Bill Hudd, head of the working party which was responsible for the handling of works of art, but instead accessed computerised information. Peter Wilson (who had initially joined the Gallery as an intern in the Conservation Department) and his colleagues spent four years researching the best means by which art could be packaged and transported. In general, an increase in professionalisation brought a tightening of standards, particularly in the field of conservation, which had repercussions that went far beyond the Tate. Even so, unforeseen disasters occurred. On 19 June 1984 the lower glass pane in Richard Hamilton's recreation of Duchamp's *The Bride Stripped Bare by her Bachelors, Even (The Large Glass)* shattered as a result of what the glass manufacturers called 'spontaneous stress relief', brought about by the presence of micro-particle impurities in the glass. Then in May 1988, while on loan to the Nationalgalerie in Berlin, Lucian Freud's gem-like portrait of Francis Bacon was stolen. Though covered by British Council indemnity, this as yet unrecovered work remains an irreparable loss.

The appointment to the Board in 1985 of Gilbert de Botton and Mark Weinberg, both financial experts, had represented a further attempt to strengthen the financial arm of the Tate. At the 15 September 1985 Board meeting Bowness's insistence 'that the government had a responsibility to see that national collections were properly supported and financed' met with a riposte from Weinberg: 'the government would not bear the cost of development and ... the trustees would have to look to the private sector'. This exchange was indicative of the continuing conflict that existed between Trustees and Director. And when Bowness informed the Trustees in 1987 that he would retire the following year, on reaching the age of sixty, as he had been offered the Directorship of the Henry Moore Foundation, Mark Weinberg offered to pay for a consultant to look into the role of the Trustees and their relationship to the Director and the staff, as a prelude to setting the terms of the appointment of the new Director. The Trustees welcomed Sir Mark's generous proposal and accepted his choice of Dennis Stevenson.

Bowness, aware that the Trustees themselves were divided into factions, continued to insist that it was at Board meetings, at which attendance was often poor, that the role of the Trustees became significant. A feeling was still prevalent that the Trustees wanted to have more involvement with the running of the Tate – an idea which many of the staff deplored, feeling that it was the Director who mattered. Where this difference of opinion became openly apparent was in the course of meetings of the Exhibitions Sub-Committee.

A mixed exhibition programme, including exhibitions drawn primarily from the collection, had continued to thrive at the Tate during the mid-1980s. One of these was Ronald Alley's *Forty Years of Modern Art* in 1986. It proved a fitting climax to his career, which had included the publication of his long-awaited *Modern Foreign Catalogue* (1981), its precision and thoroughness setting a standard for cataloguing that was taken still further by Leslie Parris in the Historic British Collection and by Richard Morphet, who became Keeper of the Modern Collection after Alley's retirement in 1986. The programme as a whole benefited from

Corinne Bellow's skill at raising sponsorship (at the time of her retirement in 1988 she had raised almost £2 million); for instance, United Technologies Corporation had funded the 1986 Kokoschka exhibition, and AT&T the Hockney exhibition which arrived from Los Angeles and New York in the autumn of 1988.

Staff and artist-Trustees met at the Exhibitions Sub-Committee where it was customary for the most senior Trustee to take the Chair. When Patrick Heron joined the Committee he was surprised to discover that it met only once a year and then largely to approve the programme put before it. At the 1985 meeting he pushed the agenda aside and announced that he had a proposal. He then outlined in considerable detail a suggestion that the Tate should mount the largest Matisse exhibition the world had ever seen, which would bring together the fifty-five Matisses in Russia with loans from America and elsewhere. He went on to explain how he envisaged it should be hung, with *Dance* and *Music* visible at the end of long vistas, which were to be achieved by removing certain walls in the 1979 extension. According to Heron, his proposal was met with silence on the part of the curatorial staff, and when the minutes of the meeting appeared, his long peroration was summed up in a couple of lines.[13]

Heron spent the next four and a half years working hard on what came to be known as the 'Matisse Project'. He found supporters in John Golding, Anthony Caro and Richard Rogers, and was not alone in feeling that, because the Matisse Project was the result of Trustee initiative, the staff were never fully behind it. Letters were sent at Heron's request to American museums, but the replies, as reported, seemed unsatisfactory and unreliable. Nevertheless, they cumulatively suggested that loans from America would not be forthcoming, and Heron therefore pinned his hopes on the Russian Matisses, which, having been shut away in the Soviet Union for decades, would make a world-class event if brought to London and shown at the Tate. Yet further disappointments were in store. One instance of this was the reply received from the British Ambassador in Moscow, in answer to a letter from Bowness: the Russians would never lend their Matisses, but they might be willing to send reproductions. Heron was so incensed by this reply that he and Richard Rogers decided to bypass the Gallery and go straight to Mrs Thatcher, who was shortly to make a visit to Moscow. A letter, written by Heron in Rogers's house and biked round the next day, received a prompt and encouraging reply: the Prime Minister would mention the Tate's interest in the Russian Matisses to Mr Gorbachev and she advised them to go themselves to the Soviet Union.

A visit, arranged for 21–4 October 1987, was cancelled at the last moment by the Russians, as it coincided with the fiftieth anniversary celebrations of the 1917 Revolution. Not until 10 February 1988 did Bowness, Rogers and Heron finally set out, Heron clutching a model of what he hoped the entire exhibition would look like. After talking with the authorities at the Pushkin Museum in Moscow, Bowness had to return to London in order to be present at the opening of a David Bomberg exhibition at the Tate. Heron and Rogers went on to the Hermitage in Leningrad where it was suggested that in return for their Matisses the Russians would receive a survey exhibition of British art from Hogarth to the Pre-Raphaelites. Aware that the talks had not been conclusive, Rogers afterwards wrote again to Mrs Thatcher, asking for help at high ministerial levels in order that pressure could be maintained on the Russian authorities.

When Patrick Heron at the Hermitage had produced his model of the exhibition, on the side of which was imprinted 'Tate Gallery: Henri Matisse – paintings and sculptures from the Soviet Museums', Dr Vitaly Suslov had raised his eyebrows. 'Already?' he asked. In the experienced eyes of Ruth Rattenbury, the Tate's exhibitions organiser, the Matisse Project seemed 'a folly'. Nevertheless, it was still in the air after Bowness's departure from the Tate in August 1988.

Knighted for his services to art in the New Years' Honours in January 1988, Bowness left the Tate pleased that the Clore Gallery had at last done justice to Turner's great Bequest and that with the opening of the Gallery in Liverpool the Tate had a presence outside London. He was, however, saddened that his academic expertise had not been fully used and that he, as a specialist in the classic period of modern art, had not had the right funds to purchase more in the field of French painting. He had always been aware that his period of office would be short in comparison with that of his two predecessors and that he would have to hurry to get things done. But his chief regret was that he had served under Conservative governments generally indifferent to public museums and galleries.

17

Past, Present and Future

When Nicholas Serota took over as Director of the Tate Gallery in September 1988, his succession seemed to many as inevitable as that of Alan Bowness in 1979. Yet in some ways Serota's appointment was a more daring, less obvious choice. Among his competitors at the final stage were Norman Rosenthal, Exhibitions Secretary at the Royal Academy; Dr John Elderfield, Director of the Department of Drawings at the Museum of Modern Art, New York, and an internationally renowned scholar; and Julian Spalding, Director of Manchester City Art Galleries. What Serota lacked in comparison with the last two individuals was the museological experience involved in the care of a collection. Having begun his career, like Bowness, as a Regional Arts Officer with the Arts Council, he then directed the Museum of Modern Art at Oxford for three years before moving to the Whitechapel Art Gallery in 1976. There, with the help of Loveday Shewell, his very able administrator, he developed further his skills at selecting, organising, editing and installing major exhibitions – often working closely with the artists involved and learning much from them about the display of art. But Whitechapel shows, with their recurrent focus on international, avant-garde artists, were often reviewed negatively owing to an ingrained prejudice against innovative contemporary art in the English press. Serota, whilst becoming increasingly respected among his peers in the international art world, had remained a little outside the English establishment.

At the Whitechapel he had both travelled widely and focused on the near at hand. In keeping with the missionary impulse that had led to the foundation of the Gallery, he had encouraged a vigorous programme of involvement with local artists and East End communities. The Gallery's educational activities, run by Jenni Lomax, were not art-history led but developed out of direct engagement with contemporary art or artists. An active educational programme was pursued even when the building closed for two years for much-needed refurbishment. Owing to the acquisition of a sliver of land, the architects Colquhoun & Miller were able to incorporate into the new scheme a first-floor gallery, a lecture theatre, restaurant and video and study rooms, all of which opened off a generously proportioned new staircase. Though the sophisticated architectural solution, decidedly modern yet reminiscent of turn-of-the-century Glasgow and Vienna, was widely admired when the Gallery reopened in September 1985, the rebuilding had taken longer and cost more than had been expected, leaving the Whitechapel with an overdraft of £250,000. What could have been the cause of administrative embarrassment was rectified in 1987 by the success of an auction of work donated by artists at Serota's request. The fact that this auction raised £1.4 million, paid off debts to builders and contractors, and established an endowment fund which made it possible for the Whitechapel to continue showing the kind of challenging, innovative work by younger artists unlikely to attract a commercial sponsor, was no small factor in Serota's appointment to the Tate.

All the short-listed candidates for the Tate Directorship had been asked to submit a seven-year plan for the Gallery. In the opinion of Richard Rogers, Serota's submission revealed that he had done his groundwork thoroughly, and stood out far above the rest. Entitled 'Grasping the Nettle', it managed to cover in the space of two sides of A4 paper all the key areas of concern and made terse, ambitious but realistic proposals with regard to the collection and access to it; exhibitions; buildings; fundraising and public affairs; and management. It was premised by an acute appraisal of the Tate's current situation, and the impending crisis that loomed over it owing to constraints in government spending, rising prices in the art market and a changed climate of management in the public sector. It concluded that many aspects of the Tate's policy and operation were in urgent need of review and that, though the Tate was loved, it was not sufficiently respected.

Support for his appointment came from Howard Hodgkin who readily endorsed the new Director in the *Sunday Times*. 'Nick Serota has enormous energy and demonstrated at the Whitechapel a tremendous sense of diplomacy. He is a passionate man, and indeed is quite unusual in this country in his commitment to modern painting and sculpture.'[1] A contrary view was voiced in *Modern Painters* by Peter Fuller who launched a vitriolic attack, claiming Serota had neither the experience nor inclination to maintain and preserve a collection of historic British and modern Western art. Such criticism was to be negated by Serota's decision to base his entire policy on the premise that the collections must remain at the heart of the Tate's enterprise.

Nine months were to pass between Serota's appointment and his arrival at the Tate. In the intervening period a slight awkwardness prevailed, in that Bowness, who had a number of things to achieve during the final months of his Directorship – including the opening of Liverpool – did not wish for any overlap, fearing that any suggestion of there being two Directors would have a disruptive effect. The dispute with Palumbo had also left Bowness very nervous over access by Trustees or outsiders to Tate staff. Though Serota, while still in the employment of the Whitechapel Art Gallery, visited the Tate on a monthly basis, for a couple of hours' talk with Bowness, he was discouraged from making contact with any staff, many of whom he knew socially. At the same time Richard Rogers, whose Chairmanship of the Tate in January 1988 was extended for another year, was anxious to get moving with future plans and agreed to hold an informal discussion group at his house on 10 May 1988. After this, three Chairman's study groups met with Serota at the Millbank Lodge in June. An air of conspiracy hung over these meetings, owing to the association of the Lodge with the Tate Gallery Foundation and to the fact that out of respect for Bowness no Tate staff were invited. Each meeting involved small but diverse groupings of people and the three areas under

81 Sir John Rothenstein with Richard Morphet and Nicholas Serota in 1988,
in front of Sir Hubert von Herkomer's 1897 portrait of Sir Henry Tate

investigation were: goals and strategies; the Tate as a business; and its organisation and management. Among the conclusions drawn were that not enough was
being made of the Tate's role as the national collection of British painting and that
the Tate's education programmes had still not become an integral part of the
Gallery's operation. Overall, few wholly new ideas emerged, but instead a feeling
that the Tate now had the opportunity to draw together policy strands which had
been in the air for some years. Serota reported on these study groups at his first
Board meeting in September.

One of the first things he did on arrival was to hold an artists' party. He had
heard several say that they had not had the chance to see properly the *Late
Picasso* exhibition, which had three weeks still to run. He recognised also that
unless artists were closely involved with the Tate it was unlikely to flourish. As a
result special viewings for artists were to become a regular feature at the Gallery.
In addition, Serota continued Bowness's habit of celebrating birthdays and
anniversaries connected with senior figures in the art world. On 5 December 1988
a lunch was held to mark the fiftieth anniversary of Sir John Rothenstein's
appointment as Director of the Tate Gallery. Four Tate Directors attended it, as
did all living former Chairmen.

In the opinion of Richard Rogers, a new feeling of optimism had been underlined by Serota's opening party. Yet the situation at the Tate was far from rosy.
There was a backlog of work in the Conservation Department which, now that it
incorporated Paper and Sculpture Studios, required additional funding. The store
at Gorst Road in Acton had a leaking roof and, by modern standards, inadequate
security. The older parts of the Millbank building were in poor structural condition, while at Tate Gallery Liverpool the top floor remained incomplete and
unused.

It had become apparent that Liverpool, despite the success of its inaugural exhibition, *Starlit Waters*, and that of its follow-up, *Angry Penguins and Realist Painting in Melbourne in the 1940s*, had opened too soon, with inadequate funds and with certain aspects of the first stage of building still incomplete. An increase in the Grant-in-Aid for 1988–89 had been intended to reflect the Tate's additional responsibility with regard to Liverpool, but it did not cover the shortfall in running costs and left Serota with no alternative but to close certain galleries in Liverpool soon after he arrived. In November 1990 the 1988 scheme was modified to make possible better education facilities, a larger café and the removal of the bookshop to the ground floor; but the top floor of the building, as part of Phase 2 in the Gallery's development, remained untouched, having to await further funding. Despite other minor problems with the building, which were eventually solved, and a persistent shortage of money, Tate Gallery Liverpool maintained an ambitious outreach programme run by Toby Jackson, Curator of Education. This was in addition to workshops held in the Gallery; study days for sixth formers, and day-schools and adult education classes run jointly with Liverpool University. Jackson and his assistants worked closely with the other curators, now led by Lewis Biggs, who took over in 1990 after Richard Francis decided to return to London where Serota invited him to animate discussion about the Tate's future. Biggs and Jackson, coming respectively with experience of the Arnolfini in Bristol and the Museum of Modern Art, Oxford, brought with them the kind of progressive views associated with independent, Arts Council-funded arts institutions and applied them to the situation at Liverpool. Biggs and his Assistant Curator, Penelope Curtis, continued to mount exhibitions which were theme-based, adventurous, innovative and, in their close co-operation with education services, setting a precedent for possible implementation in London.

Incomplete and inadequately funded, Tate Gallery Liverpool was nevertheless regarded by the Minister for the Arts as a shining example of the government's regional cultural policy. This left the Tate in an anomalous position — committed to the concept of regional outstations yet unable to find sufficient revenue for one that was already in existence. Since the mid-1980s plans had been afoot to build a gallery in St Ives, and South West Arts and Cornwall County Council had negotiated with Alan Bowness an agreement by which the Tate was committed to lending some sixty works by the St Ives school. Now, following the immense publicity that had accompanied the opening of Tate Gallery Liverpool, two other cities – Bristol and Norwich – began to seek the establishment of similar institutions. When Serota arrived at the Tate he found both Rogers and another Trustee, David Puttnam, Director of Anglia Television, actively supporting the idea of further regional development and arranging discussions with local authority representatives and with businessmen. Though the Bristol initiative soon ran into the sands, the idea for a centre of modern art in Norwich was picked up by Timothy Colman, Lord Lieutenant of Norfolk, director of several companies and Pro-Chancellor of the University of East Anglia. He organised a series of meetings in Norwich and the proposal gathered momentum. By the spring of 1989 a Steering Group had been established, the Tate maintaining at all times that the Trustees were willing to lend pictures, but that the capital and revenue costs of such a project had to be the responsibility of local initiative.

As a result of a feasibility study, two options emerged: one, a riverside building in the centre of Norwich, part of a redevelopment scheme; and the other, to collaborate with the Sainsbury Centre at the University of East Anglia, using their existing buildings. The prospect of the first alternative receded with the onset of the economic recession, but a further idea arose which involved the conversion of certain rooms within the Castle Museum. Meanwhile, negotiations with the Office of Arts and Libraries over St Ives had confirmed that there was no likelihood of finding any revenue costs for a 'Tate Gallery Norwich' from this source. Though the idea of an East Anglian outstation eventually collapsed, a positive outcome emerged from all these discussions: two Tate exhibitions, *Stanley Spencer* and *Transformation of Appearance* (the latter focusing on the 'School of London'), were shown in Norwich in 1991. In addition a lasting agreement was reached with the Castle Museum concerning joint projects and regular loans, a partnership which may serve as a model for future collaboration between the Tate and major regional museums.

The debate over the viability of outstations made it clear that Serota had taken over the running of the Tate at a moment of transition and reassessment. During the 1980s the Gallery had undergone considerable expansion, its staff rising from 245 in 1980 (excluding Publications and Restaurant) to 406 in 1988, and the energies of the institution had been greatly absorbed by important initiatives, notably the opening of the Clore Gallery and Tate Gallery Liverpool. Consequently, there had been little opportunity to reflect on the Tate's policy and programme. The generous gift from Nomura Securities, secured by Gilbert de Botton, had given rise to a scheme hurriedly put together by the Tate with John Miller, who had been appointed by the Trustees as their architect on the main building in 1986, for a works-on-paper gallery to be built over the boiler-house yard. Serota soon discovered this had not been fully costed, that John Miller had not had time to relate it to an overall plan for the Gallery and that, if built, the new gallery would block circulation routes.

Instead, the Nomura gift was redirected towards one of the main galleries leading into the Clore. Miller's brief was not only to restore the original appearance of the architecture, but also to install all the services and controls necessary to meet the highest international museum standards. With its new floor, new wall linings, newly glazed roof, sun-screening, air-cooling and circulation system, the Nomura Room personifies the best in the upgrading of a Victorian building and it also sets the model for future upgrading in the older parts of the original building. The Nomura project proved additionally beneficial in that it provided the opportunity to move the Gallery Shop to a new and larger location alongside the Nomura Room, and at the same time to build a new plant room in a nearby hidden courtyard.

In the course of a fairly continuous programme of gallery redecoration and refurbishment, the curatorial staff moved out of the main building into the Hospital's central administration block at the back of the Clore and a new Friends' Room was created. Dr Mortimer and Theresa Sackler, encouraged by Gilbert de Botton in his role as Chairman of Tate Gallery Foundation, made possible the renovation of the Octagon in the Duveen Sculpture Galleries which was given a new roof and new lighting. This key space, at the building's centre, has since been known as the Sackler Octagon.

Whereas Bowness had opened up the Tate and seeded new initiatives, Serota quickly recognised the need for management reorganisation, to make viable the running of the huge and complex institution he had inherited. A full corporate plan, first drawn up in 1987 at the request of the Office of Arts and Libraries, had been slightly revised in 1988. Early the following year a new version was requested and in March Rick Haythornthwaite was seconded from British Petroleum (BP) in order to assist with it. The outcome – 'A Review and Forward Plan' – appeared in 1990 and set the precedent for subsequent forward plans, which from now on became an important aspect of Tate administration.

In the persistent thoughtfulness, assiduous attention to detail, careful analysis and bold planning that over the next few years transformed every aspect of the Tate, Serota was partnered by Dennis Stevenson who had joined the Board of Trustees three weeks after Serota took over. There had been earlier meetings, for Serota, soon after the announcement of his appointment as the next Tate Director, obtained a copy of Stevenson's 1987 report clarifying the relationship between the Director and the Board of Trustees in the wake of the Palumbo/Bowness confrontation, and went to see him, realising from this document that Stevenson knew more about the current situation at the Tate than almost anyone else. It was also clear to the Trustees that the person who wrote the Report would make an excellent Chairman; and, despite controversy in the press as to who would take over from Richard Rogers in January 1989,[2] following Mrs Thatcher's rejection of John Burgh, former Director-General of the British Council, Stevenson was voted Chairman-Elect as soon as he joined the Board, and his close working relationship with Serota lay behind many of the successes registered by the Tate in the early 1990s.

By his own admission, Stevenson had only a limited knowledge of art (though his mother was a keen collector of work by contemporary Scottish artists and he himself collects work by young painters), but he had a reputation as a brilliant 'corporate fixer', owing to the success of the management consultancy, SRU (Specialist Research Unit), which he had set up with Peter Wallis (also known as the writer on style, Peter York). By the age of thirty Stevenson, owing to the proliferation of his interests and commitments, had found himself responsible for tens of thousands of people; for alongside his incisive business sense ran a pronounced interest in public service. An article he had written for the *Financial Times* about unemployment among young black people had caught the attention of Peter Walker, then Housing Minister in the Heath Government, and led to his appointment, aged twenty-six, as Chairman of the Peterlee and Aycliffe new town corporation, charged with creating a new town in one of the worst unemployment areas in north-east England. He successfully wooed to the area some of the first Japanese investors in Britain.

Stevenson went on to chair other government committees, but his appointment to several high-profile public jobs was vetoed by Margaret Thatcher, who disliked this enterprising business man with liberal views. In the course of his 1987 report on the relationship between the Tate Trustees and Director, Stevenson had upheld the power of the Director, especially in relation to acquisitions, and had also commented on the need for close and mutually supportive agreement between Chairman and Director. The insight this report had given him into the running of the Tate made him an ideal candidate for a Tate Trusteeship. However, Mrs Thatcher refused to appoint him when his name was first proposed. Serota spoke with Mark Weinberg who contacted Tim Bell, former Chairman of Saatchi & Saatchi and close adviser of Mrs Thatcher. Bell, who knew Stevenson well enough not to ask his approval of the line he was about to take, told Mrs Thatcher that 'Stevenson's political views had mellowed'.[3] Consequently, Stevenson, having spent much of the 1980s building up his reputation in the City, arrived at the Tate richly endowed with connections, confidence and energy.

Having learnt of the often bitter and querulous debate over potential acquisitions in Bowness's era, as well as the bureaucratic procedure that had developed inside the Tate for generating proposals, Stevenson was determined that the Trustees should delegate more authority to the Director, trusting in Serota's 'eye' and his ability to lead a definite acquisition policy. Stevenson thought it absurd for a group of strong-minded Trustees to take formal votes on acquisitions where personal value judgements were paramount, and, under his Chairmanship, it was agreed that the amount which could be spent at the Director's discretion, without the Board's approval, should be raised from £20,000 to £100,000. However, Trustees received background notes on potential acquisitions which dealt not only with the art-historical importance of the work, but also with how it should be seen in relation to the Tate's collection. It was expected that Trustees, especially artist-Trustees, would make their opinions known to the Director between meetings. They also had a strong voice in the overall policy towards acquisitions when each year a paper was presented on this topic. Careful thought went into the breakdown of the acquisitions budget for specific categories within the overall collection, and objectives were clearly identified. Serota was particularly aware that new thinking about the art of the past had revealed whole areas of British and foreign art of the twentieth century which had been previously neglected but were now much admired. This, combined with the tenfold rise in art prices in the last decade, and the fact that in 1990 the Purchase Grant (£1,815,000) remained below that allocated in 1980 (£1,888,000), left the Gallery with no alternative but to seek additional funding from the private sector. It was also thought desirable that stronger relationships should be established with collectors as a means of drawing important works into the orbit of the Tate before they came on to the market.

Throughout February and early March 1989 Serota and Stevenson held a series of meetings with staff to examine some of the fundamental issues facing the Tate Gallery in the 1990s. These discussions helped shape the move towards the Forward Plan, which recognised the need to reorganise the responsibilities beneath the Director. Since responsibility for all Tate buildings and estate had been transferred from the Property Services Agency to the Trustees on 1 April 1988, it was thought advisable to create a post within the Gallery to manage this huge additional responsibility. Peter Wilson, who had extended his specialist training in conservation to cover an interest in museum buildings, now combined this with a personal enthusiasm for contemporary architecture and became Head of Gallery Services. At the same time it was agreed to appoint a Deputy Director, who would take responsibility for financial and business matters so that the Director could devote the greater part of his time to the collection. New lines of reporting were also created. A Management Board would from now on meet monthly to consider policy and resources, while a Collections Board also met once a month to discuss policy and plan the future programme, and the minutes of both Boards were to be circulated widely through the Gallery. In the course of staff restructuring, the former Turner and British curators were brought together in the British Collection and by 1991 had been redeployed in five 'cells': Tudor and Stuart painting, eighteenth-century painting, early and mid-nineteenth-century art, Turner, and late nineteenth- and twentieth-century art. Each cell was to be led by a senior curator supported by one or more juniors. Most of the junior Turner specialists from now on worked on other periods, and were relieved of their duties in connection with the Study Room, which was to be managed by a trained registrar and technicians.

Among the various aims behind these rearrangements were two prime objectives: to make best use of individual skills and to promote greater unity of purpose. The Exhibitions Department, under Ruth Rattenbury, now constituted a team which took on the entire administrative responsibility for all major exhibitions, special displays, the Turner Prize and touring shows at home and abroad. No longer was it teamed with Technical Services and Art Handling, which now joined the Registrar's Office and Conservation under Collection Services headed by Viscount Dunluce. The marriage of these departments aided the development of a computerised locations index and a database, making possible significant administrative improvements. A central record system for the Gallery, which had broken down into several mini-registries in the 1980s owing to the creation of new departments, was re-established and transferred to a newly created section of the Archive which was later to be known as Gallery Records. At the same time the Registrar's Office increasingly occupied a key position, acting as a kind of secretariat for the management of the collections and the building.

The recognition of the need for a Deputy Director resulted in the arrival of the forty-nine year old Francis Carnwath in January 1989. His appointment was controversial and questioned in Parliament, as he came not from the museum profession but from a merchant bank, having taken early retirement in order to seek an alternative career. He agreed to take on the job for three years and in that time was to introduce modern financial systems into the Gallery. Despite the fact that his father had been a founder member of the Friends of the Tate Gallery for many years, and had served as its Treasurer, as Carnwath had also done for several years in the mid-1980s, he was unprepared for the antiquated methods that he encountered. On his first day at the Tate Francis sought out the Accounts Department and on the top floor in a distant part of the Hospital site he found John Ashfield, a genial, bearded man, who sat surrounded by paper doing all the accounts himself, by hand. Astonished to learn that the Trustees never received any breakdown of the annual accounts, Carnwath soon realised that to achieve a full divisional breakdown was going to take six months.[4] He was later to take the lead in establishing a Finance Committee which in 1993 began meeting three times a year.

Other significant developments at this time included the promotion of Andrew Wilton to the Keepership of the British Collection following Martin Butlin's retirement in January 1990; the appointment of Teresa Gleadowe (formerly Assistant Director of the Visual Arts Department of the British Council) as Head of Information Services; and the creation of a Development Office in the Lodge to co-ordinate and lead fundraising. This last was an especially important move as it embraced the various fundraising activities already in existence – the Friends, Patrons and Foundation – all of which had their own agendas and did not work together. Though Robert Horton had recently succeeded Gilbert de Botton as Chairman of the Tate Gallery Foundation, its initial impetus had diminished while its continued existence slightly confused the purpose of the Friends. The departure of Cherry Barnett, who had for many years run and developed the Friends' organisation, created an apt moment to relaunch this institution, which needed to grow in size, but lacked the necessary infrastructure to do so. By bringing all these fundraising activities under the overall organisation of a Development Office which was responsible to the Director's Office, Serota carried through one of the tenets of his initial seven-year plan, reasserted the Trustees' authority in determining policy and made it clear that the Foundation's role was to support that policy.[5] What the Foundation did have at this time which proved very useful was sufficient money to pay certain salaries for a limited period in order to get the Development Office up-and-running. Though the annual cost of this department was questioned at the November 1990 Board meeting, Serota responded with the firm insistence that it was necessary to provide sponsors and benefactors with a first-class service, and that this could only be achieved by adequate staffing. What had begun informally under the auspices of Edwina Sassoon, was placed on an official footing and developed into a purposeful, professional unit with multiple responsibilities by Fay Ballard, who, formerly in charge of Press and Publicity at the Royal Academy, became Head of Development in November 1990.

It had become clear that the Tate, like other national museums, was moving towards a position of greater self-reliance, with regard both to its funding and its administration. This was to be legally affirmed by the 1992 Museums and Galleries Act which gave the Tate corporate status and vested all its property, rights and liabilities in the Board. From now on the institution could act like a company, could acquire or dispose of land or property and could enter into contracts and other agreements regarding the occupation and management of the Tate Gallery. The number of Trustees rose from eleven to twelve, while their term of office was reduced from seven to five years, though they could be eligible for reappointment. After further 'untying' from the Civil Service in 1996, the terms and conditions of employment for Tate staff would be determined by the Trustees working within Treasury guidelines and with the approval of the Department of National Heritage.

Among the new powers vested in the Board was a constrained right to deaccession. There had been unsuccessful attempts, as the Bill was being drafted, to get the deaccessioning clause removed – partly in order to establish parity with the National Gallery. However, though both the advantages and disadvantages of deaccessioning have since been the subject of discussion at Board level, and a policy has been established, the issue has not yet been seriously tested.

Further benefits to the Tate and its public resulted from the decision in 1991 to reorganise the Education Department. Following the immediate success in 1990 of his compendium, *The Tate Gallery: An Illustrated Companion*, Simon Wilson, Head of Education since 1980, was made Curator of Interpretation, in which role he oversees the way in which material is presented to the public. His deputy, Richard Humphreys, who had been responsible for the *Pound's Artists* exhibition in 1985, successfully applied for Wilson's former post. Humphreys, who was keen to acknowledge and learn from the educational work done in Liverpool, immediately set up a working party to help towards the formulation of a new educational policy. Previously the pattern of the Tate's educational activities had been especially good for the general visitor and for schools. Now it was thought necessary as well as desirable to forge closer links with universities and teachers and to play a more active role in public debates on educational issues, even if this carried the risk of involving the Gallery in political conflict. In time Humphreys was to divide the department into two programmes – for Adults and Young Visitors – run, respectively, by Andrew Brighton and Colin Grigg. An increasing programme of lectures, seminars and conferences – many of them attracting speakers with an international reputation – as well as an increase in educational literature and the creation of the Writer-in-Residence scheme, all helped prove the Tate's determination to do more in the realm of education, with varying but more focused activities.

Further transformation was achieved by the decision to launch a new house style, created by Pentagram Design Ltd, for all the Tate's promotional literature. It first appeared in January 1990 to coincide with the *Past, Present, Future* display, and in the 1988–90 Biennial Report, published that autumn, gave visible expression to the increased sophistication that was gradually infiltrating every aspect of the Tate – not least its entertaining, which, in keeping with the Gallery's growing reliance on private benefaction, began deliberately to court more prominent aspects of society.

The Gallery's most notable failure at this time concerned the Matisse exhibition, which remained unresolved at the time of Bowness's departure. Serota, recognising the need to make it a priority, had invited Patrick Heron to continue working on the project, even though his Trusteeship had ended in 1987. When the Soviet Minister of Culture visited the Tate in April 1989, Serota and Heron received him and, owing to rumours originating with museum colleagues in America and France, they were led to believe that the Russian museums were committed to the Tate's proposal for a Matisse exhibition. In October 1989 Heron and Serota pursued the project further by visiting Moscow and Leningrad, and in the course of discussion it was suggested that some twenty-seven Matisses would be available in return for the loan of the Tate's works by the Pre-Raphaelites and their followers, as well as, at a later date, certain Henry Moores. It was therefore a shock to learn the following year, from the Museum of Modern Art in New York, that its own proposal for a Matisse exhibition, also to be shown in Paris, had won greater favour with the Russian museums. Heron's anger and frustration with the entire history of this project fed into an article by Michael McNay in the *Guardian*, entitled 'How the Tate Missed Matisse'.[6] Not mentioned in this article was the possibility that the Russians' volte-face was in part a consequence of the government's prohibition on Anglo-Russian cultural links in the early 1980s, following Russia's invasion of Afghanistan. As Serota discovered on his visit to Russia in 1989, between 1979 and 1985, while British museums were forbidden to make contact with their Russian counterparts, French and American curators were making regular visits and building bridges for future projects.

Despite improvements of all kinds, the Gallery still remained vulnerable to the unexpected hazard, such as that which occurred on 19 February 1989, when a visitor accidentally hit his head on the frame of Nathaniel Dance-Holland's *Thomas Nuthall with a Dog and Gun* while mounting the stairs. Angered by the discovery that the blow had been sufficient to draw blood, he returned to the stairs a few moments later and punched the bottom left-hand corner of the painting, causing multiple tears. He then ran off before anyone could apprehend him, escaping into Millbank through the revolving door. A more drastic incident occurred on 16 December 1992 when a man, who termed himself a frustrated artist, drove a Triumph Spitfire sports car up the front steps of the Gallery. He came to a halt very near the top, jumped out, poured petrol over the bonnet of the car and into its interior and was about to ignite it when a member of the maintenance staff, who was cleaning the steps at the time, stepped in and with the help of a warder prevented him. The emergency procedure was immediately activated and the Fire Brigade arrived within about six minutes. In this instance disaster was avoided, but not for long. On 29 July 1994 the Tate suffered its greatest loss when two paintings by Turner, *Shade and Darkness – The Evening of the Deluge* and *Light and Colour (Goethe's Theory) – The Morning after the Deluge – Moses Writing the Book of Genesis*, were stolen while on loan to the Schirn Kunsthalle in Frankfurt.

★   ★   ★

255

In one of the many interviews that he gave soon after his appointment to the Tate, Serota was recorded as saying that he saw museums 'as offering a series of arguments, rather than simply a collection of pictures'.[7] When he began to put this into practice at Millbank he quickly realised that it was not individual rooms that needed changing but the whole frame. The galleries for the Historic British Collection were in poor decorative state, had not been significantly rehung or rethought for a decade or more, and were clogged with new acquisitions. In the Modern section insufficient recognition was given to the achievement of certain British artists, such as Stanley Spencer. Serota wanted to improve the British representation, whilst also bringing out the interconnections between British art and parallel developments in Paris, New York and, more recently, continental Europe.

Taking the courageous decision to rehang the entire Gallery, he began working closely with about ten curatorial staff on a new scheme. At the same time the galleries underwent renovation. All false ceilings, claddings and partitions were eliminated, floors were cleaned and re-sealed, the skylights in the North Duveen and the Octagon were uncovered, and the screen walls in the Sculpture Galleries removed and the stonework cleaned. In the north-west quadrant the marble door surrounds were regilded and throughout the Gallery the wall-colours were reduced to four in number – a warm terracotta, a greenish grey, a lighter grey and white. For several months these alterations caused parts of the main building to close on a rotating basis, and in January 1990 the entire Gallery was closed to the public for just under two weeks, prior to the formal opening of the new display on 24 January, which was attended by the Prime Minister.

82 Rodin's *The Kiss* in Gallery 28 before refurbishment, 1989

The title given to this first new hang – *Past, Present, Future* – reflected Serota's awareness that the Tate not only provides a perspective on the past but has a responsibility to the present to collect contemporary art as a frame through which future generations will judge our culture. The enormous vistas opened up returned the building to its original grandeur and recovered the impressive central axis made by the Sculpture Galleries, the central rotunda and the entrance hall. The actual arrangement of the galleries allowed the display of the collection to flow from historic to modern for the first time without the sharp break that had been present in earlier presentations. But the solution had met with considerable opposition from within the British Collection, as the starting point for the collection in the new display had been thrust back to the far north-west corner of the building. In addition, the numbers of eighteenth- and nineteenth-century paintings had been slightly reduced, to make possible a slight increase in the amount of twentieth-century work on show.

In general, there was a shift from the treatment of works of art as historical artefacts to objects in their own right. The hanging was spacious, the decoration did not pander to any desire for historical reconstruction, and each work was given its full weight and dignity. It was argued that the new hang not only placed greater emphasis on display, but also made possible, in the long term, greater access to the collection, as the intention was to make further changes on an annual cycle. Furthermore, public access to the work was assisted by the simple introductory texts to each room and the extended labels, which followed a practice that had earlier been adopted in the Clore Gallery.

One intention behind the new hang was a desire to unsettle or destroy the assumption of an institutional view or a received 'history'. The work of Stanley Spencer was given a fresh viewing, as it had been at the opening of the 1979 extension, and he once again emerged as a great artist, with his *Resurrection, Cookham* no longer hung like an embarrassment on a staircase wall but given pride of place in a gallery filled with his pictures, as well as items by other English visionaries and intense realists. Vorticism and Bloomsbury were also well displayed, in opposition to each other, in the same gallery; and much was made by the press of Duncan Grant's *Bathers*, painted in 1911 as a wall decoration for the Borough Polytechnic, which had only been exhibited at the Tate for about a month in the previous fifty years.

'The display is everywhere limpid, unhurried and uncrowded,' wrote John Russell in the *New York Times*.[8] Sasha Craddock in the *Guardian* found the new hang exhilarating 'because it lets us look again and question our preconceived notions'.[9] However, many visitors were disconcerted that certain old favourites had disappeared and that there were no works on view by Sickert, the Camden Town artists, the Euston Road School, or the St Ives group. The demise of the purpose-built, low-light Blake gallery on the principal floor caused William Feaver to note the disappearance of the 'Property Services Agency Twilight Suite',[10] while others felt it to be a serious loss. In keeping with the overall policy, everything (except for works on paper) was now exhibited on the main floor.

The startling, provocative connections uncovered by this and subsequent *New Displays* chimed with the post-modernist distrust of master narratives. Suddenly the Tate, far from upholding an accepted canon, dug into unexpected corners of its collection, and in so doing unsettled its former emphasis on the modernist tradition. In 1993 Brian Sewell, art critic to the *Evening Standard*, acknowledged the 'subdued but subtle beauty' presented by William Rothenstein's *Jews Mourning in a Synagogue*,[11] which had been shown for less than six months during the past twenty-two years. But he disliked the policy of constant change, refused to find interest in the realignments and became the most trenchant and unremitting critic of the *New Displays*. Twice he stated that the sponsors, British Petroleum, should withdraw their support. As BP's generosity, not just to the Tate, but also to the National Portrait Gallery, at a time of falling oil revenue, was one of the great stories of British sponsorship, Sewell was in turn criticised for his irresponsibility.

The transformation of what had been a relatively permanent museum display into a more challenging set of temporary alliances, drew further protest from the art establishment. Robin Simon, editor of the magazine *Apollo*, berated the 1992 *New Display* partly because the teaching of British art 'has suffered severely through the selectivity of the hang and its unpredictability'.[12] The opportunity to respond allowed Serota to acknowledge the difficulties attendant on the Tate's dual role – as the national collection of British painting and of modern foreign art. He also pointed out that because work by certain major figures was dispersed among several national collections, it was impossible to show their full achievement; and lack of space at Millbank meant that an attempt to demonstrate the breadth and richness of the collection inevitably resulted in a loss of some of its strengths.[13]

After the Tate celebrated the work of Adrian Stokes (a former Trustee) in one of the *New Displays*, David Sylvester arranged to bequeath to the Gallery the eight pictures he had lent to this display and which had been given to him by Stokes over the years. He had approached the Tate with this in mind in the 1980s, but had received little active encouragement, and as a result had begun making other arrangements which he now cancelled. The Tate's renewed interest for collectors helped attract loans which were used to extend the argument in various quarters of these *New Displays*. They, too, established useful connections with private collectors and other public institutions. In some cases, loans filled gaps which were impossible to fill by other means. One instance in the 1992 display was Hogarth's magnificent, humane portrait of Thomas Coram, the sea-captain turned philanthropist, whose Foundling Hospital became the first government-registered charity. This painting was made available by the Thomas Coram Foundation after a long-standing informal liaison was put on a formal footing: in return for professional advice on conservation, display, description and interpretation of the Coram collection, the Tate had been granted the right to borrow occasional works for specific displays.

Even before the full height and sweep of the Duveen Sculpture Galleries had

83 The *New Display* in the Duveen Galleries, 1990

been made visible, Serota had conceived the idea of inviting individual artists to produce work specially for this dramatic sequence of spaces. It had been admirably filled in the first *New Displays* with work that ranged from Rodin's *The Kiss* and Sir William Reynolds-Stephens's *A Royal Game* of 1906–11 – in which Queen Elizabeth I challenges Phillip II of Spain to a game of chess, using their respective fleets as chess pieces – to a Richard Long stone circle. But still more striking were the installations achieved by single artists, such as Long, Rebecca Horn and Richard Serra, when they were given command over the entire area. These installations helped to create a whole new audience for modern sculpture. The most effective challenge to the space within these oppressively tall, grandiose galleries, was Serra's decision to leave the Sackler Octagon empty and to place in the galleries on either side two vast solid steel blocks, centred on line with the main axis. Owing to the effect of perspective, the blocks looked identical in size but revealed their differences as the viewer walked between them. Their absolute austerity, in David Sylvester's opinion, had a transformative effect on the surrounding architecture, diminishing its theatricality.[14]

The installation of these three-ton blocks proved exceptionally problematic, for it was discovered that the Gallery's floor could not sustain more than two tons in weight. Bruce McAllister, Head of Art Handling, eventually found a solution: pinions, which went down through the floor to the basement, supported the steel blocks which hovered just a fraction above the floor but seemed to rest upon it.

Critical reaction to the *New Displays*, new acquisitions and the Turner Prize increased the pressure on the Tate to determine the shape of its future. Serota asked Richard Francis to develop a Masterplan that looked at the collections, their size and predicted future growth, and at the space needed to house them. This problem was becoming ever more critical, as, with three-quarters of the collection not on view, the lack of space was a significant discouragement to potential donors and lenders. The need to break the collection into elements had, in principle, been accepted in the 1980s, when Stirling had begun work on the New Museums project. But the divisions then proposed seemed to Serota unsatisfactory in that they worked against a holistic approach to the art of any one period: as part of his initial seven-year plan, he had suggested abandoning the concept of separate museums devoted to 'new art' and 'sculpture', and instead returned to the concept of a Museum of Twentieth-Century Art. A desire to bring clarity to an institution all too often regarded as an unwieldy hybrid increasingly inclined Serota, once in office, towards the notion of dividing the Tate into 'British' and 'Modern'. This idea had taken root before Richard Francis's Masterplan registered the conclusion that the Tate had insufficient space at Millbank for its present requirements, let alone for its future needs. But the lengthy consultations on which his Masterplan was based legitimised the search for an alternative site for a Museum of Modern Art.

84 Richard Serra, *Weight and Measure* 1992,
exhibited in the Duveen Galleries in 1992

From Gasworks to Power Station

One of the most surprising developments in the Tate's history is its connection with the small town of St Ives. Out of this grew one of the most successful arts projects in recent history, which has not only helped transform the economy of St Ives but also set a useful precedent for the Tate's subsequent involvement with Bankside.

Surrounded on three sides by the sea, St Ives has a clarity of light which has attracted painters to the area ever since the Victorian railway made it accessible. A further attraction was that the empty sail lofts, left behind by the declining fishing industry, made excellent studios. In the late nineteenth century Julius Olsson, renowned for his nocturnal seascapes, set up a painting school in one of these lofts; and his enormous studio later provided the first permanent exhibition space in the town when it was taken over by the St Ives Society of Artists, founded in 1927.

The goal of most St Ives artists, however, was to exhibit in the Royal Academy Summer Exhibition, and each year an entire railway carriage was filled with paintings that were sent up to London. The artistic situation changed during the Second World War when Ben Nicholson, Barbara Hepworth and Naum Gabo all moved to the area, their presence transforming this far-flung outpost into an internationally renowned centre for modern art. With the formation of the Penwith Society of Artists in Cornwall in 1949, the split between the traditionalists and modernists became pronounced. The Penwith Society made use of premises in Fore Street for exhibitions and helped promote a growing body of diverse artists – some taking up permanent residence in the area, others remaining summer visitors, but all in some way pursuing a dialogue between nature and abstraction. Opening the Penwith Society's Summer Show in 1958, the art-historian J.P. Hodin suggested that artists should co-operate with local authorities in the creation of a permanent art centre in St Ives.

This idea had, in fact, first been mooted in 1919: a retiring mayor, welcoming back men from the war, proposed the founding of an art gallery where local talent could be displayed as a means of honouring those who had fought for their country. The notion of a permanent gallery in St Ives was revived in the 1960s; but when the St Ives Town Council began transforming part of a gasworks site into flats for the elderly, the Penwith Society's request for two rooms was turned down. An alternative gallery space was found in an old pilchard-packing factory where eventually, housed in an extension, a permanent display of St Ives painting and sculpture was set up. But in 1980, following the Arts Council's withdrawal of the Penwith Society's grant, the display had to be dismantled.

Meanwhile, there was growing support for the St Ives School in high places. Following the death of Sir Herbert Read, the Tate Director, Sir Norman Reid, had taken over the presidency of the Penwith Society. Tom Cross, Principal of Falmouth School of Art and Chairman of the Penwith Society, began writing his book on the St Ives School, *Painting the Warmth of the Sun*, the appearance of which was hastened to coincide with the opening of the major *St Ives* exhibition held at the Tate Gallery in London in 1985. Curated by David Brown, with considerable assistance from the Director Alan Bowness, the show demonstrated the diversity within the St Ives School, while its catalogue and archival display put on record, for the first time, the friendships, jealousies and conflicts that had made the St Ives artistic community so lively and disputatious.

The Tate first gained a foothold in St Ives when it took over the Barbara Hepworth Museum. However, when Martin Rewcastle, Director of South West Arts, began negotiating with Cornwall County Council for a public art gallery and with the Tate for the loan of St Ives paintings, it seemed unlikely that the Tate, if it agreed to lend, would commit itself further, as it was at that time struggling to find the money with which to open Tate Gallery Liverpool.

The original idea was to convert Stennack School in St Ives. Bowness visited the school in the summer of 1986 with Patrick Heron, and afterwards advised the Trustees that, providing the conversion met Tate Gallery standards, the loan of St Ives art should be approved. In November of that year the Tate learnt that this scheme had fallen through, but sufficient momentum had been created for Cornwall County Council, together with Penwith District Council and South West Arts, to set up a Gallery Steering Group, chaired by the County Councillor Richard Carew Pole, who proved a vital force. A delegation from Cornwall visited the Tate in July 1988 to take further the idea of a publicly funded gallery in Cornwall. Again Bowness expressed willingness to lend some sixty paintings and sculptures on a rotating basis; but he also made it clear that this would be the limit of the Tate's involvement.

The search had begun for a site by the time Serota took over in September. He made his first visit to St Ives as Director on 14 and 15 December 1988. As well as inspecting the new studio roof at the Barbara Hepworth Museum and the state of the garden, which had suffered badly from severe frost early in 1987, he visited the four sites on which the architects Katharine Heron and Julian Freary had done a feasibility study. Of all these sites, the one favoured by the architects was that which Julian Freary had spotted while walking around Porthmeor Beach: a derelict gasworks which, built into the side of the hillside, overlooked the Atlantic Ocean. Serota visited the gasworks in the company of Richard Carew Pole, Martin Rewcastle, Patrick Heron, Des Hosken from Penwith District Council, Sandy Nairne, Director of Visual Arts at the Arts Council, and others, and gave this particular site his wholehearted support. Subsequently, on 9 January 1989, the Steering Group met and formally agreed that the gasworks was the preferred site.

Soon after, the two gas holders were removed and a desirable piece of real estate was revealed, for, though the site sloped steeply, it offered spectacular views out over a part of the coast which is regarded as a surfers' paradise. British Gas agreed to forego their normal policy of inviting competitive tenders and allowed the County Council six months in which to find the £200,000 necessary to buy the site. In the meantime, plans for an architectural competition went ahead. Cornwall County Council consulted the President of the Royal Institute of British Architects (RIBA) and set up a single-stage competition according to RIBA guidelines. Five architectural practices were approached and invited to submit designs for a new gallery. The brief concentrated less on the actual galleries than on those aspects of the gallery that were likely to yield revenue. It also stated:

> Apart from the obvious attraction of the exhibits, the Gallery should attract visitors in its own right in the way that the Pompidou Centre and the Lloyds Building do ... the building should be stimulating, imaginative and excellent. It should be equally attractive to the art enthusiast and to the family on holiday ... The view from the site is considered to be a major asset, and this should be enjoyed from both inside and outside the building.[1]

The winning architects were the husband-and-wife team, David Shalev and Eldred Evans, who were already known in the area for their designs for the Crown Courts in Truro. They impressed the Assessors with the inventiveness of their exterior façade, which began with a ramp that led up to a small amphitheatrical space (the Loggia) through which the visitor passes in order to reach the entrance to the building. At a higher level this circular space allows for a curved window overlooking the Atlantic Ocean. Inside, on the second floor, five studio-like exhibition rooms were arranged in a simple sequence around a secret courtyard which is only discovered at the end of the journey. Boldly imaginative in its use of the site, the Evans and Shalev scheme was also felt to be architecturally the most in sympathy with St Ives, for its spaces and routes were intended to echo the visitor's experience of the town, with its various walkways and sudden vistas. Many of the features Evans and Shalev had used in their prize-winning design for the Crown Courts at Truro were to be repeated at St Ives; among them the circular meeting space, slim triangular pillars, glass bricks and plain white surfaces. But the dominant concern was, as David Shalev said in an early interview, that the building should be 'in dialogue with the landscape and seascape of the place'.[2] In this way it was hoped that the gallery itself would provide 'some insight into the artists' inspirations and aspirations on this remote and magical island'.[3]

Though Serota had been one of the Assessors, the Tate had not been closely involved in the competition brief. But its requirements were incorporated into the planning at a later stage, through discussion with the architects and through the decision to ask Peter Wilson, Head of Gallery Services, to assist the architects with the refinement of the designs. It was his suggestion that the doors in the back run of galleries should be moved from the centre line towards the back wall, so as to

85 Tate Gallery St Ives

allow for a larger hanging space, and also that provision should be made for cupboards between galleries to contain services and to keep display spaces uncluttered. At a later date, when it became apparent that the building would exceed available funds, the Tate Gallery's role changed from advising on additional items to suggesting what could be omitted.

The final cost of the actual building was not to exceed £1.5 million and the overall cost of the project, as stated in the initial brief, was £2 million. This was the maximum that Cornwall County Council thought could be raised by subscription and grants. Richard Carew Pole was indefatigable in his pursuit of private and public funding, and was helped by Sir Geoffrey Holland, Permanent Secretary at the Department of Employment, who wrote letters to the Chairman or Chief Executive of some forty major companies. The Henry Moore Foundation put up £250,000; a further £150,000 came from the Foundation for Sports and the Arts; and £40,000 was obtained from the Rural Development Commission. The largest single local donation came from Northcliffe Newspapers which published a number of newspapers in the South-West; and at an advanced stage of planning the European Community finally approved the County Council's bid for a £887,500 grant from the European Regional Development Fund. Of crucial importance to the development of the project was the creation of the St Ives Tate Action Group (STAG), which helped raise £100,000 towards building costs (and later £35,000 towards equipping the Education Room) and did much to raise awareness of the project and to generate and sustain local support. Chaired by Steve Herbert, Chairman of the St Ives Hoteliers and Guest House Association, STAG also drew on Lady Holland's gift for public relations and Janet Axten's willingness to write, design and print the group's publicity and to help co-ordinate the expertise of other members.[4]

The running of the gallery, as it was initially conceived, was to be in the hands of a local Trust. The press referred fairly consistently to the gallery as 'the Tate of the West', and this made Serota and others anxious about the use of the Tate's name for a venture which was to be outside the Tate's administration. The Conservation Department was also concerned about control over the display of St Ives art lent by the Tate. While spending part of his holiday during the summer of 1989 in a cottage at Zennor, Serota recognised that the high standards of display and curatorial control evident at the Hepworth Museum would be difficult to achieve without greater Tate involvement. After further discussion with Carew Pole, Serota therefore put forward a suggestion to the Trustees in May 1990: the charitable company put in charge of the new gallery should lease it to the Tate Trustees. In this way, Cornwall County Council would remain responsible for the fabric and maintenance of the building, but the Tate could assume responsibility for staff, and the education and exhibition programme, and would have greater control over the use of the Tate's St Ives collection. In other words, the Tate would manage the gallery and be paid for doing so by local revenue funding, with the hope that in time the government would match this funding. This idea proved acceptable and Francis Carnwath at the Tate began negotiating the terms of the lease with Richard Lester, Deputy Clerk of the Council.

Owing to complications that arose with the building of the substructure and superstructure of the Loggia, the completion of the building was delayed by several months. In the meantime, the Grant-in-Aid for 1992–3 was increased by £100,000 as a 'one-off' contribution towards the establishing of Tate Gallery St Ives, as it was to be called. Much thought was given to the core display and exhibition programme, both of which were intended to present varying perspectives on twentieth-century art as it relates to Cornwall and St Ives. In May 1992 a group of staff from the Tate met with the newly appointed Curator Designate, Michael Tooby, to talk through the present and future hanging of the Gallery; the commissioning of artists' projects; and initial decisions on signs, publications, equipment, education and outreach programmes. It was agreed that Barbara Hepworth's late 1940s studies of surgeons in the operating theatre should form the first thematic display, and thus provide an unexpected contrast with the primarily abstract work elsewhere. And though the Tate's St Ives collection did not extend to pottery, Bernard Leach's contribution to the area was acknowledged through two long-term loans: Cornelia Wingfield Digby's collection of pots by Leach and his circle, and the Hamada collection belonging to his widow, Janet Leach.

St Ives artists had played a key role in helping focus support for the gallery, and among the artists' projects associated with the new venture was a floor-to-ceiling banner designed by Terry Frost for the main stairwell. In the final stage of building construction a large coloured-glass window, designed by Patrick Heron, was swung into position without mishap. Heron had deliberately designed it without leading. Instead, the coloured glass had been cut into shape and laminated on to Pilkington's float glass by Studio Derix of Wiesbaden, Germany. Once installed, this immense window flooded the entrance hall of the pristine white gallery with colour. Its striking effect was matched by the elegant detailing which sharpens and enhances the visitor's agreeably labyrinthine journey through a building of great calm and architectural distinction.

One contentious aspect of Evans and Shalev's design was the curved wall in Gallery Two, which, with its curved window on the opposite side, looks out over Porthmeor Beach. The inspiration behind this space was the circular gallery in the National Museum of Wales in Cardiff. Another gallery that makes use of curvilinear space, owing to its continuous spiral viewing ramp, is Frank Lloyd Wright's Guggenheim Museum in New York – a building that remains controversial as it is thought to be unsympathetic to the display of art. The Tate was nervous about hanging paintings on a curved wall. Yet, when Tate Gallery St Ives finally opened (Prince Charles making a tour of the building during the three-day opening ceremony), it was this gallery, above all the other spaces and routes, that made the building such a memorable experience. For in this somewhat quirky space, the building is most clearly held in dialogue with the surrounding landscape and seascape. Here and elsewhere, as Deyan Sudjic observed, the building 'doesn't shut the world out' but, as architecture, is 'open and outgoing'.[5] Its appeal was demonstrated by the attendance figures: within the first six months came 120,000 visitors – 50,000 more than the original target for the entire year.

★　　★　　★

The decision to redefine the collection through the creation of the Tate Gallery of British Art and a Tate Gallery of Modern Art in London – together with the future policy and building plans attendant on this scheme – was announced by the Chairman at a press conference in December 1992.[6] The reactions, in the press and elsewhere, were immediately favourable. None of the anticipated cavils arose over the division of displays on two separate sites, nor was it suggested that the claims of the regions had been ignored. Instead, the idea of a museum of modern art gained wide acceptance.

As yet the Tate did not know for certain how it was to fund this development. However, under John Major, developments were afoot that were to have radical implications for the arts. The Department of National Heritage had come into being and had taken over the responsibility of the Office of Arts and Libraries for the performing arts, museums and galleries, as well as sport, film and tourism from other ministries. The Department had a budget approaching one billion pounds and was led by a minister of Cabinet rank, initially David Mellor. One of its first tasks was to devise a National Lottery. This had been firmly opposed by Mrs Thatcher, whose Methodist background determined her attitude to gambling – even though Britain was at this time the only country in Europe without a state lottery. Under Major this situation changed and the National Lottery Bill

86 Gallery 2, Tate Gallery St Ives

was published on 17 December 1992. Immediately afterwards it was announced that proceeds from the Lottery would be divided between charities, the arts, sport, the Heritage Lottery Fund and a Millennium Fund.

The last of these was to be administered by a new Millennium Commission, the creation of which owed much to Peter Palumbo. Since 1989 he had been Chairman of the Arts Council and in this role had been asked by Mrs Thatcher for ideas for the millennium. He had proposed the rehabilitation of the cultural glory to be found in Britain's cathedrals, churches and other public buildings, with the intention of creating a mood of celebration to boost morale and rouse expectations.

This proposal gathered momentum and, after the Lottery was approved, became directed less towards the restoration of the old than the creation of the new. Once the Millennium Fund was set up, the Commission began inviting bids and ideas from the public for projects to celebrate the year 2000. Two days after Dennis Stevenson had announced the Tate's need of a new site for the Modern Collection, the Secretary of State for National Heritage, announcing that Lottery proceeds could be used for buildings, instanced a 'dance house' or a 'museum of modern art'. From this grew the public assumption that the Tate was one of the front runners for consideration as a Millennium project.

The Tate now began thinking about how it could secure, by the early summer of 1994, a site, an architect and an outline design, together with commitments of £20 to £30 million from the private sector. It brought in Loveday Shewell, formerly administrator at the Whitechapel Art Gallery and now a freelance arts consultant, to fill part of the void left by Richard Francis who had left to take up an appointment in Chicago. Shewell's brief covered the development of both the new museum and Millbank which from now on, for planning purposes, were renamed in accordance with their future roles as the Tate Gallery of Modern Art (TGMA) and the Tate Gallery of British Art (TGBA).

Serota was anxious that the glamour of a new gallery of modern art should not cause Millbank to falter in its appeal. He was aware that a museum devoted to the national school can be somewhat worthy and dull, but that this pitfall could be avoided by giving renewed emphasis to the achievement of British artists and by developing imaginative strategies for displaying the collection. In order to think through these and other ideas, six round-table discussions were organised by Richard Humphreys and chaired by the cultural historian Robert Hewison, involving art historians with a special interest in British and modern art, as well as critics and curators from other national institutions, and these helped shape certain policy decisions regarding the future of Millbank. These included the desire to take the story of British art up to the present day and to maintain a single administration for both TGMA and TGBA, so that the benefits of the congruity of the two collections could be maintained.

At the same time that the Tate embarked on this major project it was also pursuing three other building proposals. One was the development of the North-West Quadrant. This had been part of the Gallery Masterplan for Millbank which John Miller had proposed after he had been appointed as the Gallery refurbishment architect in 1987. Though his plan had never been endorsed by the Trustees, it had remained a point of reference in connection with the carrying out of smaller projects such as the Nomura Room. Miller now proposed the demolition of three galleries and the Sargent staircase at the far end of the building in order to create three new galleries, a double-height space and a more impressive, central staircase close to a new entrance in Atterbury Street. In this new scheme the lower galleries would become a major new exhibition area which could form, with select amenities such as the restaurant, a self-contained 'envelope' capable of more flexible opening hours than the rest of the building.

87 Southwark Store

The second proposal was to complete Phase 2 of Tate Gallery Liverpool. A revision of the original scheme had been agreed by James Stirling before his sudden death in 1992. The firm James Stirling Wilford and Associates remained committed to this project and the four prime objectives were an increase in galleries, improved vertical circulation, enhanced education facilities, and more office space. After the scheme was costed at £7 million, hopes were expressed that money could be obtained through European funding and the National Lottery.

While steps were taken to raise funds for Liverpool, a still more urgent priority was the need for a new store. It had been assumed at one point that in order to achieve the space needed at a reasonable price, the Gallery would have to look outside London. But the recession had left developers hard-hit. A number had gone bankrupt, leaving unfinished or unlet buildings in the hands of financial backers who were willing to agree generous terms. In an old railway yard at Bricklayers Arms, off the Old Kent Road, were seven warehouses, each including a small office, owned by the National Rivers Authority. Agents working on behalf of the Tate negotiated a deal which included two-and-a-half years rent-free, an initial capital contribution from the landlord and an option to buy after the first five years. An even more advantageous deal could have been secured for the nation if the Department of National Heritage had been prepared to support a Tate plan to acquire the freehold outright in 1994.

When it came to replanning these warehouses, the Tate used as its model the store built by Washington's Smithsonian Institute. This was the first museum to realise that diverse collections made a centralised storage facility unworkable. Instead it created what is in effect a covered-over street, with stores on one side and workshops on the other. Likewise, the Tate was to build linking art-handling routes along the back and personnel access at the front of Bricklayers Arms warehouses. Given the large car-park area, there were also hopes that eventually it might be possible to establish Sculpture Conservation on the site, together with the Registrar's office and a services centre.

After the Secretary of State for National Heritage announced that the Grant-in-Aid, previously allocated in three separate amounts (to cover running costs, building and maintenance, and the purchase of works of art), would be merged into one grant, the Trustees had greater flexibility in their use of funds. If the downside of this single grant system, which began in 1992–3, was that it made it more difficult to isolate deficiencies in funding, it also stimulated the need to identify clear goals.

One indication of changing priorities was the decision to set up a Tate magazine. The first issue of *tate: The art magazine* appeared in September 1993 and represented a major development for the Gallery, chiefly because it helped promote wider discussion of the Gallery's fields of interest. It was given semi-independent status and published in association with Wordsearch, which, founded in 1984, had made its name with *Blueprint*, the award-winning design and architectural magazine. Tim Marlow, a former part-time lecturer at the Tate, was apponted as editor. He was guided by a strong editorial board, and problems that emerged in the first couple of issues, with regard to both content and presentation, were quickly attended to as the magazine grew in strength and interest.

It also proved a key promotional tool for recruiting Friends of the Tate Gallery – now headed by Rachel Johnson – and was a part of the general overhaul of the Tate's press and promotional activities which took place in 1993. New systems of working with the press were established, and on the suggestion of Damien Whitmore, Head of Communications, the press consultancy Bolton and Quinn were asked to advise on working methods and to develop strategies for increasing the visibility of the Gallery. The press list was radically reduced and a more sophisticated system introduced which allowed for better targeting. At the same time a new, unifying corporate identity was created by Pentagram Design Ltd for the three Galleries in London, Liverpool and St Ives. This proved helpful in the summer of 1993 when, following discussions with Fay Ballard and Rachel Johnson, the Tate Friends St Ives was set up, which, though it had its own committee and organised its own events, paid its subscriptions to, and came under the auspices of, the London office. The good relations which it enjoyed with the London administration owed much to the enthusiasm of its first Chairman, Lady Holland. It took longer for this same office to persuade the separate membership charity, Liverpool Supporters, to follow suit.

That same year, 1993, the Deputy Director, Francis Carnwath, announced that he would be leaving in the spring of the following year. This created an opportunity to review senior management and to adopt a new structure designed to create new and more logical groupings of departments. Now that Serota's Directorship was firmly established, it was possible to place more operational decisions with senior managers, thereby freeing the Director to concentrate on the collection, new buildings and overall strategy. As a result, two new posts were created: a Director of Finance and Administration and a Director of Public Services. The first was filled by the thirty year old Alex Beard who came from the Finance Department of the Arts Council, where, in the course of his responsibility for appraisals of flagship companies, including the Royal Opera House, he had caught the attention of Dennis Stevenson. The second post was filled by the forty year old Sandy Nairne.

At this time the Turner Prize began to enjoy a more definite status in the mind of the public. However, conferring establishment approval on art at the cutting edge proved a tricky task and placed the Tate in an awkward position. For, unlike the Book Trust – which is a neutral administrator of the Booker Prize – the Tate plays an active role in according recognition to contemporary art; and this had troubled its role in relation to the Prize in the eyes of some critics, despite the fact that all the members of the jury, apart from the Tate Director, come from outside the institution. Adverse criticism and the collapse of its sponsors, Drexel Burnham Lambert, almost led to the termination of the Turner Prize in 1990 – even though Channel 4 had immediately expressed interest in taking over the sponsorship. The Tate accepted this offer but suspended the Prize for one year in order to reconsider its merits and think through possible modifications. As a result, since 1991 the Prize has been limited to artists under the age of fifty, a rule that helped avoid the embarrassment of senior artists being pitched against younger artists. At the same time a requirement was introduced to ensure that a nomination was linked to a particular public presentation of the artist's work in the previous year, rather than being tied simply to general admiration for that artist's work.

The Tate was also concerned to improve the means by which the work of the shortlisted artists was mediated to a lay audience, and therefore made a more wholehearted commitment to exhibiting their work. Overall, there was anxiety that the fierce criticism the Turner Prize aroused, and the trivialisation of the issues in the press and the media, did a disservice both to the artists and to the Tate. But in 1993 the Prize suddenly seemed to come of age. It attained a higher profile than ever before, partly because Vong Phaophanit's *Neon Rice Field* had considerable news value, as did *House* – Rachel Whiteread's cast of the living space within a Victorian terraced house in Hackney. In addition, improvements in the exhibition display and in the television coverage helped turn the Prize into an event of sufficient common currency that mention of it began to appear in plays, jokes and cartoons.

The response to the Turner Prize highlighted the widening gulf between senior critics, collectors and establishment figures in the London art world and a younger, exhibition-going public who reacted to contemporary art with immediacy and excitement. The Tate acknowledged the needs of this younger audience when it decided in 1994 to convert the Garden Room at the back of the 1979 extension into the Art Now room. It also mounted displays and exhibitions, such as *Rites of Passage: Art for the End of the Century* (1995), which dealt with the plurality, fragmentation and sense of crisis in contemporary art practice. At the same time, however, the Tate also sought to answer its critics. For it was aware that a hostile climate would have a deleterious effect on its foremost campaign – the relaunch of Millbank as the Tate Gallery of British Art and the creation of the Tate Gallery of Modern Art at Bankside.

★   ★   ★

Acquisitions remain the single most public and emotive issue on which the Tate is judged. Stevenson's decision to limit the Trustees' direct involvement with regard to the purchase of individual works of art has given Serota considerable leeway. However, his acquisitions have been directed by a clear and purposeful statement of policy, strategy and procedure, which is annually reviewed and approved by the Trustees. The needs of the collection, which is divided into specific categories, are reassessed annually, and priority lists drawn up. Acquisitions are underpinned by careful research, intelligent networking, a certain amount of wheeler-dealing and the successful courting of artists and collectors. Despite the fact that the Tate operates on a broad front, it has been accused of being in the pockets of a few fashionable dealers in contemporary art. Critics also like to take one of two lines: either that the Tate is too cautious about contemporary art, buying too little too late, or that it takes too many risks in its readiness to acquire new work. Scant recognition is given to the fact that Tate curators often see value in paintings not regarded as fashionable, as in certain recent seventeenth- and eighteenth- century acquisitions where works important to an understanding of the evolution of British art have been acquired at low cost. Similarly, when Maggi Hambling's powerful portrait of Frances Rose came up at auction, at a time when interest had moved away from her early work, and was knocked down cheaply, it surprised many to learn that the Tate was the buyer.

By the 1990s the Tate could look back on controversial acquisitions with pride. Now that Carl Andre's work was fetching up to £150,000 on the open market, the £2,297 paid by the Tate in 1972 for *Equivalent VIII* had to be seen as a good investment. But the vast increase in the price of art was also to the Tate's disadvantage. During the art boom in the late 1980s prices had risen fivefold and, in some areas, tenfold; but the purchase grant during the first four years of Serota's Directorship

88 Lucian Freud, *Standing by the Rags*, 1988–9

remained at £1,815,000 – the level that had first been set in 1980. The Warhol *Marilyn Diptych*, purchased in 1980 for £200,000, a sum that then represented one-tenth of the Grant-in-Aid, would in the 1990s have cost at least £2 million – more than a whole year's purchase grant. This was, by the 1990s, equivalent in value to a small part of a Constable, or a still smaller section of a Picasso or a Francis Bacon triptych. For this reason donations, bequests, presentations in lieu of tax and gifts became increasingly important, and were sought with persistent diplomacy and much behind-the-scenes negotiation. There was also the possibility of obtaining substantial contributions for heritage items – from the National Art Collections

Fund and the National Heritage Millennium Fund – which enabled the Gallery to double its purchasing power. And in one instance, the Gallery agreed to purchase a Gainsborough jointly with Gainsborough's House in Suffolk.[7]

Serota's first major acquisition had been Lucian Freud's *Standing by the Rags*. In the same year, 1989, he bought Giuseppe Penone's *Tree of 12 Metres*, with the Chairman's authorisation, as its price slightly exceeded the £100,000 which was the Director's discretionary amount. Serota's interest in British and European sculpture of the 1980s did not always find support from the senior artist-Trustee, Sir Anthony Caro, who, after the Penone came to the Board, reiterated his concern at the amount that the Director could spend at his own discretion. In subsequent years Serota's acquisition policy was to be assisted by a significant shift in generation among the artist-Trustees, Caro, Heron and Golding giving way to Michael Craig-Martin, Christopher Le Brun and Richard Deacon – this middle generation of artists proving more sympathetic to work by younger artists.

Aware that the Tate lacked a major unique installation or environment by Joseph Beuys, Serota persuaded the Trustees to buy *The End of the Twentieth Century* in 1991. Composed of thirty-one basalt stones – each with cone-shapes cut

89 Wright of Derby, *An Iron Forge*, 1772

out and then rebedded with a lining of felt – this elegiac, austere work gives expression to Beuys's concern with the environment and with creativity. But its price – £942,408 – was the subject of controversy when it formed part of the 1992 *New Displays*. Though not a unique installation (four different versions exist), it proved a haunting representation of this most influential and charismatic artist who had died in 1986.

The catholic nature of the purchasing policy has confounded many of the Tate's critics. The decision to go for outstanding masterpieces of the British School has resulted in a number of impressive acquisitions, including Wright of Derby's *An Iron Forge* and his *Vesuvius in Eruption, with a View over the Islands in the Bay of Naples*. But astute purchasing is reflected in many pockets of the collection; for instance, in the acquisition of a major Kitchen Sink painting from the 1950s, Edward Middleditch's *Flowers, Chairs and Bedsprings*, David Hockney's *The Third Love Painting* and his *Tea Painting in an Illusionistic Style*, Bridget Riley's *Nataraja*, or Norman Blamey's *The Lavabo*, as well as Bill Viola's video-sound installation, *Nantes Triptych*. Meanwhile, the Tate has continued to benefit from major bequests, including that of Gustav Kahnweiler, younger brother of the Cubist dealer Daniel-Henry Kahnweiler, and his wife Elly, whose deed of gift, originally made on 12 March 1974, was activated by the death of Mrs Kahnweiler in 1991. In addition, paintings and sculptures that had belonged to E.J. Power, England's major collector of contemporary art during the post-war period, came to the Tate in lieu of death duties, valued at more than £4.3 million.

When the Tate first announced its ambitious plans for the Millennium in December 1992, it mentioned as an interim idea the possible establishment of a temporary Tate Gallery of Modern Art. Though this was soon abandoned, attention had focused for a period on Billingsgate – the former London fish market – which was leased to Citibank and converted in 1985–6 by Richard Rogers and Partners to provide a major dealing-room in the City, but had never been used. Though it had good environmental conditions and spectacular views over the river, there were a number of drawbacks to this building; and when Millennium

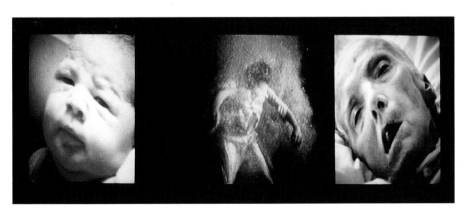

90 Bill Viola, *Nantes Triptych*, 1992

funding became a strong possibility, the Tate decided to put all its energies into the search for a permanent site.

Before long, Stuart Lipton, of Stanhope Properties, had produced a detailed analysis of sites within central London that might be suitable for the size of the building which the Tate had in mind. It was thought essential that the site should be easily accessible by public transport and in reasonable distance of Millbank. At first, the most suitable location seemed to be the car-park on the west side of Hungerford Bridge overlooking Jubilee Gardens, which was owned by the Arts Council and leased to the South Bank Board. Its close proximity to other major arts facilities, as well as to Millbank and the National Gallery, made it a landmark site. But its principal drawbacks were the limited space available and planning constraints which prevented the building of more than one storey in height on a large proportion of the site.

Various other alternatives had been considered, including a number of commercial sites principally on the south side of the river between Vauxhall and Tower Bridge, as well as sites in public ownership likely to be developed over the next ten years, such as hospitals and stations. Mention had been made of Sir George Gilbert Scott's Bankside power station, which had been decommissioned in 1981, but it had not properly caught the attention of the Tate. Sitting on the far side of the Thames between Blackfriars and Southwark bridges, it seemed remote and, despite its size, remained one of the unknown buildings of London. Even though this immense brick building is regarded as Gilbert Scott's masterpiece, and a far finer piece of work than his Battersea power station, it was in danger of being demolished, as its owner, Nuclear Electric, had recently obtained a certificate of immunity from listing. The Twentieth Century Society had begun to take action to try and save it, and in this way it came to the attention of Peter Wilson, who mentioned it to Francis Carnwath, then still Deputy Director at the Tate. Carnwath went to see Bankside in his role as Chairman of the London Advisory Committee for English Heritage. His visit coincided with that of a BBC television film crew who were making Bankside part of the 'One Foot in the Past' series, as part of the campaign to get the building listed. Carnwath was filmed leaving the building and his opinion on it was sought by the architectural historian, Gavin Stamp, who, in the course of their conversation, flung out the suggestion that Bankside would make a marvellous Tate Gallery of Modern Art.

That same day Carnwath returned to the Tate where Nick Serota, on hearing of his visit to Bankside, asked him to describe it. The building sounded impossibly large. But that evening Serota, on his way home, went via Bankside and obtained an estimate of its size by counting his steps as he walked, first alongside it on the river path, and then, with more difficulty, as it was impossible to walk in a straight line, around the side of the building. This gave him a figure of 500 × 200 feet, and he then worked out that the square footage at Bankside was more or less on a par with Millbank. This reckoning made the vastness of Bankside suddenly seem more manageable.

In the course of further meetings with Stanhope Properties, it was decided to

91 Bankside power station

investigate the conversion costs of Bankside and to compare these with the costs of a new building at the South Bank. At the same time the Gallery asked Stanhope to investigate the privately owned Effra site at Vauxhall Cross, as it seemed the least problematic and would therefore offer a 'base cost' against which other sites could be effectively judged. But what soon removed this third site from the agenda was the discovery that underground railway tunnels ran very close to the surface and the expense of building over them would have been very great.

Further research revealed more limitations in connection with both the Effra and South Bank sites, whereas the limitations at Bankside, which had been evident at the start, began to disappear when the Tate began negotiations with Nuclear Electric, the owners, and Southwark Council.

The Trustees made their first visit to Bankside in July 1993 and were bowled over both by the location and the sheer size of the building. It was far bigger than anything they could ever have hoped to build. At first reckoning, this industrial cathedral, with its immense turbine hall running the full length of the building, was said to offer 390,000 square feet on four floors and a further 170,000 square feet below ground. It was also immediately recognised that the 325-foot chimney (just a few feet shorter than the dome of St Paul's) had potential as an observation tower and that if a footbridge could be built between Bankside and the steps opposite, leading up to St Paul's Cathedral, it would place Bankside within five minutes of the City. And despite the uncertainty that hung over the Jubilee line extension, this too was seen to be a factor in Bankside's favour, as, when built, it would undoubtedly contribute to the revitalisation of the area.

With high unemployment and a 20 per cent over-provision of offices in its borough, Southwark Council was keen to encourage culture and tourism as a growth area. The Council had recently been transformed under the leadership of Jeremy Fraser and his Chief Executive, Anna Whyatt, and in 1992 it had discovered, in the course of a survey, that the majority of the 3,000 households interviewed supported the idea of a major educational or exhibition space in their midst. Southwark Council was, therefore, fully behind the project from the start and agreed to put up the sum of £1.5 million towards the initial development costs.

To Nicolas Serota it seemed essential that, in going for Bankside, the Tate should carry its various audiences with it. No one had asked the Tate to build a new museum of modern art; there had been no ministerial edict, as there would have been in France, followed by the setting up of a committee; and therefore it seemed very necessary to show that it was for the benefit of all. At the press conference announcing the choice of site for the Tate Gallery of Modern Art, held on 28 April 1994, a number of important public figures were on the platform, including John Gummer, Secretary of State for the Environment, Michael Cassidy, Chairman of the Policy and Resources Committee for the Corporation of London, and Jeremy Fraser. Over the previous year the Tate had held further round-table discussions with interested outsiders on the nature and form of a Tate Gallery of Modern Art, and it had also undertaken a survey of the views of artists, from Britain and abroad. Information obtained in this way had fed into a discussion paper, written by Catherine Kinley and Richard Morphet with assistance from other Modern Collection curators, which, in its third draft, was presented to the Trustees in May 1994. In the weeks and months that followed the Bankside announcement, the Tate continued to hold round-table discussions with people who might be involved, from the London Borough of Southwark, English Partnerships, English Heritage and the Baring Foundation, among others. The Trustees were also approached carefully, for Serota and Stevenson were aware that to railroad them in one way or another might cause strong resentment, and with it the possibilities of a factional division. Steering this project towards its goal was to test even further Serota's skills as leader-manager of what was now a highly complex, ambitious organisation.

It proved no small advantage at this time that the Tate's Chairman, coming from business consultancy, knew how to persuade people. Soon after Bankside had been named as the site for the Tate Gallery of Modern Art, a public relations exercise went into action which was as systematic, well co-ordinated and thorough as a military operation. In order to talk the venture through and to attract funds for the start-up costs, early-morning breakfasts were held at Millbank, after which people were taken down to Bankside in groups. The Development department, though still a relatively new feature of the Tate, had gained considerable experience and expertise in the course of fundraising for the Tate's three existing sites. Whereas £1,333,000 had been raised in 1990–1, in 1993–4 the Development Office brought in £4,025,000 and now ran an annual fundraising bidding process to decide on internal priorities. It had also structured itself into four main areas – charitable giving, events, corporate sponsorship and Friends – and, at Fay Ballard's insistence, maintained high standards of entertaining. As a result, when MORI published the results of a research enquiry in 1993, it was discovered that the Tate had become one of the most prestigious arts venues in London for corporate entertaining and that more MPs attended corporate events at the Tate than at any other venue.

'A really imaginative conversion', Serota was quoted as saying in the *Guardian*, 'can be more exciting than a new building.'[8] Proof of this in recent years could be found in several successful museums and galleries that had resulted from the conversion of existing factories, warehouses or stations, such as Max Gordon's conversion of 98A Boundary Road for Charles Saatchi, Richard Gluckman's DIA Foundation in New York or the Musée d'Orsay in Paris. However, while negotiations proceeded with Nuclear Electric over the price of Bankside, the decision to convert an existing building rather than build a new one aroused a certain amount of dissent; especially while the power station remained full of redundant machinery and fetid drifts of pigeon-droppings. Interestingly, the negative response was similar in tone and argument to that which, a century before, had been used against the choice of Millbank for Henry Tate's original building.

> It presents a vertical acre of the ugliest-ever bricks to the City and to the river, unredeemed by any masterful detailing. Despite some art deco styling, previously associated with high spirits, the building still casts a miasma of depression.
>
> The station always was a flop. It operated for less than ten years, spreading vast quantities of sulphurous fumes across the centre of the city. The taller chimney originally designed was rejected for being higher than St Paul's.
>
> Its monstrous size blocks some 200 yards of Bankside from the river, and its back elevation is lined with an obsolescent sub-station … The complex

sterilises a large hinterland of office buildings that are themselves obsolete. Its construction was a disaster in urban planning, which its retention perpetuates.

Does the Tate propose to spearhead a joint redevelopment project to change this almighty mess into a visionary precinct, with new buildings representing the best of British architectural talent, as it meant to do with the Turner Gallery? It proposes instead to camp in the machine rooms, perpetuating the blight and the muddle, and preventing state-of-the-art development. How backward-looking; how necrophiliac; how very Britain of the Nineties.[9]

So Lawrence Hansen, Director of the Southwark Environment Trust, wrote in a letter to the *Independent*, stirring considerable further comment, including the following letter from C.M. Rogers:

Refurbished, cleaned and lit in the same dramatic manner as the Lloyds building, Bankside would make a stunning beacon of culture among the commercial dross of that part of the Thames … Let the Tate have Bankside, and rejuvenate an awe-inspiring building to provide some much-needed refinement to the Southwark desert.[10]

This was the view also favoured by the architectural critic Deyan Sudjic.[11] For him, as for many others, one overriding argument in favour of Bankside lay in the opportunity it brought for large-scale urban renewal. And the Tate, itself, knew that, in addition to its desire to show its collection more completely, it needed this broader argument.

★　　★　　★

The decision to transform a temple of power into a power house of art won the Tate favour with the conservationists. Momentum had begun to build up in favour of Bankside in the course of positive discussions with various government departments and organisations, including the Departments of National Heritage and Trade and Industry, and English Heritage. An inspection by Ove Arup, the structural and service engineering consultants, proved the building to be structurally sound and the bricks in good order. Nuclear Electric was now anxious to sell as soon as possible as the government was keen to move quickly in privatising the industry. Eventually the building was transferred to Magnox Electric, which remained the public-sector arm of the nuclear industry. Originally offered at £10 million, the price was renegotiated after an open-market valuation gave it a lower value, owing to the cost of deplanting and the need to rectify contaminated land. Eventually Magnox agreed to accept £8.5 million and to undertake deplanting. The sub-station, however, far from being obsolete, had to remain, as it was part of the National Grid system, but engineers were confident that noise infiltration could be abated.

A new phase in the history of Bankside began on 13 July 1994 when the Tate held a press breakfast to announce details of the architectural competition for Bankside. Six days before, it had faxed the same announcement to the Official Journal of the European Community, and architects the world over were able to access information on it through their computers. From then on a full-scale press campaign in support of this project was maintained by the Tate, in collaboration with the press consultants, Erica Bolton and Jane Quinn. In addition, Karl Sabbagh obtained a commission from Channel Four, and permission from the Tate, to film strategic moments in the creation of the Tate Gallery of Modern Art over the next six years for Skyscraper Productions. The excitement increased when it was discovered that by 26 August, 205 registrations had been received, among them some of the most celebrated architects of the day, as well as a strong field of highly regarded younger European and British architects. The shortlist was to be announced on Monday 26 September at the Biennial Report press conference. The reason for such haste was that the huge amount of press comment provoked by the scheme had begun to generate a sense of impatience among the Tate's supporters. Further delay would have given the impression of uncertainty. Moreover, the need to submit an application to the Millennium Commission was dependent on the Tate having agreed an architect.

In selecting the jury for this competition, Serota and Stevenson were clear that, though the Trustees were to be represented on it by Janet de Botton and Michael Craig-Martin, it should be a body independent of the Trustees. It was agreed that the jury should comprise those with extensive architectural expertise and knowledge: Hans Hollein, designer of several museums in Europe; Sir Philip Powell, designer of the distinguished Christ Church Picture Gallery in Oxford; Richard Burdett, Director of the Architecture Foundation and knowledgeable on the work of younger architects; and Richard Koshalek, Director of the Museum of Contemporary Art in Los Angeles, who had overseen the building of two museums. They were joined by Caryl Hubbard, a former Tate and National Gallery Trustee, and member of the building committee that had overseen the creation of the Sainsbury Wing at the National Gallery; Joan Bakewell, a member of the Friends Council and a television presenter with an interest in visual arts, who was to represent the people's voice; and Sir Simon Hornby, an experienced committee chairman with a long track-record of interest in the field of design, and no obvious preference for a particular kind of architecture. It was thought that his influence might be helpful at a later stage in the City.

What the Tate was seeking was an architect capable of inventing form and volume, and of handling light as well as suppressing it, in a way that would create a variety of gallery and public spaces, and at the same time give coherence and legibility to the building as a whole. It was also thought essential that the architect should have real respect and sympathy for art, so that there would not be any apparent division inside the building between the desires of the curators and Trustees and those of the architect. In this way, it was also hoped to avoid the tense disagreements between curators and architect that had made the last stages of the Clore Gallery so difficult.

The shortlist, announced in September 1994, included top international names. In the final countdown there had been 148 submissions and from these thirteen architectural practices had been chosen – six of them British and the rest from abroad. Among them were two of the best-known architects from Japan: Arata Isozaki, who had designed the covered stadium for the Barcelona Olympics; and Tadao Ando, whose major projects include the Naoshima Contemporary Art Museum in Okayama. Also listed was Renzo Piano, Italy's top architect, who had designed the Centre Georges Pompidou with Richard Rogers; and Rafael Moneo, who had done much to foster the recent renaissance of contemporary architecture in Spain. Among the British firms listed were Michael Hopkins and Partners and David Chipperfield, a younger architect, who had won much respect for his work for smaller cultural institutions. In October all were assembled for a briefing session at the Tate and then taken down to Bankside to get an initial impression of the challenge they faced. On the same day a photocall of the entire gathering was taken in the Turbine Hall and widely reproduced in the press.

Because Bankside, despite its weighty appearance, is actually clad with the thinnest of brick skins and relies for its strength on a steel-frame structure, the shortlisted architects could reinvent the building with great freedom. Their designs and models, which later went on display at the Tate, revealed startlingly different solutions. Four presented designs that preserved the existing structure of the building and followed its main lines. Others made dramatic additions or altered the alignment of the building, played with the outline of the roof or added extra elements that broke up the monolithic outline. In terms of the internal plan, the architects had to consider a layout that divided the museum into six suites of gallery spaces – five of which were intended for the display of the permanent collection, and one of which was to be for temporary exhibitions. The spaces, though differently sized, were not intended to be infinitely flexible, as the Tate was clear that it wanted solid walls and definite rooms.

In November 1994 the jury reduced the shortlist to six contenders who were each given £15,000 to refine further their ideas. The six names that went forward were Tadao Ando, David Chipperfield, Herzog and de Meuron, Rafael Moneo, Rem Koolhaas and Renzo Piano. During December the jury, both individually and as a group, began visiting a number of sites with which these architects had been connected. The following January the jury began their search for a winner. In their assessment of the designs they now began to penetrate beyond aesthetic matters to questions of cost and buildability. They spent two days interviewing the six candidates and in the course of these discussions the three younger contestants – Koolhaas, Chipperfield and Herzog and de Meuron – moved forward, partly because it became evident that they had listened more carefully to what the Tate had been saying and were able to prove themselves more responsive to the client. Koolhaas's design played on the tension between old and new by dividing the interior space into various zones – reached by stairs, escalators, lifts and ramps at varying speeds. Chipperfield's decision to take down the tower, and replace it with a shorter, more block-like glazed tower, seemed a bold move, though it was finally concluded that not enough seemed to be gained by it. There were also doubts about the kind of gallery spaces he proposed. The final decisions were chaired with great skill by Sir Simon Hornby and the jury came out unanimously in favour of Herzog and de Meuron.

Their design offered extreme simplicity. As Deyan Sudjic has observed, 'Rather than make monumental gestures of their own or create spectacle out of structure or services, their scheme allows both the art works and the power station's impressive form to speak.'[12] The building's framework and character, and therefore a memory of its past life, remained clearly visible; yet at the same time subtle alterations and the introduction of more light helped transform its impermeable bulk into a crisp and purposeful modern interior. By placing the gallery suites on the north side, behind a new screen wall, Herzog and de Meuron had decided to minimise intrusions into the turbine hall. This is to remain a huge, raw, public space in which can be placed artworks at least as big as Rachel Whiteread's *House*. The design of the gallery spaces had the attraction of offering great flexibility – as each floor was to be different in height – and the rooms, though all rectangular, presented a variety of configurations, light conditions and sizes. On either side of the chimney stack were to be open-ended spaces where art could be shown in a more everyday environment, alongside activity rooms, concourses and other ancillary requirements. But the most prominent feature in Herzog and de Meuron's design was the addition of a 'light beam' – a glass construction running the full length of the roof, intended to house the truss from which the exhibition floors will hang; to provide light for the top-floor galleries and restaurant; and to advertise the presence of the building to the outside world.

News that they had won the competition reached Herzog and de Meuron in an unexpected way. Pierre de Meuron's mother heard it on the Swiss radio several hours before Nick Serota telephoned with official confirmation. The speed at which the news was then relayed to the public meant that at the official press conference only three of the four Herzog and de Meuron partners could be present. But the Tate now had an architect, and the architects had a project which was not only on a scale far vaster than anything they had so far achieved but was also to arouse steadily growing international interest.

★   ★   ★

Soon after Serota's arrival at the Tate the Exhibitions Sub-Committee had began to meet more frequently. The ambition now was to mount at least three major shows a year, which were to be complemented by a range of smaller exhibitions and by the Art Now programme which began in 1995. Overall, the policy was to achieve a balance between the Tate's responsibilities towards British, modern and contemporary art. Among its successes were *On Classic Ground: Picasso, Léger, de Chirico and the New Classicism 1910–1930*, which set a new benchmark for survey exhibitions; and *Picasso: Sculptor/Painter*, which combined high scholarship with great art, and had immense popular appeal.

The tradition that a different artist each year should decorate the Christmas tree in the rotunda began in 1988 with Bill Woodrow. Far from restricting themselves to the decorations, the artists became increasingly inventive with their solutions to this commission, Shirazeh Houshiary hanging her tree upside-down and gilding the roots, Cathy de Monchaux wrapping her tree and making it part of a complex installation, and Julian Opie opting for a forest of fabricated trees.

The diverse nature of contemporary art, and the variety of materials employed, continue to set new problems for the Tate's Conservation Department, which maintains a high reputation internationally. In September 1995 it hosted an innovative conference on the techniques and conservation of modern sculpture – 'From Marble to Chocolate' – which attracted 200 delegates from around the world and dealt with such topics as laser cleaning and the problems connected with conserving plastics. Earlier that year Viscount Dunluce had retired after thirty-one years in the department, and in his place James France became Director of Collections Services and Roy Perry, Head of Conservation. The year before, another long-standing figure, Iain Bain, Head of Publications, had retired after developing a notable range of fine exhibition catalogues and prints. His successor Celia Clear was encouraged to broaden the publishing list and to increase revenue from retail and marketing in support of the Tate's ambitious programmes. In 1995 the Millbank shop was extended and a year later a limited company was set up, Tate Gallery Publishing, which is wholly owned by the Trustees and covenants its entire profits to the Gallery.

Increased efficiency of communication within the Gallery was made possible by the installation of a new telephone and voice-mail system. The staff could now also communicate by e-mail, which helped speed messages between not only the far-flung corners of Millbank but also the four different sites on which the Tate was now operating. But, until Bankside opened, nothing could be done to alleviate the pressures on the space at Millbank, where it was felt necessary to impose an overall limit of 3,500 people in the building; and the Tate had sometimes to shut its doors on Sunday afternoons to prevent over-crowding. On 5 November 1994 a demonstration was staged outside the Tate against the current ruling which limited the number of wheelchair-users to only six at any one time – a limit that had arisen from the Home Office Fire Officer's ruling that this was the number which might safely be evacuated in the event of fire. The cause of the crush was the *Whistler* exhibition which had attracted many elderly visitors and more wheelchairs than usual. A revised evacuation process was therefore implemented which allowed twenty, rather than six, wheelchair-users on the main gallery floor.

Overcrowding at Millbank became still more noticeable at the time of the 1996 *Cézanne* exhibition. It brought together nearly a hundred of Cézanne's greatest paintings and had been Serota's idea, though the complex negotiations required to stage an exhibition of this stature were largely undertaken by Joseph Rishel at the Philadelphia Museum of Art, with assistance from Françoise Cachin, Director of the Musées de France. There had been many other occasions when London

92 Christmas tree by Shirazeh Houshiary, 1993

had been passed over as a possible venue for major touring exhibitions, such as the 1992 Matisse exhibition and the showing of the Barnes Collection in 1993 – a fact that highlighted its need for a new showcase for art. The argument that the Tate Gallery of Modern Art would significantly enhance Britain's ability to host world-class exhibitions of modern art became part of the full application to the Millennium Commission, which the Tate submitted in April 1995 with the help of McKinsey & Co, who were guided by a steering committee comprising key members of the Tate executive team.

Talking with the shortlisted architects in the course of the competition, the Tate team had learned a great deal about the building on which they had exchanged contracts in December 1994. These conversations had also helped clarify and increase ambitions for its development. Thus the Millennium Commission application proudly claimed that 'the TGMA's opening in 2000 will be a cultural event of worldwide significance'. Elsewhere it argued: 'At the heart of the capital, it will establish a new landmark and an outstanding public space for the nation and enhance London's position as a world centre, bringing cultural, social and economic benefits to millions of people in the nation as a whole.' Three million pounds had already been raised to ensure that the necessary preparatory work

93 Plant removal in progress at Bankside, 1995

94 Computer-generated image of the Tate Gallery of Modern Art
with footbridge across the River Thames

had been done properly, and the total capital cost of the project was estimated at
£106 million. The Tate was therefore asking for the maximum grant of £50 million, on the understanding that it would have to match this with £56 million from
the private, corporate and public sector. Some £12 million of this had already been
received from English Partnerships, the urban regeneration agency. In addition,
the Tate claimed to have identified income streams to cover 60 per cent of the
annual operating costs of the project. And it could rightly claim proven ability
to work effectively with public and private agencies on major projects, having
opened and then managed three new galleries. But on every point – on the architects, the project implementation, finance and schedule – the document rang
with conviction and authority.

Already the task of stripping Bankside of machinery had begun. This huge
dismantling job, which took fifteen months, was made additionally difficult by
the fact that explosives were excluded from the contract, and the machinery and
concrete supports had to be removed from the building without damaging its
structure. Immediately before this work began, a number of artists had gone
into Bankside to make a visual record of its pre-conversion appearance. Of these
artists, Anthony Eyton was the most persistent, working over a period of six
months and only stopping when the process of deplanting made it impossible for
him to continue. Meanwhile, the cost of protecting the fabric of the building had
been met by English Heritage, and the idea of a footbridge linking Bankside with
St Paul's had been taken further. Serota did not think it advisable that the Tate
should take a lead on the bridge, and welcomed the offer of the *Financial Times* to
run an international competition for its design. This eventually found its winner
in the pairing of the architect Norman Foster with the sculptor Anthony Caro,
while the project was taken over by a consortium which included London's Cross-
River Partnership. Meanwhile, the rapid escalation of responsibilities in relation
to Bankside made it necessary to appoint a Project Manager to co-ordinate five

executive teams (fundraising, building, programme, finance and legal, and communication), and Dawn Austwick took on this role in March 1995.

The design team had first begun work in March 1995. Comprising members of the Tate staff, engineering and service consultants and the architects, it met either in London or in Basel, where the Herzog and de Meuron team worked from a modest set of offices. By October 1995, when the Millennium Commission was due to announce its first allocation of grants, the entire project, though now well advanced, was in a fragile state owing to the tense anxiety over the Tate's application. There had been criticism in the press that London seemed likely to benefit from an unfair share of Lottery money, and it was thought possible that the Millennium Commission, in response to this adverse view, would defer its decision with regard to Bankside. But at 8 am on the morning of Monday 30 October a letter arrived by fax from the Commission informing Serota that the Tate had got its £50 million grant. There were two principal conditions: that the outstanding co-funding of the overall capital costs would be in place by April 1996 and that by that date the Tate had also to satisfy the Commission that it was able to finance the operational costs from non-Millennium Commission sources. The Commission further agreed to provide interim funding up to a maximum of £2.8 million over the next six months, while the Gallery worked to meet these conditions.

★   ★   ★

95 Computer-generated night view of the Tate Gallery of Modern Art

The following day the exhibition of works by artists shortlisted of the Turner Prize opened. Certain of the Tate's advisers had warned against the showing of Damien Hirst's controversial *Mother and Child, Divided* at the same time that the news of the Millennium grant was being released. But what initially kept this work of art hidden from view was a slight leak in one of the cases which had been specially made with extra thick glass at the Tate's request. Because this work involved the use of formaldehyde, elaborate precautions had been taken, the floor relined and additional ventilation introduced, in order to satisfy the requirements of the Health and Safety Executive, which two months before had come down heavily on the Tate after a sculpture by Hamad Butt had broken and released iodine vapour. When finally *Mother and Child, Divided* went on view, it became the focal point of the show which ended with Hirst becoming the 1995 winner of the Turner Prize. One member of the jury, William Feaver, afterwards wrote: 'Damien Hirst got the prize for panache and effrontery ... He has been the leading brainstormer of his generation of artists, a goad and corrective, showing up the solemnity of professional art curators while demonstrating that art's main concern has to be the way we live now.'[13]

The Tate was now moving forward on a number of fronts, and to the staff it sometimes seemed as if they were being carried along by a huge gathering wave. In July 1995 the decision had been taken to apply for Heritage Lottery Funding for the transformation of Millbank into the Tate Gallery of British Art. John Miller & Partners had previously been commissioned to redevelop the North-West Quadrant but work on this project had been delayed. Miller was now invited to review his Millbank Masterplan and to extend his plans beyond the North-West Quadrant. This £31 million Centenary Development, as it became known, involved the creation of five new galleries, the renovation of nine others, and the provision of new exhibition space on the lower floor which would be served by a new entrance in Atterbury Street. The staircase at the back of the building was to be removed and another built, close to the Atterbury Street entrance, in a double-height hall that would transform the relationship between the two floors and would bring the visitor more directly into the centre of the building. Not only did Miller's design offer the prospect of introducing a new dignity and airiness into the older parts of the building, but it also took account of possible future developments: the strong central west–east axis at the lower level is intended to create an important link between the Atterbury Street entrance and a building that might in time be centred on the east side of the 1979 extension.

At the same time Drivers Jonas, the consultant surveyors who had been involved with the Tate since 1987, began to develop proposals for Millbank's immediate surroundings, recommending improvements to the gardens, railings and gates, and the creation of more easily identified routes to all entrances. This led to the appointment of the architects Allies and Morrison, who are currently redesigning the garden in front of the Clore.

A Tate Gallery of British Art Project Group was set up in 1995, chaired by Sandy Nairne and assisted by Beth Houghton, Head of Library and Archive. At the same time Sir Richard Carew Pole, who had joined the Board of Trustees in 1993, began chairing the TGBA Development Committee, and Anne Beckwith-Smith took charge of the Capital and Gifts Campaign connected with it. By the time the Heritage Lottery Fund awarded the Tate £18.75 million in February 1997, most of the necessary matching funding had been raised, and, in addition to the £7 million donated by Sir Edwin Manton at the time of the announcement of the TGBA/TGMA divide (which had provided the cornerstone to the whole scheme), more than £7.5 million had come from private sources.

The aim was to relaunch Millbank as the Tate Gallery of British Art in 2001, when it could benefit from the space released by the opening of TGMA. By bringing out of storage most of the important works, devoting certain rooms to key artists, and where necessary drawing on loans from other institutions, it was hoped that a far more extensive and coherent presentation of British art would be made possible; and the Gallery effectively rededicated to Sir Henry Tate's original purpose. In order to achieve this aim, the Tate began negotiations with other national collections, building on relations which had been carefully nurtured in recent years. Given the problems in the past over transfers between the Tate and the National Gallery, both Nicholas Serota and Neil MacGregor, Director of the National Gallery, had been keen to establish a mutually acceptable policy regarding their respective collections, though awkwardness had arisen in 1990 when the Berggruen collection, which was rich in Picassos, went on loan to the National Gallery. As a result, in September 1996 the Trustees of the National Gallery and the Tate made a joint announcement that they had agreed to exchange works for a period of four years, so that nineteenth-century foreign painting would be consolidated at the National Gallery and the twentieth-century paintings consolidated at the Tate. This concord might not have been so startling had there not been a long history of friction in the relationship between the two Galleries.

The future role of the Tate as the National Gallery of British Art was affirmed in 1996, when, with the help of a £3.77 million grant from the Heritage Lottery Fund, it spent £5 million on the Oppé collection which comprised some 3,000 works. This acquisition demonstrated the Tate's ambition to become a pre-eminent centre for the study of British art, and not simply the study of British painting – for the Oppé collection was one of the last great collections of British drawings and watercolours still in private hands. It had been created by the civil servant, also the distinguished scholar and collector, Paul Oppé, who had been responsible for the 'discovery' of certain key artists such as Francis Towne and Alexander Cozens. The core of his great collection focused on the golden age of English watercolour painting, 1750–1850. One of its greatest treasures was Francis Towne's *The Source of the Arveyron*, which, in its stark simplicity seemed to prefigure, if not surpass, the use by the twentieth-century artist Paul Nash of sharply analytical design. A further positive side-effect of this acquisition was that it became imperative for the Study Room in the Clore to open more frequently and for longer hours.

In May 1997 the Gallery started its centenary celebrations by opening its eighth

96 Artist's impression of the new entrance to the Tate Gallery of British Art

rehang. Spread through the *Centenary Displays* were the Tate's own type of hit-parade – a hundred paintings or sculptures deemed by the curators to be either acknowledged masterpieces or to possess some particular point of art-historical interest. TateInform, the digital audio-guide system first introduced in 1995, provided information on the displays which overlapped with a celebration of the tercentenary of Hogarth's birth. Through the inclusion of several significant loans, some of them newly discovered works, this special display reaffirmed the vigour and directness of his art. A further cause of celebration was the announcement that a leading art collector, Janet de Botton, had offered to donate a significant part of her collection to the Tate.

At the venerable age of one hundred, the Tate and its reputation seem unassailable. But if its early struggles and disasters, troubles and omissions, are a thing of the past, it still courts controversy and attracts criticism as well as praise. The news that all four shortlisted artists for the 1997 Turner Prize were women was accepted as a welcome redress to the gender imbalance of previous years. But those with an interest in the history of print-making remain critical of the Tate's failure to honour the extensive gifts of prints made in the 1970s. At Tate Gallery St Ives a greater than expected net operational deficit in the year 1993–4 has made necessary an internal review, and the implementation of a new forward plan, in an attempt to put this part of the institution on a better financial footing. Meanwhile, Tate Gallery Liverpool received less money than was hoped for from the European Regional Development Fund, and suffered a delay in the start of its Phase 2 building programme. Bankside, too, underwent a testing period in December 1995, when the Tate subjected it to a cost-cutting exercise, so as to retain public confidence in the Gallery's ability to keep within the demands of budget and schedule. In order to save £4 million, Herzog and de Meuron had to accept the removal of certain aspects of their design, including a mezzanine floor, as well as subtleties and modifications, the loss of which would leave the building more spare. Its out-turn cost, which took into account inflation up to the year 2000, was £130 million. At the time of the centenary £100 million had already been found and the public appeal, which will partly assist with the remaining £30 million, had not yet been launched. Similarly with the Tate Gallery of British Art, effective fundraising had found the greater part of the £31 million, leaving £4 million outstanding until a few days before the Tate's centenary, when it was disclosed that Sir Edwin Manton had given the promise of £5 million towards the scheme, in addition to the £7 million he had earlier given anonymously. It was also disclosed that he would be leaving to the Tate a recently discovered Constable, *The Glebe Farm*.

Sir Edwin Manton was publicly thanked by Dennis Stevenson at the Tate Centenary party, held chiefly for artists, on 21 July 1997, at which Prince Charles was the Guest of Honour. Earlier that month another centenary celebration, a fundraising dinner in aid of the Tate's redevelopment appeal, was attended by many celebrities, including Diana, Princess of Wales. She was celebrating her birthday, and appeared in a sleek full-length dark-green evening dress at what proved to be one of her last official engagements, and one mentioned by her brother in his address at her funeral.

There had been a few days in September 1996, between the deplanting of Bankside and the start of construction work, when the shell of the building had been open to visitors. Among these was the artist Richard Wentworth, whose opinion on Bankside was sought by Karl Sabbagh for his film on the making of the Tate Gallery of Modern Art. 'The problem for the English is always to do with the past and the future,' Wentworth remarked, 'and maybe what makes this an intriguing place is that it's actually saying rather vigorously goodbye to the past and boldly trying to say hello to the future.' For Wentworth, as for other visitors to Bankside at that time, the tension between the building's past and its envisaged transformation was exhilarating. And the challenge of the Tate remains this continuing dynamic – between the ever-growing richness of its past and its hopes and ambitions for the future.

Notes

Place of publication is London, unless otherwise stated.
TGA = Tate Gallery Archive

1

The Potent Tate

1 Information on this collection, which became one of the cornerstones of Tate's National Gallery of British Art in 1987, can be found in Robin Hamlyn, *Robert Vernon's Gift*, exh. cat., Tate Gallery 1993.
2 An account of this and other developments in Henry Tate's career is included in J.A. Watson, *Talk of Many Things: Random Notes Concerning Henry Tate and Love Lane*, Tate & Lyle Refineries Ltd 1985.
3 A useful source on Henry Tate's philanthropic activities is Tom Jones, *Henry Tate 1819–1899: A Biographical Sketch*, Tate & Lyle Ltd, 1960.
4 This suggestion was first made by Kenneth Ouncy, Librarian of Liverpool University. See J.A. Watson, *The End of a Liverpool Landmark: The Last Years of Love Lane Refinery*, Tate & Lyle Refineries Ltd 1985, p.77.
5 Harcourt's boast formed part of his speech at the opening ceremony of the National Gallery of British Art on 21 July 1897. It was reported in *The Times* the following day.
6 For further information on the penitentiary and the history of the Millbank site see Krzysztof Z. Cieszkowski, 'Millbank before the Tate' in *The Tate Gallery: Illustrated Biennial Report, 1984–86*, pp.38–43.
7 The various signifiers encoded in Sidney Smith's choice of architectural detail are drawn out by Brandon Taylor in 'From Penitentiary to "Temple of Art"', in *Art Apart: Art Institutions and Ideology across England and North America*, ed. Marcia Poynton, Manchester University Press 1994, pp.9–32.
8 Memorandum by W.V. Harcourt [Sir William Harcourt] of an interview with Henry Tate, 22 Feb. 1893: Public Records Office, WORK, 17, 60.
9 Quoted in *The Times*, 22 July 1897.

2

The Search for Identity

1 Alfred Thornton, *Fifty Years of the New English Art Club*, Cowan Press 1935, p.6.
2 Uncertainty over the nomenclature of the Gallery led the periodical *Truth* to run a list of possible names in September 1897. Among its suggestions was 'the Tate-and-up-to-date Gallery'.
3 Minutes of the National Gallery's Board of Trustees' meeting, 5 July 1898. Mrs Heimpel's death is reported in the Minutes of the National Gallery's Board of Trustees meeting, 12 Dec. 1911: National Gallery Archives.
4 Henri Alain-Fournier, *Towards the Lost Domain: Letters from London, 1905*, ed. W.J. Strachan, Carcanet Press, Manchester 1986, p.129.

5 George Moore, quoted in *Chantrey and his Bequest: A Complete Illustrated Record of the Purchases of the Trustees, with a Biographical Note, Text of the Will, etc.*, Cassel & Co. 1904, pp.32–3.
6 D.S. MacColl, *The Administration of the Chantrey Bequest*, Grant & Richards 1904, p.20.
7 Crewe Inquiry, *Chantrey Trust, Report, Proceedings and Minutes of Evidence*, Select Committee of the House of Lords, 1904, UK Parliamentary Papers, 357, v. 498.
8 See Cordon Fyfe, 'The Chantrey Episode: Art Classification, Museums and the State, c.1870–1920' in *Art on Museums. New Research in Museum Studies: An International Series*, Athlone, London, and Atlantic Highlands, N.J. 1995, pp.5–41.
9 This fact is upheld by Maureen Borland in *D.S. MacColl: Painter, Poet, Art Critic*, Lennard Publishing, Harpenden 1995.
10 *Saturday Review*, 28 Nov. 1896.
11 Ibid.
12 D.S. MacColl, *Confessions of a Keeper*, Alexander Maclehose & Co. 1931, p.4.
13 Ibid., p.6.
14 Ibid., p.3.
15 Ibid., p.7.
16 D.S. MacColl, 'Desiderata List', 1909: National Gallery Archives.

3

The Curzon Report

1 John Rothenstein, *Brave Day, Hideous Night: Autobiography 1939–1965*, Hamish Hamilton 1966 (hereafter referred to as BDHN), pp.10–11.
2 Ibid., p.11.
3 William Rothenstein, *Since Fifty: Men and Memories 1912–1938*, Faber & Faber 1939, p.63.
4 Charles Aitken, 'Suggestions by the Keeper of the National Gallery of British Art for the Consideration of the Trustees', Jan. 1912, National Gallery Archives 215.4.
5 Ibid.
6 A clause in the deed of gift for Henry Tate's original building provides that it should be used for British art only and for no other purposes. This clauses, however, did not apply to the galleries built in the 1920s by Sir Joseph Duveen for modern foreign art as they were outside the boundary of the original site and therefore not bound by this condition.
7 Not at the Tate Gallery, as stated in Dennis Farr's *English Art 1870–1940*, Oxford, Clarendon Press 1978, p.346. This detail aside, Farr's chapter 'Patronage and Collecting 1870–1940' is an invaluable source of reference for this period.
8 See the letter which Maureen Borland quotes in *D.S. MacColl: Painter, Poet, Art Critic*, 1995, p.208.
9 Manson's interest in French Impressionism led him to form the short-lived exhibiting society, the Monarro Group, and to act as its secretary. Its title was derived from a conflation of the surnames of Monet

and Camille Pissarro, and Monet was its *Président d'honneur*.

10 Charles Holroyd to C.H. Collins Baker, 8 May 1915: National Gallery Archives.

11 Further information on how the consortium divided up the Dante drawings can by found in Krzysztof Cieszkowski's 'The Formation of the Collection' in *William Blake, 1757–1827* (Tate Gallery Collections: vol.5) by Martin Butlin, 1990, pp.12–13. A still more detailed account has been published by Cieszkowski in the *Blake Quarterly*, Winter 1989, pp.166–171.

12 This passage from the Curzon Report is quoted by Ronald Alley in *Catalogue of the Tate Gallery's Collection of Modern Art*, Tate Gallery 1981, pp.viii–xix.

13 *Nevermore* was eventually purchased by Samuel Courtauld in 1927, at a reduced price on the understanding that it would eventually come to the nation.

14 S.N. Behrman, *Duveen*, Hamish Hamilton 1952, p.1.

15 See minutes of the National Gallery, Millbank Board meeting, 21 May 1920. I am also grateful to Krzysztof Cieszkowski for his paper 'Boris Anrep's Mosaics in Gallery 16' (unpublished).

16 *Burlington Magazine*, vol.38, May 1921, p.209. Further information on this brouhaha can be found in 'Tate and Miss Davies's Cézannes' a collection of letters in the Tate Gallery Archive (TGA 736), in which it is recorded that MacColl, as a Tate Trustee, was persuaded to reconsider the Cézannes in 1922 while they were hanging in an exhibition at the Burlington Club, and as result he and other trustees informed Blaker that they had been mistaken about Miss Davies's Cézannes. Aitken subsequently wrote to her asking if *Midday, L'Estaque* (now in the National Museum and Gallery of Wales, Cardiff) could be sent to the Tate when the Burlington Club exhibition ended. But angered by their cavalier rejection, Miss Davies refused to lend to the Tate in 1922, or again in 1926, and did not finally do so until the 1950s.

17 This list was published by Madeleine Korn in 'The Courtauld Gift: Missing Papers Traced', *Burlington Magazine*, vol.138, April 1996, p.256.

18 After 1927 the Courtauld Fund came to an end, apart from small contributions towards a Camille Pissarro landscape in 1932, and a watercolour by Dunoyer de Segonzac in 1939. It was partly revived in 1944 by the sale of a Renoir which was thought to be below the otherwise very high standard.

19 Both versions of the speech can be found among Lord D'Abernon's papers: British Library, Manuscript Collection, 48931, vol.xv.

20 *Defining Modern Art: Selected Writings of Alfred H. Barr, Jr*, eds. Irving Sandler and Amy Newman, New York, Harry N. Abrams, 1986, p.71.

4

The Flood and After

1 Charles Aitken to C.J. Holmes, 29 Nov. 1924: National Gallery Archives, 215.3.

2 *The Times*, 20 Aug. 1968.

3 Chief Surveyor's Report on Flood Damage: Public Record Office, Work 117/1160.

4 Charles Aitken to Lord D'Abernon, 16 July 1928: British Library, Manuscript Collections, 48931, vol.xv.

5 Charles Aitken to the editor of *The Times*: National Gallery Archives 215.5. Published 1 May 1929.

6 Roger Cole, *Gaudier-Brzeska: Artist and Myth*, Sansom & Co., Redcliffe Press, Bristol 1995, pp.166–7.

7 H.S. Ede, tape-recorded conversation with Corinne Bellow: TGA, TAV 620A.

8 H.S. Ede to Charles Aitken, 28 Oct. 1927: National Gallery Archive 215.4.

9 See note 6.

10 H.S. Ede to C.H. Collins Baker, 10 April 1927: National Gallery Archive 215.4.

11 C.H. Collins Baker to H.S. Ede , 11 April 1927: National Gallery Archive 215.4.

12 These three sculptures and seventeen drawings were eventually purchased from H.M. Treasury, not by the Tate, but by Frank C. Stoop for £160, and presented by him through the CAS in 1930.

13 H.S. Ede to Ben Nicholson, 18 April 1929: TGA 8717.1.2.853.

14 H.S. Ede to Ben Nicholson, 26 Feb. 1929: TGA 8717.1.2.852.

15 H.S. Ede to Ben Nicholson, n.d. [early summer 1929]: TGA 8717.1.2.852.

16 Medical report on H.S. Ede, 8 Nov. 1929: National Gallery Archive 215.5.

17 Charles Aitken to Mr Mennell, 15 Nov. 1929: National Gallery Archive 215.5.

18 William Rothenstein, *Since Fifty: Men and Memories 1927–1938*, 1939, p.65.

19 Charles Aitken to Lord D'Abernon, 28 Nov. 1929: British Library, Manuscript Collection, 48931, vol.xv.

20 Lord D'Abernon to Sir Ronald Waterhouse, 5 May 1926: British Library, Manuscript Collection, 48931, vol.xv.

21 Charles Aitken to Lord D'Abernon, 22 May 1926: British Library, Manuscript Collection, 48931, vol.xv.

22 Lord D'Abernon, quoted in the minutes of the National Gallery, Millbank Board meeting, 23 June 1930.

23 Lord Duveen to John Rothenstein, 26 July 1938: TGA 087.

24 Kenneth Clark, *Another Part of the Wood: A Self-Portrait*, John Murray 1974, p.233.

25 *Studio*, vol.77, 1919, pp.21–5.

26 William Gaunt in the *Daily Telegraph* (24 Nov. 1967) quotes a letter Manson wrote to Lucien Pissarro: 'My Trustees are hopelessly hostile to modern art. It makes me furious. They have the point of view of nearly fifty years ago.'

27 Minutes of the Trustees' Board meeting, 27 June 1933.

28 *Sunday Times*, 31 July 1932.

29 H.S.Ede, in a tape-recorded conversation with Corinne Bellow: TGA, TAV 620A.

30 Lillian Lee, in a tape-recorded conversation with Corinne Bellow: TGA, TAV 1267A.

31 C.J. Holmes, *Self & Partners (Mostly Self)*, Constable 1938, pp.329–30.

32 Kenneth Clark, 'Notes on the Relations between National Gallery and Tate': typescript, National Gallery Archive 215.8.

33 Kenneth Clark, *Another Part of the Wood*, p.232.

34 David Fincham to J.B. Manson, 25 Jan. 1938: TGA 806.1.316.

35 Clive Bell to Vanessa Bell, 6 March 1938: Charleston Papers, TGA 8010.5.371.

36 Peggy Guggenheim, *Out of this Century: Confessions of an Art Addict*, André Deutsch 1979 (reprinted 1995), pp.173–4.

37 Quoted in David Buckman, *James Bolivar Manson: An English Impressionist, 1879–1945*, Maltzahn Gallery 1973.

5

A New Beginning

1 Clark's opinion is reported in a letter from Elizabeth Rothenstein to Philip Hendy, n.d. [Dec. 1952]: TGA 8726.3.23.

2 John Rothenstein, *Summer's Lease: Autobiography, 1901–1938*, Hamish Hamilton 1965, p.2.

3 Ibid., p.100.

4 Ibid., p.131.

5 Ibid., p.132.

6 Rothenstein appointed a local artist and picture restorer, George H. Constantine, to set up a conservation studio in the Graves Art Gallery. Constantine was already known to Alderman Graves and sometimes acted as buffer between Graves and Rothenstein. A book, in the possession of Constantine's son, Frank Constantine, is inscribed: 'To G.H. Constantine thanks to whom I am still (Dec. 25, 1936) Art Director in Sheffield. John Rothenstein.'

7 Kenneth Clark, *Another Part of the Wood*, p.232.

8 BDHN, p.5.

9 See BDHN, p.4: 'not one had been placed on exhibition'. The minutes of the Trustees' Board meeting, 20 July 1937, record Maclagan's protest that only four of the nineteen pieces by Rodin were on show.

10 Quoted in BDHN, p.9.

11 Quoted in BDHN, p.8.

12 BDHN, p.5.

13 *Listener*, 27 Oct. 1938.

14 Rothenstein hoped that an opportunity would arise to lend these paintings to another institution. In time another huge Watts, *A Story from Boccaccio*, was sent on long-term loan to Keble College, Oxford, but *The Court of Death* appears to have gone missing.

15 Quoted in *'Degenerate Art': The Fate of the Avant-Garde in Nazi Germany*, Los Angeles County Museum of Art and Harry N. Abrams, New York 1991, p.135.

16 *New Statesman and Nation*, 16 July 1938.

17 BDHN, p.47.

18 Quoted in BDHN, p.21 (where the painting is referred to as 'Battle'), also in the minutes of the Trustees' Board meeting, 22 Nov. 1938.

19 Kandinsky's letter is not in the Gallery Records, but a description of it can be found in the Director's Report in the minutes of the Trustees' Board meeting, 21 Feb. 1939.

20 As reported by Herbert Read to Douglas Cooper, 20 March 1939: Getty Research Institute for the History of Art and the Humanities.

21 BDHN, p.24.

22 Ibid., p.54.

23 Ibid., p.54.

6

The Hidden Tate

1 John Rothenstein to Frank Tribe, 19 Oct. 1939: TGA 8726.3.9.

2 Sir William Rothenstein to John Rothenstein, 21 March 1940: TGA 8726.4.3.

3 E. Hale to Sir Edward Marsh, 10 April 1940: TGA 8726.3.9.

4 BDHN, p.83.

5 Ibid..

6 'Mr Fincham', supplement to minutes of the Trustees' Board meeting, Sept. 1941.

7 One instance occurred in 1947, when a Mrs Blundell requested the return of Richard Dadd's *Portrait of William Dollond*, which had been offered to the Tate in 1931 and had remained in the Gallery for consideration as a loan. Fincham, to whom the picture had been entrusted had, without knowledge or approval of the Trustees, taken the picture to be cleaned, and in 1945 sold it to the Leicester Galleries for fifty guineas. He claimed the owner had made a present of it to him on hearing that it was beyond repair. Mrs Blundell strongly denied this assertion and still had an official Tate Gallery receipt signed by Fincham. The Treasury Solicitor approved a settlement of fifty pounds and in time a cheque was extracted from Fincham to cover this amount.

8 One owner admitted, in a letter to Fincham, that she had offered the use of her home as a refuge house in order to avoid having to take in slum children, as the authorities were pressing her to do ('we would much rather take in inanimate than animate!').

7

Post-War Revival

1 Information supplied by John Richardson, in conversation with the author.

2 In 'The Future of Painting', *The Listener*, 2 Oct. 1935.

3 *Listener*, 9 Oct. 1935, signed with the pseudonym 'Douglas Lord'.

4 Quoted in James King, *The Last Modern: A Life of Herbert Read*, New York, St Martin's Press 1990, p.236.

5 Herbert Read to Douglas Cooper, 7 Aug. 1945: Getty Center, Research Institute for the History of Art and Humanities, 860161, Box 1.

6 These two exhibitions caused the artist Frank Emanuel, Vice-President of the Society of Graphic Art, to interrupt the proceedings with a shouted protest against French art being shown in a British national institution. He was shouted down by fellow artists, who formed a significant part of this well-attended event.

7 Quoted BDHN, p.168.

8 Ibid.

9 As recalled by Sir Norman Reid, in conversation with the author.

10 The owner of *The Red Studio*, David Tennant, had offered in 1927 to lend to the Tate a work by Matisse then entitled *Interior of a Studio*, which was very probably *The Red Studio*. The Trustees turned it down (minutes of the Trustees' Board meeting, 18 Oct. 1927).

11 Graham Sutherland to Douglas Cooper, 16 Nov. 1948: Getty Research Institute for the History of Art and Humanities, Douglas Cooper Papers, 860161, Box 2.

12 BDHN, p.200.

13 *Harper's Bazaar*, Jan. 1951.

14 Minutes of the Trustees' Board meeting, 18 Nov. 1948.

15 Maurice Collis, in *Time and Tide*, 30 Aug. 1947.

16 Henry Lamb, as recorded in the minutes of the Trustees' Board meeting, 18 March 1948.

17 *New Statesman and Nation*, 15 Jan. 1949.

18 Minutes of the Trustees' Board meeting, 20 Jan. 1949

19 I am grateful to Mrs Natalie Brooke for access to papers concerning the Tate kept by her late husband, Humphrey Brooke. These include minutes from the Trustees' Board meeting, 16 Dec. 1948, which were

omitted from the official record, and other papers, including Brooke's unpublished autobiography. A brief account of the whole episode, from John Rothenstein's point of view, can be found in his letter to Sir Edward Playfair, [*c.* Dec. 1952]: TGA 8726.3.23.

8

Iago

1 In 1950 John Richardson argued in the *Listener* (30 Nov. 1950) that the availability of Picasso's *Bust of a Woman* had been known to Rothenstein for two years before it was purchased.
2 Douglas Cooper to Philip Hendy, 6 Feb. [1950]: National Gallery Archives, 215.16.
3 John Rothenstein to the Rt Hon. Lord Jowitt, 15 Nov. 1951: TGA 8726.3.25.
4 *Illustrated*, 25 Oct. 1952.
5 Lord Harlech to the Rt Hon. Lord Jowitt, 14 Nov. 1951: TGA, Dennis Proctor Papers.
6 Douglas Cooper to Sir John Rothenstein, Nov. 1952: Getty Research Institute, Resource Collection, Douglas Cooper Papers, 860621, Box 2.
7 Details concerning the negotiations and events that attended the purchase of the Degas bronze can be found in BDHN, pp.262–75; and in the seven-page document prepared by LeRoux on the subject: TGA, Dennis Proctor Papers.
8 The Rt Hon. Lord Jowitt to Sir Thomas Barnes, 17 Nov. 1952: TGA, Dennis Proctor Papers.

9

The Tate Affair

1 This act of vandalism took place on 15 March 1953. The Hungarian Laszlo Svilvassy gave as his motive: 'Those unknown political prisoners have been and still are human beings. To reduce them – the memory of the dead and the suffering of the living – into scrap metal is just as much a crime as it was to reduce then into ashes or scrap. It is an absolute lack of humanism.' Quoted in *Contemporary Masterpieces*, ed. Colin Naylor, St James's Press 1991, p.43.
2 Anthony and Theo Kloman to John and Elizabeth Rothenstein, 2 May 1953: TGA 8726.3.24.
3 Cooper protested against the 'national prejudice, the parochialism, the personal affections' to which Rothenstein 'blithely confessed', in the *Times Literary Supplement*, 30 Oct. 1952.
4 Douglas Cooper to John Rothenstein, 13 June 1953: TGA 8726.3.10. Quoted, together with its postscript, in BDHN, p.28.
5 There are certainly grounds for assuming Rothenstein was antagonistic to Clark. In a letter to Philip Hendy (TGA 8726.3.24) Elizabeth Rothenstein stated her belief that Clark had prevented her husband from serving office on certain wartime art committees. The mistrust that had developed may have been instigated by Rothenstein's long absence in the United States during the first nine months of the war. Clark says noticeably little about Rothenstein in his memoirs.
6 But not as inaccurate as John Rothenstein suggests in

Brave Day, Hideous Night, where he says that LeRoux ascribed some forty infringements to the Tate (p.203). This is one of several examples of small exaggerations or omissions to support his point of view and which made necessary Dennis Proctor's unpublished paper, 'Brave Day, Hideous Night: Some Comments by the Then Chairman of the Trustees': TGA, Proctor Papers. Roger Berthoud was the first to publish an alternative to Rothenstein's account in his *Graham Sutherland: A Biography* (1982), in which he benefited from first-hand consultation with Sir Dennis Proctor, Sir Colin Anderson, John Piper and Sir William Coldstream.
7 Sir Colin Anderson, unpublished autobiography: Mrs Catriona Williams.
8 Humphrey Brooke to Douglas Cooper, 22 Jan. 1954: Getty Research Institute for the History of Art and Humanities, Resource Collection, Douglas Cooper Papers, 860161, Box 5.
9 Denis Mahon to Douglas Cooper, 22 Jan. 1954: Getty Research Institute for the History of Art and Humanities, Douglas Cooper Papers, 860161, Box 7.
10 *Sunday Express*, 31 Jan. 1954; quoted BDHN, p.313.
11 Dennis Proctor, 'Brave Day, Hideous Night: Some Comments by the Then Chairman of the Trustees: TGA, Proctor Papers.
12 A taste of this letter can be obtained from the following:'To do anything like justice to the situation we should have to tell John Rothenstein that we don't think he told the truth about the *Courtauld infringements*; that the misuse of the Kerr fund was most culpable and the laxity with the *Knapping* a matter for serious blame; that the reference at the beginning of his apology, to *Reid as the officer responsible for allocations to funds* bears an implication that we prefer to forget; that the most elementary *records* have been revealed to be in a state which no process of reorganisation can excuse; that to perpetuate such records in a printed catalogue argues a grave unawareness of a Director's fundamental responsibility; that we find the *temporary labels* under his direction deficient and the *permanent ones* haphazard; that his behaviour in connection with *K. Clark's trusteeship*, even overlooking any evidence from sources now open to doubt, was dishonourable and damaging both to Gallery and Board; that the negotiations for the '*Little Dancer*' were, at the very least, grossly incompetent; that his actions to his staff must never again lend colour … to the impression that he disciplines them with the threat of actions for slander … that *Zsa Zsa Gabor* remains unmentioned rather than forgotten by those who have the dignity of the Gallery at heart; that an intelligent ear to the views of his staff … might prevent him again finding himself in a position so dubious as he was in connection with the *Publications Department's tradings in rationed paper*; … and that he must on no account promote his next recruit over the *head of a man* whom he has better cause to thank than he is likely to know.' (emphasis in italics Proctor's own): TGA: Proctor Papers.
13 BDHN, p.373.
14 See note 7.
15 Later, after Beaverbrook himself had experience as an employer of LeRoux, he went out of his way to make amends, obtaining for Rothenstein an honorary degree at Fredericton, New Brunswick, and himself paying for Rothenstein's airfare to Canada.
16 See note 11.
17 See note 7.

10

An Independent Tate

1 A description of how this painting was bought can be found in a letter from Dennis Proctor to Douglas Cooper, 25 May 1957: Getty Research Institute for the History of Art and Humanities, 860161, Box 7: 'My absolute outside limit was 6700 gns. which I gave to Alec Martin only ten minutes before the auction began.' Patrick Lindsay, his letter continues, was bidding for an American client and had bid 6,500 gns. 'Alec Martin, seeing that he would be left without his last bid if he merely raised it by 100, raised it by 200 and bid 6,700, at which it was knocked down. Patrick Lindsay thought it was his the bidding had gone very rapidly and he evidently fluffed the fact that Alec Martin had skipped a step with his last bid – but Alec Martin claimed it for the Gallery. He told me it was the auctioneer's right to do this if there are two disputed bids and one of them is the Auctioneer's – ie. in such a case the Auctioneer's bid overrides a bid from the floor – but if both of the bids have been from the floor, he would have had to call on one of them to go further. In other words, Alec Martin did a bit of a coup to get the picture for us in a way no one else could have done.'

2 Bryan Robertson, speaking at the memorial party for Sir John Rothenstein, held at the Tate Gallery, 8 June 1992.

3 John Richardson to Anthony Lousada, 15 Oct. 1957: TGA Proctor Papers.

4 Dennis Proctor to Douglas Cooper, 25 May 1957: Getty Research Institute for the History of Art and Humanities, 860161, Box 7.

5 A further instance of which is the £100,000 Sir Robert Adeane gave to the Fitzwilliam Museum, Cambridge, to be directed towards the building of a new wing.

6 See note 4.

7 Speaking at Sir John Rothenstein's memorial party.

8 Sir John Rothenstein to Dennis Proctor, 26 March 1954: TGA Proctor Papers.

9 Sir Colin Anderson, Report, quoted in Dennis Proctor's unpublished memoir, 'The Tate Gallery Troubles': TGA Proctor Papers.

10 Norman Reid to Richard L.York, copy, [1970]: TGA 260.43.

11 See Stefan Slabczynski, 'The large vacuum hot-table for wax-relining of paintings in the Conservation department of the Tate Gallery', Studies in Conservation, vol.5, 1960, pp.1–5.

12 'Chief Restorer's Report on his Visit to the Conservation Departments on the Continent. June 1957', typescript: Tate Gallery Conservation Department Archives.

13 Ibid.

14 Oldham Evening Chronicle, 18 March 1975

15 Sir John Rothenstein's tribute appears in the Director's Report in the minutes of the Trustees' Board meeting, 19 June 1958.

16 Lionel Robbins to Douglas Cooper, 10 Oct. 1957: Getty Research Institute for the History of Art and Humanities, 860161, Box 2.

17 See minutes of the Trustees' Board meeting, 16 May 1957.

18 Recollected by Sir Norman Reid, in a tape-recorded conversation with Corinne Bellow: TGA, TAV 944A.

19 John Rothenstein, Time's Thievish Progress: Autobiography III, Cassell, 1970, p.148.

20 Alexander Dunluce, in a tape-recorded conversation with Corinne Bellow: TGA, TAV 968A.

21 Sir Lawrence Gowing, in a tape-recorded conversation with Corinne Bellow: TGA, TAV 624A.

22 Time's Thievish Progress, p.157.

23 In the third volume of his autobiography, Rothenstein argued that the abstract work of artists such as Mondrian, Kandinsky, Nicholson and Hepworth represented a 'total break with the European tradition based upon the phenomenal world'. Further on he adds: 'The influence of abstraction has been to sever the link between the artist and the phenomenal world, and I believe that the severance is disastrous in its disintegrating effects.' Time's Thievish Progress, pp.227, 229.

24 Earlier, however, neither Rothenstein nor his Trustees had shown any interest in Francis Bacon's Figure Study II, bought by the Contemporary Art Society in 1949. It sat in the Tate Gallery basement until 1952 when the curator of Batley Art Gallery, Mr Gelsthorpe, claimed it.

25 Time's Thievish Progress, p.160.

26 The Earl of Crawford and Balcarres to Sir Colin Anderson, n.d. [Oct. 1964]: Mrs Catriona Williams.

27 Time's Thievish Progress, p.160.

11

Whaam!

1 Sir Anthony Lousada, 'The Tate Gallery', unpublished memoir: TGA.

2 Sir Dennis Proctor, 'Postscript on the Tate', unpublished memoir: TGA, Proctor Papers.

3 Lawrence Gowing to Sir Colin Anderson, 30 Nov. 1961: Mrs Catriona Williams.

4 Procter quotes from the reference that he wrote for Reid in his memoir (see note 2). It also provides a major source for the period leading up to Reid's appointment. I am also grateful to Sir Alan Bowness for information on his involvement with Gowing on the '54–'64 Gulbenkian exhibition. According to David Sylvester, another factor in Gowing's non-appointment was his stutter, which one influential Trustee felt was a serious impediment to his taking public office.

5 30 July 1964.

6 Lawrence Gowing, in a tape-recorded conversation with Corinne Bellow: TGA, TAV 624A.

7 Nevile Wallis in the Spectator, 7 Aug. 1964, TGA.

8 BDHN, p.220.

9 Observer, 9 Oct. 1966.

10 Recollected by Sir Norman Reid in conversation with the author, 21 May 1996.

11 Sir Colin Anderson to Sir Dennis Proctor, 15 March 1965, copy: Mrs Catriona Williams.

12 Tate Gallery Report 1965–66, 1967.

13 The Times, 21 Feb. 1967.

14 See note 1. Lousada's recollection of this incident exaggerated the length of time that Pasmore remained absent.

15 Notably in the pages of the Sunday Times after its Colour Section carried a reproduction of the Matisse on its cover on 14 October 1962 and The Snail went on show in the Sculpture Hall the next day.

16 As the Friends of the Tate Gallery put up £10,000 to cover the cost of the Giacomettis, the labels on all these works credit the Friends, but not the artist's

generosity in offering them at half what the Tate was prepared to pay.

17 Peggy Guggenheim, *Out of this Century: Confessions of an Art Addict*, André Deutsch 1979, p.369.

18 As recalled by Sir Norman Reid in notes for the author.

19 As reported in the *Guardian*, 27 Oct. 1971.

20 *Studio International*, March 1971, pp.92–3.

21 See note 10.

22 See note 18.

the Director, Alan Bowness, persuaded the Trustees to accept it.

13 Sir Norman Reid, in a tape-recorded conversation with Corinne Bellow: TGA, TAV 944A.

14 The title given here for the Sol LeWitt is as reported in the minutes of the Trustees' Board meeting, 19 July 1973. In the *Concise Catalogue of the Tate Gallery*, 1991 ed., it is listed as *A Wall Divided Vertically into Fifteen Equal Parts, Each with a Different Line Direction and Colour, and All Combinations*.

12
The Fourth Quarter

1 *The Times*, 31 Jan. 1966.

2 *The Times*, 1 Feb. 1966.

3 *Art and Artists*, Jan. 1970.

4 As recalled by Sir Anthony Lousada in a tape-recorded conversation with Corinne Bellow: TGA, TAV 621A.

5 Quoted in *Mark Rothko 1903–1970*, exh. cat., Tate Gallery 1987, p.86.

6 Ibid., p.58.

7 In 1987, when the Tate Gallery mounted a Rothko exhibition, the Rothko Foundation gave three more important examples of his work to the Gallery, as well as financial support for the catalogue. In addition to being shown in London, Rothko's original gift has also been shown at Tate Gallery Liverpool, and in 1996 three Rothkos were exhibited at Tate Gallery St Ives, where they formed the centrepiece of the *Mark Rothko in Cornwall* exhibition.

8 *Daily Telegraph*, 12 Nov. 1968.

9 *The Times*, 26 May 1967.

10 *The Times*, 27 May 1967.

11 *The Times*, 1 June 1967.

12 Recalled by Sir Robert Sainsbury in a tape-recorded conversation with Corinne Bellow: TGA, TAV 621A.

13 *The Times*, 1 July 1969.

13
The Fierce Light of Publicity

1 *Listener*, 23 Nov. 1950.

2 Pat Gilmour refers to this in a tape-recorded conversation with Corinne Bellow: TGA, TAV 1575A.

3 Discussion of exhibition policy forms a part of Michael Compton's tape-recorded conversation with Corinne Bellow: TGA, TAV 945A.

4 *Sunday Times*, 15 March 1970. The reference is to Eckermann's *Conversations with Goethe*.

5 *New Statesman*, 4 Dec. 1970.

6 *Guardian*, 17 Feb. 1971.

7 *Evening Standard*, 30 April 1971.

8 *New York Times*, 23 May 1971.

9 Mentioned by Corinne Bellow, in her tape-recorded conversation with Laurence Bradbury: TGA, TAV 979A.

10 *Guardian*, 28 Feb. 1972.

11 Sir Norman Reid, 'Note for the Chairman by the Director': TGA Beuys File, PC10/1/296, Pt 1.

12 *Fat Battery* was later offered by E.J. Power through the Friends of the Tate Gallery as a gift in 1984, and

---

14
Brickbats and Bouquets

1 See Robert Hewison, *Culture and Consensus: England, Art and Politics since 1940*, Methuen 1995, p.xiv, for the argument 'culture … is the shaping, moral medium for all society's activities, including the economic'.

2 'Letter from London', *New Yorker*, 20 Feb. 1976.

3 The fundamental error in Cooper's criticism of the Boccioni sculpture was his assumption that the Tate cast had been made from an existing bronze, whereas it had been cast from the original plaster with Madame Boccioni's permission. After Cooper queried the authenticity and legality of the sculpture, Lord Bullock, in a letter to *Books and Bookmen* (Aug. 1976), pointed out that the shrinkage which Cooper had observed had occurred in the casting and was consistent with the technique of surmoulage; that the Tate was not encouraging 'the pirating of established works' and that the legal casting rights were not exhausted in 1952 when the work was sold by Marinetti's widow to Matarazzo Sobrinho.

4 *Sunday Times*, 15 Feb. 1976.

5 *Daily Mirror*, 16 Feb. 1976.

6 *Daily Mail*, 17 Feb. 1976.

7 *The Times*, 18 Feb. 1976.

8 *Daily Telegraph*, 18 Feb. 1976.

9 'Editorial', *Burlington Magazine*, vol.118, April 1976, p.187. Ronald Alley had drafted a press release concerning 'The Bricks' in response to the public outcry, but Reid vetoed it, on the grounds that the fuss would soon blow over.

10 *New York Times*, 20 Feb. 1976.

11 'He [the Chairman] felt that by amassing the anti-Tate material in this way it further promoted antagonism and gave little chance for the serious article to be read sympathetically.' Minutes of the Trustees' Board meeting, 17 Feb. 1977.

12 *Times Educational Supplement*, 18 April 1975

13 *Tate Gallery 1974–76: Illustrated Biennial Report and Catalogue*, 1976, p.12. The fuller description of this picture found in this Report is now thought almost certainly to be wrong, and that given in the Catalogue of Acquisitions for 1974–76 more likely to be correct. It is there concluded that the seated woman holding an infant is likely to be, not a maid, but the second wife.

14 Quoted in the Minutes of the Trustees' Board meeting, 20 April 1967.

15 Minutes of the Trustees' Board meeting, 15 March 1973.

16 Minutes of the Trustees' Board meeting, 20 Oct. 1977.

17 See minutes of the Trustees' Board meeting, 19 July 1979.

18 John Pope-Henessy's remark was recalled by Andrew Wilson in conversation with the author, 12 Dec. 1996.

19 Sir Hugh Casson, quoted in the *Economist*, 5 Nov. 1977.

20 Minutes of the Trustees' Board meeting, 21 Oct. 1977.

21 Ibid.

22 *Evening News*, 20 Dec. 1977.

23 Recollected by Sir Norman Reid in conversation with the author, 21 May 1996.

24 *Observer*, 4 March 1979.

25 For instance, Hockney had berated the Tate for not buying Edward Hopper's *Hotel Room* which, Reid explained, had been turned down not for lack of money or will, but because of an adverse report on its condition. Reid also rebutted Hockney's claim that the Tate had been offered his *A Bigger Splash* for £400 in 1968, by saying that as far as he knew it had always belonged to Lord Dufferin. Hockney here seems to have been confusing *A Bigger Splash* with an earlier painting, then titled *Picture of a Hollywood Swimming-Pool*, offered by Kasmin in 1965 for £300, which the Tate turned down. The Tate did, however,try to acquire *A Bigger Splash* from Lord Dufferin in 1977 but he did not then wish to sell. It was finally acquired by the Tate in 1981.

26 *Observer*, 11 March 1979. Reid's final sentence – 'It helps to have an amiable and loyal wife (as I have had) and, need I say it, a certain understanding, and sympathy even, for what makes artists behave as they do' – was interpreted as a slur on Hockney's homosexuality. However, Reid had originally used the word 'companion and only changed it to 'wife' at the newspaper's suggestion, for the sake of clarity.

27 *New Statesman*, 22 June 1979.

28 Recollected by Sir Norman Reid, in a tape-recorded conversation with Corinne Bellow: TGA, TAV 944A.

29 Lawrence Gowing, 'The New Tate', *Encounter*, Aug. 1979, reprinted in *The Tate Gallery 1978–80: Illustrated Biennial Report*, pp.102–4.

15

Brinkmanship

1 The following were shortlisted: Alan Bowness, Michael Compton, Joanna Drew, Dennis Farr, John Hayes, Norbert Lynton and Kynaston Shine.

2 In 1955 Bowness, told that he was not civil service material, lost out to his contemporary at the Courtauld Institute of Art, Martin Butlin, for the post of Assistant Keeper. He applied again in 1964, at the time of Rothenstein's retirement, and was thought to be too young for the post of Director. His third application was in 1965 for the Keepership of the Modern Collection, which went to Ronald Alley.

3 Minutes of the Trustees' Board meeting, 16 Nov. 1978.

4 Alan Bowness, 'Covering Note for the Trustees', 7 Jan. 1980: TGA.

5 Minutes of the Trustees' Board meeting, 19 May 1983.

6 Ibid.

7 Minutes of the Trustees' Board meeting, 21 Jan. 1983.

8 Recollected by Corinne Bellow in some memoir notes on sponsorship at the Tate: Corinne Bellow.

9 For further details of Hans Haacke's critique of Mobil, together with a reference to the Tate exhibition, see *Hans Haacke: Unfinished Business*, The New Museum of Contemporary Art, New Yor and MIT Press, Cambridge, Mass., .1986, pp.272–7.

10 The speakers were James Joll from Pearson's,

Timothy Clifford, Director of the National Galleries of Scotland, and Waldemar Januszczak. A transcript of the debate was afterwards published by the Tate, edited by David Coombs, editor of *Antique Collector*.

11 An account of Peter Palumbo's paper, together with the Director's reply, can be found in the minutes of the Trustees' Board meeting, 16 July 1981.

12 *Sunday Times*, 29 April 1984.

13 Peter Palumbo, in a tape-recorded conversation with Corinne Bellow: TGA, TAV 1242.

14 Patrick Heron in conversation with the author, 4 March 1997.

15 *Sunday Times*, 29 April 1984.

16 Alternative funds had to be found for the refurbishment of the Restaurant and it was paid for by an unexpected bequest from an American, Carroll Donner, a regular summer visitor to the Tate. The bequest was also used to acquire works by Cecil Collins and Winifred Nicholson, two artists she admired.

17 John Golding mentions this in his tape-recorded conversation with Corinne Bellow: TGA, TAV 1576.

16

Tate in the North

1 Richard Rogers, from a document connected with his entry in the Beaubourg competition.

2 A summary of the Woodstock conference was reported in the minutes of the Trustees' Board meeting, 21 Feb. 1985.

3 Minutes of the Trustees' Board meeting, 19 Dec. 1968.

4 Minutes of the Trustees' Board meeting, 21 June 1973. Probably the first person to associate the concept of an outstation with Liverpool was Herbert Thearle, who wrote to the *Sunday Times* (21 July 1969) arguing that if three-quarters of the Tate's holdings were out of sight, then the dispersal of the collection to the provinces should be considered. He concluded: 'In this event, Liverpool should be at the head of the queue; Sir Henry Tate … was a Merseyside "sugar boiler", beginning with grocer shops on both sides of the river here.'

5 The future of the Walker Art Gallery after the abolition of the Merseyside County Council was resolved by the creation of the National Museums and Galleries on Merseyside.

6 For a detailed account of the pre-history of the Clore see Robin Hamlyn's essay, 'The Clore Project: The Shaping of a Gallery', in Robin Hamlyn (ed.), *The Clore Gallery: An Illustrated Account of the New Building for the Turner Collection*, Tate Gallery 1987.

7 James Stirling, interviewed by Charles Jencks in *The Clore Gallery: An Illustrated Account*, p.53.

8 Minutes of the Trustees' Board meeting, 20 July 1985.

9 Minutes of the Trustees' Board meeting, 16 July 1987.

10 *Tate Gallery Biennial Report 1984–86*, 1986, p.28.

11 Alan Bowness to Lord Goodman, 12 June 1986: TGA 55/6.

12 *Guardian*, 30 May 1984. Januszczak's praise of Bowness's buying policy was in response to Palumbo's criticism that the Tate had been buying too much 'fashionable' art.

13 Patrick Heron, in conversation with the author, ran through the salient points concerning the Matisse

project. Further details can be found in Heron's tape-recorded conversation with Corinne Bellow (TGA, TAV 1517A) and in Michael McNay's 'How the Tate Missed Matisse', *Guardian Review*, 14 March 1991.

13 Nicholas Serota, 'The Dilemmas Facing the Tate: The Director's Reply', *Apollo*, June 1992, pp.393–4.

14 David Sylvester, *About Modern Art: Critical Essays, 1948–96*, Chatto & Windus, 1996, p.394.

17

Past, Present and Future

1 *Sunday Times Magazine*, 3 Jan. 1988.

2 Following an interview Serota gave to Andrew Graham-Dixon in the *Independent*, Lord Hutchison wrote a letter to the newspaper protesting about remarks in the article, and ending with a rare outburst. Serota's success as Director, he argued, 'will depend upon the long-delayed decision by the Government as to which millionaire, tycoon or Tory bigwig will be appointed as his chairman' (*Independent*, 16 Sept. 1988). This comment was picked up by Robin Stringer (*Evening Standard*, 6 Oct. 1988) in an article, 'Trawling for the Right Faces', which looked at recent government appointments to the boards of art institutions. It was observed that national galleries and museums were increasingly becoming arms of government, at the same time that government policy was to run down central support for the arts, while encouraging increased private support.

3 Information on the background to Dennis Stevenson's appointment was supplied by Stevenson in conversation with the author (29 April 1997) and by Nicholas Serota.

4 Recollected by Francis Carnwath in a tape-recorded conversation with Corinne Bellow: TGA (not yet catalogued).

5 The need for a single team to deal with all aspects of fundraising had first been mooted by Serota in his seven-year plan 'Grasping the Nettle'. He was unaware at the time of writing this proposal that Stevenson's report, 'The Relationship between the Tate Trustees and the Director', had concluded that fundraising should not be left as a part-time initiative on the part of certain Trustees, but was a matter for full-time executive action.

6 *Guardian*, 14 March 1971.

7 *World Link*, Nov. 1988.

8 *New York Times*, 25 Feb. 1990.

9 *Guardian*, 22 Jan. 1990.

10 *Observer*, 21 Jan. 1990.

11 *Evening Standard*, 18 Feb. 1993. This article, titled "Miserable Sum of the Tate Parts', was the first in which Sewell advised British Petroleum to withdraw their sponsorship of the annual *New Displays*. He was criticised for his remarks by Richard Dorment in the *Daily Telegraph* (26 Feb. 1993), but Sewell merely reiterated his criticisms in his reply (*Daily Telegraph*, 2 March 1993). In the *Evening Standard* (2 Sept. 1993) he again urged BP to apply their shareholders' funds to better purpose elsewhere. After complaints from the Tate Chairman and Director to the Editor, the *Evening Standard* published, on 7 Sept. 1993, both a letter from Serota and an article by Robin Stringer, praising BP's sponsorship and arguing that business and art need each other.

12 Robin Simon, 'The War between the Tate: The Fate of the Historic British Collection', *Apollo*, June 1992, pp.207–8.

18

From Gas Works to Power Station

1 Quoted in Janet Axton, *Gasworks to Gallery: The Story of Tate St Ives*, privately published by the author and Colin Orchard, 1995, p.109.

2 Quoted ibid., p.111.

3 Ibid., p.109.

4 For a fuller account of the significance of STAG, see ibid., pp.131–48.

5 Quoted ibid., p.207.

6 The press announcement, released 15 Dec. 1992, was headed 'Tate Gallery announces plans for the Millennium and first steps in their implementation.'

7 Gainsborough's *Peter Darnal Muilman, Charles Crokatt and William Keable (The Muilman Group)*, was purchased jointly by the Tate Gallery and Gainsborough's House from the Edward Janes Foundation in 1979 for £235,000.

8 *Guardian*, 2 Nov. 1993.

9 *Independent*, 5 Nov. 1993.

10 *Independent*, 10 Nov. 1993.

11 Writing in the *Guardian*, 9 Nov. 1993.

12 Deyan Sudjic, Rowan Moore and Clare Melhuish, *Tate Gallery of Modern Art: Selecting an Architect*, Blueprint 1995, p.5.

13 *Observer*, 3 Dec. 1995.

Tate Gallery Exhibitions

Exhibitions are listed chronologically by date of opening.

When an exhibition was organised by another institution, this is given in square brackets.

AC = Arts Council; BC = British Council; CAS = Contemporary Art Society; CEMA = Council for the Encouragement of Music and the Arts; NG = National Gallery, London; RA = Royal Academy; TG = Tate Gallery; V&A = Victoria & Albert Museum

1911
Loan collection of works by Alfred Stevens
Works by English Pre-Raphaelite painters lent by the Art Gallery Committee of the Birmingham Corporation

1912
Loan collection of works by Alphonse Legros
Loan collection of works by James McNeill Whistler

1913
Loan exhibition of works by Pre-Raphaelite painters from collections in Lancashire
Loan exhibition of works by William Blake

1915
Cartoons, paintings and drawings by Alfred Stevens for the decoration of the dining room at Dorchester House, lent by Sir George Holford and Mr Alfred Drury

1921
Loan exhibition of works of J.D. Innes, 1887–1914
Exhibition of the 'Liber Studiorum' by Turner: drawings, etchings and first state mezzotint engravings with some additional engravers' proofs and 51 of the original copperplates

1922
Cotman exhibition: exhibition of works by John Sell Cotman and some related painters of the Norwich School, Miles Edmund Cotman, John Joseph Cotman, John Thirtle

1923
Exhibition of earlier British water-colours lent by the Whitworth Institute, Manchester
Book illustration of the Sixties
Loan exhibition of paintings and drawings of the 1860 period
Loan exhibition of drawings by Aubrey Beardsley, 1872–1898

1924
Loan exhibition of the Burrell Collection

1925
Loan exhibition of works by Richard Wilson

1926
Opening exhibition of the Modern Foreign Gallery
Opening exhibition of the Sargent Gallery

1927
Exhibition of sculpture, sketches and fragments of monuments executed in cities in Sweden by Carl Milles
Loan exhibition of works by Charles Conder, 1868–1909
Rowlandson centenary exhibition, and British drawings 1750–1850

1929
East London Art Club: works selected by Sir Joseph Duveen from an exhibition held at the Whitechapel Gallery, Dec. 8–22 1928
Loan exhibition of works by P. Wilson Steer

1930
Exhibition of Jugoslav sculpture and painting. *Under the auspices of the Jugoslav Society of Great Britain and the Friends of Great Britain in Jugoslavia*
Exhibition of paintings of scenes of Gaucho life in the Province of Entre Rios by C. Bernaldo de Quirós
Exhibition of oil paintings by Camille Pissarro, 1830–1903
Exhibition of Turner's early oil paintings, 1796–1815

1932
Loan exhibition of works by George Chinnery, R.H.A., 1774–1852
Memorial exhibition of drawings in water-colour by Professor W.R. Lethaby, 1857–1931

1933
Centenary exhibition of paintings and drawings by Sir Edward Burne-Jones, 1833–1898

1934
An exhibition of cricket pictures from the collection of Sir Jeremiah Colman
Sporting pictures at the Tate Gallery from the collection of Mr H. Arthurton

1935
Centenary exhibition of paintings and water-colours by William McTaggart, R.S.A., 1835–1910
An exhibition of paintings by Joanna Mary Boyce [Mrs. H.T. Wells], 1831–1861

An exhibition of sculpture by Paul Manship
Silver Jubilee exhibition of some of the works acquired by the Contemporary Art Society, 1910–1935
Loan collection of paintings, drawings and engravings by contemporary British artists, recently exhibited in New Zealand and Australia under the auspices of the Empire Art Loan Collections Society

1936
Exhibition of works by Professor Henry Tonks

1937
Centenary exhibition of paintings and water-colours by John Constable, R.A., 1776–1837

1938
Exhibition of paintings and sculpture by the late Glyn Philpot, R.A., 1884–1937
A century of Canadian art [National Gallery of Canada]

1939
Mural painting in Great Britain, 1919–1939: an exhibition of photographs

1941
Walter Richard Sickert [TG in conjunction with NG]. *Held at NG*

1942
The Tate Gallery's wartime acquisitions. *Held at NG*
A selection from the Tate Gallery's wartime acquisitions [CEMA]. *Touring to 12 British venues*

1943
Memorial exhibition of the work of Philip Wilson Steer, O.M., 1860–1942. *Held at NG. Selection toured by CEMA 1943–4*

1944
Two centuries of British drawings from the Tate Gallery [CEMA]. *Touring to 12 regional venues*
British narrative paintings from the Tate Gallery, from the Regency to the 20th century [CEMA]. *Touring exhibition*
The Tate Gallery's wartime acquisitions: second exhibition [CEMA]. *Touring to 9 regional venues*

1945
A selection from the Tate Gallery's pre-war collection
Paul Klee 1879–1940 [TG]. *Held at NG then toured by AC*

1946

Tate Gallery continental exhibition: modern British pictures from the Tate Gallery. Exhibited under the auspices of BC. *Touring to 9 European venues (later shown at TG, 1947, and toured in British provinces by AC 1947–8)*

The works of James Ensor [AC]. *Held under the auspices of TG and NG, in rooms in NG allocated to TG*

Braque and Rouault [BC, La Direction générale des rélations culturelles and L'Association française d'action artistique]

Paul Cézanne: an exhibition of watercolours [AC]

A collection of contemporary English painting

American painting, from the eighteenth century to the present day [National Gallery of Art, Washington]

The Contemporary Arts Society: an exhibition of a selection of acquisitions of the Contemporary Art Society, from its foundation in 1910 up to the present day

Drawings and paintings by Alexander Cozens. *Previously at Graves Art Gallery, Sheffield*

1947

Tate Gallery 1897–1947: pictures from the Tate Gallery Foundation Gift and exhibition of subsequent British painting

Modern British pictures from the Tate Gallery [AC]. *Subsequent to 1946–7 continental tour and the showing at the TG. Toured to 12 British venues*

William Blake, 1757–1827 [BC]. *Previously in Paris, Antwerp and Zurich*

Hogarth–Constable–Turner [NG, V&A and TG for the Art Institute of Chicago. *Previously shown in venues in USA and Canada*

Vincent Van Gogh, 1853–1890: an exhibition of paintings and drawings [AC]

J.M.W. Turner, 1775–1851: exhibition of paintings [TG and BC]. *Touring to 6 European venues*

1948

Marc Chagall: an exhibition of paintings, prints, book illustrations and theatre designs, 1908–1947 [AC]

Paul Nash 1889–1946: memorial exhibition: paintings, watercolours and drawings [AC and TG]

Westminster regained [Architectural Review]

Samuel Courtauld memorial exhibition [TG and Courtauld Institute]

Pictures for schools: S.E.A. exhibition [Society for Education in Art with the support of AC]

An exhibition of paintings by Jack B Yeats [AC]

Contemporary South African paintings, drawings and sculpture [South African Association of Arts for the Union Government]

Pre-Raphaelite Brotherhood, 1848–1948: a centenary exhibition

David, 1748–1825: an exhibition of paintings and drawings [AC by courtesy of the French Government]

1949

An exhibition of pictures by Richard Wilson and his circle [City Museum and Art Gallery, Birmingham]

Art treasures from Vienna [AC]

A memorial exhibition of works by James Pryde 1866–1941 [AC]. *Previously in Brighton*

1950

Fernand Léger: an exhibition of paintings, drawings, lithographs and book illustration [AC and L'Association française d'action artistique]

The Index of American Design [National Gallery of Art, Washington]

The private collector: an exhibition of pictures and sculpture selected from the members of the Contemporary Art Society's own collections [CAS]

Sir William Rothenstein, 1872–1945: memorial exhibition. *Subsequently toured by AC*

Modern Italian art: an exhibition of paintings and sculpture [AC]. *Held under the auspices of the Amici di Brera and the Italian Institute*

D.S. MacColl memorial exhibition

1951

Edward Wadsworth 1889–1945: memorial exhibition

Exhibition of the Eton leaving portraits

Sculpture and drawings by Henry Moore [AC on the occasion of Festival of Britain 1951]

The Turner Collection from Petworth House

William Hogarth, 1697–1764 [AC on the occasion of Festival of Britain 1951]

An exhibition of theatrical pictures from the Garrick Club

William Dobson, 1611–1646: an exhibition of paintings [AC]

Edvard Munch: an exhibition of paintings, etchings lithographs [AC]

1952

Seventeen collectors: an exhibition of paintings and sculpture from the private collections of members of the Executive Committee of the Contemporary Art Society [CAS]

Slade School: past students: an exhibition of paintings owned by the Slade School

Ethel Walker–Frances Hodgkins–Gwen John: a memorial exhibition [AC and TG]

XXth century masterpieces: an exhibition of paintings and sculpture [Congress for Cultural Freedom and AC]. *Previously in Paris*

Degas [Sponsored by the Edinburgh Festival Society and arranged jointly with the Royal Scottish Academy and AC]. *Previously in Edinburgh*

Epstein [AC]

1953

An exhibition of the sculpture of Matisse and 3 paintings with studies [AC for Exhibition

of Mexican Art from Pre-Columbian times to the present day] [under auspices of the Mexican Government, by AC]

International sculpture competition: The Unknown Political Prisoner

An exhibition of paintings and drawings by Graham Sutherland [AC and TG]

Thomas Gainsborough, 1727–1788: an exhibition of paintings [AC and TG]

Matthew Smith: paintings from 1909 to 1952

National Art-Collections Fund: fiftieth anniversary, 1953

Renoir. *Sponsored by the Edinburgh Festival Society and arranged jointly with the Arts Council of Great Britain; selected from larger exhibition previously shown in Edinburgh*

Yugoslav medieval frescoes (replicas) [AC]

Figures in their setting, painted at the invitation of the Contemporary Art Society

1954

Raoul Dufy: an exhibition of paintings and drawings [AC and Association française d'action artistique]

Charles Ginner, 1878–1952: exhibition of paintings and drawings [AC]

The Pleydell-Bouverie Collection of Impressionist and other paintings lent by the Hon. Mrs. A.E. Pleydell-Bouverie

Manet and his circle: paintings from the Louvre [AC and l'Association française d'action artistique]

Masterpieces from the São Paulo Museum of Art [AC]

An exhibition of paintings by Cézanne. *Sponsored by Edinburgh Festival Society and arranged jointly with the Royal Scottish Academy and the AC. Previously in Edinburgh*

George Frederic Watts, O.M., R.A. 1817–1904 [AC]

David Jones: an exhibition of paintings, drawings and engravings [Welsh Committee of the Arts Council]. *Previously in four British venues*

George Morland: an exhibition of paintings and drawings [AC]

1955

Harold Gilman, 1876–1919 [AC]

Works by Paul Klee from the collection of Mrs Edward Hulton

Ben Nicholson: a retrospective exhibition. *Selected from BC touring exhibition at Venice Biennale; travelling to four European venues*

Four French Realists: André Minaux, Ginette Rapp, Roger Montané, Jean Vinay [AC]

An exhibition of paintings, engravings and sculpture by Paul Gauguin [AC and Edinburgh Festival Society]. *Previously in Edinburgh*

Stanley Spencer: a retrospective exhibition

1956

Modern Art in the United States: a selection from the collections of the Museum of Modern Art, New York [Museum of Modern Art, New York, and AC]

The Seasons: an exhibition of paintings and sculpture organised by the Contemporary Art Society

Hundred years of German painting, 1850–1950 [Government of the German Federal Republic]

Wyndham Lewis and Vorticism

Autour du Cubisme: an exhibition of paintings lent by the Musée d'art moderne, Paris [AC]

G. Braque: an exhibition of paintings [AC and Edinburgh Festival Society]. *Previously in Edinburgh*

Modern Italian art from the Estorick Collection [AC and Italian Institute, London]

1957

An exhibition of paintings from the Solomon R. Guggenheim Museum [AC]

An exhibition of works by Wilhelm Lehmbruck, 1881–1919: sculpture, paintings, drawings, etchings [AC]

British painting in the Eighteenth Century [BC]. *Subsequently touring to Montreal, Ottawa, Toronto and Toledo*

A selection of pictures, drawings and sculpture from the collections of Sir Edward and Lady Hulton

Claude Monet: an exhibition of paintings [AC and Edinburgh Festival Society]. *Previously in Edinburgh*

Constant Permeke: paintings and drawings [AC]

William Blake bicentenary: the Gallery's entire collection of works by William Blake

Art books: an exhibition of current books on painting, drawing, sculpture and prints [National Book League]

1958

Paintings by Kandinsky from the Solomon R. Guggenheim Museum, New York [AC]

Joseph Wright of Derby, 1734–1797: an exhibition of paintings and drawings [AC]. *Touring to Liverpool*

The Niarchos Collection: an exhibition of paintings and sculpture [AC]

The religious theme: an exhibition of painting and sculpture organised by the Contemporary Art Society

The Moltzau Collection: from Cézanne to Picasso

Paintings from the Urvater Collection [AC]. *Previously in Leicester and York*

Touring exhibition: watercolours of the 20th century from the collection of the V&A and the Tate Gallery (1958) [V&A and TG]. *Not shown at TG*

1959

Evie Hone, 1894–1955 [AC]. *Shown at TG and at AC Gallery*

Lovis Corinth: an exhibition of paintings [AC]

The new American painting [Museum of Modern Art, New York, and AC]

Francis Gruber, 1912–1948 [AC]

Duncan Grant: a retrospective exhibition

The Romantic Movement: fifth exhibition to celebrate the tenth anniversary of the Council of Europe [AC]. *Shown at TG and AC Gallery*

From Hodler to Klee: Swiss art of the Twentieth Century: painting and sculpture [AC and Prohelvetia Foundation, Switzerland]

Sculpture by Jacques Lipchitz [AC]

1960

James Ward, 1769–1859 [AC]

Contemporary Art Society 50th anniversary exhibition: the first fifty years 1910–1960: an exhibition of a selection of works given by the Contemporary Art Society to public galleries [CAS]

Sickert: paintings and drawings [AC]. *Touring to Southampton and Bradford*

Picasso [AC]

The Blue Rider Group [AC and Edinburgh Festival Society]. *Previously in Edinburgh*

Giacomo Manzú: sculpture and drawings [AC]

P. Wilson Steer, 1860–1942 [AC]

The John Hay Whitney Collection

1961

Zadkine [AC]. *Touring to Newcastle-upon-Tyne and Bristol*

Toulouse-Lautrec, 1864–1901 [Association française d'action artistique and AC]

Contemporary Yugoslav painting and sculpture [AC]

Daumier: paintings and drawings [AC]

Max Ernst [AC]

Epstein [AC]

1962

Modern Spanish painting [AC and Directorate General of Cultural Relations, Madrid]

Sonja Henie-Niels Onstad Collection [AC]

Ecole de Paris [AC]

Francis Bacon

Alexander Calder: sculpture, mobiles [AC]

Kokoschka: a retrospective exhibition of paintings, drawings, lithographs, stage designs and books [AC]

Jean Arp: sculpture, reliefs, paintings, collages, tapestries [AC]

1963

Australian painting: Colonial, Impressionist, Contemporary [Commonwealth Art Advisory Board]. *Previously shown in Australia, and travelling to Ottawa*

John Opie 1761–1807 [AC]. *Previously shown in 5 regional venues*

Private views: works from the collections of twenty Friends of the Tate Gallery [Friends of the Tate Gallery]

British painting in the Sixties [CAS]. *Section 1 in TG, section 2 in Whitechapel Art Gallery*

Ivon Hitchens: a retrospective exhibition [AC]. *Touring to Bradford and Birmingham*

Modigliani [AC and Edinburgh Festival Society]. *Previously in Edinburgh*

Chaim Soutine, 1893–1943 [AC and Edinburgh Festival Society]. *Previously in Edinburgh*

Dunn International: an exhibition of contemporary painting sponsored by the Sir James Dunn Foundation [AC]. *Previously in Fredericton, New Brunswick*

Art books [National Book League]

1964

Canadian painting, 1939–1963 [National Gallery of Canada]

Painting and sculpture of a decade, '54–'64 [Calouste Gulbenkian Foundation]

London Group 1914–64: jubilee exhibition: fifty years of British art [London Group]

The illustrated books of William Blake [William Blake Trust]

Joan Miró [AC]. *Touring to Zurich*

Painters of the Brücke: Heckel, Kirchner, Mueller, Nolde, Pechstein, Schmidt-Rottluff [AC]

The Peggy Guggenheim Collection [AC]

1965

British sculpture in the sixties [CAS and Peter Stuyvesant Foundation]

Arshile Gorky: paintings and drawings [AC]

Victor Pasmore: retrospective exhibition 1925–65

Alberto Giacometti: sculptures, paintings, drawings 1913–65 [AC]

Max Beckmann, 1884–1950: paintings, drawings and graphic work [AC]

William Roberts ARA: retrospective exhibition [AC]. *Touring to Newcastle and Manchester*

1966

Gauguin and the Pont-Aven Group [AC]

Naum Gabo: constructions, paintings, drawings [AC]

Jean Dubuffet: paintings [AC]

The almost complete works of Marcel Duchamp [AC]

David Smith, 1906–1965 [AC]

Rouault: an exhibition of paintings, drawings and documents [AC and Edinburgh Festival Society]. *Previously in Edinburgh*

L.S.Lowry RA: retrospective exhibition [AC]. *Previously in 3 regional venues*

1967

Young Contemporaries at the Tate 1967: an art exhibition organised by students of the Royal Academy Schools, The Royal College of Art, and the Slade School of Fine Art. *Subsequently toured by AC*

David Bomberg, 1890–1957: paintings and drawings [AC]

Zoltan Kemeny, 1907–1965: an exhibition of relief sculptures and drawings [AC]

Marzotto Prize 1966–1967: European community contemporary painting exhibition: Metropolitan scene: images and objects. *Previously exhibited in Valdagno, Copenhagen, Amsterdam; touring to Paris*

Picasso: sculpture, ceramics, graphic work [AC]

Marcellus Laroon: an exhibition of paintings and drawings [Paul Mellon Foundation for British Art]. *Previously at Aldeburgh*

Cubist art from Czechoslovakia: an exhibition of painting and sculpture by Czech and French artists [AC]. *Previously in Paris*

Recent British painting: Peter Stuyvesant Foundation Collection

1968

Roy Lichtenstein. *Previously in Amsterdam; touring to Bern and Hanover*

Barbara Hepworth

Peter Lanyon [AC]. *Touring to 3 regional venues*

Alfred Wallis [AC]. *Touring to 3 British venues*

Henry Moore [AC]

Balthus: a retrospective exhibition [AC]

Art Books [National Book League]

John Crome, 1768–1821: an exhibition of paintings and drawings organised by the Arts Council to mark the bicentenary of the artist's birth. *Previously in Norwich*

Willem de Kooning [AC and Museum of Modern Art, New York]

1969

Plans and models for the extension to the Gallery

Magritte [AC]

The art of the real: an aspect of American painting and sculpture 1948–1968 [AC and Museum of Modern Art, New York]

Ben Nicholson

The Annenberg Collection

The Elizabethan Image: painting in England 1540–1620

1970

Endymion Porter and William Dobson

Sir Herbert Read Memorial Gift: display of works donated in memory of Sir Herbert Read by Henry Moore, Barbara Hepworth, Ben Nicholson and Naum Gabo

Richard Hamilton. *Touring to Eindhoven and Bern*

Larry Bell, Robert Irwin, Doug Wheeler

Claes Oldenburg [AC and Museum of Modern Art, New York]. *Previously in Amsterdam and Düsseldorf*

Julio González

British painting and sculpture 1960–1970 [TG and BC]. *Held at National Gallery of Art, Washington*

Léger and Purist Paris

1971

'Shock of Recognition': the landscape of English Romanticism and the Dutch seventeenth-century school [AC]. *Previously in The Hague*

Warhol. *Previously in Pasadena, Chicago, Eindhoven and Paris. Travelling to New York*

Tate Gallery extension plans [Department of the Environment]

Robert Morris

John Constable: the art of nature

The Alistair McAlpine Gift: David Annesley, Michael Bolus, Phillip King, Tim Scott, William Tucker, William Turnbull, Isaac Witkin

Eduardo Paolozzi

William Hogarth

William Blake's water-colour designs for the poems of Thomas Gray [William Blake Trust]

1972

Seven exhibitions: Keith Arnatt, Michael Craig-Martin, Bob Law, Joseph Beuys, Hamish Fulton, Bruce McLean, David Tremlett

William Scott: paintings, drawings and gouaches 1938–71

Barnett Newman. *Previously in New York and Amsterdam; touring to Paris*

Tate Gallery 75th anniversary: an exhibition of designs and projects for the original building of the Tate Gallery

Action space

Caspar David Friedrich, 1774–1840: Romantic landscape painting in Dresden

Photographic imagery in prints

Sidney Nolan: paradise garden

The age of Charles I: painting in England 1620–1649

1973

Barbara Hepworth 70th birthday display

Process, mark making, structure, space: scales in British abstraction in the sixties [Education Department]

Adrian Stokes memorial exhibition

Robyn Denny

The Friends of the Tate Gallery 15th anniversary exhibition

Modernism in England, 1910–1920: the Vorticists and their circle

Paul Nash's photographs: document and image

Edward Burra

A child of six could do it!: cartoons about modern art

William Turnbull: sculpture and painting

Kidsplay [Education Department]

Henry Moore to Gilbert and George: modern British art from the Tate Gallery [TG and BC for Europalia 73 Great Britain]. *Held in Brussels*

Bridget Riley: Fragments and 19 Greys

Landscape in Britain, c.1750–1850

1974

Yves Klein

Piero Manzoni: paintings, reliefs and objects

The late Richard Dadd, 1817–1866. *Toured by AC to 3 regional venues*

Stubbs and Wedgwood: unique alliance between artist and potter

Picasso to Lichtenstein: masterpieces of twentieth century art from the Nordrhein-Westfalen Collection in Düsseldorf

Ben Nicholson [: exhibition to celebrate the award of the Rembrandt Prize]

J.M.W. Turner, 1775–1851 [TG in association with RA]. *Shown at RA*

John Martin's last masterpieces

1975

Duncan Grant: a display to celebrate his 90th birthday

Henry Fuseli, 1741–1825

Kenneth Martin

Henry Moore: graphics in the making

I.A.A. Print Portfolio

Richard Smith: seven exhibitions 1961–75

Four new Surrealist acquisitions

Paul Nash: paintings and watercolours

Ian Tyson prints

1976

Peter Phillips' prints

Bernard Cohen prints

John Constable: paintings, watercolours and drawings

For John Constable [: A portfolio of prints by 18 contemporary artists, commissioned by Bernard Jacobson]

Ceri Richards, 1903–1971

Howard Hodgkin prints

Video show: installations by Tamara Krikorian, Brian Hoey, Stuart Marshall, David Hall, Steven Partridge, Roger Barnard

Works from permanent collection of the Print Department

Samuel Colman, fl.1816–1840: four apocalyptic themes

William Townsend: paintings and drawings

John Latham

Michael Moon

Mechanistic imagery in Paolozzi and Dine

Prints by Gordon House

Kasimir Malevich

George Stubbs, anatomist and animal painter

The González Gift: drawings by Joan and Julio González presented to the Tate Gallery by Mme Roberta González-Richard

Prints by Colin Lanceley

Ben Nicholson: paintings and prints

Prints by Alan Green

Naum Gabo: the constructive process

Gainsborough's 'Giovanna Baccelli'

Sculpture for the blind and partially sighted

1977

A programme of films by Marcel Broodthaers

Artists at Curwen: a celebration of the gift of artists' prints from the Curwen Studio

Recent acquisitions: prints

British Art and St Ives: works from the permanent collections

British Artists of the '60s, from the collections of the Tate Gallery [CAS]

Prints by Julian Trevelyan

Whistler and his influence in Britain

Richard Hamilton: Release stage proofs and related works 1968–9 and 1972

Four paintings by Mondrian

Jules Olitski: prints

Kim Lim graphics

Turner: a special loan exhibition of 20 rarely seen paintings

Art in one year: 1935: an exhibition drawn from the permanent collection

Carved, modelled, constructed: three aspects of British 20th century sculpture

Prints from White Ink

Series. *A display from the permanent collection*

1978

Watercolours from the Turner Bequest, lent by the British Museum

Alchera: prints by Joe Tilson

All is safely gathered in: an exhibition of British paintings of harvest scenes to celebrate the acquisition for the Nation of 'Haymakers' and 'Reapers' by George Stubbs

William Blake

A selection from the Print Department

Artistic Licence

Some old favourites and other works

The drawings of Henry Moore. *Previously in Toronto and touring to 5 Japanese venues*

The Henry Moore Gift: a catalogue of the work of Henry Moore in the Tate Gallery collection, published to celebrate the artist's recent gift of sculpture

J.M.W. Turner: early works before Turner's first visit to the continent: watercolours from the Turner Bequest loaned by the British Museum

The Pier Gallery, Stromness, Orkney. *Touring to Aberdeen and Glasgow*

Patrick Caulfield prints: some poems of Jules Laforgue, and the still life theme

Recent acquisitions for the Print Collection

1979

Turner and the country house view tradition: watercolours and sketches from the Turner Bequest loaned by the British Museum

Tate '79 exhibition: works from the modern collection

Edna Clarke-Hall: 100th birthday tribute

Turner's first visit to the Continent: watercolours from the Turner Bequest loaned by the British Museum

Archive display 1979–80: Artists International Association, Naum Gabo, Paul Nash, Richard Long

Paul Mellon Gift. *Archive display*

Tom Phillips. *Archive display*

J.M.W. Turner: Sea, sky and sun: watercolours from the Turner Bequest, loaned by the British Museum

1980

Abstraction: towards a new art: painting 1910–20

Images of ourselves: printmakers and figurative themes

Mary Potter: 80th birthday display

Marcel Broodthaers

Salvador Dalí. *Previously in Paris*

David Hockney: Travels with pen, pencil and ink [Petersburg Press]. *Previously in New Haven, and touring to other venues in the USA*

Kelpra Studio: an exhibition to commemorate the Rose and Chris Prater Gift: artists' prints 1961–1980

'JMWT PP': a selection of drawings made by Turner to illustrate his Royal Academy lectures as Professor of Perspective. *Loaned by the British Museum*

Victor Pasmore: etchings and aquatints 1972–1980

Thomas Gainsborough

Algernon Newton R.A., 1880–1968. *Archive display*

Recent acquisitions of the Print Department

Sir Jacob Epstein centenary

Sporting pictures from the Halifax Collection

1981

Jasper Johns working proofs. *Previously in Basel; and touring to 7 European venues*

Augustus Wall Callcott

Yugoslav prints

Chantrey Bequest: recent acquisitions

Turner's first visit to Italy, 1819: watercolours from the Turner Bequest, loaned by the British Museum

Robert Rauschenberg

Landscape: the printmaker's view

David Jones. *Touring to Sheffield and Cardiff*

Ceri Richards. *Touring to Swansea*

The prints of Cecil Collins

Sculpture for the blind: an exhibition for the blind and partially sighted

Artists and performance

Charlie Hooker: Behind bars (performance)

Chris Welsby: Shoreline One and Shoreline Two

Marc Camille Chaimowicz: Partial eclipse ... (performance)

Tim Head

Video and film

Nicolas de Staël. *Previously in Paris*

Patrick Caulfield: paintings 1963–81. *Previously in Liverpool*

Turner and George the Fourth in Edinburgh, 1822. *Touring to Edinburgh*

Prints by six British painters: Stephen Buckley, Robyn Denny, Howard Hodgkin, John Hoyland, Richard Smith, John Walker

Artists' Christmas cards. *Archive display, on loan from Sheffield City Art Gallery*

Memorial display for John Lennon

S.W. Hayter 80th birthday display: six prints

Approaches to landscape

1982

Turner and the sea: watercolours from the Turner Bequest, loaned by the British Museum

Painting the town: modern murals in Britain [AC]

Acquisitions for the modern collection since April 1980

Sir Edwin Landseer. *Previously in Philadelphia*

Meredith Frampton

Lionel Constable

The Battersea Mural: the good, the bad and the ugly. *A photographic display*

The Print Collection: a selection

Ben Nicholson memorial display

Six Indian painters: Rabindranath Tagore, Jamini Roy, Amrita Sher-Gil, M.F. Husain, K.G. Subramanyan, Bhupen Khakhar

Graham Sutherland

Watercolours and drawings by D.G. Rossetti

Paint and painting: an exhibition and working studio sponsored by Winsor and Newton to celebrate their 150th anniversary

Julian Schnabel

Turner in the open air: watercolours from the Turner Bequest, loaned by the British Museum

Giorgio de Chirico [Museum of Modern Art, New York]. *Previously in New York*

Prints and works on paper, drawn from the permanent collection

Bequest by Mrs. F. Ambrose Clark to the British Sporting Art Trust

Matthew Smith and Augustus John

Artists and sound

The Art Record

Audio Arts: live to air

Gerald Newman

Ian Breakwell

James Coleman

Patrick Keiller

Philippe Regniez

Sharon Morris

Sonia Knox

Stuart Brisley

Tim Head

Tinguely. *Touring to Brussels and Geneva*

Howard Hodgkin's Indian Leaves

James Ward's 'Gordale Scar': an essay in the Sublime

Richard Wilson: the landscape of reaction. *Touring to Cardiff and New Haven*

Jennifer Bartlett: At the Lake, Up the Creek, In the Garden

Eric Gill and Wyndham Lewis: a selection from the permanent collection

The Print Room Gallery: a selection from the permanent collection

Stephen Willats: Meta Filter and related works

1983

J.M.W. Turner: studies for finished watercolours (c.1825–40): watercolours from the Turner Bequest, loaned by the British Museum

James Barry: the artist as hero

Peter Blake

Paule Vézelay

Documents: works from the Print Collection which document other works

Songs and Proverbs of William Blake *(14 poems and texts by Blake interpreted as dance, with choreography by Erica Knighton and music by Benjamin Britten)*

The essential Cubism: Braque, Picasso and their friends 1907–1920

Harold Cohen

Turner abroad: watercolours from the Turner Bequest loaned by the British Museum

The Clore Gallery: architects' drawings

Henry Moore at 85: some recent sculptures and drawings

Making sculpture: a working studio on the lawn. *Display of prizewinners*

Summertime at the Tate Gallery: Woman's Hour/Radio Times painting competition

New Art at the Tate Gallery 1983

New Art audio visual

Reg Butler

John Piper

Richard Hamilton: image and process:

studies, stage and final proofs from the
graphic works 1952–82
Turner and the human figure: watercolours
from the Turner Bequest, loaned by the
British Museum

1984

Hans Haacke
The Mrs A.F. Kessler Bequest to the Tate
Gallery
The Pre-Raphaelites
Cedric Morris
Beckmann's 'Carnival', 1920
Anglo-French video exchange: an exchange
show [Pompidou Centre in Paris and
London Video Arts and TG in London}
Sculpture on the lawn 1
The hard won image: traditional method and
subject in recent English art
American art: minimal expression
New acquisitions to the moderncCollection
David Jones 1895–1974. *Archive display*
Sculpture on the lawn 2
Turner watercolours: Turner's tour of
Richmondshire / Yorkshire: in Turner's
footsteps through the hills and dales of
Northern England
A.R. Penck: 'Brown's Hotel' and other works
Richard Wentworth: making do and getting
by
Have you seen sculpture from the body?:
sculpture on the lawn 3
Mary Martin
New acquisitions: prints and drawings
Tate Gallery Patrons of New Art [selected by
the Acquisitions' Sub-committee]. *Shown at
Warwick Arts Trust*
George Stubbs 1724–1806. *Touring to New
Haven*
The Turner Prize *(shortlist: Richard Deacon,
Gilbert and George, Howard Hodgkin, Richard
Long, Malcom Morley)*
William James Müller, 1812–1845
Susan Rothenberg [Los Angeles County
Museum of Art]
Suffering through tyranny: 1933–1953

1985

John Walker: prints 1976–84
St Ives 1939-64: twenty five years of painting,
sculpture and pottery
St Ives: people, places and politics, 1939–1964.
Archive display
Richard Deacon
John Banting book designs. *Archive display*
The political paintings of Merlyn Evans,
1930–1950
Susan Hiller: 'Belshazzar's Feast'
British film and video 1980–1985: the new
pluralism
Francis Bacon. *Touring to Stuttgart and Berlin*
Posters of the Thirties, part 1. *Archive display*
Sculptural alternatives: aspects of photo-
graphy and sculpture in Britain 1965–82
Bruce McLean
Pound's artists: Ezra Pound and the visual
arts in London, Paris and Italy [Kettle's
Yard, the Cambridge Poetry Festival
Society and TG]. *Previously in Cambridge*

Braco Dimitrijevic: 'Triptychos Post
Hictoricus'
Performance art and video installation
Howard Hodgkin: prints 1977 to 1983
Scott Burton
Posters of the thirties, part 2. *Archive display*
Turner Prize 1985 *(shortlist: Terry Atkinson,
Tony Cragg, Ian Hamilton Finlay, Howard
Hodgkin, Milena Kalinovska, John Walker)*
Kurt Schwitters [Museum of Modern Art,
New York]
Posters of the Forties and Fifties. *Archive
display*

1986

Forty years of modern art, 1945–1985
David Hockney: moving focus – prints from
Tyler Graphics Ltd
The 'English landscape' prints of John
Constable and David Lucas
Terry Winters: eight paintings
Barry Flanagan: prints 1970–1983
Oskar Kokoschka, 1886–1980. *Touring to
Zurich and New York*
Oskar Kokoschka: aspects of a life. *Archive
display*
Jasper Johns: 'Savarin' monotypes
Stephen Cox
Henry Moore memorial display
Sol LeWitt: prints 1970–86
Recent acquisitions 1984–1986:
documentation of works in the Tate.
Archive display
Painting in Scotland: the Golden Age.
Previously in Edinburgh
The Turner Prize 1986 *(shortlist: Art &
Language, Victor Burgin, Gilbert and George,
Derek Jarman, Stephen McKenna, Bill
Woodrow)*
The Lipchitz Gift: models for sculpture
Ideas about Schwitters [Education
Department]
British and American Pop art, drawn from
the Print Collection of the Tate Gallery
New Art from the Tate Collection, drawn
from the Permanent Collection

1987

Selections from a gift, drawn from the
Permanent Collection
Naum Gabo: sixty years of Constructivism
[Dallas Museum of Art]. *Previously in
Dallas, Toronto, New York, Berlin and
Düsseldorf*
Land Art alive [Education Department].
School display
Three projects for the Tate Gallery: James
Stirling, Michael Wilford and Associates
*(architects' plans for Clore Gallery, Tate
Gallery Liverpool, and the New Museums)*
Art from Europe: works by Ulay and Marina
Abramovic, René Daniels, Marlene Dumas,
Astrid Klein, Pieter Laurens Mol, Andreas
Schulze, Rosemarie Trockel
Recent acquisitions 1984–1986, part 2: Michael
Ayrton 1901–1975. *Archive display*
Winifred Nicholson. *Touring to 5 UK venues*
Mark Rothko, 1903–1970
George Price Boyce

Prints and drawings from the Permanent
Collection
William Tucker: gods: five recent sculptures
Prints and drawings from the Permanent
Collection
'"Gordale Scar" revisited' [Education
Department]. *Primary school project*
Manners and morals: Hogarth and British
painting 1700–1760
Turner and the Channel: themes and
variations, c.1845
The Turner Prize 1987 *(shortlist: Patrick
Caulfield, Helen Chad wick, Richard Deacon,
Richard Long, Declan McGonagle, Thérèse
Oulton)*
Beatrix Potter, 1866–1943: the artist and her
world
John Piper: photographs of buildings and
landscapes in Britain, 1935–1985. *Archive
display*
Performance art: Tina Keane and Richard
Layzell

1988

Young Turner: early work to 1800:
watercolours and drawings from the
Turner Bequest 1787–1800
Douglas Cooper and the masters of Cubism
[Kunstmusum Basel]. *Previously in Basel*
David Bomberg. *Touring to Seville and New
Haven*
Hans Hofmann: late paintings
Turner and architecture
David Mach: '101 Dalmatians'
'Lloyds 1986': a print in the making, by
Brendan Neiland. *Archive display*
Richard Deacon: sculpture in the garden
Late Picasso: paintings, sculpture, drawings,
prints 1953–1972 [Musée nationale d'art
moderne, Paris]. *Previously in Paris*
Turner and Natural History: the Farnley
project. *Previously in Leeds*
David Hockney: a retrospective [Los Angeles
County Museum of Art]. *Previously in Los
Angeles and New York*
Jacob Epstein: letters to his daughter
1948–1959. *Archive display*
Turner Prize 1988 *(no official shortlist)*
Pat Steir: prints 1976–1988 [Musée d'art et
d'histoire, Geneva]. *Previously in Geneva*

1989

Turner: the second decade: watercolours and
drawings from the Turner Bequest
1800–1810
The arts for television [Los Angeles Country
Museum of Art]. *Previously at 12 venues in
Europe and USA*
Portrait of the artist: artists' portraits
published by *Art News and Review*
1949–1960. *Archive display*
John Martin 1789–1854: 'Belshazzar's Feast',
1820
Jacques-Laurent Agasse, 1767–1849 [Musée
d'art et d'histoire, Geneva]. *Previously in
Geneva*
Francis Danby, 1793–1861. *Previously in Bristol*
Turner and the human figure: studies of
contemporary life

Tony Cragg, winner of the 1988 Turner Prize

Cecil Collins: a retrospective exhibition. *Smaller version travelling to Southampton*

F.E. McWilliam: sculpture 1932–1989

Paul Klee: the Berggruen Collection in the Metropolitan Museum of Art, New York, and the Musée nationale d'art moderne, Paris [Metropolitan Museum of Art, New York]. *Previously in New York and Tübingen*

Turner at Petworth

Within these shores: a selection of works from the Chantrey Bequest 1883–1985. *Shown in Graves Art Gallery, Sheffield*

Summer miscellany: watercolours from the Turner Bequest

Colour into line: Turner and the art of engraving

1990

Gods in the studio: the classical ideal in painting and sculpture

Past, present, future: a new hang of the permanent collection

Recent acquisitions. *Archive display*

The third decade: Turner watercolours 1810–1820

Wright of Derby. *Touring to Paris and New York*

Thomas Lowinsky. *Subsequent tour to Coventry and Sheffield organised by South Bank Centre*

On classic ground: Picasso, Léger, de Chirico and the New Classicism 1910–1930

Painting and poetry: Turner's 'Verse Book' and his work of 1804–1812

W.R. Sickert: drawings and paintings 1890–1942. *Previously at Tate Gallery Liverpool*

W.R. Sickert: Dieppe 1907–1923: drawings and letters. *Archive display*

Anish Kapoor: drawings

Richard Long: Tate Gallery, 1990–91. *Touring to Tate Gallery Liverpool*

Turner's papers: a study of the manufacture, selection and use of his drawing papers 1787–1820

The paintings of William Coldstream, 1908–1987. *Touring to 3 regional venues*

Charles Keene: drawings and wood engravings 1847–1890. *Archive display*

Lisa Milroy: Christmas tree

1991

New displays 1991

Turner: the fourth decade: watercolours 1820–1830

Max Ernst: a retrospective. *Touring to Stuttgart, Düsseldorf and Paris*

Pop prints: aspects of printmaking in Britain and the USA 1959–1977

From Turner's studio: paintings and oil sketches from the Turner Bequest. *Touring exhibition, travelling to 8 British venues*

Josef Herman: drawing a rich seam: Ystradgynlais 1944–1955. *Archive display*

Oil sketches from Nature: Turner and his contemporaries

Constable

William Blake and his followers

Sir John Rothenstein: 90th birthday display. *Archive display*

The Helena and Kenneth Levy Bequest

Turner's rivers of Europe: the Rhine, Meuse and Mosel. *Touring to Brussels*

The transformation of appearance: Andrews, Auerbach, Bacon, Freud, Kossoff. *Exhibited at Sainsbury Centre for the Visual Arts, University of East Anglia, Norwich*

Anthony Caro: sculpture towards architecture. *Touring to Paris and Baltimore*

Gerhard Richter

The Turner Prize 1991 *(shortlist: Ian Davenport, Anish Kapoor, Fiona Rae, Rachel Whiteread)*

Giorgio Morandi: etchings. *Toured by the South Bank Centre to 3 regional venues*

1992

Canaletto: 'The Old Horse Guards from St James's Park'

New displays 1992

Turner: the fifth decade: watercolours 1830–1840

David Hockney: seven paintings

Unit One 1933–5. *Archive display*

Brice Marden: prints 1961–1991. *Touring to Paris and Baltimore*

Otto Dix, 1891–1969. *Previously in Stuttgart and Berlin*

William Blake: the apprentice years

Turner and Byron

Richard Hamilton. *Touring to Dublin*

Georg Baselitz: prints 1964–1990. *Previously in Geneva and Valencia*

The painted nude: from Etty to Auerbach

Robert Adams, 1917–1984: a sculptor's record. *Archive display*

Richard Serra: Weight and Measure 1992

Turner as Professor: the artist and linear perspective

The swagger portrait: Grand Manner portraiture in Britain from Van Dyck to Augustus John, 1630–1930

The Turner Prize 1992 *(shortlist: Grenville Davey, Damien Hirst, David Tremlett, Alison Wilding)*

Beardsley to Bomberg: British drawings and watercolours 1870–1920

Ivon Hitchens: the Cecil Sharp House Mural. *Archive display*

Visualising masculinities

1993

New displays 1993

Turner: the final years: watercolours 1840–1851

Robert Ryman [TG and Museum of Modern Art, New York]. *Touring to Madrid and 3 US venues*

Robert Vernon's Gift: British art for the Nation 1847

Georges Braque, printmaker

Ian Hamilton Finlay: artists' books and prints. *Library display*

William Blake: independence and innovation

Paris Post-War: art and Existentialism 1945–55

Turner's painting techniques

Burne-Jones: watercolours and drawings

Terry Frost: the camera as notebook. *Archive display*

Turner's vignettes

Ben Nicholson. *Touring to Saint-Etienne*

Writing on the wall *(works from the collection by women artists selected by women writers)*

The Turner Prize 1993 *(shortlist: Hannah Collins, Vong Phaophanit, Sean Scully, Rachel Whiteread)*

A decade of collecting: Patrons of New Art gifts 1983–1993

1994

New displays 1994

Picasso: sculptor/painter

Turner's 'Rivers of England' and 'Ports of England'

Fluxbritannica: aspects of the Fluxus movement, 1962–73

Naum Gabo: the creative process

The essential Turner

The Wilkie Gift: contemporary art from the collection of David Wilkie (1921–1992)

R.B. Kitaj: a retrospective. *Touring to Los Angeles and New York*

Sculptors' drawings, presented by the Weltkunst Foundation

Sutherland sketchbooks. *Archive display*

William Blake: art and revolution

Turner's Holland

Turner miscellany

Rebecca Horn *(in both TG and Serpentine Gallery, London)* [Solomon R. Guggenheim Museum, New York]. *Previously in New York and 3 European venues. Touring to Grenoble*

James McNeill Whistler. *Touring to Paris and Washington*

The Turner Prize 1994 *(shortlist: Willie Doherty, Peter Doig, Antony Gormley, Shirazeh Houshiary)*

1995

New displays 1995

Through Switzerland with Turner: Ruskin's first selection from the Turner Bequest

Willem de Kooning: paintings [National Gallery of Art, Washington]. *Previously in Washington and New York*

British sporting art

Matthew Barney: OTTOshaft. *Artnow 1*

Turner in Germany. *Touring to Mannheim and Hamburg*

Rites of passage: art for the end of the century

Marc Quinn: Emotional detox. *Artnow 2*

William Blake and patronage

Artists' books. *Library display*

Geneviève Cadieux: Broken memory. *Artnow 3*

Sketching the sky: watercolours from the Turner Bequest

Dynasties: painting in Tudor and Jacobean England 1530–1630

The Turner Prize 1995 *(shortlist: Mona Hatoum, Damien Hirst, Callum Innes, Mark Wallinger)*

Miroslaw Balka: Dawn. *Artnow 4*

Picturing blackness in British art: 1700s–1990s

1996

Bill Woodrow: fools' gold. *Touring to Darmstadt*
Cézanne [Philadelphia Museum of Art]. *Previously in Paris; touring to Philadelphia*
Georgina Starr: Hypnodreamdruff. *Artnow 5*
Turner's 'Drawing book': the Liber Studiorum
Paul Graham: Hypermetropia. *Artnow 6*
Leon Kossoff
Hans Hartung: works on paper 1922–56 [in association with Fondation Hans Hartung et Anna-Eva Bergmann]
Tacita Dean: Foley artist. *Artnow 7*
Grand Tour: the lure of Italy in the eighteenth century. *Touring to Rome*
Turner in the north of England, 1797. *Touring to Harewood House*
The Turner Prize 1996 *(shortlist: Douglas Gordon, Craigie Horsfield, Gary Hume, Simon Patterson)*
Brancusi to Beuys: works from the Ted Power Collection
Nicholas Pope: the Apostles speaking in tongues. *Artnow 8*

1997

Luciano Fabro
Lovis Corinth. *Previously in Munich, Berlin and Saint Louis*
Turner's watercolour explorations 1810–1842. *Touring to Southampton*
Hogarth the painter
Kathy Prendergast: City drawings. *Artnow 9*
Michal Rovner. *Artnow 10*
Ellsworth Kelly. *Previously in New York, Los Angeles and Munich*
Francis Towne. *Touring to Leeds*
Henry Tate's Gift
Mondrian: nature to abstraction, from the Gemeentemuseum, The Hague
Beat Streuli. *Artnow 11*
The Oppé collection of British drawings and watercolours
Turner's rivers of France: the Loire
The age of Rossetti, Burne-Jones and Watts: symbolism in Britain 1860–1910. *Touring to Munich and Amsterdam*
The Turner Prize 1997 *(shortlist: Christine Borland, Angela Bulloch, Cornelia Parker, Gillian Wearing)*

TATE GALLERY LIVERPOOL

1986

Events Summer 1986: Steven Campbell: a billboard painting; Tony Cragg: a sculpture; Bruce McLean, David Ward: a new performance

1988

Surrealism in the Tate Gallery Collection
Starlit waters: British sculpture, an international art, 1968–1988
Mark Rothko: the Seagram Mural Project
Modern British sculpture from the Collection
Angry Penguins and Realist painting in Melbourne in the 1940s [South Bank Centre and Australian National Gallery. *Previously at Hayward Gallery, London*
I CAN paint: the art of the handicapped child [ICAN (Invalid Children's Aid Nationwide)]. *Previously at other UK venues*

1989

The Surreal object
Video positive 89: international video festival [Merseyside Moviola]. *In 4 locations in Merseyside*
Towards a bigger picture: contemporary British photographs from the collection of the Victoria and Albert Museum. *Previously at V&A*
W.R. Sickert: drawings and paintings 1890–1942. *Touring to TG*
Minimalism
Brian McCann: 'Recognition: drawings from a series' *(works by the first MoMart artist-in-residence)*
Distant drums: a video installlation by Marion Urch
Art from Köln
Degas: images of women
World War Two: a display of pictures from the collection to mark the 50th anniversary of the outbreak of war in September 1939

1990

Lifelines: four British artists *(Helen Chadwick, Susan Hiller, Ian McKeever, Boyd Webb)* [Organised with BC]. *Previously in Ludwigshafen*
Dancers on a plane: John Cage, Merce Cunningham, Jasper Johns. *Previously at Anthony d'Offay Gallery, London*
Francis Bacon: paintings since 1944
Expression and engagement: German painting from the collection
Funny pictures: cartoons about modern art
New North: new art from the north of Britain. *Touring to 4 UK venues*
Jean Hélion. *Previously in Valencias*
Out of the wood: Die Brücke woodcuts and woodcarvings
Laura Godfrey-Isaacs: Pink: paintings from a series produced as MoMart artist-in-residence 1990
New light on sculpture

1991

Richard Long
Strongholds: new art from Ireland. *Touring to Tampere*
Alberto Giacometti: the artist's studio
Dynamism: the art of modern life before the Great War
Video Positive 91: international video festival [Merseyside Moviola]
Alison Wilding: Immersion: sculpture from ten years
Original eyes: progressive vision in British watercolour 1750–1850
Echo: works by women artists 1850–1940
Maud Sulter: Hysteria
Malcolm Morley: watercolours. *Previously in Maastricht and Basel; touring to Southampton, USA*
A cabinet of signs: contemporary art from post-modern Japan [Japan Foundation and Tate Gallery Liverpool]. *Touring to Whitechapel Art Gallery, London, and Malmö*
Ian Hamilton Finlay and the Wild Hawthorn Press 1958–1991

1992

Lucian Freud: paintings and works on paper 1940–1991 [BC]. *Previously in Milan; touring to Utsonomiya and Tokyo*
Myth-making: Abstract Expressionist painting from the United States
Stanley Spencer: a kind of heaven
New realities 1945–1968: art in western Europe: a changing display from the National Collection
Working with nature: traditional thought in contemporary art from Korea
Natural order: recent European sculpture from the Tate's collection

1993

Gilbert and George: the Cosmological pictures 1989 [Haags Gemeentemuseum]. *Previously in 8 European venues; touring to Stuttgart*
Roy Lichtenstein
David Hockney: paintings and prints
Joseph Beuys: the revolution is us
Video Positive 1993
Robert Gober. *Previously at Serpentine Gallery, London*
Elective affinities
Antony Gormley: testing a world view [Oriel Mostyn, Llandudno]. *Touring to 5 UK venues*

1994

Ann Hamilton: mneme
Gary Hill: in light of the other. *Previously in Oxford*
Venus re-defined: sculpture by Rodin, Matisse and contemporaries
Moral tales
Africa explores: 20th century African art
Barbara Hepworth: a retrospective [Tate Gallery Liverpool and Art Gallery of Ontario]. *Touring to New Haven and Toronto*

1995

Sigmar Polke: join the dots

Video positive 1995. *In 5 locations in Liverpool*

Witness: photoworks from the Collection

Michael Sandle: memorials for the twentieth century

Andreas Gursky: images

Making it: process and participation: Janet Hodgson, Sarah Raine, James Reilly, Padraig Timoney, Daphne Wright, TEA

Vital: three contemporary African artists: Cyprien Tokoudagba, Touhami Ennadre, Farid Belkahia

Testing the water: a collection display selected by the Young Tate

Home and away: internationalism and British art 1900–1930

1996

Susan Hiller

Characters and conversations: British art 1900–1930

Wandering about in the future: new Tate acquisitions

New Contemporaries 96

Joan Miró: printmaking, from figuration to gesture

Rachel Whiteread: shedding life. *Touring to Madrid*

1997

Paula Rego. *Touring to Lisbon*

TATE GALLERY ST IVES

1993

Barbara Hepworth's hospital drawings

Trevor Corser

Andy Hughes: sea fever. *Collaboration with Surfers Against Sewage and the British Surf Association*

Terry Frost: walk along the quay

1994

Bryan Wynter: IMOOS

Alison Wilding: new works at Tate Gallery St Ives

Equivalents for the megaliths

Peter Randall-Page: recent work

Peter Appleton: the state of sea

Martell Linsdell: to the megaliths

Peter Lanyon: generation

Phil Mawdsley: medical records. *Collaboration with ArtCare*

John Bedding

1995

Guido Morris: a fine printer

John Aiken: Aresta cortante: a project for Cornwall and Portugal. *Collaboration with Centro de Arte Moderna, Fundaçáo Calouste Gulbenkian, Lisbon*

Porthmeor Beach: a century of images

Lulu Quinn: submerged identities

Paul Feiler: form to essence: theme and development

Maggie Meadows: Merry Maidens I–IV

David Kemp: wild works. *Collaboration with Kneehigh Theatre and British Trust for Conservation Volunteers*

Jason Wason

1996

Mark Rothko in Cornwall

Paul Mason: carvings and drawings

Christopher Wood: a painter between two Cornwalls. *Touring to Quimper*

Triplicate: three galleries, six artists. *Collaboration and simultaneous exhibition with Southampton City Art Gallery and Towner Museum and Art Gallery, Eastbourne*

Karl Weschke

Clive Bowen

1997

Peter Fluck and Tony Myatt: chaotic constructions

A quality of light. *Collaboration with St Ives International, Newlyn Art Gallery, Falmouth College of Arts, South West Arts, INIVA*

Roy Walker: Skylight III

An instrument of truth: sketchbooks and related paintings by Roger Hilton

The Marlow Moss Reconstruction Project by Florette Dijkstra

Ralph Freeman: Foundations and fragments

Trustees of the Tate Gallery

Plans

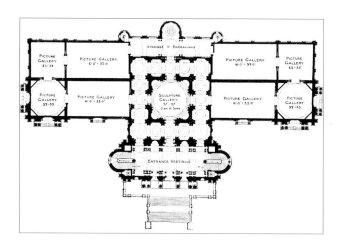

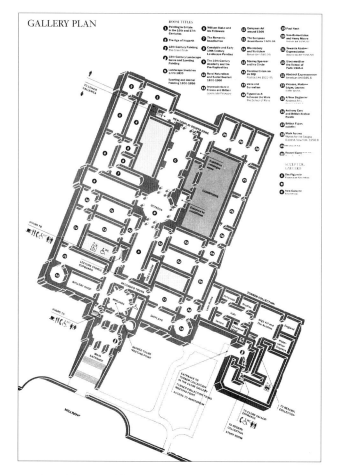

Plans of the ground floor of the Gallery: as it first opened to the
public in 1897 (top) and at the time of the first *New Displays* in 1990

Index

Credits